Practical Game Design

Learn the art of game design through applicable skills and cutting-edge insights

Adam Kramarzewski
Ennio De Nucci

BIRMINGHAM - MUMBAI

Practical Game Design

Commissioning Editor: Amarabha Banerjee
Acquisition Editor: Larissa Pinto
Content Development Editor: Francis Carneiro
Technical Editor: Diksha Wakode
Copy Editor: Safis Editing
Project Coordinator: Devanshi Doshi
Proofreader: Safis Editing
Indexer: Pratik Shirodkar
Graphics: Jason Monteiro
Production Coordinator: Deepika Naik

First published: April 2018

Production reference: 1130418

Published by Packt Publishing Ltd.
Livery Place
35 Livery Street
Birmingham
B3 2PB, UK.

ISBN 978-1-78712-179-9

www.packtpub.com

`mapt.io`

Mapt is an online digital library that gives you full access to over 5,000 books and videos, as well as industry leading tools to help you plan your personal development and advance your career. For more information, please visit our website.

Why subscribe?

- Spend less time learning and more time coding with practical eBooks and Videos from over 4,000 industry professionals

- Improve your learning with Skill Plans built especially for you

- Get a free eBook or video every month

- Mapt is fully searchable

- Copy and paste, print, and bookmark content

PacktPub.com

Did you know that Packt offers eBook versions of every book published, with PDF and ePub files available? You can upgrade to the eBook version at `www.PacktPub.com` and as a print book customer, you are entitled to a discount on the eBook copy. Get in touch with us at `service@packtpub.com` for more details.

At `www.PacktPub.com`, you can also read a collection of free technical articles, sign up for a range of free newsletters, and receive exclusive discounts and offers on Packt books and eBooks.

Contributors

About the authors

Adam Kramarzewski is a game designer who, at the age of 19, dived straight into the pre-smartphone mobile games industry of 2007. He has gathered over a decade of experience with the likes of Gameloft, Square Enix, and Space Ape Games, and has worked on over 30 game projects and many world-class IPs, including Lara Croft, Deus Ex, and Transformers. Adam is an avid gamer, and a fan of cinematography, psychology, and all things science. He also sat on the jury for game design at the 2017 BAFTA Video Game Awards.

I'd like to extend my gratitude to my loving girlfriend, Shan, for putting up with me throughout this project, and to my brother Chris, my parents, and everyone at Space Ape Games who helped me out with feedback, fresh ideas, and words of encouragement. Special thanks to Andrew Munden and Bill Robinson, for great suggestions that helped improve this book.

Ennio De Nucci is a game designer and developer. He works as a game designer since 2011 and designed both digital video games and physical board games. He worked for a variety of video game developers, such as the Italian PM Studios Srl, Supermassive Games, and the multinational IGT. Since November 2014, he has been a part of the BAFTA Crew Games. Currently, he works at Another Place Productions in London, where he designs mobile RPGs.

My first thanks to Barbara, who supported me in the long hours of writing and studying for this book. Thanks to my parents, my friends, and all my colleagues at Another Place Productions, who welcomed me into the most amazing dev team. Finally, my gratitude to Fabio Belsanti and Fabio Abbattista, who believed in me and sparked my passion for game design.

About the reviewers

Zoë O'Shea is a PhD candidate studying at Goldsmiths University, London, and is part of the Intelligent Games/Games Intelligence Center for Doctoral Training (IGGI). Originally from Dublin, Ireland, Zoë has previously studied 3D modeling, game design, and games theory. Her current research is centered around player psychology and behavior. When not working on her thesis, Zoë undertakes a wide selection of freelance work and enjoys playing Final Fantasy XIV Online.

Bill Robinson has been developing games for almost 30 years, and has been doing so professionally for over 10 years. He currently works at Space Ape Games in London and worked for Jagex in Cambridge earlier.

Packt is searching for authors like you

If you're interested in becoming an author for Packt, please visit `authors.packtpub.com` and apply today. We have worked with thousands of developers and tech professionals, just like you, to help them share their insight with the global tech community. You can make a general application, apply for a specific hot topic that we are recruiting an author for, or submit your own idea.

Table of Contents

Preface

As the authors of this book, we promise you an honest, unfiltered, and highly practical guide to the art and craft of game design.

To begin with, we have to acknowledge that there are great benefits to learning more about the history of games, the nature of human behavior, and the theory of play. Also, there's great material out there (some of it referenced in this very book) that we can wholeheartedly recommend that you explore!

However, our medium is rapidly evolving, and when it comes to working as a game designer in the modern day and age, there appears to be a gap; we took upon ourselves the tremendous task of trying to fill it.

Our goal is to not only share our knowledge on game design but also to shed light on how to work in a modern development team. From game concept to release and well into live operations, years of experience, blood, sweat, and post-crunch tears and distilled into practical and applicable knowledge.

We've done our best to gather actionable insight and valuable advice on game design across genres, development platforms, and business models, and we are very humbled by the ability to share it with the world!

Who this book is for

Whether you are a student just approaching the discipline, an existing game designer, or a developer looking to expand your knowledge, this book will equip you with the fundamental know-how and best practices to help you succeed in your career.

What this book covers

Chapter 1, *Introducing the Game Production Process*, explores the basic machinations of the games industry, teaching you about various game design roles, responsibilities of designers, production methods, and development milestones.

Chapter 2, *Game Concept*, teaches you how to write a game concept and your responsibilities as a game designer in the process of doing so. Practical tips and real-life examples will help you create your very own game concept based on an original idea or an existing game.

Chapter 3, *Scoping a Game Project*, covers the concepts and relationships between the game's overall scope, its structure, and its content. We'll explore real-world examples and help you build an understanding of how to better document the size, complexity, and dependencies in your game, as well as help you estimate your tasks.

Chapter 4, *Design Documentation*, explains everything you need to know about writing game design documentation: from the tools and techniques to numerous pieces of practical advice.

Chapter 5, *Adaptation of Mechanics*, approaches the definition of game mechanics and will give you an idea of how to create your own game using pieces from existing games. This chapter also introduces the concept of dynamics and features as a set of mechanics that form a bigger part of the game.

Chapter 6, *Invention of Mechanics*, explores the theory behind game design and the creation of mechanics that are fun to play. You'll learn how a new mechanic is taught and how the core loop of a game is formed. Finally, you will learn about the roles of conflict, combat systems, game complexity, and depth.

Chapter 7, *Prototyping*, demonstrates how to prototype a game idea or concept. This chapter will cover both paper and digital prototyping, with all the pros and cons of both techniques. You will read about a practical example from a real-life scenario, easy to replicate as an exercise.

Chapter 8, *Games and Stories*, highlights the importance of narrative elements in games and helps you design strong characters, intriguing worlds, and compelling stories.

Chapter 9, *Level Design*, introduces you to processes and techniques used to create highly playable game content. You'll learn about creating believable spaces, manipulating light and geometry, and making the best of the available game mechanics.

Chapter 10, *Characters*, explains the different kinds of characters that populate virtual worlds and how to make the best use of them. In this chapter, you will also get a closer look at a practical character-design example for an existing game, from which you'll be able to get some inspiration to try and do your own character design, a great exercise for any game designer.

Chapter 11, *User Interface and User Experience,* outlines the complexities of input mechanics, camera systems, and effective game feedback. You'll then gain practical insight into the processes behind UI and UX design, helping you create interfaces and experiences that are informative, empowering, and delightful to interact with.

Chapter 12, *Accessibility,* dives into how to make your games more *accessible,* that is, easier to use, understand, and relate to. You'll then learn about usability testing and arm yourself with the expertise required to plan and execute your very own playtesting sessions.

Chapter 13, *Balancing,* combines the knowledge from previous chapters and explores the ways in which you can pace, structure, and adjust the rules and content of your games to create experiences that capture and hold the interest of your audience.

Chapter 14, *The Final 10 Percent,* takes you through the processes that need to take place before a game is finally released. You will also read about the difficulties and pitfalls of closing and be releasing a video game, and how to avoid them.

Chapter 15, *Games As a Service,* distills the knowledge required to turn your game into a successful service—from monetization tips and live operations strategy to addressing game balancing, understanding analytics, customer support, and the tools required to run your games sustainably.

To get the most out of this book

We've done our best to explain any industry-specific terms and practices in order to make this book as accessible as possible.

The contents of this book require no prior experience with game development. However, a basic knowledge of some popular video games (such as *Call of Duty: Modern Warfare, The Elder Scrolls: Skyrim, Hearthstone,* and *Starcraft*) will be helpful.

Download the color images

We also provide a PDF file that has color images of the screenshots and diagrams used in this book. You can download it here: https://www.packtpub.com/sites/default/files/downloads/PracticalGameDesign_ColorImages.pdf.

Conventions used

There are a number of text conventions used throughout this book. An exercise is styled as follows:

> **Exercise**
> This is your first exercise. If you have a game idea already in your head, try to put it on paper: a couple of pages would be enough. If you don't have any particular game idea in mind, try to describe a game that you have played and loved enough to know all its rules and secrets.

Italics: Indicates new or highly specific terms as well as titles of games, books, or articles.

Bold: Is sometimes used within the body text to put extra emphasis on certain terms and sentences.

Important notes and information appear like this.

Tips, tricks, and interesting techniques appear like this.

Get in touch

Feedback from our readers is always welcome.

General feedback: Email feedback@packtpub.com and mention the book title in the subject of your message. If you have questions about any aspect of this book, please email us at questions@packtpub.com.

Errata: Although we have taken every care to ensure the accuracy of our content, mistakes do happen. If you have found a mistake in this book, we would be grateful if you would report this to us. Please visit www.packtpub.com/submit-errata, selecting your book, clicking on the Errata Submission Form link, and entering the details.

Piracy: If you come across any illegal copies of our works in any form on the Internet, we would be grateful if you would provide us with the location address or website name. Please contact us at copyright@packtpub.com with a link to the material.

If you are interested in becoming an author: If there is a topic that you have expertise in and you are interested in either writing or contributing to a book, please visit authors.packtpub.com.

Reviews

Once you have read and used this book, why not leave a review on the site that you purchased it from? Potential readers can then see and use your unbiased opinion to make purchase decisions, we at Packt can understand what you think about our products, and our authors can see your feedback on their book. Thank you!

For more information about Packt, please visit packtpub.com.

Disclaimer

The screenshots used in this book are for illustrative purposes only. We do not recommend you to misuse these in any way. For more information please consult the terms and conditions of the publishers mentioned here.

Electronic Arts(EA) : https://www.ea.com/terms-of-service

Nintendo : https://www.nintendo.com/terms-of-use

Interplay Productions : http://www.interplay.com/about/terms.php

Mobygames : http://www.mobygames.com/info/terms

Valve Corporation : http://store.steampowered.com/privacy_agreement/

Activision : https://www.activision.com/legal/privacy-policy

Capcom : http://www.capcom.com/capcom/legal_privacy/privacy.html

Blizzard : http://tw.blizzard.com/zh-tw/company/about/privacy.html

Frozenbyte : https://www.frozenbyte.com/privacy-policy

**Microsoft
Studios** : https://www.microsoft.com/en-us/legal/intellectualproperty/copyright/default.aspx

Bethesda Softwares : https://www.rockstargames.com/privacy

THQNORDIC : https://www.thqnordic.com/

Introducing the Game Production Process

Welcome to the games industry! It's an ever-changing world where competition is fierce, publishing platforms and business models come and go (crowdfunding has appeared and seemingly peaked in just a few years), whole genres of products disappear (only to be revived or reinvented 15 years later), and big publishers and small independent studios alike fight for an ever-limited resource: player attention. We're often giving away more and more (if not all) of our content for free, hoping to monetize users later down the line.

At the time writing, Valve's Steam dominates publishing on PC, while Sony, Microsoft, and Nintendo keep fighting for their share of the console pie. Exclusively handheld consoles are on the back foot, quick being replaced by phones and tablets. The mobile industry itself is all but dominated by Google's Play Store and Apple's App Store and while the mobile market keeps on growing, it has become much, much harder for small developers to break through and make a profit. User acquisition is extremely challenging (read: expensive) and lack of support from the platform holder can sink your profitability. Premium (paid-for) mobile games are a minority, and most financially successful products are what we consider *freemium* or *free to play*. In this crowded market, games are becoming more and more expensive to make, market, and operate. What worked in 2010 works no more; the best bet for small groups of indie devs is now with Steam, though that market has also been flooded with the introduction of the now-defunct Steam Greenlight. According to the data exposed by `http://steamspy.com/`, there were 379 games published on Steam in 2012; by 2016, that number grew to 4,207. Developers now face a market that's increasingly hit-driven, and unless you sit on a billion-dollar brand such as FIFA or Call of Duty, playing it safe is no longer an option. If you do not adapt and innovate quick enough, you're sure to face commercial failure. As the stakes go higher, teams either balloon out of proportion or grow ever leaner.

Now, the reality might have sounded a little grim, and make no mistake, while it's very difficult to make a great game, it's even harder to make it successful. But for those who keep on trying, for those who do not hold back and surrender after their first, fifth, or even twentieth canceled or failed game, this can be the best industry on the planet and within it, being a game designer can be the most rewarding and fulfilling job.

We'll start this book by delving briefly into the basic machinations of the games industry, exploring game design roles and responsibilities, production methods, and development milestones. There's a lot to cover, and probably much more exciting stuff to follow so... Are you ready? Let's begin!

Game design roles

Game designers come in all shapes and sizes. We've got generalists that work on *everything* as well as highly specialized craftsman put in charge of a single system. Creative leads often work on a high level, maintaining a cohesive vision for the game and shaping it through feedback, with typically little to no hands-on involvement.

There's no universal distinction, with roles and responsibilities varying between companies, but game designers can be roughly divided into:

- **Generalists**: Junior and senior game designers, as well as lead designers and creative directors. A generalist will often take care of (or feedback on) all areas of game design not already covered by someone else on the team.
- **Economy designers/monetization specialists**: A role very likely to be encountered in the mobile games industry as nearly all products require someone with expertise in designing and implementing a fitting monetization strategy, as well as balancing the game economy.
- **Level designers**: Often a crossover between a designer and a 3D artist. Some level designers only take care of the gameplay side of the level, while others are capable of delivering a finished stage.
- **Mission/content designers**: Rather than working on new features and game mechanics, these designers specialize in adding and balancing in-game content, from buildings, vehicles, NPCs, and weapons to quests, puzzles, achievements, and more!
- **Narrative designers**: Tasked with writing, designing, and implementing narrative elements in games. Often work hand-in-hand with level and mission designers to help craft a playable experience.

- **Systems designers**: A catch-all term for all designers focusing on the more high-level design of game mechanics, loops, and systems rather than content creation and balancing. Big game projects will often have a specialist taking care of multiplayer game modes, player progression, or combat.
- **Technical designers**: A term usually reserved for highly qualified mixtures of a gameplay programmer and a game designer, or used for a game designer empowered by tools and scripting languages. They design and implement new game features and mechanics, be it independently or by bridging the gap between design and programming teams.

Specialization and T-shaping

More specialized positions only make practical sense in a big team or a large company that can support them. Look carefully at the opportunities available to you as well as your interests. If you have another passion, explore it; there's a high chance it will become useful or inspiring. An interest in creative writing and storytelling can lead towards a career as a narrative designer. An artistic aptitude and interest in 3D modeling and world-building will naturally lead you towards level design.

On the opposite side of heavy-specialization lies T-shaping: broadening your skill set and the spectrum of tasks you can handle. Developing a broad range of skills (even at an entry level) is always a good idea.

Ultimately, your job is not to design the perfect gameplay system and walk away. You are there to help realize the game's potential, turning it into the best possible experience for your players. Sooner or later on a project, you'll find an area outside of your core responsibilities that you'd like to improve, and often it's much faster and easier to just work on it yourself rather than to create a *ticket in the system* for someone else to eventually (if ever) address. For the record, I am not advising you to be a rogue agent who constantly messes with other people's work and tries to sneak things past the quality assurance team. I am simply asking you to be very proactive and constantly seek opportunities to improve things. The difference between good and great is that extra attention that often wasn't planned for and isn't necessarily part of the original specification. When things are good enough, derailing other team members just for a tiny improvement is not warranted or productive. In these situations, a wide skill set can enable you to turn great into excellent. Just make sure to share the changes you've made with others—leave the surprises for the players, not for your team!

A variety of skills will turn you into a more helpful and independent team member, allow you to communicate more effectively with experts from different fields, and even improve your creativity. One of the most coveted ones is programming. However daunting it sounds, taking even the most basic scripting courses and tutorials will be hugely beneficial. It will improve your understanding of how games work (including the constraints and possibilities at hand) and perhaps even allow you to create or tweak parts of the game without having to rely on programmers. Just make sure they review your work and decide it's up to their standards!

When it comes to tools, word processors, spreadsheets, and presentation software are absolutely essential, but don't forget about the powers of pen and paper! Even the most basic drawing can help clarify your ideas and avoid confusion. On top of that, having a working knowledge of popular game engines such as Unity and Unreal is highly desirable, and both offer easy-to-follow tutorials. Any generalist should also look into learning 2D and 3D art software, audio and video editing suites, as well as looking into the **VFX** (**visual effects**) editors built into the aforementioned game engines.

As for personal growth beyond tools and game theory, I suggest self-studying in psychology (especially cognitive science), creative writing, physics, and economics. But remember, you learn most when you're having fun. Focus on something you enjoy or wish you could do. Take things at a manageable pace and stay on the lookout for new tasks and opportunities to jump on. Experiment, stay curious and don't believe everything you see or hear.

Development teams

In tiny independent teams, there can often be no space for designated product people (a term used to describe producers, game designers, and live operations managers). In such situations, game design responsibilities are distributed between the artists and programmers.

However, while a team with no designer may work well on a small indie scale (one to four people), the prospect of running a game team of more than five people without a designated designer is a very risky one. With the freedom of distributed design (colloquially called *design by committee*) often comes a lack of ownership and accountability. Making good design decision becomes increasingly difficult as the game is being pulled in different directions and lacks a cohesive vision. In such teams, even the most pressing gameplay issues can go unaddressed. Everyone loves to chip in with their ideas, but nobody feels compelled to work on design problems, be it for the fear of associating themselves with them, or the conflict of going against the rest of the team.

You're most likely going to be a part of a small or mid-sized team. Anything with 15 to 30 people would be considered a medium-sized team, and this number will always fluctuate depending on where you are in the development cycle and includes a total of two to four design-oriented staff members. A smaller operation has a headcount of 5 to 12 people, and one or two other design-oriented people at most. It's also quite common, especially for a senior designer working on games with a relatively manageable scope, to be the only designated game designer on the project.

Each company has its own approach to managing human resources. And while various artists and even programmers jump in and out of projects to help the teams around critical milestones, designers are often in it for the long run, that is, from preproduction until the game is released, and most likely some more after that. This is not only because of the importance of having a unified design direction but also due to the sheer amount of time and effort required to get to know the game and make meaningful design decisions.

While bigger teams have hugely varying structures, with space for a very low-level specialization, medium and small teams usually share a similar setup across the industry. As a great example of the strategy of small teams, let's look at the creators of *Clash of Clans*, the Finnish game company *Supercell*, who by definition are an assembly of independent cells. Each cell is a small team consisting of a producer, a few artists and coders, at least one tester, a generalist game designer and potentially a monetization/live operations-oriented person. People rotate in and out of their cells slowly as games are kicked off or *killed* (canceled). Each team can also count on support from a stable of people who work for the whole company, taking care of player analytics, finance, social media, operations, customer support, marketing, user acquisition, and more. The goal of Supercell's structure is to create an environment that facilitates creativity, and gives each team the power to make decisions on a game's design and direction.

Responsibilities of a game designer

The tasks and responsibilities of a game designer vary dramatically and are affected by the team structure, project type, and the development phase.

To shed some light on what you might be required to do, let's look at a real-world example. Here is a list of tasks I undertook when working with a mid-sized team at a London studio, *Space Ape games*, on a mobile game, *Transformers: Earth Wars*. The game could be classified as a part of the *Build & Battle* genre—similar to *Clash of Clans*, but with a multitude of unique characters, all with their own attacks and abilities.

In the two and a half year period (one year to soft launch, half a year to polish the game, and a year of live operations), my tasks included:

- Writing the **GDD** (**game design document**) and most of the subsequent feature specs (smaller documents explaining game features and content required).
- Communicating the design vision (face to face, and in writing) and overseeing the implementation of game mechanics, features, and content.
- Creating user flows and sketching user interface designs.
- Prototyping, designing, and implementing new gameplay systems and content including characters (with varied classes, stats, behaviors, weapons, and special abilities), game modes, achievements, buildings, and defenses.
- Level design and creation of single-player campaigns.
- Planning, scripting, and tweaking tutorials, achievements, and cutscenes.
- Balancing gameplay with dozens of special abilities and over 100 unique characters.
- Writing and integrating in-game text and dialog.
- Requesting and integrating new VFX. Over time, I also started doing more and more particle effects on my own by tweaking and combining existing ones (thus enabling that artist to work on other games).
- Planning a future content roadmap: new characters, game features, and story developments.
- Managing an external writer and audio engineer, creating a list of tasks for them, feeding back on their work, and integrating it.
- Addressing the community via weekly Twitch Live Streams, YouTube videos, Q&As, and more.

Now, this sure sounds like a lot to handle! Fortunately, I had another senior designer working with me during the first year of development. We also had the entire game economy handled by our monetization specialist. This included setting up and fine-tuning the income and spending of in-game currency, level up and upgrade curves, building timers, in-app purchases, and more. We also had a live operations expert who joined later and took care of our weekly special events, in-app purchase promotions and content rollout. All of these tasks can, and often will also fall on the game designer.

Do not worry though! Throughout this book, we'll shed light on these confusing terms and technical jargon, and build an understanding of how to approach your daily tasks as a game designer! First up, how are game projects run?

Software development models

We'd like to help you better understand the production process and the path a game project takes. To achieve that, let's take a brief look at the two most common software development models, Waterfall and Agile.

Waterfall

Waterfall, as we understand it today, is a sequential approach to production with no space for iteration. The product is supposed to go through six rigid phases in a specific order (always trickling down, such as a waterfall):

1. Listing all software requirements
2. Analyzing requirements
3. Designing the whole product and its architecture
4. Writing and implementing all of the systems and content
5. Testing and debugging
6. Operations, support, and maintenance of a completed product

Since this process allows for no iteration, its use in games development is highly limited. It can, however, be applied on a small scale, be it on a part of game's content (asset production) or a single game feature with already proven mechanics and rock-solid specification. Applying waterfall on the whole product (with unproven mechanics and systems) would most likely result in a broken game that ticks all the boxes but is not fun to play at all.

Agile

Creating a highly polished and fine-tuned work of art is not easy, which is why games benefit greatly from extensive iteration. These iterative cycles are at the core of the Agile methodology of software development. The Agile Manifesto (http://agilemanifesto.org), which popularized the movement, has led to the development of several frameworks; Scrum is one of the most popular in the games industry.

Scrum

Scrum is traditionally best suited for teams of 10-15 people; for larger teams, there are modified versions such as Large-Scale Scrum and Scrum of Scrums.

Scrum itself usually relies on sprints (development cycles) that last a few weeks (usually between one and three), as well as short daily standup meetings (where relevant progress is being shared). Longer development cycles can be used but anything spanning more than four weeks hampers the iterative process and becomes very hard to plan. Flexibility is a core tenet of Scrum, and it has to be preserved by adhering to short (but still meaningful) sprint cycles.

In Scrum, a product owner (usually the producer) represents the interests of an end user and ensures that all development tasks are divided into a set of comprehensive tickets.

 Tickets are virtual reminders of the work you have to do. Most teams use online ticket and bug tracking systems such as *Jira*, which offer easy to use dashboards and manage everything, from feature and content creation tasks to bugs and issues that come out of testing. Work done in each sprint cycle has to be properly tracked as tickets so it can be planned and tested.

A task to create a resource trading feature would probably take the shape of a user story (a task that's described from the point of view of the end user), starting with *As a player, I can easily trade resources with my guildmates...* and would be followed by a detailed set of functionalities and acceptance criteria, and possibly paired with a user interface mockup or a link to a relevant design document. These tasks are placed in the product backlog and wait for the end of the current development cycle. The backlog itself is a database of all tasks and bugs. It's usually handled by tracking software such as *Jira* and requires regular oversight from the production staff (including the designer).

On top of using software dashboards, many teams opt for a physical sprint board often placed on an actual office wall or a large whiteboard. The sprint board is where all relevant *tasks* end up, often in the form of sticky notes. Bugs rarely live on these boards as they are too small to track with such scrutiny. Moreover, bugs rarely follow the workflow of new feature and improvement tickets.
A physical sprint board is a great visual indicator and serves as the epicenter of daily standup meetings, where people working on each task share their progress and move the ticket across the board to reflect their progress. Commonly, sprint boards are divided into four columns: to do, in progress, testing, and done.

The sprints themselves can consist of multiple phases. For example, in a game that has already been released, a three-week sprint might have two weeks of development (after which all features are locked into place) and a week fully dedicated to bug fixing, testing, and a store submission of the improved version of the game. Each sprint formally ends with a retrospective and starts with a planning meeting. During sprint planning, any upcoming tasks are pulled from the backlog, estimated by their respective disciplines, and slotted into the newsprint.

Game designers working in Agile teams will greatly benefit from their iterative nature and increased flexibility, but only if they stay diligent! Once the development cycle begins, it is unlikely you'll be able to sneak in extra feature work. Any improvements and ideas you'd like to put into the game will have to be turned into concise and actionable tickets and brought to everyone's attention during sprint planning or backlog grooming (a regular analysis of all open tickets). Design documents and spreadsheets will rarely be seen by your teammates unless you include them in the tickets themselves.

Production schedule and milestones

Due to their ever-changing nature, game projects are incredibly difficult to plan. By now, most gamers are very familiar with the frustration of having their most anticipated game delayed and pushed back multiple times. In such situations, no one suffers more than the developer; publishers rarely pay for extended development.

Games vary in size, and teams vary in velocity. Still, the main production phase can span anywhere from several months for some of the smaller mobile games, to three or four years for big PC and console titles.

Game projects are divided into specific phases and milestones, and each milestone has a set of criteria that has to be fulfilled. If the project is being funded by a publisher, the developer will only be paid once the milestones are delivered, reviewed, and approved by the publisher.

The production process allows for better structure development, estimating its costs and increasing the chances of finishing the product on spec and on time. Unfortunately, big design pivots, unforeseen technical issues, licensing problems, and financial pressures are commonplace in our industry. Experienced producers always push for a buffer of an additional 15-25% development time on each milestone, and quite often that still isn't enough.

These production processes are essential even if you're working on your own or as a part of a tiny independent operation. A set of deadlines and even loosely defined short and mid-term goals to work towards will help you focus, stay motivated, and increase the chances of finishing the project.

Greenlight gates and vertical slice

As we already know, game development is risky and expensive. To minimize the risk, during the life cycle of a project it will likely have to go through at least one greenlight gate—a point at which the fate of the game is being decided. A failure to greenlight will force the team to go back and iterate on the idea or result in the game being canceled altogether.

Before real production starts, game designers work with their producers to create and present the initial greenlight documentation to the key stakeholders in the company, hoping to convince them that the concept being proposed is a wise investment of time and money.

Once development starts, a version of the game itself is what's being shown. It's a common practice to start the project with the aim of spending the first several months on creating a so-called Vertical Slice. Vertical Slices are essentially demo versions of the main game hoping to showcase its potential, prove the artistic vision, and validate basic gameplay mechanics. Think of them as vertical slices of a cake: it may cover a very small area of the final product but contains all major ingredients (game systems are essentially horizontal layers). It serves as a good indication of whether it's worth the commitment to make the whole cake/game.

It's not uncommon to use Vertical Slices to present the game to the press, create teaser trailers, as well as to try and get external investors or publishers on board with funding the project. However, at diligent studios, many games will get canceled before they get that far.

Traditional milestone structure

While each studio and game producer can have their own way of running a project, a variation of the traditional set of milestones and production phases (borrowed from the movie industry) is employed by most:

- **Concept phase**: An idea is born! A concept document (usually in a form of a 5-20 slide presentation) is created and pitched to key stakeholders. If the project is given the go-ahead, the initial preproduction team is assembled and tasked with expanding the concept.

- **Preproduction**: A crucial period where the most important design decisions are likely to be made. Core gameplay mechanics are being validated by prototyping. The game's scope, art direction, technical requirements, production schedule, and team size are all being established. At the end of preproduction, the GDD should be finalized by the designer and approved by key stakeholders.
- **Production**: The team begins to execute on the agreed design, writing production-quality code, art assets, and content. As a rule of thumb, the further the game is into production, the harder it becomes to make large changes in product design.
  - **Pre-alpha**: Depending on the length of the project, several interim production milestones are usually set, with the aforementioned Vertical Slice often being one of them. These give the team a defined mid-term goal to work towards and are useful even if there is no publisher (and therefore payment) associated with them.
  - **Alpha**: At the end of the Alpha stage, the product should be *feature-complete*, meaning the game is playable from start to finish (should it have one) with all functionalities and content roughly in place. That said, the quality will be far from final, with many bugs left to be fixed and various improvements and changes to be made, often based on the results of playtesting.
  - **Beta**: Beta represents a much more complete version of the game. In theory, all of the content is locked in place and the only changes being made from there on are bug fixes, balancing changes, tweaks, and polishing. Some companies will conduct public beta tests that are either closed (invite only) or open to everyone.
  - **Gold candidate**: Once all important issues have been addressed, a release candidate can be approved by the publisher to put the game on the path to distribution! The gold status itself goes back to the old practice of creating a **GM** (**Gold Master**)—a version of the game that would be signed off and used for mass duplication of the final product.
  - **Release**: It's time to celebrate! Your game has beaten the odds! Making games is hard and expensive, and the vast majority never see the light of day.

- **Post-release**: Depending on the post-release support plan, the team will either drop the milestone structure and handle improvements and additions on a sprint-by-sprint basis or create additional milestones around the creation of **DLC** (**downloadable content**) and larger expansions.

Validation funnel in-game development

Let us delve into a slightly less traditional and more experimental approach to game production. While most game studios avoid talking publicly about unreleased and failed game projects, companies such as *Supercell* and *Wooga* often talk about the huge amount of games they have *killed* (canceled) at various stages of their life cycle. Some projects get canceled as late as during a *soft launch* that is, a test release in one of the smaller market such as Canada, Australia, Philippines, or the Netherlands.

Isn't canceling 9 out of 10 games hugely wasteful? And why would a nearly finished game ever get shelved?

Companies that adopt this model often operate in the mobile market, where the costs of marketing and user acquisition far outweigh the entire development cost. As the mobile market is a hit-driven one and studio resources are limited, to release a poorly performing product would mean to not work on something with a potentially much bigger upside—an opportunity cost, you may say.

The process of gradually culling less promising projects is what validation funnel is all about, and there's much to learn from it, no matter the type of game you work on and the markets you operate in. For one, games are never sure-fire hits. To allow for a high cancellation rate (especially in the early stages of the development) is to enable your team to take more risks and be creative. It's also important to give the teams the power to kill their product, rather than to have that decision flow from senior executives—the former is empowering and inspiring, the latter antagonizes and demotivates. If the decision has been made well into production, a *postmortem* presentation should follow. The aim of the postmortem is to analyze the production process, explain the reasoning behind key decisions, and share any learning from the project across the entire company.

The following is the validation funnel and game development process employed at *Space Ape games* at the time of writing. At the core of the process are small teams supported by shared company resources and outsourcing. While this funnel is focused on free to play mobile games, a similar approach could be taken with any digital product:

- **Ideation**: At *Space Ape games*, roughly a day per month is dedicated to an initiative during which the company can come together to form self-directed mini-teams that collaborate on something outside their day-to-day duties. This initiative often has a set objective and creative constraint; it may be around T-shaping, branding, improving existing games, or coming up with new ideas and prototypes. If new games are the focus, the lineup of game concepts and prototypes is voted on by the wider company. Ideas that are popular and deemed viable are then expanded upon and taken into preproduction, or put in the backlog awaiting a more suitable time. The key differentiation here is that new game ideas are not dictated by the executives or creative directors; they form and gain traction organically from within the whole company.
- **Preproduction**: A team is formed around the idea and works on its design. Core game loop, game pillars, target audience, brand, art, and technical direction are all being defined. The preproduction phase of *Space Ape games* is kept short and often ends with market sizing.
- **Market sizing**: This validation phase usually includes market research (looking into industry trends and competition) as well as testing our idea for a brand and potential user acquisition costs. To do the latter, we will often create a set of test advertising campaigns using a few potential art styles and brands for our game. The game will only pass if there's space for the product in the market and potential user acquisition costs are acceptable. It's possible to delay market sizing and begin the work on the internal prototype, but ultimately, all games need to make sure they can acquire an audience if needed.
- **Internal prototype**: The game concept is now ready for execution and a more polished and feature-rich prototype is being created. The team will now extensively iterate on gameplay and gather feedback from internal and external playtesting. At the end of this phase, a company-wide test is held. If the team is satisfied with the feedback and believes in the product, and if there are no *red lights* on the horizon, the game idea will live on!

- **Alpha**: The team switches over to writing production-quality code and continues to develop and playtest the game. The difference here is that Alpha builds can be used to gather external validation. This only happens if the team itself decides to seek real-world insight into certain aspects (such as experimental controls or multiplayer code). In such cases, a test version of the game will be released in a small territory, often with a placeholder name and under the umbrella of a brand new publishing name. The only way to test unknown quantities is to release the game to a real market and see how it fares. As everything is subject to extensive changes and most of the game will still be missing, these early versions of the game do not allow for any in-app purchases and are not ready to provide real insight into important stats such as user retention.

- **Beta**: A natural expansion of the Alpha stage with production going full Steam ahead. As always, company playthroughs, playtesting, and external validation help to push the game in a more refined direction. At the beta stage, the metagame should be validated (at least internally); this means the inclusion of long-term progression and features focused on improving player retention. The game is still likely to undertake major changes and will abstain from including any in-app purchases.

- **Soft launch**: At this stage, the game is released in a few territories, with the official title and branding. The game will remain in soft launch for several months as the team works on additional features, balancing, and polishing the product and improving the **KPIs** (**Key Performance Indicators**). Such KPIs include user acquisition costs, player retention, purchase conversion rate, estimated LTV (lifetime monetary value of a retained user), game session length, and frequency.

- **Release**: As the game is nearing worldwide release, the company will work on the game's marketing and user acquisition strategies. By then, the platform representatives (in this case Google and Apple) might already be aware of the product and its upcoming release, increasing the chances of receiving the ever-elusive featuring (for example, a prominent promotional banner on the virtual storefront).

- **Live ops**: The worldwide release of a free to play game marks the end of the official development phase and the beginning of the live operations era. The game team will continue to work on designing and implementing new features and content, and the game's live operations managers will ensure a steady stream of engaging events. In this world, the release is just the beginning.

Thanks to market sizing, frequent playtesting, and multiple stages of internal and external validation, teams at *Supercell* and *Space Ape games* can take risks with their ideas, yet minimize the unknowns when launching a finished product. It may be difficult for a game to make it to the end of the funnel, but once it does, it's much more likely to become critically and commercially successful, warranting ongoing support and investment.

As always, it's important to note that no process is set in stone. While every phase described here is important, the funnel approach is likely to shift and evolve along with industry practices, the company, and its culture.

Role of a games publisher

It's possible that a game project you'll be working on will have a publisher other than your studio. The relation between the publisher and the studio can either be internal (in which case they own the developer) or external (the publisher is connected to the studio).

Whatever the relation to the developer, the publisher will not only release the product under its own name and market it, they are also very likely to cover all of the costs of development. Deals and royalty structures vary greatly, but in most cases, publishers are the ones who keep the cash flowing between all involved parties and are the ones who are set to gain (or lose) the most. Publishing can get very complex; sometimes more than one studio will work on a single game, other times an external owner of an **intellectual property** (**IP**) will be involved (the IP itself can be a brand, a book, video game, or movie universe).

When a publisher is engaged in the project, the detailed milestone structure mentioned previously will be of paramount importance as it will carry financial outcomes for the developer. Publishers will have to approve the GDD and provide feedback on each and every milestone; this can, of course, limit the flexibility of the developer, but it will also help ensure the project stays on track and has a chance of being released. Sometimes, publishers also take care of initial ideation and seed the game pitch to the developer.

Summary

As you surely realize by now, game development is quite complex and game design itself can be a very broad and elusive subject...

We might have just scratched the surface, but so far we've looked at how games are being produced, what kinds of teams make them, and what responsibilities a designer can assume within a development team.

Some games might have no real ending, but every game project has a start! We'll now put some of that industry knowledge into perspective, and start looking at how to work on a game idea and turn it into a presentable game concept.

And remember, your job is not to design the perfect gameplay system and walk away. You are there to help realize the game's potential and turn it into the best possible experience for your players. Put your personal preferences and biases aside and focus on what's good for the project, even if it requires you to scrap ill-fitting ideas and throw away weeks or months of work in the process.

Game Concept

2

Every game starts with a concept, an idea of what the player experience will be—a vision of a world coming to life on screen.

The challenge, once this idea takes shape in the creator's mind, is to fix it and communicate it to everyone involved in the game development process.

In this chapter, we're going to learn how to write a game concept and your responsibilities as a game designer in the process of doing so.

We are going to cover topics such as:

- Defining what a game concept is
- The formal structure of the game concept document
- How to compare your idea to what's already out there
- What are themes, fantasy, and mood, and why are they important at this stage?

We are going to use some practical examples from real-life scenarios and you will be able to follow the tips in each paragraph of this chapter and create your own game concept, based on your own idea or an existing game.

What is a game concept?

Imagine a game that you have played from beginning to end or one that you have simply loved and played for a long time. Would you be able to write a two-to-five pages short presentation on that game? A presentation that describes why is it fun, how you play it, what it looks like, and for what kind of player it is going to be a great experience?

Now imagine that you've never played that game, that it doesn't even exist yet. Would you still be able to describe it?

That vision is the game you want to make and the presentation is a game concept.

The purpose of the game concept is to describe a game with enough detail *to distill and communicate its vision* to the reader. To explain what makes it fun, who'll enjoy playing it, and why we should make it a reality.

One of the main responsibilities of every game designer is to make sure that, at every stage of development, the vision behind the game is clearly documented and communicated to the team.

The earlier you are in the development cycle, the more abstract this documentation will be. What starts with a short high-level concept will eventually turn into a full game design document that can easily span over a hundred pages. Later on (especially if you work in an Agile team), your documentation efforts are likely going to shift into feature specs (a focused design document that only will be used to explain a single standalone element of the game) and small *user stories* or *tickets* mentioned in Chapter 1, *Introducing the Game Production Process*.

As one of the very first steps in the development process, the game concept is the most abstract document, so it is paramount that it stays focused on the core aspects of the game.

After all, you only have a few pages to describe the whole thing. You don't really want to linger on your main protagonist's story for four pages and then describe how the game works in the remaining few lines of the last page.

A game concept is a holistic view of the game; it describes the game and what the team is going to put into it (not just the designers; it contains early artwork and technical and marketing information):

Exercise
This is your first exercise. If you have a game idea already in your head, try to put it on paper: a couple of pages would be enough. If you don't have any particular game idea in mind, try to describe a game that you have played and loved enough to know all its rules and secrets.

There's no need to read the rest of Chapter 1, *Introducing the Game Production Process*. Do the exercise now, before knowing anything more.

Once this is done, keep going with the reading and the exercises. You will be able to compare your initial work with what we're going to see, expand it, and find and correct any eventual mistake by yourself.

Structure of a game concept document So, how do you write a game concept? And what do you need before starting?

There is some information that any game concept should always contain:

- Introduction (sometimes called a *hook* or *elevator pitch*)
- Description/game overview
- A list of key features, including its **Unique Selling Points** (**USPs**)
- Game genre
- Platform
- Target audience

It is clear from this list that your role as a game designer is not about deciding all this. The game idea or hook may come from any other team member, from an external client, from a publisher, or from some lead/director within the company.

The games industry offers a lot of freedom and possibilities; there are companies that make games to make a profit or indie developers that follow their passion and make their games because they have something to say—there are even people working on games in their free time just because they love it.

Regardless of the motivations or the goals of a developer, it's always a good idea to treat a game such as a commercial product. This means that, in order to justify the existence of the game, there must be people willing to buy it, play it, and hopefully even talk about it. This is why the game concept needs to go beyond a simple description of a game; you have to think about a game concept as a sales tool.

The audience may vary (and so do the formality and the structure of the document) but the goal stays the same: whoever reads the document must understand and see what the development team wants to do, and needs to get excited about that!

The reader might be a publisher to which you are presenting the idea. Presenting really means selling, in this case. But the reader could be the programmer who is going to implement the game or an artist who is going to create all the artwork or graphical assets, or even just a possible player. All these people will look at the document in a different way, but one thing is for sure: if they get what the document is trying to present they will get excited about the project and look forward to whatever it is they have an interest in, from giving the money needed for its development, to working on it or to just playing it!

Exercise

Try to compare the work you have done in your first exercise with what you have learned in this paragraph. Does your concept include information such as genre, platform, or target audience?

Read on to understand what are we talking about and why these things are as important as the mere description of the game.

The "hook" or "elevator pitch"

You have a couple of sentences, three maximum, to describe what your game is going to be. The introduction has to condense all the information that you will expand in the rest of the document. This is your first page and if it doesn't catch your reader's attention, nothing else you have to say will.

It's not only that; by stripping your whole game down to such a fundamental description, you are focusing on what's really important. It's like a mantra you will have to follow during development because that's your promise to your players.

It's called *a hook* because the reader wants to know more. Some call it an *elevator pitch* because it's what you can say to a stranger in a 30-second elevator ride. A great example comes from a well-known game developer, Rami Ismail. He and his team, Vlambeer, made a game called *Ridiculous Fishing*, a hit mobile game from 2013.

What is it? In his own words, it's *Fishing with machine guns*.

In just four words, this sentence tells a lot about the game, but also makes you wonder *how?* (and probably *why?*). You're hooked. You want to know more. Great introduction!

 There are no strict rules on how to put together your introduction. In a multimedia world, some games are introduced with a short video, a set of mood boards, or concept art. These are all powerful tools that can be used to communicate the game vision. Don't limit yourself to just words on a page; after all, a picture is worth a thousand words. At the same time, keep in mind your audience, be sure that the person who is going to read your concept can clearly understand your intentions. As your audience changes (from peers to high-level executives), you might need to change things around and adapt your concept.

Description

In a few paragraphs, a page, or a few slides, this is where the game is described. All the main elements should appear in this section:

- The core gameplay mechanics

- The narrative
- Mode and setting
- Information about the characters and the game world

The idea is to give to the reader a clear picture of how the final experience is going to be. This is also the section with more space for multimedia. Concept artwork can juxtapose text to reinforce it, but also to give directions about the art style.

Sometimes audio and soundtracks will be a defining part of a game concept (just think about musical games), and for games that would require an extensive use of audio, such as narrative games with voice acting, including these details early in the concept is as important as defining the core gameplay mechanics.

 A common mistake while writing the description is to include too specific information or yield to the temptation of exaggerating. Describing the game combat as *driven by a revolutionary artificial intelligence* is not a good idea if developing that AI is not part of the plan (or the budget). And in case it is, there's no need to go into the details of how such an AI will work, even though a few words to describe why it's defined as *revolutionary* might be required.

Key feature set

This is a list of the features that make your game a great experience for your players. There's no need to include all the system you will be designing, but it is expected that a game concept includes all the main ones. This means that a healthy development cycle starts with a fundamental feature set that remains largely unchanged (unless things don't work out as expected and you find yourself in dire need of a big design pivot).

Some common key features are game modes, multiplayer guild systems, battle systems, playable characters, progression systems, and technical features (such as advanced AI or particular graphics). The list is as long as a designer's imagination can go, so make sure to include only the ones really relevant to your game.

To look at some practical examples, the App Store gives some very good insights. Most App Store descriptions contain a list of the game's key features. *Hearthstone*, for example, markets itself with the following messages:

> *JUMP RIGHT IN: Fun introductory missions bring you into the world of Hearthstone's intuitive gameplay.*

BUILD YOUR DECK: With hundreds of additional cards to win and craft - your collection grows with you.

HONE YOUR SKILLS: Play in practice matches against computer-controlled heroes of the Warcraft universe. Thrall, Uther, Gul'dan - they're all here!

COLLECTION TRAVELS WITH YOU: Your card collection is linked to your Battle.net account - enabling you to switch your play between tablet and desktop with ease.

AND FIGHT FOR GLORY: When you're ready, step into the Arena and duel other players for the chance to win awesome prizes!

As you can see, Blizzard did an excellent job of mixing technical and gameplay features, describing them with taglines that make players excited about their trading card game. These messages were obviously written by the marketing team for the finished product, but they are a perfect example of clearly and efficiently communicating the key feature set to the target audience.

Finding your USP

What makes your game different? What is its USP?

Finding the USP is a fundamental step in defining your key feature set, especially if your concept is intended for a publisher or an investor.

The USP determines that unique mechanism or takes on your genre that are going to make your game stand out from the competition, the reason why players out there will be interested in dedicating their valuable time to your game instead of the many others that they already have or are interested in trying.

To help you understand the idea behind the USP, sometimes also called *breakthrough*, let's have a look at some widely popular and successful games. The *Assassin's Creed* franchise came out in 2007 and it revolutionized the action-adventure game genre by introducing its famous *parkour* mechanic. The ability to traverse on the vertical axis by freely climbing buildings was a fresh and innovative feature and helped set the game apart from its competition. The public response was immensely positive, and despite some major flaws in that original game, Assassin's Creed became one of the biggest game franchises in history.

Another famous example, on a different platform: *Supercell's Clash Royale*. The core gameplay is based on collecting cards and battling with them in an arena with other players. The game is full of fresh takes on different mechanics, but it has one very clear USP: real-time **Player vs Player** (**PvP**). When the game came out in mid-2016, very few mobile games were relying on synchronous PvP. Most titles at the time were either turn-based or real-time vs AI (the other player being controlled by an artificial intelligence). Clearly, it was a consequence of the technical challenges of creating synchronous PvP games on mobile.

Like in any market, an unexplored area is both a risk and an opportunity. *Supercell* was successful in pushing the boundaries of mobile multiplayer games towards synchronous PVP and created a billion-dollar game in the process.

The USP concept seems to be another one more concerning marketing and sales. Indeed, the two questions: *Why should I buy your game?* and *Why should I play your game?* have very similar answers, but as a game designer, your job is to answer the latter. However, most of the time, that will answer the former too!

> **Exercise**
> Have you clearly defined the USP for your game concept? Try to add it to your document.
> Is it unique enough to make the concept stand out from similar games?
> Do you know any other examples of game franchises that owe their popularity to a specific USP? Think about a few of them and compare their USP with yours.

Platform

This refers to the hardware on which the game will be played or a particular distribution platform. Hardware such as PCs, games consoles, mobile devices, and virtual reality headsets are considered *platforms*, but also specific environments such as Facebook or iMessage are platforms themselves. Each platform brings a unique set of requirements and opens up very different possibilities, both on the technical and creative sides.

Choosing the right platform for your game has to be one of the earliest decisions. The platform on its own can have an immense influence on the game design, from the target audience and business model to controls, user interface, and performance requirements. Platform choice in itself sets certain expectations towards the game you're making. There's a good reason why match-three puzzle games are not swarming the console market.

From an audience perspective, a card solitaire game may work really well on smartphones but is unlikely to be as popular on consoles. Similarly, but from a hardware angle, a strategy game that relies on precise controls provided by mouse and keyboard might not translate very well to the console or handheld input methods.

There are many unspoken rules to game design, and knowing when to break them is part of the art. Introducing a complex strategy game to the smartphone market and tackling the challenges of the platform head-on might result in a very innovative and interesting product. But remember, such experiments are risky, so make sure you know the rules before you try to break them!

Each platform has also a very tangible impact on how the game will be designed. The most evident example is about input controls: an action game would pose completely different challenges on a mobile device than on a console controller...

Those difference in design are not limited to the platform technology; the way the player expects to interact with games on different platforms is important too. A mobile game would be usually characterized by short sessions where the player is able to complete the whole game loop in just a few minutes, while a PC game could require the same amount of time just to go through a single cutscene.

Audience

There is a huge difference between an educational game for little kids and an 18+ rated zombie shooter.

Defining the audience is part of the initial creative process. Even if it seems such as a consequence of the kind of game one wants to make, it is important to spend some time thinking about it and having a clear idea of who is going to play the game. The kids/adult example is an easy one, but identifying an audience means asking yourself questions such as who is interested in this game? Which other similar games does he or she play? What are they expecting from a new game in their favorite genre?

Mere demographics are still an important factor in defining an audience, but in our modern world, amazingly, pretty much everyone plays video games and there's no such thing as a *young hardcore gamer* or an *average casual gamer*.

These are concepts from the past that it is important to leave behind. Everyone is a potential gamer in today's world, but each and every gamer is interested in very different game experiences. Internet and online communities give game developers an incredible tool to find out about people's desires and fantasies in terms of what they'd love to play. User research is done by many developers, submitting rough concepts, trailers, or marketing materials of games that don't yet exist to test and learn from those desires.

Video game audiences are also constantly evolving. There is a great article written by Meg Jayanth (the writer behind 80 Days) for The Guardian in 2014 titled:

> *"52% of gamers are women – but the industry doesn't know it"*.

(`https://www.theguardian.com/commentisfree/2014/sep/18/52-percent-people-playing-games-women-industry-doesnt-know`). Give it a good read! Industry reports available online can also give you a great idea of the different (and, sometimes, unexpected) types of audience out there.

When you define your target audience, try to go beyond a generic definition. Define your audience by their interests.
Casual players who have a few spare minutes on their commute is incredibly more accurate than *an average casual gamer*.
Hardcore players who grew up playing strategy games such as Dune II and Fallout Tactics are not quite the same as *hardcore strategy game players*.
A more precise target audience definition is extremely helpful because it gives you something to design around already. Just look at the information contained in *casual players who have a few spare minutes on their commute*. You don't only know that your game is for casual players, you also know that the average game session should last no more than *a few minutes* and that the game might have some problems working online, as commuting usually means unstable mobile networks.

Age rating systems

You surely have heard about PEGI or ESRB. Age-based rating systems are important in the game industry and they should be taken into consideration by developers. Knowing beforehand that you are developing a game that is supposed to be PEGI 7, for example, already says a lot about the game design itself.

The same goes for mature-rated games.

Sometimes, the very fact that they are mature-rated is part of the concept.

In fact, the idea of including an *expected* age-based rating in the concept might help in creating a game actually suitable for that age restriction.

There is an everlasting debate about these systems and how they are (or are not) useful to consumers, especially parents choosing a game for their children. As will often be the case in this book, we strongly recommend you explore the topic on your own; but for now, keep in mind that they are not just tools to rate a finished game, but also useful guidelines to keep a project on track so it's suitable for a particular audience.

Genre

If you think about movies, since there's no interactivity involved, the narrative theme is enough to define an entire genre: thrillers, war movies, romantic movies, comedies, and so on.

Since games are an interactive medium, talking about a *war game* doesn't really tell us much about it. Therefore, in games, the *genre is more informative than the theme and the setting*. And so our genres, such as a **First Person Shooter** *(FPS)*, are heavily related to the gameplay at hand. An FPS can take place in different settings and explore different themes: from historic, to present day or even sci-fi.

Genre tells the players what kind of game they will be playing, and it's a very useful way to classify games. There are quite a lot of genres and each genre might have many sub-genres. Also, smart game designers are constantly redefining genres and pushing the boundaries of what a genre means. Nonetheless, it is safe to say that some genres are universally recognized by both developers and players as standard.

Some examples are FPS, platformers, **role-playing games (RPG)**, sports games, **mass multiplayer online games (MMO)**, **Multiplayer online battle arenas (MOBA)**, strategy games, and simulations. The list goes on and on.

Defining the genre, or having a genre as a starting point for redefining one, is a crucial part of creating a game concept, certainly the one that will most influence the entire design process:

Exercise
How many genres are you familiar with? Make a list of all the genres you know and then highlight the ones you have never played. Get yourself some games in those genres and familiarize yourself with them. Everyone has their favorite genre, but by becoming a game designer, you can't afford to ignore the genres you don't like to play. You are not a mere videogamer

```
anymore!
Have a look at this great list on Wikipedia and keep learning about old
games and genres you might have missed!
https://en.wikipedia.org/wiki/List_of_video_game_genres
```

Business model

The business model (or revenue model) is simply a system by which the game is going to make money. Remember, a game is ultimately a product that needs to be sold, even the most artistic one—surprisingly enough, even the ones that will be given away for free. As we already mentioned, a game concept is not a one-man job by the game designer. Just like game design, creating a game concept is a collaborative work in which the whole team participates and there might be also requirements coming from outside. This includes the business model, and the team needs to have a clear idea of how it will work.

You might think that this is something about marketing that doesn't really concern you, but the business model will have an impact on how the game is designed; therefore, it is absolutely your concern and has to be clear from the beginning.

 Some developers think that business models are some kind of virus that infected the game development world in recent years. That great games *are going to sell because they are great,* so there's no need to think about it. Or maybe, that smaller games made by a handful of developers don't need to waste time on marketing stuff.
Sometimes, indeed, this is true, especially because there are many reasons to make a game with no intention of selling it.
That said though, the rest of the time (which is most of the time) games have to be sold and the job of the game developer is to make games for a living. So keep the business model in mind, and design around it from the beginning. *Create something so great that players are willing to pay for it.*

There are three main business models through which a game can generate revenue:

- **Premium**: A premium game is paid upfront and then it can be played virtually forever by the player. It is still the dominant business model for console and PC games. Some examples include *The Elder Scroll V: Skyrim, The Sims,* and *The Legend Of Zelda: Breath of the Wild.*

- **Subscription**: Games with subscriptions require the player to pay a monthly fee in order to continue to access the game. The most popular subscription-based games are MMOs such as *World of Warcraft* or *Eve Online*.
- **Free to Play**: **Free to Play** (**F2P**) games can be downloaded and played for free and rely entirely on optional microtransactions. Extensive information on this business model can be found later on, in `Chapter 15`, *Games As a Service*.

Sounds simple enough, right? Like every aspect of game development, there's a whole lot under the surface! Each of those three main models can be implemented in a variety of different ways and also intertwined with each other.

Premium games can be given out for free as a demo (only a limited amount of content available for free) or for a limited amount of time (free weekends are really popular for competitive multiplayer games such as Overwatch). Premium games can also be enriched with further content releases of **downloadable content** (**DLC**). This is new and fresh content (levels, characters, game modes, and so forth) made available later to keep players interested and engaged in a game. Usually, DLC is sold for extra money, but sometimes it might be free (for everyone or just for players who purchased a particular edition of the game).

A great example of an innovative business model is Episodic games, popularized by *Telltale games*, with their series of licensed titles such as *The Walking Dead* and *Back to the Future*. This is essentially an evolution of the old shareware (demo) or trial model but naturally divided and reinforced by the narrative. Usually, the first episode is given away for free, and the player can decide to purchase each additional episode individually or *subscribe* and gain access to the entire season.

F2P games can generate their revenues in even more creative and new ways. Offering virtual goods or in-game currencies for real money is just one possibility. F2P games can make money through advertisements (yes, just like TV shows!) and then sell players the ad-free version, or they can ask players to watch an ad to get an in-game reward, or maybe to subscribe to the game to get the same reward without having to watch any ads.

There are many possibilities, but regardless of the business model you chose for your game, one thing must not be forgotten: the business model and the game design are intertwined.

Creating a game and thinking about its business model as the last step before release is a huge mistake. Switching between vastly different business models in the middle of the development process (for example, turning a premium game into an F2P one) is a very dangerous move that can seriously derail the product. This is why the business model is an essential part of the game concept. Like anything else in it, it sets important guidelines for the entire development:

Exercise
Did your initial concept include something about the business model?
Think about it and include it in your concept. Does it change your idea of
the game? What are players going to pay for?

Know your competition

There is another reason why a game concept is such an important milestone in starting to create a new game. Once your game genre, audience, and platform are defined, it is possible to take a look at what's out there in the market: your competition. Understanding games similar to the one you will be developing is crucial to the project's success. It is very likely that the developers of those other games have already faced and solved (or maybe not!) many of the problems you will encounter at some point during development.

Communities of players already playing those games might be discussing them in depth online. This is an invaluable resource for you, as you will be able to fix known problems or add features to your game, based on what real players are willing and hoping to play.

 Other ways of gaining insight into the competition include game postmortems (first-hand reports on what went right and wrong on a particular game project), user research, analytics, and industry press.

Your competition also defines the state of your game's genre, giving you a clear direction regarding your design. Once you have analyzed your competition, you can ask yourself questions such as:

- *Is my game too similar to what's already out there?*
- *How is it different?*
- *Does it offer a better and novel experience to its target audience?*
- *If I was a fan of my competitor's game, would I be interested in trying out this new game?*

Answering these questions honestly will help you establish and test your USPs.

The ideation process

We have already explored defining and communicating game ideas to others through the game concept document, now let's pose a more fundamental question. How do we generate the game idea in the first place? How do we get to the point of having something to write down in the concept document?

Before we begin, let's make it clear that the game designer is not the *ideas guy*. It is not their job to have a constant flow of new game ideas. These can (and should) come from anyone in the company or even from people outside your organization. It's very common in our industry to have publishers *commission* a game idea to the developers, an owner of an **intellectual property** (**IP**) such as *Star Wars* or *The Witcher* to seek out licensing, or game studios themselves providing outsourcing services to other developers.

A game idea could be driven by market research, a game vision, or even, in a more artistic way, by the urge to say something or tell a story. What is really important for you as a game designer is to have what I like to call the *designer mindset*. The designer mindset allows you to process raw ideas analytically. You should be able to imagine a finished product being played by your audience. You will need to predict any major problems and issues, have a clear idea of the competition, and some intuition about possible USPs.

There are no shortcuts to developing this mindset; you have to play games and create them, to know what works and what doesn't, to keep a critical eye on everything you play and see. Ideally, you will strive to become a true expert in the genres you are more interested in (both as a designer and as a player), but to do so, you'll often need to explore all sorts of games. You might not be keen to play certain types of game, but you must still try and understand what makes them fun for their intended audience. A truly great designer will be able to point out good and bad design decisions in anything from a pony nurturing game to a horror shooter.

Every developer (not just game designers) dreams of working on their dream game, but as a professional who's trying to make a living, you will have to adapt your skills and career goals to what's required of you. Shift your expectations to the available opportunities and embrace the challenge of working on something that isn't your forte. Your job will rarely allow you to create a perfect representation of your dream game; until that time arrives, be resourceful and make the best possible game, treating your constraints as interesting problems rather than depressing limitations. Learn from your mistakes and do the best you can for the players and the team!

The designer mindset and the game designer profession are something you develop with experience and dedication. Like any other discipline, you will need to study and work hard.

Coming up with ideas

As we said, ideas can come from many different sources, so let's try to recap them in a practical list of activities that can help you come up with interesting concepts for future new games:

- Play tons of video games, especially ones outside your favorite genres
- Watch movies, TV, and theatre, and read books
- Travel
- Think how to turn your interests outside gaming into a game (bricolage, wine, fitness, art, music, traveling, and so on)
- Analyze the market and think about unique games that are not quite there
- Ask other people what they'd like to play that is not quite there
- Deconstruct your favorite games, focusing on what would make them better
- Go to game jams where you'll have a very restricted amount of time to create a game around a given theme
- Give yourself a theme and try to make a game around that in a very short time
- Learn the basics of a game engine and do some stuff! Anything: follow online tutorials, try to recreate some game mechanics, just mess around with example projects

Twisting familiar mechanics

As a game developer, your goal will always be to create new interesting games, but as we can learn from other game developers' success stories, a successful game is always a mix of novelty and familiarity. If you think about most of the games available today, you can clearly see how each of them is an iteration of an older game or well know mechanics. Very few games are completely new and with *never-seen-before* core mechanics.

In fact, your role as a game designer is not to invent a completely new set of mechanics every time, but to pick a set that works well with the game you're making. Using existing mechanics, refining well-known concepts, and falling back on clichéd settings is totally fine (if you think about it, many multimillion dollars franchises do exactly that). Just make sure that you have a very clear goal of what you want to achieve and how the mechanics you picked are helping you deliver on your vision.

Don't be afraid, there will be plenty of space for innovation and creativity even working on proven mechanics. More importantly, there will be plenty of occasions to work on truly innovative games in your career. Just keep in mind that, as a professional game designer, your goal is to design compelling game experiences and not to do something new and different at all costs.

It must be clear at this point that everything that goes into the game concept will have a direct impact on how the game is going to be designed. This is why it is so important that it is defined as a first stage and must be kept in mind for the whole development process.

It must act as the ultimate reference, a guide to keep the vision clear and the project on track during the difficult and exciting times ahead when the proper development begins.

Creativity through constraints

The main risk of defining and refining a game concept when is in its ideation stage is to underestimate the project scope or the actual ability of the team to accomplish such effort. The fact that these limits exist is all good news though. Imagine having a blank canvas and being told to draw a beautiful painting, or having a blank page and having to write a short story. This is when artists experience *artist's block*: the inability to produce any new work or let their creativity flow.

Your blank canvas is your ideation space. The more constraints you can identify, the more that space will shrink, allowing you to focus on ideas that could actually work! The size of your team, the expertise on the platform, your budget, the available technology... They all help to inform what you can and cannot realistically do. Every design decision you will make will be somehow constrained. You have to embrace those limits and create something that works within them. Game design is problem-solving, which usually means compromising.

Finding the fun

What do you think about this?

A game where you play as an astronaut who watches Planet Earth being destroyed from a space station?

Or this?

An augmented reality game in which you use your phone to find clues and solve mysteries.

These may sound like good hooks for a game concept (if you think about that first one, that could be a hook for a book or a movie as well), but the most important thing when you are ideating your game is: How can this be fun? What do you do in that game? Is the space station game a survival adventure or a horror? Is it about managing resources or survival? Is it a space shooter? Think about the games you love, what makes them fun? And what is fun anyway? Is it the joy of learning and mastering new systems, of exploring and interacting with the virtual worlds, making interesting choices?

We'll be exploring the connection between *fun* and game mechanics in further chapters while trying to avoid any unnecessary immersions in the theory. That said, it doesn't mean that you don't have to! There are entire books dedicated to the topic of *fun*. Raph Kostner's *Theory of Fun* and Nicole Lazarro's *Four Keys to Fun* are just two of many noteworthy examples.

Good designers are fluent with practical game design techniques and well informed in the theory. Excellent game designers are experts in both. Fun in games comes from the player experience, which is ultimately related to the core game mechanics. As you can imagine, if those core mechanics are not fun, no one will be interested in the game.

Of course, you cannot wait until the game is finished to try it out and see whether it's fun... So how do you do it?

There's only one answer to this question, and it is by prototyping.

Prototyping

We will talk about prototyping in detail later; for now, let's just get some basics:

A prototype is an early sample, model, or release of a product built to test a concept.

Only 15 years ago, building a prototype for a video game concept or to just try out some mechanics was out of the question for most game developers. Today, with tools such as Unity and other accessible game engines, prototyping is extremely quick and efficient, and most importantly, not only a prerogative of games programmers.

Imagine that you want to make a 3D game where two armies clash in battle. Developing a playable demo of such a game, with 3D models of every soldier, the battleground, and the rules behind movement and fighting, is a massive amount of work.

And what if after everything is ready, you find out that the battle is not as fun as you thought it would be?

Prototyping means focusing on the essentials and answering particular gameplay questions. Once it is clear what we want to test out with a prototype—in this case, whether the battle mechanics are fun—we realize that we don't need fully rendered 3D models for soldiers and accurate terrain. We probably don't even need the soldiers.

By abstracting, we'll find out that we will just need some cubes moving on a flat plane. Setting up a plane and some cubes require 5 minutes of work in Unity. Clearly, the challenge would be to make them move and act as if they were soldiers on a battlefield, but since that's what we need to focus on, we can do just that. Eventually, you will find out that the concept of *two armies fighting* was too generic to have a meaningful or realistic prototype. You have to search for the fun at an even more abstract level. You have to ask yourself other questions. What kind of battle are you trying to represent? A medieval battle is very different from a battle between tanks in the Second World War.

 If you're planning to show the prototype to a less imaginative audience, you might want to replace the abstract cubes and shapes with some basic models and images found on the internet. The likes of Unity Asset Store can be a great source of effective prototyping assets! Just make sure that the audience realizes that you're not trying to represent the final look of the game.

Iteration

While prototyping, you essentially *iterate on the concept*, stripping it down to its core.

For example, you may find out that the essence of the game you're trying to make can be described as your unit charging the enemy in a medieval battle. That's your next direction for prototyping, just focus on the charge element, on the enemy's reaction. They can flee if you're charging from one side, or react by firing arrows or standing their ground if you're charging from the front.

All you will see on your screen is going to be just colored cubes chasing each other. But that's already a great start. The sooner you have something playable, the sooner your vision will become more tangible and you will have real feedback not only on its playability but also on its feasibility.

Remember, there's no need to prototype something that's already been proven. There's no point in prototyping running and jumping for a 2D platformer if you already have a strong reference to them. Your prototypes should focus on the USP! For example, the portal gun and its mechanics in *Portal* are more important to prototype than the behavior of the automated turrets.

Defining the fantasy

The common association in the part of the word *fantasy* is with a fictional world populated by magic and fantastic creatures. Let's leave that idea of fantasy behind for now. By *fantasy* here, we mean the *activity of imagining things*, not necessarily things that cannot happen in our real world. You can fantasize about being a doctor, an athlete, or a gangster. That's what we mean by *fantasy*. Defining the fantasy means establishing the imaginary settings and environments for the game world and the actions the player is able to use in it.

The fantasy is not something that needs to be explicitly stated in the game concept, as it emerges from how the game is designed around the initial vision.

In the example we made previously in the *Prototyping* section, we were creating a strategy battle game set in a medieval past. Through iterations, we strip the game to its core, imagining the fun of issuing orders to our units, commanding a charge through enemy lines.

What we did there is come up with a fantasy. The fantasy of being a general ordering troops to charge into battle and conquer enemies. Note how the genre influences the fantasy. A strategy game with many different troops to command implies the player is the *strategist*, therefore the fantasy is being a general of a medieval army.

If the concept (and the prototype) was about a first-person action game where you command a Knight during a charge on the enemy lines, we would have a completely different fantasy (the player being the heroic knight leading the charge). Different fantasy, same setting (and same battle).

Other common fantasies in games include being a hero through his journey to save someone (from *Super Mario* to *Legend of Zelda*) or controlling a team in a specific sport. Again, a fantasy always suggests a genre, but it describes something more telling: a bigger story about the player's actions. Clearly, defining a fantasy means setting up more guidelines that will drive the entire development and any design decision down the line.

Creating the fantasy through game mechanics

Let's go back to the charging knight example we just made. You want that charge to be spectacular, tense, and ultimately satisfying for the player; that means designing the enemy reaction and behavior (and even the game physics) in a way that is meaningful for that fantasy. Imagine if the combat system doesn't include any physics and the Knight simply stops in front of his target after the charge and begins a static fight where both he and his enemy just swing their weapons until one is defeated. Wouldn't it be so much better if the momentum built by the charge sends the enemy through the air and the Knight continues advancing until the momentum is gone (and many enemies have been knocked out). Creating such a game requires the design of the core mechanics to be built around a very specific fantasy.

The mood, or "how the game looks and feels"

Part of the identity of any video game is how it looks on screen and how the combination of its mechanics, visual, and audio creates an *aesthetic* of the game. This combination evokes an emotional response from the player and defines the mood of a game.

The mood is very much part of the design like any other element, as important as gameplay or story. Games such as *Limbo* and *Journey* are essentially designed around a mood, with the specific intention of evoking certain emotions in the player as a central part of the experience.

Usually, it's not the game designer's job to define the mood of a game, but as we have seen, the mood influences the design and vice versa, so it is always an ongoing conversation within the team. Artists create amazing content that can define the mood and the soul of any game and sometimes it's the designer's responsibility to put it together. He might be the first one to actually see it "in-game." Keeping in touch with the art team is crucial to the final quality of the game; designing new content that the art team will have to create is not unidirectional. Make sure to get as much input as you can from the art team about any work they will have to do based on your design!

Exercise

It is time to go through the document you have written, taking into account everything we have been saying. If you chose to create a concept for your own game idea, try to write a new one for an existing one, and vice versa. Try to have someone else read your game concept and give you some feedback. Did they understand the game? Did they get the vision you had in mind while writing? Discuss your results online or with other designers or developers. **Don't be afraid of sharing your ideas**. Yes, there might be a chance that someone will steal them. But there is a far greater chance that someone will like them, and might even hire you for them!

Summary

We have learned some basics about how to conceptualize a game idea and present it to other people, as well as understanding the importance of early prototyping and iterations.

We have discussed how having a game idea is only the tip of the iceberg and how the role of the game designer is to communicate ideas that might come from anyone inside or outside the team.

We clarified the importance of marketing your game from the very beginning and finding the correct audience for what is, above all, a product that has to be sold (even if it's free).

We had a glance at some practical techniques game designers use to develop and create games, which we will explore in more depth in the next chapters.

We also made some paperwork. The time you have put into creating a sample concept document is time well spent, I guarantee you that. Learning game design is about getting hands-on experience, and there's a lot you can do only with a text file or even just pen and paper. Keep doing it. I hope you are able to go back to all your homework some day and meditate on how far you have come.

In Chapter 3, *Scoping a Game Project*, we're going to discuss the importance of understanding the size of a game project, how the scope determines the constraints you will have to consider in your design decisions and that you will have to respect if you want to complete your game.

3
Scoping a Game Project

In this chapter, we'll teach you the concepts and relationships between a game's overall scope, its structure, and its content. We'll explore real-world examples and help you build an understanding of how to better document the size, complexity, and dependencies in your game, as well as to help you estimate your tasks.

The game's **scope** is a term used to define the project's perceived size and complexity. Without knowing the scope in advance, any production scheduling, costing, and staffing would be nigh on impossible. The scope is usually well defined by the time you wrap up the first version of the game design document.

As a game designer working on establishing the initial scope, it's your responsibility to list all of the game's features, functionalities, and systems, as well as to approximate the entirety of the game's content. This includes the quantity and complexity of gameplay mechanics, playable levels, missions, cutscenes, storylines and dialog, sound effects and music, playable and unplayable characters, weapons, power-ups, items, and so on.

Once the project enters production, you're likely to keep using your scoping expertize whenever you work on a new feature proposal or design revision.

 It's always good to make sure your ideas are not too costly or beyond the possibilities of the technology or the team (constraints can channel and boost your creativity) but do not overthink the scope too early! Writing down the scope only makes sense once the structure and core gameplay ideas are well defined.

Beware of feature creep! Sometimes less is more; deciding what to remove is harder but more important than dreaming of new features. The term **feature creep** is often used when describing scenarios (or even whole projects) in which we attempt to resolve our problems and make the game more compelling by adding more and more features and content, rather than working out the issues living deep within the base game systems and mechanics. Knowing what to keep and what to cut is an essential skill for any game designer. Changes *on paper* and during prototyping are the easiest and cheapest to make. Don't be afraid to propose cuts early on, as later may end up being too late.

After the first drafts of the **GDD** (**game design document**) and **TDD** (**technical design document**, usually maintained by the lead developer) are finalized, the representatives of various disciplines from your team and studio will be able to estimate the amount of time needed to deliver on the project. This, in turn, allows the producer to create and agree upon the schedule and budget.

Since game development is highly unpredictable, you can expect the scope and estimations to be frequently revised and a 20-40% uncertainty buffer added to each estimation (some people go as far as to double their initial estimates).

On a side note, it's important to acknowledge that in certain projects you could deal with continuous iteration. This means that your scope will stay relatively undefined and flexible for the duration of the project. Such scenarios are rare, require clear short-and mid-term objectives, and should not become an excuse to generate an unsustainable amount of work for yourself or others. After all, even if time and resources are not an issue, you rarely want to spend ten years on a single game, only to have the entire industry move towards a different direction, distribution platform, and technology.

Game structure

To have any chance of scoping and sizing your game accurately, you first need to define its structure. For the purpose of this book, the structure refers to the way different segments of the game all link together and the journey players take during play.

With the structure defined, it becomes much easier to divide the game into independent sections and assess the size, complexity, and dependencies of various parts of your game.

As a designer, you need to decide on the player's journey and the experience you're offering. Do you foresee a single predestined path through your game? Is it branching? Or perhaps you only want to provide the players with various tools and let them take things from there? Is the experience designed to be highly replayable, or is it simply a puzzle to solve or a fixed story to be told and experienced? Answering these questions will tell you a lot about the structure of the game you're making.

The structure of games not only depends on the desired gameplay experience, but also on the applied business model.

Video games might have found popularity in arcades, but they soon made their way into our homes—filling them with dedicated consoles and adding to the reasons for owning a PC. Most games gradually drifted away from high score-driven challenges and sports-like competitions, and towards more defined experiences that told a story or posed a challenge that can be solved, mastered, and exhausted. Limited replay value was not necessarily an outcome of basic game mechanics, but rather of a desire to raise the quality of games, control their difficulty with predefined challenges, and thoroughly utilize all assets and playable content.

Finite experiences provided by console and PC titles not only made for more balanced games, they were also perfectly in sync with the available business model:

1. Buy a new game
2. Finish the game
3. Buy another game

In such a world, having a product with incredibly high replay value might have been used to generate word-of-mouth recommendations, but was not particularly good for long-term business. Nowadays, thanks to a highly competitive market, improved digital delivery methods, and the possibility of monetizing customers repeatedly, we have highly connected games that often offer endlessly replayable experiences, deep multiplayer interactions, and a huge variety of user-generated content. Some argue that games were better in the old days; I'd say they were definitely simpler to produce...

There are many ways of dissecting and classifying video games. Many products blur the lines with their expansive game modes and complex structures. Before we delve into some examples, we'll need to take a peek at some of the most common terms and tools used when planning the game's structure, its relationship with content, and the effects of individual decisions on the scope and lifetime of the end product.

Game content

In the context of scope and structure, game content refers to games that are designed to be experienced (or consumed). This would include things such as game levels, items, characters, abilities, vehicles, achievements, weapons, missions, and storylines. Since the main gameplay mechanics and rules are the essential foundations upon which everything is built, you generally do not treat them as parts of the game content. Instead, you focus on anything that builds upon your foundations, adds value, and increases the lifetime of your game.

In the case of a simple racing title, the content would include all of the tracks, cars, and car parts (including cosmetic items such as paint colors and stickers you can put on your car), as well as the breadth of available game modes (such as time-trial, single-race, tournament, multiplayer head-to-head, and so on). Sounds, music, and the story would also be included, but these components are admittedly less likely to make or break the product. After all, it's safe to assume that many players will quickly lose interest once they master the game mechanics and familiarize themselves with all tracks, cars, and modes, no matter how much story and music we put into the product.

A game designer is often faced with important decisions on the relationships between rules and content. Try to look well ahead and predict the areas that might change and expand. Think carefully about the following questions:

- Is everything hand-crafted by the development team? Or will you use randomization and/or procedural generation?
- Will you expand game content after the game is released? Which parts? How often and to what extent?
- Do you plan to use user-generated content? How will you ensure its quality? How will you moderate it?

That's a lot to think about, so let's unpack the content-specific terminology and help you answer these questions!

Always disclose your intentions within the design specification of each game feature. Let's say you're working on a collection feature. Not knowing that the initial set of 10 collectible items will be later expanded to 100 can have very dangerous consequences. The entire user interface around the feature might need to be remade and the code for creating, storing and displaying these items rewritten. In a sample scenario with only 10 items, your User Interface designer may opt for using large, animated objects, but as soon as that number grows to 100 the inventory becomes hard to navigate and the game's performance suffers and all because the rest of the team were not prepared to support your final intentions. The art assets themselves might even go through an entirely different (and more systemic) pipeline once the aspirations for a large quantity are known. You could even end up using an art outsourcer or automating large parts of the creation and implementation processes!

Content burn

As players interact with your game, they will not only gain mastery over game mechanics and systems, they will also grow more familiar with the contents of your game. Humans love to learn, and good learning opportunities are rewarded with feelings of accomplishment and satisfaction. We easily get excited by anything new—a fresh challenge, an untold story, an undiscovered land. While this part of the human condition leads to our players seeking out and enjoying our games, it also leads to them being bored by repetitive and unchallenging tasks or familiar stories. Boredom is what we try to avoid, and unfortunately for we designers, people are as good at learning as they are at spotting patterns. The same brain that can spot animals in the shapes of clouds, or a human face within a picture of a Martian rock, will be exposed to seeing your game—often for hours on end. The sole act of exposure to the same set of 3D props and art pieces used to create a seemingly unique dungeon will lead to a feeling of fatigue and boredom. The same fate befalls any content that players interact with repeatedly, including mechanics and systems that do not seem to hold any secrets and potential learning. All of this means that our players don't just enjoy the content of our games, they burn through it, permanently diminishing its value.

Avoiding content furnace

The term *content furnace* is often used when describing games that heavily rely on fresh content to sustain the interest of their players.

There's nothing wrong with creating highly focused, hand-crafted stories, but unless you're consciously aiming to deliver an experience with highly limited replay value, you'll have to plan for ways to keep the game seem fresh for longer. There are several ways in which you can limit content burn (or increase the amount of content to burn through) and hopefully keep your players' interest for longer.

Depth and possibility space

You have probably heard about some games being described as *deep*. Depth in this context means that a game has a lot of complex systems and interesting choices hidden beneath the surface. Remember hearing about games that are *easy to learn but hard to master*? This cliche refers to a perfect-world scenario in which a game is accessible and understandable, yet filled with intricacies that take years of practice and offer near limitless replay value.

To create a game with a wide possibility space is to create a game with potentially endless combinations of interesting and unique scenarios to explore. Do games like that exist? Wouldn't they require an enormous amount of content to begin with? The answers are yes and no.

Think of classic games such as *Chess* or *Go*, these games rely entirely on their elegant rule sets. These rules enable an incredibly deep set of gameplay scenarios that can entertain players for years. There are 20 ways in which you can open up a game of *Chess*. By the time your opponent responds, the number of possible board states skyrockets to 400—each being more or less a valid and meaningful move. These games rely not on supplying new content but on the availability of interesting move sets and challenging opponents to play against (you can play chess against an AI, but it's arguably much less fun without a human opponent). You can say that, through a wide possibility space provided by the rules, these games have avoided becoming a content furnace.

Does that translate into modern video games? Yes, it does! At the time of writing of this book, I have amassed over 2,000 hours of playtime in *DOTA2*, *Valve's* famous **MOBA** (**multiplayer online battle arena**), not to mention several years spent playing *League of Legends* beforehand. In these games, the level design stays largely fixed. It becomes an unchanging avenue for the moment-to-moment displays of skill, short-term decisions, and long-term strategy. These are games that achieve replayability via deep choices and a wide possibility space, an outcome of:

- Interconnected content that creates millions of combinations:
    - A large number of playable characters with unique abilities. Given that these games are played in teams of five, the number of possible team combinations is enormous.
    - A large number of items to purchase in-game that can have a meaningful impact on your character's (and your team's) performance.
- Rules and mechanics that test a variety of skills:
    - Physical skill tests such as timing, aiming, and reaction times
    - Tactics and short-term decision-making, including environmental awareness, item and skill development decisions and enemy movement prediction
    - The long-term strategy, often based on spotting play-patterns and predicting enemy team behavior
    - Communication, coordination, and leadership
- The challenge and satisfaction of playing against human opponents. These games wouldn't be as engaging and popular if they were played against AI opponents. It's incredibly difficult to create effective but seemingly natural AI opponents, and even harder to have them work together and make interesting choices.
- An ever-changing *meta*—the way in which the game is being played by the community evolves with the game itself. If a certain strategy becomes dominant, the community naturally evolves by learning to expect and counter it.

I am just scratching the surface of what makes these two games replayable, though now you may be wondering *do I need 100 items and 100 characters to create a replayable game?* The short answer is no, you don't! The slightly longer answer is, look at games such as *Rocket League*—a game that could be described as *football played with cars*. The rules and victory conditions are simple and elegant: get the ball to the enemy goal by hitting it with your car. The amount of content required for this gameplay to work is impressively small—one arena, one car, a boost pad, and a ball. The game is played in small teams (from 2 to 4 players per team), where each player controls a single car that drives in a familiar way, but players can also jump and steer their car in the air and use a rocket boost to propel themselves. Hit the ball with your car and try to get it to the opponent's goal and... that's it! Simple, right? Yet, for many, the replayability is through the roof! The way *Rocket League* achieved its elusive easy-to-learn, hard-to-master status is all down to the simplicity of the rules paired with the incredibly high skill ceiling of precisely controlling the movements of your car in relation to the ball and each of the surrounding players. It's a highly kinetic game where great timing and team play are absolutely essential.

Even though the human factor can hugely help in providing fresh challenges, depth and a wide possibility space are not exclusive to multiplayer arena games. Think of strategy games such as *Sid Meier's Civilization* and the *Total War* series, or simulations such as *SimCity* and *Dwarf Fortress*. One could argue that even if you removed most of the visual assets and reduced the amount of content, the effect of interactions between the player and the systems powering the game could still provide dozens of hours of fun, filled with interesting decisions and engaging outcomes.

Creating deep games is a very difficult craft and can take more time and expertize than crafting heaps of content surrounded by more shallow mechanics. As you increase the number of combinations and possibilities within your core gameplay mechanics, you expose your systems to a range of extreme (and potentially game-breaking) scenarios. Before you add any new rule or feature in the hopes of extending the game's lifespan/depth/complexity, your team will need to make a set of important decisions. Widening the possibility space can (and almost surely will) bring currently unforeseen consequences. Will you have the time to explore these new options? How certain are you that the new addition will be a positive one and make the game more fun to play for longer? Would your time be better spent by simply adding more consumable content to the already working systems?

We'll delve into ways of creating engaging mechanics and broadening your possibility space in later sections of the book; for now, let's look at other ways of limiting your content burn!

Randomization and procedural generation

Randomization and procedural generation are two interconnected terms. While randomization is mainly concerned with the application of chance-based mechanics (think card shuffling, critical hit chance, and randomized loot drops), procedural generation is focused on creating new content based on carefully crafted rules.

Let's focus on looking at the effects of randomization first!

To be effective at prolonging your game's lifespan, randomization has to be constrained and applied in a careful, deliberate way. If done right, it can add thrills and make the game slightly less predictable, without undermining the player's ability to plan ahead. Do it badly and you'll end up with an unplayable mess where player actions seem to have little influence over the end result and it's impossible to predict and prepare for what's going to happen next.

Anything that becomes randomized is at risk of making the game rules less understandable, as well as breaking the balance of the game (making it either too easy or impossible to win). Moreover, due to *negativity bias*, most humans pay significantly more attention to negative outcomes of randomization than to positive ones. This means that fully randomized effects can lead to players feeling cheated by the game and losing the sense of agency.

 A fellow designer, Keith Burgun, makes interesting points on randomness that are worth sharing at `https://www.youtube.com/watch?v=2qfFEP_-LkI`. Keith distinguishes between two types of randomness: input randomness and output randomness. Input randomness is described as one that informs player's decisions, for example, map generation. Players cannot affect or predict it in advance, but will able to make decisions based on what they've been served. On the other hand, we have output randomness, which defines the outcome of a player's actions, for example, a die roll that determines whether the action (which you've already committed to) was successful or not. Be very careful when you inject your game with output randomness! The feedback on the player's actions can become confusing and may limit satisfaction from performing good decisions, as well as the opportunity to learn from one's mistakes. A valid move can be met with a failed result, while a mistake on the player's part could yield a positive outcome.

There are many great examples of using randomization. Some games use it to prolong the lifespan of the game's content; others put it at the heart of their game mechanics. Card games such as *Magic The Gathering* or *Hearthstone* would lose most of their appeal if the decks always produced the cards in a predefined sequence. As for *Hearthstone* itself, the designers have added a wide selection of cards that provide randomized effects after they're played – a great example of using the aforementioned output randomness. It's a polarizing set of cards that can result in both moments of great elevation (*Oh my, I got so lucky!*), as well as ones of great frustration (*This? Really? I quit!*). Unless you can provide your players with a clear indication of risk and uncertainty, you should shy away from using output randomness in key areas of the game.

Another great use of randomization is within reward systems. In games such as *World of Warcraft*, groups of players would often replay the same dungeon several times in order to get a chance at the desired item. An extreme version of reward randomization is found in a game that uses a Gacha-based (*Gacha*, from the Japanese word *gachapon*, refers to capsules sold in vending machines and containing random toys inside) business model. In such games, the most important items in the game that gate player progression are stashed away in randomized loot boxes. It's important to know that not every implementation of *gacha* rewards is the same (and therefore always fully randomized). A so-called *box-gacha* refers to a reward set with random chances but no duplicate rewards. Imagine a box with a strictly defined set of 10 items. Even if one of these items has a tiny 0.1% chance of dropping, you can be sure that you'll get the item within 10 tries. The worst case scenario is that you'll need to pull out 9 other items first.

If you rely on reward randomization, make sure you carefully prepare to handle filler content and duplicate rewards—there's nothing more demotivating than getting a *useless* reward or no reward at all. In case of duplicates of unique items, perhaps you can convert them into useful resources? More on this type of rewarding and Gacha-based business model can be found in Chapter 15, *Games As a Service*.

An outstanding example of smartly utilizing randomization can be observed in *Valve's* 2008 first-person shooter *Left 4 Dead*. In *Left 4 Dead*, four players work together across one of several campaigns. A campaign is a predefined string of levels, and each level has a mostly linear path, with a fixed entrance and exit. The game offers just a handful of weapons and items, a few special enemy types, and no differences between characters. On first glance, it does not seem like a hugely replayable game. However, the makers of the game made some very smart design decisions...

Left 4 Dead features an *AI Director*. The Director's role is to provide the survivors (players) with a varied and exciting experience that matches the chosen difficulty level. To do that, the director will track a variety of attributes for each player such as health, state, skill level (accuracy, kills, and so on) and position (are they in a group or alone, ahead or behind). Based on this information, the AI Director is capable of making each play-through unique through a variety of gameplay adjustments, the most prominent being:

- Spawning hordes of common infected (think fast-moving zombies). The director picks one of the available spawn zones. The quantity and frequency all operate within set limits and are decided by the director.

- Spawning special enemies. Types and locations vary and there are limits as to how many special foes can be alive at a time. Some very difficult foes are set to only spawn a set amount of times per map, in one of a few predefined locations, no matter the state of the survivors.
- Spawning weapons, health, and ammo in one of several predefined locations. Again, there are upper and lower limits, but if your team is hurt they are much more likely to find life-saving medkits rather than temporary painkillers.

The Director also takes care of much more subtle features, such as triggering weather effects or dynamic dialogs between survivors (these often refer to their current location or the enemies they face).

Since the AI Director plans some elements of the level before the game starts, you could say it dabbles in procedural generation, but the true powers of using procedural generation to create new content go way beyond that!

We can delve into the fully procedural worlds of *Minecraft* and *Terraria*, as well as *No Man's Sky*, which not only assembles an entire universe full of planets but also populates it with living creatures! It's important to acknowledge that such extensive procedural generation is an art form in itself, and requires immense technical expertize.

On the less extreme (and more controllable) end, we've got the cult action-RPG *Diablo*, an RPG shooter *Borderlands,* and countless modern examples of *Roguelikes* (*Enter the Gungeon, Nuclear Throne,* and *Rogue Legacy* to name a few). Looking a bit closer at *Diablo*, it uses procedural generation to create its special monsters, magical items, and even assemble dungeon layouts, but the designers chose to retain a much higher level of control over the most important aspects of the game. The best gear in *Diablo*, all of the bosses, the overall story, objectives, and order of dungeons and environments are all handcrafted and pre-planned.

When designing your game, try to find parts of it that would naturally benefit from randomization and procedural generation, but remember there are tradeoffs! Writing good procedural generation code will take a lot of time (and it will take even longer to test and fine-tune it), and this can have a huge impact on the scope of the game. Moreover, procedurally generated worlds/items/stories rarely feel as special as handcrafted ones. There's a lot you can do by simply randomizing a few elements rather than creating them from scratch. If your game requires a high quantity of content and you need to rely on procedural generation, think of ways in which you can maintain a level of control over the critical parts of it.

User-generated content

Do you want a lot of content but don't want it to come from a *soulless* algorithm? Encourage your players to create and provide new content for each other!

There are many ways in which you can do this. In the past, PC games have often come with a set of map editors and content creation tools some of the best maps in games such as *StarCraft* and *Heroes of Might and Magic* were made by fans. Empowering and supporting an active modding community can also be a valid solution for prolonging your game's lifespan and appeal. However, it can also be very time-consuming and expensive to run, support, and moderate. Therefore, it makes the most sense for big, premium games such as *Fallout* and *Elder Scrolls*.

Nowadays, the online architecture can enable player generated content to be immediately and seamlessly integrated into the core experience. We've got *Super Mario Maker* featuring thousands of great maps and the likes of *Little Big Planet* that let players create and share entirely new types of gameplay experiences that can play nothing like the main game. However, the quality of such free-flowing player creations is often questionable. Without proper moderation tools, as well as ways of promoting quality content, things can go south pretty quickly. As much as you'd want things to run themselves, such features will surely require constant oversight and inflate your game's scope significantly.

Maps and mods are great! Unfortunately, not every player wants to spend hours crafting content for others. Fortunately, there are ways in which you could make your players produce high-quality content unintentionally! All you need is to turn that content creation into a significant part of your game. In games like the mobile smash-hit *Clash of Clans*, player generated maps are used front and center for everything (apart from a relatively short and insignificant single-player campaign). The game has dominated what we now call a *build and battle* genre, a mix of a real-time strategy and a tower defense game. In these games, players build and upgrade their bases (carefully placing their defenses to protect themselves), recruit troops, and attack other players to take their resources. Incentivizing players to protect their resources drives each and every player to create a new, highly playable map for everyone else. Moderation impact is minimal for the developer, and since players are ranked and match-made against each other, the difficulty is properly maintained.

Managing content treadmill

Teams working on live games often have to resort to adding new content in order to maintain their current audience engaged. We sometimes call such situations as being stuck on a *content treadmill*—if you stop putting out new content, then you run the risk of losing your players.

There are many ways of addressing such situations and it's often up to the whole team to come up with solutions of the streamlining production process or lowering the reliance on new content. Still, this is a practical book and we aim to provide some practical ideas, such as:

1. **Remixing**: Content does not need to be entirely new to still feel fresh. Mirrored tracks in racing games are a great example. Another one would be using old bosses as late-game enemies—players only fought them once, why not give them a second life? Recoloring and resizing your assets can also be a very powerful tool!

2. **Replaying**: Systems such as *prestige levels* (reset your progression in exchange for a token or badge of elite status that can be seen and highly admired by other players) and *New Game+* (replay the game at a higher difficulty but keep your progress) are both great ways of giving your players an excuse to keep playing once they reach *the end*.

3. **Resurfacing**: Why not encourage players to play with content they long grew out of? Special objectives and challenges or game modes/custom rule sets can do just that!

4. **Increasing depth or altering rules**: Another way to answer the need for content is to provide more variation outside the content, giving it new life by limiting the repetitiveness of the main game loop. Think of *The Arena* mode in *Hearthstone*; it uses exactly the same cards as the main game but allows players to draw randomized cards and create custom decks that always feel fresh and unique. For many players, this mode has prolonged the lifespan of the game greatly!

5. **Improving your pipeline**: Sometimes it's okay to be stuck on a treadmill, as long as you can identify the bottleneck and invest in tools or outsourcing that will make the team's life more pleasant.

Common game structures

Games are a medium for interaction and storytelling. While both of these elements often go hand in hand, there are times in which the story crafted by the developer and the player's personal story (as told by their actions and experiences) differ widely. Our medium is great at creating interactive systems and letting players loose within them, yet the stories we tell in our games often fall back onto the tropes, conventions, and static structures found in books or movies.

While it's possible to implement heavily interactive storylines with dozens of branching paths, and even systems that create and assemble the story procedurally, the same development effort is much better placed with core gameplay mechanics. After all, everyone will interact with gameplay systems, but only a small minority will explore all story branches. This is why in most cases, our games can provide a lot more freedom in their gameplay than in their storytelling.

Let's look at the possible structures for our games, noting that in many cases, the gameplay and storytelling can either go hand in hand or diverge widely. In cases like that, it's often best to first focus your efforts on the more interactive elements of the game (as they are usually the most difficult to iterate and redesign).

Linear

Linear games are likely the closest our medium can get to traditional, non-interactive media such as books or movies. The experience is pre-planned, carefully paced, and delivered in a fixed sequence, with little room for sweeping decisions or branching paths:

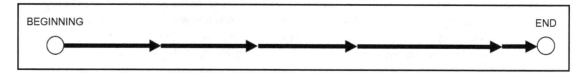

A simplified portrayal of the player journey in a linear game

The biggest and most obvious benefit of making your games linear is having the ultimate level of control over the combined storytelling and gameplay experience. If you know how to exert such control, you can grab your audience and take them through an experience they will never forget.

Nowadays, games with a fully linear gameplay and story are hard to find. Even the most restrictive ones often offer a few decision points, alternative solutions, optional paths, multiple endings, and at least a small degree of freedom in approaching the gameplay scenarios. A few examples of games I'd consider very linear (across the years, platforms, and genres) include *Super Mario Brothers*, *Uncharted*, *Heavy Rain*, *Portal*, and *Inside*.

 If you're working on a linear game, you'll need to keep the highest standards of quality across the entirety of the game, possibly reworking whole sections of the game repeatedly. In linear games, pacing and balancing are much more controllable, but also even more important. Your players cannot ignore the parts they don't like, or easily distract themselves by doing *side missions* or exploring other parts of the game—if you fail to keep their interest (or get them stuck) you put them at great risk of leaving, permanently.

Structured nonlinear

Nonlinear games take players off the rails and take advantage of the interactive nature of games - players no longer have to follow a single predefined path from start to finish. In such titles, players are asked to make meaningful choices and have a sense of agency in either gameplay, storyline, or both. However, designers of structured nonlinear games still retain a level of oversight and control over the gameplay experience. They prepare for a series of possible gameplay or storytelling scenarios and prepare the solutions and endings. The final result is a carefully balanced and structured experience that gives a level of freedom to the players, increasing replayability and allowing players to play in a way they enjoy the most:

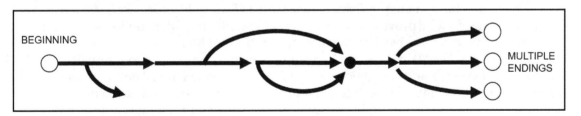

Nonlinear games with carefully planned branches, side paths, and multiple endings

There are obvious drawbacks and challenges with nonlinear games. The alternative paths should be as fun and rewarding as the main one, as the moment you encourage certain play styles is the moment you take away the choice and force many players to play the game in the *optimal* (but potentially less fun) way. Your scope will also grow substantially, especially if hand-crafted stories branch in multiple directions. You'll also create a lot of potentially time-consuming content that most players will never explore, so take that into consideration if you plan to put the coolest bits of the game behind an unlikely branch.

It's much more manageable to provide a level of expression in your gameplay while keeping the story going in a roughly similar direction. You can then rely on the player's play style and choices, and reflect them either at the end of the game or throughout it (but not in a way that derails the main branch of the story).

In games such as *Hitman*, *Thief*, *Deus Ex*, or *Dark Souls*, players are presented with a great degree of freedom in the way they approach gameplay situations, but ultimately the structure follows an order that can be predicted and planned for.

Open nonlinear

Some nonlinear games open up their structure and let the players loose. They provide a very wide possibility space and make it nearly impossible to predict how the player will reach the end. Such titles still come with a defined set of winning and losing states, and often a carefully crafted main storyline, but any attempts at plotting the player journey are futile.

In such games, players are set free to roam and explore the content and gameplay systems, making each playthrough unique. Some series, such as *Fallout*, *Elder Scrolls*, *Just Cause*, or *Grand Theft Auto*, do it by providing an open world and filling it full of optional activities and missions that can immerse their players for hundreds of hours. Others, such as *Civilization* and the *Total War* series, make their players miss on sleep by offering deep, interconnected systems and simulations with countless moving parts. Another worthy example would be the interactive fiction *80 Days*, which is a unique take on an open nonlinear game with amazing, highly adaptive storytelling and a definite ending:

A game with a defined beginning and ending, but a wide and unpredictable possibility space

There are no absolutes in game design; it's perfectly possible to retain a level of control over the structure and story of the game, while still allowing for free-form exploration. Most open-world games assume a hybrid form. They do not want players to be overwhelmed or venture too far too soon. In order to do that, you can create a set of artificial requirements that players have to meet in order to access an additional portion of the game. This unlock mechanism will let you pace the experience better and let your players focus on a more manageable amount of content:

Rather than opening your structure fully, you can divide the game into a series of hubs with players progressing through them in a controllable manner

The scope implications of an open world game can be huge, making tools for content creation and testing of paramount importance. You'll need to create a lot of content to make the world feel interesting, often with a risk of having to throw it all away as you modify and polish your gameplay mechanics. And as always, without solid second-to-second gameplay, no amount of content will save your game!

There's always an option of going after a wide possibility space through the depth of gameplay. In such case, you'll require countless hours of prototyping, playtesting, and bug fixing to ensure the system is fun and performing as intended. Deep systems and simulations can be very hard to create and especially hard to balance, as a single change can have unforeseen repercussions across the entire long-term playthrough.

Endless and sandbox

Some games do not have a defined end or victory state and can be considered *endless*. This does not stop at the *endless runner* genre (very popular a few years ago, and includes the likes of *Temple Run, Subway Surfers*, and *Despicable Me: Minion Rush*). There are multiplayer games such as *World of Warcraft, The Sims*, or *Clash of Clans* that have a finite amount of content but never really end. In these games, you can win a battle, but you can never end the war...

Sandbox games are not only endless, they are also mostly devoid of goals. Many designers argued that due to its endless and directionless nature, *Minecraft* is a toy and not a game (that was before *Minecraft* added some structure and goals via *adventure mode*).

It's easy to mistake games that support sandbox play, such as *Grand Theft Auto* or *Fallout*, for sandbox games. It's true that *GTA* allows a huge degree of freedom and supports undirected, exploratory play, but there is always a storyline, progression gates, and a potential victory state. Even if players are free to choose their path, they are often confined and locked in certain states by the game's story. A true sandbox game is free-form and often endless; it's a vehicle for player expression, a virtual world, a simulation to get lost in. This structure rose to popularity with games such as *Terraria, DayZ,* and *Rust* (and of course *Minecraft*) selling millions of copies:

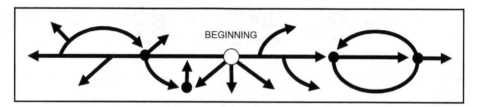

BEGINNING

Uh... Plotting a player journey? Oh well... There might be progression milestones and technology trees, but you can't really predict what your players will do next

Sandbox games are not easy to create and even harder to test. However, by adding multiplayer features, one can get away with a seemingly shallow game as long as players can express and entertain themselves by interacting with each other. Just make sure there's something to work towards, to aspire to—a fantasy that players can spend long hours trying to fulfill.

Notes on structure

As with any classification, the reality is often putting things on a sliding scale, and one product can have game modes or chapters that belong to wildly different categories. It's also possible for players to completely ignore the structure, step outside the path we laid out, and even make up their own goals. For example, some players in *GTA 5* may completely ignore the tight sequence of story missions concerning the main characters, and instead explore the world, set records in longest car jumps, and try to attract as much police attention as possible and get away with it.

Settling for a particular style of game structure within any part of your game is an important part of the design process. You need to consider:

- Do you have the expertize required to pull off this type of experience? Opening up the possibilities comes with risks and can multiply your budget.

- Do you know from the outset what kind of game you're making and what kind of play styles will you support?
- Is there a set of expectations to be met on the structure of the game? These can be internal (team) or external (your audience).

Scoping practices

The best way to approach scoping is by deconstructing the game from the top and defining the critical progression path of the player. Think of the final experience you want to deliver or the story you want to tell. Thinking about levels or any other units of player progress, can you define the minimal, optimal, and nice to have quantities? How much new content (obstacles, NPCs, game mechanics, and so on) you'll need on each part of the critical path to keep things interesting? By dividing player experience into chunks, you'll be able to easily estimate the amount of all interdependent elements.

Content lifespan

The content lifespan is a document that lists every significant piece of content and maps it against a player's journey in the game. It allows people to plan the production, estimate which elements are needed first, and identify the areas that have too many or too few new elements.

Unless you're working on a very open-ended game or a sandbox experience, it should be possible to define a player's *vector of progression*. This vector will serve as the reference point in the lifespan document. To give a couple of examples: in an open world RPG, the vector of progression might be the player's experience level; in a linear puzzle-platformer, it would be the stages themselves; and in an adventure game, it could all come down to the place in the storyline.

Content lifespan documentation can be used to:

- **Examine the progression path**: If you're focusing on improving the first hour of the game, you'll want to focus your efforts on only the relevant parts
- **Pace the end-user experience**: It's arguably the easiest way of ensuring that fresh content and game mechanics are properly spread out

- **Plan content deliveries**: You always want artists and programmers to work on things that you'll need next
- **Identify dependencies**: No need to work on that new power-up if the gameplay mechanics for it are half a year away!

Real-world examples

Normally, my content lifespan document would take the form of a long table with a single row for each element in the game (it would include buildings, obstacles, playable and non-playable characters, interactive objects, cutscenes, weapons, abilities, scenery, level design, and so on). I'd then add columns that contained the following: a short description, the first time an element is used, priority, and dependency (an obstacle that requires a special gadget obviously has to be created after said gadget).

Games have differing structures and their relationship with content varies wildly, therefore every game should be approached in a fitting way.

In *Transformers: Earth Wars*, we already had an art production spreadsheet and lists of robots and buildings; there was little point in listing all of the assets again. Therefore, I opted for a simplified graph followed by a more complex and integrated progression matrix, which I'll demonstrate further on.

The game is a mobile, multiplayer, build and battle title. For the critical vector of progression, I chose the most important building, the player's Command Center. Unlike the player's robot collection (which is the most important thing in the game, but can vary wildly), buildings follow a linear path and are strictly tied to the Command Center Level. Upgrading the CC becomes a big investment in the base and is a visible milestone. Treating it as a main vector of progression also meant we assigned and locked all of the game features and technologies directly to it.

Player progression flow

First, I mapped known features and milestones in the game against Command Center levels. This diagram has been created as a drawing inside our game design document (the GDD itself was a Google Docs text file). Once we were happy with it, I printed several copies, stuck one of them on the wall and gave out the rest to the people responsible for planning the production (producer and art director), as well as to every single programmer on the team.

Interestingly enough, we all knew that the game would go beyond Command Center 11 (we actually made data for 16 CC levels and held some back, releasing the first 14 on game launch), but we also knew no new features would be locked by or planned for that late in:

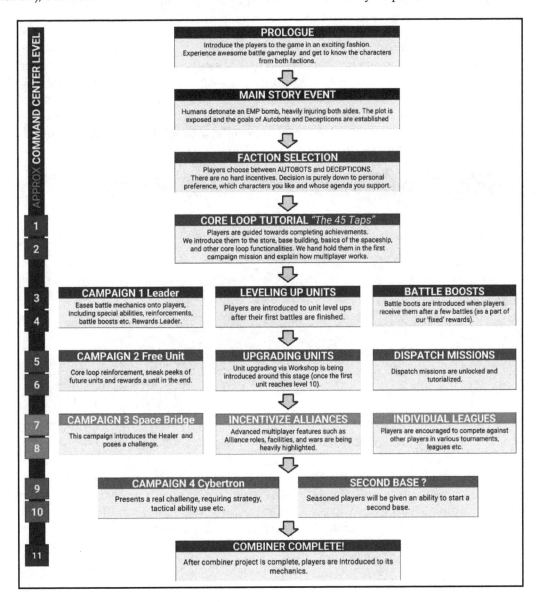

Simplified player progression flow allows to plan feature delivery and control the added complexity, ensuring we don't overwhelm our audience

Unlock matrix

Following the *progression map*, the *unlock matrix* was created; this table was also printed and handed out around the office. It may look a bit confusing and hard to read, but that's because it wasn't just a reference point. It also served a much bigger purpose…

We've integrated the *unlock matrix* into our economy spreadsheets. Through multiple lookup and match formulas, we have ended up with a single sheet that directly amended and influenced game data for our entire economy. Making changes in the *unlock matrix* would result in corrected resource costs, building times, and unlock requirements being filled in automatically for all the other sheets such an approach makes it much easier to balance and refactor player progression (more tips on how to set things up can be found in the balancing chapter of the book).

NUMBER OF BUILDINGS																	
Command Center Level		Unlock CC	1	2	3	4	5	6	7	8	9	10	11	12	13	14	15
Buildings	ID		Number of buildings														
Scanner	uti-scanner-1	3	0	0	1	1	1	1	1	1	1	1	1	1	1	1	1
Alloy Mine	res-alloyharveste	1	1	1	2	2	2	2	3	3	3	3	4	4	4	4	4
Alloy Storage	res-alloystorage-	1	1	1	1	1	2	2	2	2	3	3	3	3	3	3	3
Energon Mine	res-harvester-1	1	1	1	2	2	2	2	3	3	3	3	4	4	4	4	4
Energon Storage	res-storage-1	1	1	1	1	1	2	2	2	2	3	3	3	3	3	3	3
Hangar	uti-hangar-1	1	1	1	1	1	1	1	1	1	1	1	1	1	1	1	1
Drone Pad	uti-dronepad-1	1	5	5	5	5	5	5	5	5	5	5	5	5	6	5	5
Workshop	uti-workshop-1	4	0	0	0	1	1	1	1	1	1	1	1	1	1	1	1
Combiner Labs	uti-combiner-1	9	0	0	0	0	0	0	0	0	1	1	1	1	1	1	1
Armoury	uti-armoury	8	0	0	0	0	0	0	1	1	1	1	1	1	1	1	1
Wall	wall2x2-1	1	6	8	10	12	14	16	18	20	22	24	26	28	30	32	38
Autocannon	def-cannon-1	1	1	1	2	2	3	3	3	3	3	4	4	4	4	5	5
Outpost	def-outpost-1	2	0	1	1	1	1	2	2	2	2	2	3	3	3	3	3
Laser Turret	def-laser-1	3	0	0	1	1	2	2	2	2	3	3	3	3	3	4	4
Mortar	def-mortar-1	4	0	0	0	1	1	1	2	2	2	3	3	3	3	3	3
Stasis Mine	def-stasis-1	5	0	0	0	0	2	2	2	2	3	3	3	3	4	4	4
High-Powered L.	def-beam-1	6	0	0	0	0	0	1	1	1	1	1	1	2	2	2	2
Shock Tower	def-shock-1	9	0	0	0	0	0	0	0	0	1	1	1	1	1	2	2
Missile Launcher	def-missile-1	11	0	0	0	0	0	0	0	0	0	0	1	1	1	1	2

The first part of the matrix lists the maximum number of buildings you can build per type

Anything going from **0** to **1** in the matrix given in the preceding screenshot signifies a new type of building being unlocked. The data looks a bit hard to read but can be processed by spreadsheet formulas with ease. You can look at the flow as well as each CC level individually. For example, I was able to add a column to the footprint of each building and use it to calculate the size of the building required to fit the base. This was of tremendous help when trying to figure out how many removable obstacles (rocks, trees and so on) should be placed on the map:

MAX UPGRADE LEVEL

Command Center Level	ID	Unlock CC	1	2	3	4	5	6	7	8	9	10	11	12	13	14	15
Buildings			Maximum Upgrade Level														
Scanner	uti-scanner-1	3			1	2	3	4	5	6	7	8	9	10	11	11	12
Alloy Mine	res-alloyharveste	1	1	2	3	4	5	6	7	8	9	10	11	12	13	14	15
Alloy Storage	res-alloystorage-	1	1	2	3	4	5	6	7	8	9	10	11	12	13	14	15
Energon Mine	res-harvester-1	1	1	2	3	4	5	6	7	8	9	10	11	12	13	14	15
Energon Storage	res-storage-1	1	1	2	3	4	5	6	7	8	9	10	11	12	13	14	15
Hangar	uti-hangar-1	1	2	2	3	3	3	4	4	5	5	5	6	6	6	7	7
Drone Pad	uti-dronepad-1	1	1	1	1	1	1	1	1	1	1	1	1	1	1	1	1
Workshop	uti-workshop-1	4				1	1	1	2	2	2	3	3	4	4	4	5
Combiner Labs	uti-combiner-1	9									1	1	1	2	2	2	3
Armoury	uti-armoury	7							1	1	1	1	1	1	1	1	1
Wall	wall2x2-1	1	1	2	3	4	5	6	7	8	9	10	11	12	13	14	15
Autocannon	def-cannon-1	1	1	2	3	4	5	6	7	8	9	10	11	12	13	14	15
Outpost	def-outpost-1	2		1	2	3	4	5	6	7	8	9	10	11	12	13	14
Laser Turret	def-laser-1	3			1	2	3	4	5	6	7	8	9	10	11	12	13
Mortar	def-mortar-1	4				1	2	3	4	5	6	7	8	9	10	11	12
Stasis Mine	def-stasis-1	5					1	2	3	4	5	6	7	8	9	10	11
High-Powered La	def-beam-1	6						1	2	3	4	5	6	7	8	9	10
Shock Tower	def-shock-1	9									1	2	3	4	5	6	7
Missile Launcher	def-missile-1	11											1	2	3	4	5
Characters																	
Max Level of Bots (Workshop Dependant)			10	10	20	20	30	30	30	40	40	50	50	60	60	60	60
Bots available in battle			3	3	4	4	4	5	5	6	6	6	7	7	7	8	8

The second part of the matrix shows maximum upgrade level per CC level

When it comes to *upgrade levels*, most defenses and production buildings simply increase by 1 for each Command Center level. But that's not the case for everything; things like the *Workshop* (a research center that restricts the maximum experience level for your bots) and *Attack Shuttle* (controlling the total number of robots you can deploy in battle) are very carefully crafted.

On a side note, the confusing pink numbers were added when I was implementing the 3D models for buildings. We've only created six visually different versions of each building (apart from walls, as combined they leave a very large visual footprint on the base). So to make my life easier, I put the visually different levels in pink to help in data input. I made sure there's always a visual upgrade from level 1 to 2 (the first time you upgrade something), but I also made sure we don't use up all of the building upgrades too early (some upgrades for the most advanced buildings were left for the future).

I might have gone into quite a lot of potentially unnecessary detail here, but there is an important lesson to take away from the process. As a designer, you need to define the kinds of data you want to control and adjust, and this can be difficult if you're breaking new ground. Once you have defined your parameters, use spreadsheets, graphs, post-it notes—anything that will help you visualize and operate on the data from a new angle.

Game flow

Flow charts and diagrams are a very powerful tool that every designer has to learn to utilize. They can be used for anything from explaining the ins and outs of your game economy and gameplay mechanics, to portraying technology and skill trees.

Unless your game is trivially simple (or a near-direct copy of something existing), you'll need to create a flowchart of sorts to explain where various options and features fit in and how they are connected. Even a simple game of *Rock-Paper-Scissors* could have its flow represented by a chart:

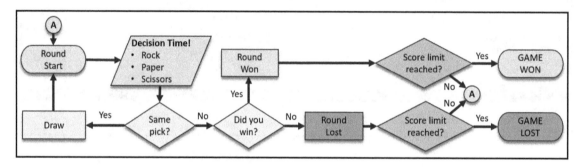

Flowchart for a game of Rock-Paper-Scissors with multiple rounds.

In the preceding example, we can see the structure of play as well as some of the rules that decide the outcome of a round. For those not familiar with the symbology:

- **Rounded squares** represent terminal blocks (beginnings and ends of processes)
- **A parallelogram** is used for user input/output
- **Diamonds** portray decisions. Use these for simple yes/no or true/false forks
- **Rectangles** are used for processes and operations
- **Arrow connectors** are used to join parts of the diagram and portray the direction of transitions
- **On-page connectors** (the circles with letters inside) allow us to avoid long and confusing arrows by connecting two remote parts of the flow

It may be a lot to take in, but for experienced people, reading such diagrams is much easier than reading paper rulesets.

Nevertheless, do not overthink the flow diagrams—we're not creating blueprints of factory processes, we're making games! It doesn't matter how many different shapes and connectors you use. As long as you do not confuse people, you can opt for a set of simple arrows and boxes.

Going to the lengths of putting a rhomboid decision box with forking outcomes for *every single thing* will likely end up as a waste of your time and potentially overwhelm the rest of your team (no one wants to read a flow with hundreds of nodes).

Ultimately, the game flow will evolve and change over time; the purpose of the initial diagrams is to help you visualize the structure of the game—do it by whatever means necessary. You can inject screenshots from reference games or earlier prototypes, comments, wireframes (rough sketches of the user interface and content)—everything flies as long as it helps you communicate effectively. If you really need a diamond decision box with forking paths—use it! But, if you're going to write up a detailed explanation of that part of the game anyway (with potentially its very own flow chart), opt for simplicity and put it all in a simple *box*.

 These days, you rarely need to install specialist software such as *Microsoft Visio* or *Inkscape*. There are countless online solutions such as *draw.io* or *Lucidchart*, and you can always fall back on something even simpler; unless you're doing something large and complex, *Google Slides* and *Powerpoint* can easily satisfy most of your needs. Some people even use pictures of whiteboards or post-it notes.

Example of a menu flow

As an example, I choose to create a simple **menu flow** for the PC version of *Blizzard's* digital card game *Hearthstone*. A few details about the game were simplified (in order to fit it on a single page), but it should still prove as a useful example!

Instead of using a conservative flow diagram iconography, I've opted for a very loose and accessible approach. Each area of the game is portrayed by a rectangle that explains available options.

Even a simplified menu flow like that, combined with the information contained in the GDD, paints a good picture of how the game can be put together, helping the whole team see the connections between the different areas of the game and empowering user interface artists to start working on wireframes, visualization of various options, and polishing the end-user experience:

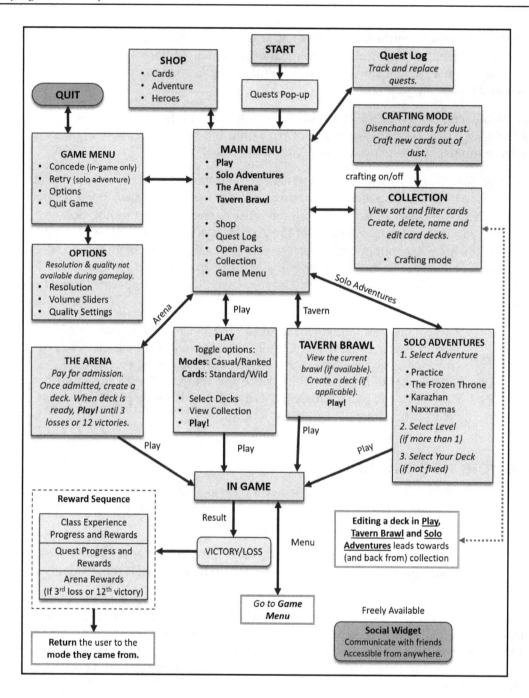

Bear in mind that in modern, collaborative teams, any flows and documents you create are not supposed to be a *final directive* of how the game will be made. Instead, treat them as a great way to present your vision, a solid starting point that enables the team to spot flaws early on and allows for a more informed discussion to take place. Do not over-explain too early and be prepared to edit and re-work everything. Again, the more changes you make on paper, the better and more efficient your team can be!

Planning design work

In the games industry, it's usually the project manager who creates and enforces production schedules. To do that, a list of task and assets to produce is assembled based on the design documentation. These tasks are then paired with estimates that (in the best-case scenario) come from the people who will actually end up doing said tasks. If the project is highly inventive and/or staff members inexperienced, more senior employees might get involved in helping with the initial schedule.

Unfortunately, in the words of strategist Helmuth von Moltke, "No battle plan ever survives contact with the enemy." First production schedules are likely to be very, very wrong. In the beginning, things will usually take longer than anticipated, and a lot of unknown problems, changes in direction, and missed tasks will emerge. Fortunately, as time goes on, your team's experience with the product grows and your tools are likely to improve, making the creation of future game content much quicker than initially anticipated. Good development studios and publishers acknowledge that games are very hard to plan accurately, and are prepared to be reasonably flexible.

In Agile game development, you're likely to encounter different levels of detail when it comes to planning and task preparation. Long-term plans tend to be loose and based on rough estimations; the game might have a shipping date from the beginning, but it's very unlikely to be the actual one. Mid-term plans (next few months), usually focus on clear goals that the team is striving to achieve for example: getting the first level playable, finishing the character customization system, testing network code. Short-term plans (next two sprints, that is, development cycles) are the most detailed and least likely to change, as they contain lists of detailed tasks, order by priority, which is either worked on right now or will be assessed for inclusion in the next development cycle.

No matter how fragile and changeable, plans need to be made right before the game can enter the production period. As a representative (or at least a valued member) of the design team, you're likely to be involved in the process. While deliverable tasks for artists (such as character models, animations, environments, and so on) are relatively easy to put into numbers and estimate, design tasks tend to be much more elusive. We'll cover some tips that might help you in tackling this problem!

Estimation techniques

Estimating the entire project upfront can be a daunting task, but there's a technique you can use when faced with any big problem - break it down into many small problems!

Your first step would be to look at a list of all features and pieces of content. Think of any design tasks that could go on that list. For example, if you're working on a first-person shooter, you'd not treat level design, weapon design, and enemy design as just three huge tasks; instead, weapon design could be broken down and estimated as a set of smaller, more manageable tasks:

- High-level design of all weapons (quantity, when are they unlocked): 2 days
- Design and implementation tasks for each weapon: 3-4 days (per weapon)
    - Ideation and prototyping (desired role and feel): 4 hours
    - Art brief and references: 1 hour
    - Initial gameplay implementation: 2-4 hours
    - Initial balancing pass: 2-3 hours
    - Art implementation and sound brief: 2-4 hours
    - Playtesting and polishing time: 6-8 hours
    - Bug fixing: 2-8 hours
- Playtesting for all weapons: 5 days
- Final balancing of all weapons: 3 days
- Final polish pass for all weapons: 5 days

Once you break things down, look at the combined time taken and see if there are any obvious mishaps, then add some contingency budget (usually at least 20%) and make sure to revisit and re-estimate the tasks in the future, based on acquired experience.

You'd be surprised how effective such breakdowns can be, especially if you approach the unknown quantities in the same way as the famous nuclear physicist *Enrico Fermi*...

Fermi was known for his ability to make very good approximate calculations with very little to no actual data. Instead, he relied on making justified guesses in which he replaced any unknown quantities with averages of possible lower and upper values. How does that translate into practice? A famous example of a *Fermi* problem is *How many piano tuners are there in Chicago?* In order to answer that question, we'd break the problem down into smaller chunks asking following questions:

- How many people live in Chicago? Let's say we have no idea, but we know it's a big city, more than 4 million but less than 15 million. An average of these two values would be 9.5 million.
- How many people are in each household on average? Surely more than 1, but probably less than 3. Let's take 2.
- How many households have a piano that requires regular tuning? Probably more than it 1 in 35, but less than 1 in 5. Let's say it's 1 in 20!
- We can also guess that regularly tuned pianos need around once a year.
- How long does it take to travel to the customer and tune a piano? More than an hour, but probably less than 4. Shall we say 2.5?
- Each tuner works 8 hours a day, five days a week. 50 weeks in a year.

With these assumptions we can do the following calculation:

(9,500,000 people in Chicago) ÷ (2 persons/household) × (1 piano/20 households) × (1 piano tuning a year) = 237,500 piano tuning tasks every year in Chicago.

Now, how many piano tunings can a tuner perform in a year?

(50 weeks/year) × (5 days/week) × (8 hours/day) ÷ (2.5 hours to tune a piano) = 800 piano tunings per year.

Now for the final calculation!
(237,500 piano tunings per year in Chicago) ÷ (800 piano tunings per year for each piano tuner) = 297 piano tuners in Chicago.

According to the Bureau of Labor Statistics (`https://www.bls.gov/oes/`), the number of piano tuners in Chicago (as of 2009) was 290. Isn't that uncanny?

This approach to estimating is not wizardry. As long as you're not consistently biased in one direction (which obviously can happen), overestimates and underestimates generally help cancel each other out. A Fermi calculation involving many factors (such as the piano tuner problem) can yield surprisingly accurate results.

Whenever you're tasked with providing ballpark estimations for something you have not done before, imagine yourself doing the job, deconstruct the problem into smaller more manageable parts, then add up the averages. There's a good chance you'll end up with a reasonable number. And as always—before you go all Fermi on a problem—don't forget also to try and refer to other, potentially more experienced people on the team or within the company. There's a good chance they've done something similar and can share their experiences. Obviously, there are limits as to how granular you can and should get, but the more alien the problem, the better the value of approaching it as a series of smaller ones.

As previously portrayed, estimation can be an art in itself! But once you get some practice, you'll be able to utilize the same set of skills when approaching game balance, as well as any other area of the game that requires a (more or less informed) shot in the dark.

Priorities and dependencies

Knowing the priority order in which things should be made is hugely important. Even the smallest changes to the story or base game mechanics can have rippling effects across the whole game, potentially leading to a lot of wasted development effort.

One way of quickly communicating and visualizing dependencies between tasks and parts of the game is to create a *dependency stack*, a diagram that lays down the various game features and pieces of content and the relationships between them (you can use the same tools as when creating a menu flow). Note that this is not a tool that helps communicate the structure or flow of the game; it's used purely to prioritize tasks.

If diagrams are too much, a simple spreadsheet can help you order and prioritize work. All you need to do is to take a list of features and content (simply expand your content lifespan sheet, or an art asset sheet), then add fields for priority and dependency.

Dependencies are not that hard to figure out. In an action game, your enemies won't work if players have no tools to defeat them, which in turn won't work if they can't control their characters, and so on.

As far as using numbers for priority, I recommend putting 0 as the least important and going up from there, this way it's easier to make something more important—simply put critical things as 1000, then start going down. Anything below a certain threshold can be treated as optional.

When designing any game feature (or game for that matter), create a list of components that would comprise your **minimum viable product** (**MVP**), that is, key elements without which you wouldn't be able to release said feature/product. If there's a strong indication of not meeting the MVP when planning the work, you might get ready to save time by cutting it all out. Defining the MVP can sound a little restrictive at first, but it helps your team focus first and foremost on what's essential for the feature/game you're working on.

Follow the MVP by clearly describing what your desiredoutcome is. And finally, don't hesitate to add a wishlist, your best-case scenario. Perhaps there's an extra behavior or a set of parameters you could use? To put this into an example, don't ask for *five power-ups*, ask for *no less than three power-ups (to make the feature viable), ideally we'd go for five. [Optional]: We could introduce three ratings for each power-up, this way we can take five power-ups and turn them into 15!*

Start from the middle

Remember when we spoke about the vertical slice (the practice of making a high-quality snippet of the full product)? It's not a secret that they rarely include the actual start of the game. There are a few reasons behind that. For one, you obviously want to show the game with its wings fully spread. You want to try showcasing how fun and engaging the mechanics can be, rather than being constrained to the slow and steady pace of the tutorial sections, which would do the game a disservice. Also, with content and mechanics likely to change, you can expect the early tutorial (or any other on-boarding experience you have) would have to evolve multiple times over the course of development.

However, there's another more important reason. Have you ever played through an expansion pack or a piece of post-release downloadable content, which felt much better than the base game? As with many things in life, practice makes perfect!

Your best work on nearly any game is the work you'll do last, built upon the breadth of experience with the product. The middle of the game is very much such as the middle of a book or a movie, no matter how good it is, if the beginning is bad no one will reach it, and if the ending sucks, that's the only thing they'll remember. Almost all games benefit from starting the development partway through the player journey, no matter how annoying it is to not have the game playable from the start for a long period of time. If you're to create a platform game with 10 stages, start on level 3 or 4, followed by more work on the middle chunk, then do the start and finally the end.

If for some reason you cannot start in the middle (say you want to do play-testing of core mechanics), make sure to set aside some time to revisit, iterate, and potentially rebuild the initial areas later on.

Remember, the very same technique of starting in the middle works on any scale and applies to individual features. For example, you're working on multiple campaigns, but you must deliver them in order, perhaps you can start each campaign in the middle? What also helps is the extra frame of reference that you gain as you start in the middle. It's more convenient to aim for medium difficulty level, then dial it up and down as needed, than to start easy and keep escalating up.

 The screenshots used in this chapter are for illustrative purposes only. We do not recommend you to misuse these in any way. For more information please consult the terms and conditions of the publishers mentioned in the *Disclaimer* section of this book.

Summary

This has been quite a chapter! By now, you should have a better idea of how to analyze the structure of games and better predict their scope. We spoke at length about game content and your role in helping to define it. We've accustomed ourselves to the content treadmill (and how it can be avoided), and looked at the differences between games that rely on the content burn and those that aim to deliver a deep possibility space. We've also analyzed popular game structures and explored ways in which you can document the scope and plan of your work.

Armed with all this knowledge, we should be ready for the part you're anticipating (or dreading) the most. It's time to delve deep into the art and craft of writing design documentation!

4
Design Documentation

Writing **game design documents** (**GDDs**) is one of the main responsibilities of every game designer. The whole point of having a game designer in a team is to ensure that someone is taking care of putting everything about the game in black and white—someone able to define and communicate ideas, mechanics, and any other information the team might need to know in order to develop the game.

Many novice game designers (and game developers in general) look online or ask friends in the industry for a game design document template that they can use as a starting point for writing their own documentation. The general misconception is that *if it worked for someone else, it will do for me.*

As opposed to a game concept document, where there are established rules and information that must be included in a certain way (due to the *selling purpose* nature of the document), a GDD doesn't follow a determined structure or format, and the information it contains can greatly vary depending on the game, on the work methodology and on the team size and dynamics.

If you search online for a GDD template, what you are most likely to find is a classic standard template. Probably it was made in Word, probably 10 to 20 years ago. The template usually contains an outline that game designers are supposed to fill with their content, a document, that once filled, will most certainly reach at least 100 pages, if not more. A monolithic bible with all the possible information you can imagine. One that no one is going to read, not even yourself. It contains chapters such as character descriptions, input controls, dialogues, and an art assets list.

Game development has changed quite a lot since that kind of document template was released. What if your game doesn't have any dialogues? Or there are no characters at all? What if the input controls can only be described in association with a specific mechanic (for example, swiping for matching candies in *Candy Crush Saga*)? What if you're working on a huge game and filling all that information would require months which you don't have? Or maybe you're part of a team of designers and each needs to start working on a different aspect of the game at the same time? How can you work on the *art assets list* if you don't even know what the level designer is going to include in his or her levels?

All these queries caused a sort of crisis of GDDs in modern game development when the very usefulness of producing such documentation was questioned by many developers.

Luckily for us, we can say that the crisis has been now resolved. The answer is that no one needs that kind of game design document anymore. But of course, a GDD is essential to any project that aims to be successfully released. The secret lies in the fact that no template is good for your game. Every GDD is unique and the format and tools and techniques are simply the ones that work for you, your team, and the project. Reading those old templates, or even GDD examples released by developers, is still a useful exercise, one that I sincerely recommend. But when the time comes to write your GDD, use what you have learned from those templates and make sure you are building a document that serves your purposes, instead of one that covers all the bullets point made by someone else for a completely different project.

As you will have guessed by now, in this chapter we won't focus on what to write in a game design document. Instead, I'm going to provide a series of tools and techniques you can use to write your own document, in a way that works for you.

The following topics will be covered in this chapter:

- The purpose of a GDD
- The characteristics of a good GDD
- The tools available for creating GDD with pros and cons for each of them
- A list of useful writing techniques
- Elegance in game design
- Maintaining a GDD

What is the purpose of a GDD?

Documentation serves two purposes:

- Providing the team with a detailed description of what needs to be done (communication)
- Acts like a sort of encyclopedia of the game, where the team can keep track of what has been done and how, and what has changed (memory)

This means that the job of the game designer is not only to spec out the game on paper before any software is written, but also to ensure that everything that is written must be up to date. Whenever something changes down the line, or it is not implemented exactly as per documentation, it is important that the doc is updated. A great practice is to add comments about why (and how) the final implementation is different from the initial design. This kind of thing happens all the time in game development. In fact, no game designer has ever handed his document to the rest of team without being asked to modify or remove something that could be implemented in a better way or cannot be implemented at all. Like we said, game design is an iterative process, and writing documentation is no different.

Characteristics of a good GDD

Let's have a look at what makes a good game design document.

The characteristics we're going to describe in the following paragraphs are something that any GDD of any game should have.

Every time you're required to write a GDD, come back to this list and make sure everything you write conforms to it.

Every time you finish writing a GDD, go back again to this list and ask yourself whether your work possesses or not these characteristics and, if not, whether it's your particular case that doesn't require it or you have to adjust something.

A good GDD:

- Is modular
- Has goals and requirements
- Is the result of a discussion

- Is clear, brief, and concise
- Is multimedia
- Leaves space for creativity and debate
- Is not necessarily only a text file
- Is online

It is modular

Generally speaking, the goal of the document is to communicate the game design to all the parties involved in game development. But it's very unlikely that the whole design is going to be covered by a single document. Some parts of the game might need to be designed as soon as possible, while others might wait for a later stage or even need to be designed after some of the features have been implemented.

A development team can reach over 200 people in AAA productions and many people will have a very specific role. Imagine if a programmer in charge of developing the multiplayer network was forced to read a 1,000-page document to understand what they needs. They will get information about levels, characters, storyline, or the balancing of the combat system... all stuff they doesn't need to understand to actually jump on what they needs to know.

Ideally, there would be a chapter just for him called *Multiplayer*. Even better, there would be an entirely separate document called *Multiplayer*. If this, let's say, 50-page document contains all the information the programmer needs, with fewer possible dependencies on other features or documents, we can call it a GDD in itself or a module.

A game document should always be modular.

What does modular mean? Let's get more technical and look at how modularity is defined for software development by Wikipedia:

> *"Modular programming is a software design technique that emphasizes separating the functionality of a program into independent, interchangeable modules, such that each contains everything necessary to execute only one aspect of the desired functionality."*

Just like modular software, a modular GDD should be composed of different modules as independent and interchangeable as possible. Remember that video games are software and as such they can (and should) make good use of software development techniques at every level, not only for coding. Unlike software, though, it's very unlikely that a video game is going to be made of parts fully independent of each other. Removing one part of the game, or changing its design, will have an impact on the others, and without one part, the entire game might fall apart and not work as intended any more. However, that is exactly why you need to keep the GDD organized in modules. If something needed to change, you'd need the confidence of knowing which part to rework and exactly how and where it is referenced elsewhere in your documentation.

Here's a very simple example: you have designed a combat system in an action game. Following the practice of modularity, you have created a separate document called *Combat System*, just for that feature, where all the details are meticulously designed. In other modules of the GDD, every time you have to reference a particular mechanic in the combat system, you simply point at the specific document on that topic. Let's say at some point during production, something in the combat system must change drastically. If your references to the combat system document are very few and always in a form like *see combat system document for details*, all you'd have to do is make the required changes in that module only, and all the references will remain relevant.

As we discussed, GDD is by definition a live document, so it will need constant updates and changes, and sometimes entire parts may be cut out or added. Modularity ensures that taking out or changing a module doesn't mean going back and updating the entire documentation. Most importantly, it guarantees that a change in one feature doesn't impact the rest of the game, or if it does it gives control over where the dependencies are. Modularity ensures another important concept inherited from software development: *reusability*. A modular GDD is reusable because every single module can be used for different projects (if conveniently adapted). Writing a modular GDD means for you, the game designer, creating a library of designs for a variety of game features and mechanics that is easy to consult, examine, and improve throughout your entire career.

Don't worry too much about creating a spectacular-looking GDD every time. The goal is to communicate in the best and most efficient way, not to show how pretty your documentation is. Reusing previous work (without violating any property rights) means not losing time reinventing the wheel and focusing more attention on what's new or different.

It starts with goals and requirements

What is the goal of what you're about to write? What do you need to achieve and what kind of requirements are there? Some of the requirements and goals of the entire game have been already specified in the game concept, but with the GDD we are stepping deeper into the game. Therefore, we need to define goals and requirements for each different module.

Let's have a look at a practical example.

Hearthstone is a famous **Collectible Card Game** (**CCG**). When it was initially released in March 2014 the game was strictly multiplayer, with only PvP matches available (and a shallow single-player mode to test out card decks). After a few months, the Adventure mode was released, offering a single-player experience to Hearthstone players.

What goals and requirement could have been set for it?

If you know the game, try to make a list before reading further, and then compare your ideas with our list.

The set goals might look like these:

- Offer a single-player experience to Hearthstone players
- Introduce new cards and game boards
- Keep non-competitive players engaged with the game
- Expand the setting with storytelling

The requirements could be:

- Keep the game accessible (avoid introducing too much new content/too many new mechanics)
- Versatile system to periodically introduce new adventures
- Keep the old cards in balance with the new
- Adhere to the Warcraft settings guidelines

Of course, these are not the official goals and requirements that Blizzard set for the development of the first *Hearthstone* adventure, *Curse of Naxxramas*, but that's how I would spec them out.

We already mentioned how important requirements and constraints are to creativity. Writing a game without knowing what can an

Writing down the goals and the requirements is also a great way to actually start writing! Blank page syndrome is well known by all game designers. Putting together ideas and creating a flow of words on paper to explain a design is not an easy task. Having a fixed structure to follow is always a great idea to start with!

Is the result of a discussion

Once goal and requirements are defined, and some ideas have popped into your mind, it's time to have an early confrontation with other designers or the rest of the team that will be in charge of developing the feature.

It's never early enough to share ideas! The earlier you start brainstorming and sharing, the earlier you'll be able to catch pitfalls in your design or evolve your ideas to a more effective level.

Don't think that this part belongs to you. What you are thinking might be not feasible for technical reasons you're not aware of. Get the rest of the team involved!

Game programmers are the most important interlocutors at this point. They are the ones who will implement your design. You want to get them involved in the creative process and you want to make sure they know what they are going to work on before giving them the final document.

 Brainstorming is an invaluable technique you need to master. There are no *too crazy ideas* during brainstorming; you have to stay open to criticism from others but avoid doing the same yourself and to anything that comes to mind. Rationalizing them and deciding what to use or not will come after the session. Wikipedia (`https://en.wikipedia.org/wiki/Brainstorming`) offers great insights on brainstorming that are worth reading.

It's only after you have interrogated your ideas and designs with others that you'll finally be able to decide what to write. Remember that everything you'll be writing will be transformed into software and will require a lot of work by many different people. You don't want to get it wrong. Small mistakes and imprecision can trigger an *avalanche* effect that can translate into a massive waste of work for the team down the line. Again, this doesn't mean that everything must be written like in an instruction manual, but whatever you decide to write down needs to reduce confusion and ambiguities, not create more! If something cannot be precisely defined at this stage, don't be afraid to write that into the document!

Is clear, brief, and concise

A game designer can produce a lot of documentation, going into the finest details and exploring all the possible scenarios, but a document is useless if no one reads it. And a very long, too-specific document that requires hours of study and reading is most likely counterproductive.

Clarity means that the reader doesn't have to put in too much effort to read and understand what you're saying. It means going straight to the point and writing only what's necessary. It also means that it is comprehensive and covers all the necessary details. Game documentation is neither an essay nor an instruction manual.

A bullet point, such as a to-do list, is most likely too concise (although, it might work for very simple games), but on the other hand a lengthy text detailing too many irrelevant details or too-technical details won't do any good. If describing a feature takes more than a dozen pages, you probably need to split the feature into sub-features and describe them in different documents.

Maybe you're working on the design of a guild system for an MMO, which might sound like a single feature, but it will turn out to be massive, as it usually includes social interactions, guild quests, guild versus guild systems, and maybe guilds halls. You should never tackle all that in a single document.

Using weak statements, or words such as *could*, *might*, or *should*, contributes to creating a sense of confusion in the reader, so avoid using those!

Is multimedial

A GDD is not just text. *A picture is worth a thousand words*, including sketches, concept art, reference pictures, or even examples from other video games (which could easily be in video format). These are great ways to convey information about how a specific system should work. In particular, using existing video games as a reference is perfectly fine.

It is unambiguous and can save both the designer and the reader a lot of time. There's no need to describe something that already exists in a lengthy manner. It's called *not reinventing the wheel*. If someone already did what you're trying to do, and you can reuse what's already been done…just do it!

As we already said, you don't have to be innovative in every aspect. On the contrary, using familiar mechanics where needed is as important as creating new breakthrough features. In the case of new mechanics, the GDD can contain a link to a playable prototype or footage of prototyped gameplay. Remember that as a designer you should always clearly describe what you're showing in any media you are presenting. Showing a video of a particular game's combat system and just stating "Our game combat system works in the same way as the one shown in the video" is clearly a very bad way of writing documentation.

On the other hand, if you're working on a turn-based RPG that uses an *initiative bar* to show the player in which order the characters attack, you can definitely use a video or an image from an existing game:

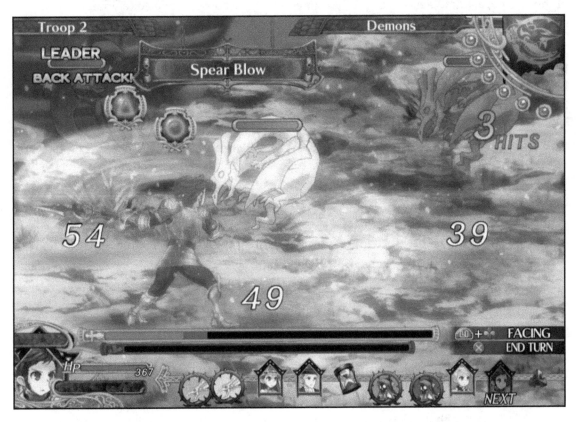

In *Grand Kingdom*, as in many turn-based JRPGs, an initiative bar shows the combat order. This image is a perfect example that can be used as a reference for your initiative bar mechanic

It leaves space for creativity and debate

A game development team is usually composed of some very talented professionals. Creating documentation that doesn't leave any space for these people to express themselves through their work most certainly means that the team's potential will remain unexpressed.

This means that if you're writing about game characters, for example, you should limit your work to what is needed from a designer. Details such as how the character is dressed, how she moves, which sounds/soundtrack accompany her, might not need a formal specification and can be left to the artist's interpretation (unless those details serve some purpose in terms of gameplay and need to be *directed* by the game design). Likewise, even if you are a highly technical game designer, and though you may be able to write code yourself, you don't want to tell a game programmer how to implement the code for a specific feature.

The idea is to communicate the *intention* rather than the *implementation*. Don't tell other people on your team how to do their job! Everyone in the team should be able and free to tackle the development challenges in the way he or she thinks is the best. It is highly probable that the same GDD handed to two different professionals will end up with the same result achieved in very different ways.

It's a matter of mutual trust; everyone trusts that your documentation is the design of a compelling feature for the player, so you have to trust that the team is going to do its best to realize it. For the same reason, don't expect to write a GDD and then just hand it over to the team and move on to your next thing.

Someone could raise questions or issues with something you've written, and these concerns have to be addressed and will eventually require an iteration on the document, fixing what doesn't work or accounting for new, cleverer solutions.

Even more probable, these problems might not arise until the actual development stage, meaning that they need prompt problem solving *on the go*. This is very much part of how game design works.

Sometimes, it might happen that the actual implementation diverged from what was written in the GDD. Never think of the GDD as some sort of dogmatic instruction manual on how to develop the game. If the actual implementation accomplishes the game vision or even does something better than the original design, it's the GDD that needs to be changed, not what's been implemented!

It comes in different formats and sizes

This should be clear already. A GDD it's not necessarily a text file written in a word processor. There are many types of software that can be used to write a GDD, which we're going to explore in the next paragraph. Different games of different sizes require different types of GDD.

The entire *Office* suite or *Google Drive* suite is usually required (*Excel*, *PowerPoint*, and *Word*, and their equivalents), but Word and PowerPoint can be replaced by a Wikia online, for example. Some games can be documented entirely on a blueprint such as document, a huge canvas where a mix of text and images can be arranged to convey the game design.

There are no fixed rules on this. You can even invent your own format if you feel like it. The only rule is to use the best tool for what you need to write.

The good news about all this variety is that most of the time, the *Office/Google Drive* suite would be more than enough, especially if you're just starting out. Learn and master as many tools as you can, and you will be able to tell which ones suit your requirements best.

It is online

This is not a choice in modern game development. If the tool you are using is not online, or you don't have a repository to upload your work and share it on the go with the rest of your team, you are simply doing it wrong.

Do yourself a favor and make the most of the incredible technology available nowadays! Even a sketchbook should always be scanned or captured with a camera and archived in digital format. Do it now, and thank yourself for having done so in a few years!
Common problems with offline documentation include files getting lost, documents shared via email and then being updated only on one end, difficulties in tracking the document version and change history, difficulties accessing files from different locations, and the list goes on and on.

Always make sure your documents are online and accessible from anywhere. And make regular backups!

Tools for writing a GDD

We have seen that there is a variety of tools a game designer can use to produce game documentation; the choice is not only about using one instead of another, but also about which one to use for any given feature.

Depending on the scope of your game, the number of documents and resources you'd have to create will vary. The most important thing is to always have an index file where all the different documents and resources are tracked and referenced. Keep it up to date and always stay organized! During development, the game designer is the *go-to* person for any questions about the game; he is the expert. Being an expert on something that doesn't exist might be a colossal challenge, but that's your job and the more committed you are to this task, the more your team will benefit from your contribution.

As we already mentioned when we talked about modularity, there's no need to have all your documentation in a single format. For the lore of an RPG game, a text file would be required, but that doesn't mean that another feature for the same game couldn't be written on a slide presentation or all the game items described in a spreadsheet.

We shall now take a look at some of the important tools required to write a GDD. Remember, always choose the right tool for what you are trying to communicate!

Word processors

A common misconception is that every GDD starts in *Word*, or *Google Drive Documents*, or another word processor. I've worked on many projects where no word processor has been used at all.

A text file is a good choice when a discursive approach is required.

Some examples would be:

- Defining the storyline of a game or describing its lore
- Describing the characters or the environments
- Defining the dialogues or the screenplay for cinematics

Here are some pros and cons in choosing word processors for your GDD.

Pros:

- Indexing is straightforward, as a particular argument or feature can easily be found by page number
- Searching for specific content or keywords is always available and easy
- Simple formatting means it is easy and fast to maintain documentation
- Minimal setup time makes this a great start for single-developer or small teams
- Using the same version control software for both documentation and code/assets means that changelogs can be directly linked from the document
- It's difficult to lose track of revisions
- It's easy to work offline and update the online version later

Cons:

- Collaborative work might be difficult; non-cloud-based word processors cannot be used by multiple users effectively
- Using multimedia links or linking other documents can become messy pretty quickly
- The page format of a word processor is not good for images, videos, or tables
- Visualizing a document made in a specific format on a different machine can create compatibility problems

Very popular word processors are *Microsoft Word*, *Apple Pages*, and *Google Documents*

Presentations

A slide-based presentation is probably the most versatile tool to write documentation.

It allows you to easily integrate images, diagrams, and multimedia files. The spatial constraint of the slide format is a great way to keep the text brief and to the point. Modularity, again, is intrinsic to the tool. You can swap slide positions, copy them in other documents, color-code your slides by arguments, and mark a slide as one with *dependencies*, meaning it would need to be reviewed and updated if the document that references it gets changed.

A presentation can also be used to make UI prototypes; using hyperlinks and integrated drawing tools, it is possible to easily create a menu or a screens flow.

Pros:

- Versatility
- Being already in a presentation format, the GDD is easy to present or talk through
- The slide format helps in keeping it short and essential
- Easy to print
- Modular format
- Good for UI prototyping and screens flows
- Can be personalized with interesting formats

Cons:

- Collaborative work might be difficult
- Not efficient for showing tables or big diagrams (spatial constraint)
- Cloud-based presentations can get slow if the file size is too big (too many slides and images)
- Can be personalized with interesting formats (yes, this is also a con; if you overdo this, or don't know how to make good-looking presentations, you can end up with really ugly things!)

Apple Keynote, *Microsoft PowerPoint*, and *Google Presentations* are all great tools for writing presentations.

Mind maps

Mind maps are diagrams used to visually organize information. A mind map might not end up in the final GDD, but nonetheless is a great way to organize ideas and draft an outline of what will be written in more detail later. Game design is about solving problems and mind maps have proven a very effective tool across many disciplines. Every game designer should try to use them whenever he feels that simple writing or brainstorming is not helping to visualize on paper his ideas and thoughts.

Sometimes, including a mind map in the final GDD proves to be a great way to communicate the rationale behind decisions. This is particularly useful when working on collaborative documents or to inspire creativity in the reader:

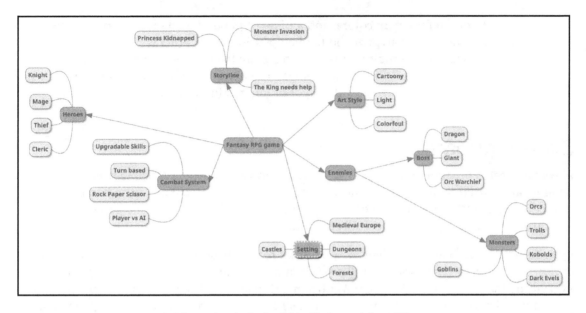

A mind map can be used to describe a high-level idea for a generic fantasy RPG game

Writing a mind map is simple:

- Start with a central idea or a concept and write it down (possibly in the center of your page); that is your *seed*.
- Write an idea or concept connected to your seed and draw a bold line that goes out from the seed and toward this new idea. It's just like a growing tree branch.
- Start again for every new concept you write, using thinner lines as you move outward.
- Use images and different colors if you like.
- Follow a radial hierarchy.

You shouldn't think too much about what you're writing or drawing; just keep working on expanding your seed for 10-15 minutes and then review your work. Usually, the results of this process will clarify your doubts or spark new ideas or solutions. This is another great technique to kick-start your writing work.

Some good pieces of software for writing mind maps are *Xmind*, *Freemind*, or *Visio*.

If you prefer a pen, colors, and a piece of paper, by all means, go for it! For a designer, it is always good, when possible, to interact with physical objects and use their hands, moving away from screens, mouse, and keyboard. If you choose to do so, by the way, never forget to scan or take pictures of your work and keep it organized in digital format!

Spreadsheets

A spreadsheet is probably the most important tool in game design. While words and images can be used to describe a game, a spreadsheet can represent an entire game in numbers and simulate its rules before a single line of code is written. Some games, at a certain level of abstraction, are basically spreadsheets.

Imagine a game such as *Age of Empires* or another **real-time strategy** (**RTS**) game. Each unit, building, and resources is nothing but a set of numbers and those numbers determine everything that happens in the game. With some skill and a lot of patience, it is possible to program and play a simple RTS or RPG only using Excel. There is more: video games can contain an incredible amount of data and very complex economies. A spreadsheet is the only way to organize, visualize, and manage that data.

We'll talk about spreadsheets in depth later, when we talk about balancing; for now just keep in mind that this is an essential tool that should be used any time a set of values or objects has to be described. Balancing, though, is a separate phase from documentation and it's usually done quite early in project development. Spreadsheets, nonetheless, have to be used from the very start.

To give you a practical example, let's think about an RPG game such as *Witcher 3*. There are hundreds of items available in the game, each belonging to a particular category and with specific characteristics. These items need to be part of the initial design, and a spreadsheet is the best tool to list and organize them. The initial list can include only a few columns, for example, the category and a name, but later in development the same spreadsheet can be improved by adding numeric values: the damage for the weapons or the items needed for crafting.

It is not only the functionalities made available from a spreadsheet that make it a great tool for a game designer. A spreadsheet can also be easily imported directly into game engines, allowing the game designer to interact with the game variables directly from it.

Pros:

- Powerful tool to simulate and describe games
- Prototype and balance simulations
- Searchable and organizable
- Perfect for lists of objects
- Can be imported right into the game

Cons:

- Increase in complexity decreases readability
- Complex systems are difficult to maintain
- Doesn't support images very well
- Cloud-based spreadsheets can get slow

Microsoft Excel and *Google Sheets* are the standard spreadsheets every game designer should know.

Project management (PM) tools

These tools are designed to plan, organize, and manage projects of different natures, game design included. For bigger games, GDDs should be separate from production documents and tools to keep track of progress and schedules, which will most likely be created and maintained by different people (producers or project managers).

As a result, using PM tools could result in the game designer using only a minimal part of the entire software functionality—a complete overkill. For smaller projects or agile teams, though, game design features can be described as tickets, issues, or tasks in a PM tool, which will serve at the same time as a GDD and as a tracking tool.

Trello is a great example of PM software that can be used as a GDD for a small game.

Pros:

- Tracking development progress of each design
- Integrated environment for bugs and issue tracking
- Allows you to assign designs to specific persons in the team
- Time tracking

Cons:

- Not as easy to use as a text file or presentation
- Underuse of the entire software package
- Weak multimedia integration
- Difficult to export in different formats or to print

The most interesting PM tool for GDD is *Trello*, but other software includes *Jira*, *Hansoft*, and *Evernote*.

Wiki

Wiki have confirmed themselves as one of the most powerful tools for game design in recent years. The growing and ever-changing amount of information needed in design documents found a perfect fit in online documentation that is designed to write, store, and organize complex information from many people over the internet.

Wikis have also become the go-to tools for player communities to store information about their favorite games. These fan-based game encyclopedias are useful tools for developers too, as it can be very difficult for a developer to discern between the development team and the player's knowledge of a game.

Pros:

- Accessibility via browser
- Built-in categorization and indexing
- Easy to search
- Easy to track changes
- Hyperlinks to web resources allow browser navigation
- Embedded multimedia files
- Can link to wiki pages directly from internal bug reports and other correspondence, making verification of a bug very easy
- Version history and revision control typically built in
- Highly customizable

Cons:

- Pages can get orphaned and unreachable
- Not as easy to use as a text file or presentation
- A wiki is not sequential, so it could be difficult to read from start to finish
- Hard to comment or annotate
- Hard to print

Some great software for creating Wikis are *Confluence*, *TWiki*, and *Wikia*.

Illustration tools

Most designers use illustration tools to draw diagrams, but some designers work on **User Interface (UI)** and **User Experience (UX)** design as well (especially for mobile and browser games). Sometimes, even more complex illustration tools can be used to draw infographics or to give a particular format to a GDD.

Illustration tools are also used to explain some mechanics that require a visual explanation. Designing actions that a character can perform in an action game is a good example; it's always a good idea to pair a textual description with an image.

Creating wireframes and click dummies is another important part of writing GDDs. A wireframe is essentially a sketch of the UI layout, made only using boxes and basic lines/shapes, without worrying about the final look. A click dummy is a prototype of the interactions the player can have on a specific screen or section of the game.

Wasting time writing how buttons work and where they lead might be a bad idea when it is possible to simply show it with a working prototype:

Using wireframes to design the UI and complement the game design is a great way to convey both the mechanics and how the player is supposed to interact with them

Another important use of illustration tools is drawing maps and designing levels. Many times in your career (all the time, if you'll be working as a level designer) you will have to sketch out maps and levels before jumping on the actual level building (using a game engine or a level editor tool). Personally, I find this one of the most interesting parts of game design. I've been doing map design since I was a kid, playing games such as *Dungeon & Dragons* and *Hero Quest*.

Creating dungeons to explore and puzzles to solve for my friends was my first approach to game design and game documentation, and I was only 12! If you haven't played those games (pen and paper RPGs, or dungeon crawler board games) I highly recommend doing so. They will provide you some great insights into game design and player behaviors. Also, they are insanely fun, and it's never too late to start:

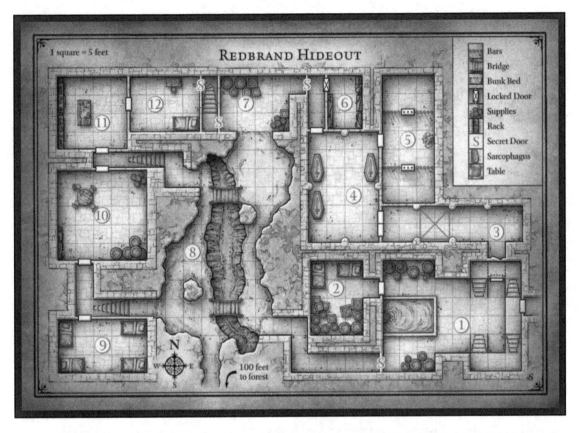

Dungeons & Dragons is the ultimate source for maps and interesting dungeon/level design. This one is from the Starter Set of the 5th Edition

If this sounds interesting, there is a lot more about level design and maps later in this book!

Some commonly used software for drawing diagrams are *Microsoft Visio* and *Dia*.

Popular tools for creating (UI) wireframes and click dummies are *Adobe Experience Design*, *PowerPoint*, and *Balsamiq*.

All-round illustration tools that allow creating actual drawings are *Adobe Photoshop*, *Illustrator*, and *GIMP*.

Writing techniques

These are techniques borrowed from creative writing, presentation design, technical documentation writing, and best practices that game designers have used and refined over thousands of game projects.

Here follows a list of useful techniques to write effective GDDs.

Use of style

The style in which you write matters; as with any other document, you need to make sure your GDD is readable and attractive to look at:

- Use plenty of white space and divide argument paragraphs
- Use a serif font for body text, bold or capital letters for headers
- Avoid any fancy or decorative fonts
- Use short sentences
- Use a hierarchical structure

Layering details

When you write about something, you should always use a top-down approach to layering complexity. The first layer should already give a good general idea of what you're talking about, and successive layers should go deeper into details.

Think about how journalists write articles for newspapers. When reading an article, you can generally always get the gist of the story by reading the headline, then the first sentence will back it up and give some explanation. The rest of the article will provide all the details needed.

Prioritize

If you are describing a complex system that will be developed in different phases, or one that will need some iterations, always describe the system design in phases: the essential part of the features can be described first and marked in a specific color (for a prototype or MVP in initial development) with other parts of the feature described later and marked as successive iterations or *nice to have*.

Use of keywords

Using keywords makes your document more readable and catches the reader's attention. Use **bold** or *italics* to emphasize keyword and important statements. A GDD is going to be read multiple times, and while the first one will hopefully be a thorough read, any successive consultation will need to focus on fewer details. The problem of using too many keywords, obviously, is that keywords will lose their importance, so think before you mark anything as more important. Remember, your document should already be lean and essential.

Table of Contents

Use a Table of Contents (always!) GDD as reference tools! Even for a shorter document, a Table of Contents with hyperlinks to the different sections is vital to access the required information quickly.

If a document goes through a lot of revisions, you might also want to consider integrating a version history.

Bullet points

Bullet points are effective and brief. They can act as a to-do list for the reader and cut off much useless and verbose writing. If you write them in a hierarchy, they also communicate priorities. Be sure not to create a wall of bullets points. If you end up with a list of more than ten elements, you're probably not focusing on the essentials, or not deconstructing your feature into small enough pieces that can be handled in separate sections or documents.

Images with captions

The use of images is almost mandatory for writing a clear GDD, but what really works is associating the images with meaningful captions. Maybe the concept you are showing is described in detail in a paragraph, but always reinforce what you are showing with an image. Even better, whenever possible try to describe the image with the caption only, or associate with an image a short bullet point list, with no other text whatsoever.

Diagrams

Many concepts of game design simply cannot be described with words. Use flowcharts to show screen flows or UX; use state machines to describe scenarios or player behaviors; use charts to represent data. Don't use too-complex diagrams that no one is going to understand, but most of all don't use diagrams to tell programmers how to do their jobs (even better, never tell anyone how to do their job!).

Variables

Avoid specifying numbers, numeric ranges, or any fixed values that are likely to change many times during development. Use *variables* instead, names that will represent those values, whatever they are going to be. This is also an effective way of writing pieces of documentation where some details are not yet defined, and automatically answers typical questions such as "How many of these are we going to have?" or "How long is this going to last?" Putting a variable in your design lets everyone know that a certain value must be kept flexible and open to change.

Redundancy

Cut unnecessary words and redundancy. Cut anything that feels like *discursive writing* or has been mentioned or explained already.

Hyperlinks

Use hyperlinks. You are not writing a printed book. Take advantage of hypertext but make sure its style is recognizable.

Write incrementally by drafting

Draft to understand the problem and write to solve it. Start writing your GDD as soon as possible and with no particular attention to detail. Make bullet points and outlines to identify the problem and use mind maps. Sometimes, even something that is clear in your mind can show its pitfalls and obscure points only when it is written in black on white. Solutions will come easily if the problem solving is part of the writing, especially when you are stuck trying to solve one problem only in your mind.

Elegance in game design

One of the most important principles of good game design is elegance. We are going to talk about elegance in game design throughout the whole book, and it is a concept that hopefully you're going to assimilate in every chapter. In your game designer career, you are going to hear it all the time: *we need an elegant solution for this, look at how elegant this tutorial is, such elegance in this feature design.* What are they talking about?

If you look at the meaning of the word elegance, two keywords are widely used to explain what it is: efficiency and simplicity.

Games are extremely complex systems, so elegance in design is not a luxury, as the word might suggest, but a strict requirement. Elegant design means features and game mechanics that are simple to learn and hard to master. It means that despite the intrinsic complexity of the system, pretty much everyone should be able to interact with it. Elegance allows accessibility.

The classic example of elegance in game design is chess, a simple yet incredibly deep game that has been played for centuries and is still compelling and exciting nowadays. There are more modern examples of elegant game design though. Supercell's Clash Royale is certainly one of those. A CCG with not many cards and a simple real-time PVP arena is one of the most-played competitive games in video game history. It is incredibly simple, yet it offers so much depth and such a clever metagame design.

It is important to notice that elegance doesn't mean quality. Some AAA games are famous for completely failing at being elegant. These games tend to be extremely complex to accommodate a demanding hardcore audience, but the greater the complexity, the lower the chances of achieving elegant solutions.

Keep it short and simple (KISS)

This principle is also known as "Keep it simple, stupid!"

A very popular design principle, it was introduced in 1960 by the US Navy. The principle simply states that a system works best if it's simple by design. As trivial as it may sound, Kelly Johnson, the lead engineer who coined it, made a very valid example to remind us how important it can be. It goes more or less like this:

Consider a jet aircraft that should be repaired by an average mechanic in the field under combat conditions with only a handful of basic tools.

Video games are complex systems, full of moving parts and made with advanced technologies. Compared to Johnson's maxim, we are talking about futuristic spaceships that only scientists in their labs might be able to repair.

To use the KISS principle as a game designer means making sure that this complexity is managed and not overused. To remove the superfluous, have a simpler system for the benefit of both the development team and the players.

As we already mentioned, iterating is a fundamental part of the development of a successful game. In order to effectively iterate and improve, at any stage of development, your game needs to be exactly like Johnson's aircraft.

The less-is-more principle

Another fundamental principle of game design is called *less-is-more*. It is a call for minimalistic design, in line with everything we have said so far.

But how do you apply this principle in practice?

The answer is pretty straightforward: while designing or prototyping a game, instead of adding features or mechanics on top of what you have, try to take something out.

This is especially true when something doesn't quite work as expected. Usually, everyone is tempted to add something to the system to make it finally work. Most of the time this is a bad idea, as adding functionalities to something problematic at its core will never solve that original issue, and just hide it at best. In this case, it is a much better idea to take the time to dig into what's already there and find out what it is that causes the problem in the first place, then just try to remove it!

If you think about games such as *Super Hexagon* and *Thomas Was Alone*, you immediately get how minimalistic design can make, for example, your game art much simpler without affecting the gameplay or reducing its enjoyability:

Super Hexagon is a classic example of minimalistic design. The player controls a small triangle, and the game world consists of a central hexagon that attracts geometrical shapes

Minimalistic design is not only about art. *Shadow of the Colossus* is a great example of an incredible-looking game with minimalistic design. The less-is-more principle here is applied to enemy encounters. The game doesn't feature any minor enemy battles; there are only 16 enemies in the whole game, and they all are bosses. This unique approach to enemies in video games made this game stand out from anything else available at the time (and even now!)

We will talk more about this principle and see how it works in the following chapters about the creation of game mechanics.

 The screenshots used in this chapter are for illustrative purposes only. We do not recommend you to misuse these in any way. For more information please consult the terms and conditions of the publishers mentioned in the *Disclaimer* section of this book.

Summary

Writing and maintaining a GDD is a huge part of an everyday game designer's responsibilities.

We have discussed the different tools for writing game documentation, with their pros and cons, and we have defined the characteristics of a good GDD.

Modularity, in particular, is what keeps GDDs still relevant in the modern game development world, characterized by fast iterations and agile methodologies.

We also explored some practical writing techniques that game designers use to write effectively and on time.

Now that we have learned how to write and communicate a game design, we are ready to delve into the next section of this book: Designing the Gameplay.

We will learn how to create game mechanics and how their interactions create what we call the gameplay.

Adaptation of Mechanics

5

We are finally ready to learn about the most exciting creative challenge for game designers: *creating the gameplay*.

There are many formal definitions of what gameplay is and what it means, and we can say the same about mechanics. Our goal with this book is not to try to give new definitions. We want to stay practical, therefore we'll go with the most intuitive definitions and leave it to you to discover all the studies and implications of those words. For the sake of simplicity, by gameplay, we mean how all the mechanics of your game contribute to creating the final experience played by the players.

We're going to have a quick look at more specific definitions of what game mechanics are later in this chapter. Again, we're going to learn from other game designers and scholars who have already done an excellent job on this, with no pretense to reformulate our own definitions.

Before learning how to create completely new game mechanics, we are going to focus on how to use existing mechanics and change and evolve them to suit your game and the gameplay you have envisioned. We have already talked about the fact that creating a new game doesn't always mean creating new and never-seen-before game mechanics. Understanding existing games and their mechanics and knowing how to deconstruct them and make them work for your game is the key to simplicity.

In this chapter, we're going to learn how to use familiar game mechanics as a starting point to create your own and we will develop a useful framework that, once mastered, will allow you to tackle the challenge of creating something new and fresh based on familiar gameplay patterns.

What is a game mechanic?

I know, this is a book about practical game design, but when it comes to game mechanics and the core elements of gameplay, we have to go through some theory.

Formally defining anything is a difficult task; I always prefer to quote definitions from different authors. All of them are equally correct and the different points of view complement each other. It is not our goal with this book to give a comprehensive definition, what's important is that a clear idea can stick in your designer mind by reading them!

Mechanics are the various actions, behaviors, and control mechanisms afforded to the player within a game context.

–'MDA: Mechanics, Dynamics, Aesthetics Framework' by Hunicke, M. LeBlanc, R. Zubek

Game mechanics are rule based systems/simulations that facilitate and encourage a user to explore and learn the properties of their possibility space through the use of feedback mechanisms.

–'A Theory of Fun' by Raph Koster

They are the interactions and relationships that remain when all of the aesthetics, technology, and story are stripped away.

–'The Art of Game Design' by Jesse Schell

Got it? Great!

It may all sound pretty simple, but those definitions took hard work and much thought to be written in black and white. Again, we are not going in-depth into these because this book is about the practical use of this knowledge more than the knowledge itself. Make sure to read the source articles and books from which we have taken these definitions; they are a must-read for every aspiring game designer.

Examples of game mechanics

Now that we have a better idea of what a game mechanic is in theory, let's have a look at some practical examples from famous games, just to clear any doubts that might still be there!

We're going to start with extremely simple mechanics, without lingering too much on how they work. What follows is a list of examples to give you a practical idea of what a game mechanic is in a game.

Jump!

Probably the most famous mechanic of all. Super Mario Bros (1983) featured only two main mechanics: running and jumping.

By pressing a button Mario can jump into the air, so he is able to stomp on enemies or reach platforms on different levels. That jump mechanic has been replicated in endless games and given birth to an entire genre: The Platformer. In the following image, we can see Mario in action:

Mario jumping in *Super Mario World*

Shooting and reloading

We have two mechanics here:

- Shooting is the action of firing a weapon
- Reloading is the mechanic by which every now and then the player has to reload the gun to keep shooting

Early shooter games didn't have any reloading involved, but modern shooter games might have quite complex reloading mechanics, each with their own unique gameplay implications.

Imagine for example a classic FPS such as **Call of Duty** (**CoD**). Every weapon has a clip of ammunition that, once unloaded, has to be reloaded. This exposes the player to incoming attacks, creating a need for strategy for when to reload and a sense of danger in doing so: a fantastic game mechanic! See it in action as follows:

In *Call of Duty*, the player can press the reload button at any given time, commencing the action of reloading their weapon

Star Wars: *Battlefront* uses a different approach. Firing a weapon for too long and too quickly causes overheat. Once overheated, a weapon cannot be used for a number of seconds. The final effect (dynamic) is clearly similar to the one we have in CoD—the overheated weapon exposes the player to attacks and creates a situation of danger, but the strategies are different. Unlike CoD, in *Star Wars*: *Battlefront* the player can pace their shooting in such a way that the weapon never overheats, at the expense of the fire rate:

In *Star Wars: Battlefront* a weapon doesn't need to be reloaded. However, if the player keeps shooting for too long, the weapon overheats and has to be cooled down by pressing the cooldown (reload) button at the right time

Action points

Typical of turn-based games, action points are a widely used mechanic. The player has a budget of points that he can spend for doing actions (each action would be a separate mechanic, such as moving, using an ability, attacking an enemy, and so forth). Usually, this point also regenerates over time or each turn:

In *Hearthstone*, the player has a number of action points called *Mana* every turn. Each card he can play has a *Mana* cost.

List of common game mechanics

Here is a practical list of game mechanics common to video games. It is by no means a comprehensive list, but it will help you better understand the meaning of the word mechanic in the context of video games:

- Turns
- Different types of movements (running, crawling, flying)
- Card drawing
- Time limit
- Resource collection/gathering
- Shooting
- Switching weapons
- Pushing
- Pulling
- Dragging
- Shooting
- Winning condition
- Losing condition
- Rock-Paper-Scissors
- Randomly Generated Numbers
- Aiming
- Quick Time Events
- Score points
- Experience Points

There are hundreds of them. It is worth noticing that, as we have seen, a mechanic could be either an action that the player can perform or a more abstract rule of the game.

Game mechanics interact with each other to develop dynamics

The moment when a game really comes to life and triggers player's real emotions is when all the mechanics work together to create experiences. Usually, these interactions are called dynamics, such as in the case of the aforementioned *MDA Framework*.

The most striking difference between a mechanic and a dynamic is that a game designer has full control of the former but much less of the latter. It is only in the hands of players that dynamics can emerge from mechanics and it is the game designer's job to make sure this happens in the way they envisioned.

Having less control doesn't mean that designing the mechanics and just hoping that they'll work will be enough. The fun of video games ultimately resides in dynamics, so getting them right is even more important than designing the core mechanics.

Mechanics and dynamics are part of a feature

We know that mechanics are the atoms of our gameplay. We've learned that the interactions among our mechanics create dynamics, and now we can finally shed some light on the term *Feature*.

A game feature is an entire set of mechanics, and designing a feature means not only describing each mechanic but also how they will generate dynamics and interact when played with.

Some feature examples are combat, multiplayer leaderboards, crafting, weapon upgrades, a world map, online mode, guilds, tournaments, and procedurally generated content; the list is limited only by the designer's imagination.

Here's a list of common features with some examples in popular games:

Character Creation	*Skyrim, Pillars of Eternity, World of Warcraft*
Combat System	*Dark Soul, Call of Duty, Chess*
Guild Wars	*Clash of Clans, Lineage II*
Crafting	*Minecraft, The Witcher*
Tournament	*Overwatch, FIFA*
World Map	*Far Cry, Fallout*

It is important to know that some features can be formed by many other smaller features—In open world games the *open world* is usually described as a feature, but an open world includes smaller features such as world map, traveling, weather and time, encounters, and many, many others.

Approaching mechanic design

Now that we have some grasp of the theory behind game mechanics and dynamics and how they are the building blocks of game features, let's look at how to work on them.

As we discussed in `Chapter 4`, *Design Documentation*, every design process should start with the definition of some goals and requirements.

When creating your mechanics, you should always keep in mind the following questions:

- What is the goal of the mechanic?
- Is the goal clear to the player?
- What are the rules that affect the mechanic?
- What is the feedback to the player?

The kind of game you are developing and its vision should guide you through the answers. Let's say you are working on an action medieval-fantasy game where melee combat is your core feature. The first mechanic you'll be focusing on is probably going to be the action of attacking an enemy.

What is the purpose of the combat system?

Regardless of the theme of your game and its vision, the fact that we are talking about an action game already provides some insights.

An action-oriented combat game challenges the player's physical skills and leverages their knowledge of the available game actions. So, one of the requirements would certainly be the use of the player's hand-eye coordination skills. It should also use memory skills, for pulling out combos or special attacks by pressing key combinations. The goal of such mechanics is usually to give to the player a skill-based system, easy to learn but difficult to master, to fight different enemies using different weapons and tactics.

Rules and game mechanics

Rules are extremely important to any game. According to different definitions of game mechanics, they might not be defined as mechanics themselves, but as a part of them. Rules for our combat system could be, for example, the number of attacks per second the player can perform. Rules can define constraints for actions or conditions to be respected (a victory condition, for example). Rules make games exciting because they determine the space in which the game's actions can take place.

Imagine a Hide and Seek game where the seeker doesn't have to close his eyes while the other players are hiding. That would be the most boring Hide and Seek game ever! The rule that states the seeker has to close their eyes and count to a predetermined number is there to force a challenge that makes the game fun—a challenge for both the seeker, who can't look where players are hiding, and the hiders, who have a limited time to hide.

We could say that this rule is not a mechanic in itself. The two main mechanics in Hide and Seek are for the seeker to *Seek* and for the hiders to *Hide*. The rule is part of the *Seek* mechanic, but nonetheless is a fundamental part of the game.

It might be difficult to distinguish between a mechanic and a rule; again, this would be a theoretical effort, which we don't want to tackle in this book.

What is important is that you understand that mechanics and rules need to come together and be considered at the same time while designing a game.

Mechanics and dynamics produce feedback

Finally, there is feedback, probably the most important part of a game mechanic in video games.

Wikipedia gives the following definition of video games:

> *"A video game is an electronic game that involves interaction with a user interface to generate visual feedback on a video device".*

The word *feedback* is part of the very definition of video games.

We could argue that the Wikipedia definition is not complete (or up to date), as that feedback is not necessarily visual. It can well be audio or even haptic (the most traditional haptic feedback is the vibration of a console controller, but haptic feedback and devices are evolving at an incredible pace with the growth of virtual reality).

Feedback is everywhere in video games and is at the core of any game mechanic. For every player's action, there must correspond a change in the game that is immediately appreciable.

The fact that *Mario* jumps on the screen when you hit a specific button on the controller is a feedback, as is the iconic *bounce* sound that he makes.

Feedback is not limited to the player's immediate actions though. An **Experience Points (XP)** progress bar is a visual feedback that provides the player valuable information about how many XP points they need for the next level. More importantly, that XP bar could flash and make a little progress every time the player accomplishes an action that rewards XP. This is a fantastic way to teach the player about cause-effect relations in the game:

The result screen at the end of every match in *Overwatch* is full of visual feedback. It does an excellent job in providing information about the player's performance, progression, and what is about to happen now that the match is over.

Feedback is also essential to understand the game's world and logic. Imagine if the same action performed in the same circumstances doesn't produce the same result (and feedback) every time. That would be extremely frustrating for the player and undermine the fun of the game. For example, you know that you can fire your weapon in a shooter game with a specific button, let's say *R2* on a PlayStation's controller. Every time you press that button, you expect your weapon to shoot. If once in a while, the same button produces a different effect, such as for example throwing your weapon at the enemy instead of shooting, we would have an infuriated player. For the same reason, if the weapon is jammed or must be reloaded before shooting, we expect the game to somehow tell us that the shooting is not available and that we need to reload. The outcome of pressing the same button, in this case, would actually be different (shoot if the weapon is loaded, don't if it's not), but the feedback given to the player must describe what is going on as best as possible.

Finding the right reference

How can you create a game mechanic based on an existing one? How do you find the right reference to start creating your own?

The first step is to look for games that include mechanics and features similar to what you are envisioning for your game. Your game concept should give you a clear idea of which games you should look at.

At this point, you should have a clear idea of who your competitors are (as we have seen in Chapter 2, *Game Concept*) and it is important to look at your competition's game mechanics with special attention. This is for two reasons:

- Here you will find the basic mechanics of your game
- It will give you a clear idea of how games similar to yours play. Your goal is to make something different in the end, not just copy-paste what's already been done!

Let's make some practical examples.

Let's say you are building a Real-Time Strategy game and need to define how resources are collected and managed:

In *Age of Empires*, the player needs to gather the resources by allocating his workers to the various resources: crops, forests, mines, and farms

You can decide to go with the classic *Age of Empires* approach, where resources are scattered around the map and you have to send a specific unit to collect them, or try a modern approach like in *Dawn of War*, where your resources are granted by capturing and maintaining strategic points:

In *Dawn of War* the player generates resource points by controlling strategic points

These two are great references that you can analyze to decide which approach suits your game better.

It is important to remember the concept of **Unique Selling Point** (USP) here. It is unlikely that your game is going have multiple USPs and that's totally fine! If resource collection is not what your game is really about, but it still needs a resource collection mechanic, just take what has already been built!

Taking mechanics that work for your game from existing games is exactly what you need if you don't want to waste time on the corollary and focus on your true USP.

Maybe you are building a classic 2D platformer game, with jumping between platforms as one of its core mechanics. The number of references you'd have to look at can be pretty overwhelming: *Super Mario, Castlevania, Sonic, Donkey Kong, Rayman, Kommander Keen*...there are hundreds of examples.

In this case, you should focus on what kind of user experience you want your players to have and trim down the list to only the games that have given you something similar.

Yes, in order to do that, you would need to play an awful lot of games, especially the ones that you wouldn't consider playing as a gamer...that's part of your job! Classifying in your mind games and genres, and categorizing them into *experiences* is a must for any game designer.

Keep a game journal. Whenever you play a game, note down your feelings and thoughts. A few sentences and the date you played would be enough. It will be valuable information later on, even years later.

Deconstructing your references

Once we have found our perfect references it, is time to deconstruct them into smaller experiences. We need to analyze these mechanics and understand why they have been developed the way they have. Then we need to understand what we need to do in order to implement them in our game and make them work according to our vision.

Let's go back to our previous platform game example.

We want to analyze the Jumping mechanic of 2D platform games. We will pick one of the classics: *Super Mario Bros*.

Jumping is, of course, a core mechanic. But can we say something else about it?

- How high can Mario jump?
- How much distance can he cover while jumping?
- Can you control the character once he's up in the air?
- Is there any rule that directly affects the mechanic?
- What kind of challenge is the player facing with the Jump action?

Let's try to address these questions.

- The longer the player holds the **JUMP** button, the higher the jump will be
- The distance covered by the jump depends on the speed of the character when he jumps and the height of the jump
- Mario hovers into the air and the player can use directional movements to line up the falling to the target
- Mario's jumps are affected by gravity—his speed in going up is slower than coming down
- The challenges are:
  - Avoiding enemies and obstacles by jumping over them
  - Landing a jump on enemies' heads to kill them
  - Avoiding falling into pits
  - Reaching a particular platform by jumping on it

Interesting findings, don't you think?

 There are various techniques to deconstruct games and game mechanics. When you want to understand a mechanic from an existing game, a great way to understand how it is made is to ask an engineer for their opinion on how he or she thinks it has been implemented. How does it work at a technical level? Getting insights on this kind of question could reveal a lot about a game mechanic!

Now that we have deconstructed the Jump mechanic in *Super Mario*, let's take another popular platform game that clearly took inspiration from the Mario: *Super Meat Boy*.

In *Super Meat Boy* the core mechanic remains the Jump action. How did the developers make a completely new and fresh game out of it?

First of all the gravity rule that affects Mario's jump is simplified: *Super Meat Boy's* jumps are symmetrical as the speed going up is the same as the speed going down.

At a first glance this seems a tiny, insignificant detail, but in reality, this simplification allows *Meat Boy* to be more reactive and controllable, with his jumps much more predictable than Mario's.

No wonder *Super Meat Boy* is a much more fast-paced game.

The predictability of *Meat Boy's* jumps serves another purpose: the player is often required to make a series of jumps which involves platforms that are off-screen at the moment he starts the sequence. So he has to take decisions and actions in a matter of milliseconds - something you can't so easily do with the weight and physics of Mario.

Another distinctive addition to *Super Meat Boy's* jump mechanic is Wall Jumping. By landing a Jump on a wall is possible to immediately Jump again in an upward and opposite direction from the wall. This is a simple addition that enables dynamics such as vertical climbing, and therefore creates a completely different and new game.

Additive and subtractive design

Our previous *Super Meat Boy* jump example is a perfect introduction to the topic we're going to discuss: additive and subtractive design.

By taking out that gravity element, *Meat Boy's* developers have subtracted from a classic jumping mechanic, while on the other hand they have added to the mechanic by allowing wall jumping.

Additive and subtractive design is the principle behind any adaptation of game mechanics.

Additive design, in particular, is what game developers have always used to create new video games. Expanding and improving existing game mechanics is the lifeblood of game design as much as introducing new groundbreaking ones.

Subtractive game design though is probably even more important.

We talked already about the *Less is more* principle and how it should be applied throughout the whole design and its documentation. Applying this principle in game mechanics is not only a matter of elegance; it can help game designers to discover (or re-discover) the fun at the core of game mechanics and their ease of use.

> '*Subtractive design is the process of removing imperfections and extraneous parts in order to strengthen the core elements. You can think of a design as something you build up, construct and let grow, but it's pruning away the excess that gives a design a sense of simplicity, elegance, and power.*'
>
> – *David Sirlin, Game Designer*

Subtractive design and examples of how it can transform good games into great games are everywhere in the history of video games.

Valve's game *Portal* is a fantastic example of minimal game design. In *Portal*, you can open two different kinds of portals using a Portal Gun—orange portals and blue portals. The core mechanic is that you can enter an orange portal and come out from the Blue portal. You have no actual weapons, there is no inventory screen, there are no NPCs or enemies (with the exception of the turrets and the final boss). The controls are ultra-simplified, with action buttons only for moving, shooting the two kinds of portals, jumping, and carrying objects:

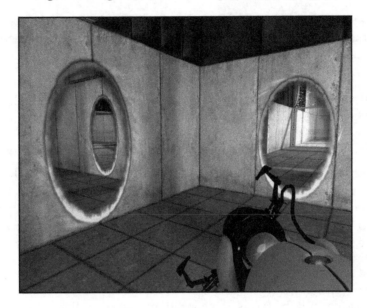

The portal mechanic in *Portal*

Portal's levels contain practically nothing except for elements that are part of puzzles, visual cues as hints about what you should do, and elements related to the story. This minimalistic design puts all the emphasis on the portal mechanic itself, which is incredibly fun. Basically, all you can do is shoot portals and move between them to solve puzzles. The fact that there are no other core mechanics in the game allows the designer to fully explore all the possibilities of the Portal mechanic, focusing on what is really fun for the player and staying away from anything distracting or out of context.

Putting it all back together

Once you have found your references, deconstructed them, taken the most significant elements as a base to develop your mechanics, and finally added or taken out whatever you needed to achieve your gameplay vision..it is finally time to test whether it really works!

At this point, you are probably not yet writing a detailed documentation to the rest of team. Most likely you are in some sort of prototyping phase. Especially with core mechanics, the only way to test your hypothesis (of fun) is to play them.

We will discuss later how to effectively prototype game mechanics and flows. For now, it is important that you understand that the process of creating new mechanics goes hand in hand with working software.

The only way to know if your character's jump needs to follow a realistic physic or not, what the speed at which it is performed should be, and the maximum height is to play the game and feel whether your design assumptions were right or not.

Or to better (and more realistically) put it, to see how they were wrong.

In this iterative process of adding and subtracting elements from your mechanics and tweaking their values you will eventually find the perfect gameplay feeling and finally fix it into your GDD...or fail and realize that some of your assumptions were wrong—don't be scared of failure though. The faster you fail, the more time you will have to get it right or decide that you're simply going in the wrong direction.

The screenshots used in this chapter are for illustrative purposes only. We do not recommend you to misuse these in any way. For more information please consult the terms and conditions of the publishers mentioned in the *Disclaimer* section of this book.

Summary

We have explored in this chapter the basic elements that form a game and how they interact, creating dynamics. We discovered the importance of playing many different games and being able to recall their core mechanics in order to find useful references for the creation of your own. We also learned some valuable design principles that will help us to adapt existing mechanics into something new and true to our game's vision.

With this solid base taken on board, we're ready to move to the next chapter, where we're going to learn an even more difficult art—The creation of new mechanics and the search for innovative gameplay.

6
Invention of Mechanics

Now that we know how to adapt game mechanics and which processes are available to do so, it's time to focus on one of the most challenging and exciting tasks for a game designer: coming up with brand new game mechanics! The difference between adapting and creating new mechanics is thin, though. We will see in this chapter how new game mechanics can be created not only as *actions* available to the players but also as different dynamics that are generated in-game by existing core mechanics.

We will discuss some of the theories behind game design and the creation of mechanics that are fun to play, and we'll dive into how a new mechanic needs to be taught to the player and how the core loop of a game is formed. Finally, we're going to have a close look at the design of a combat system and why combat and conflict are an important part of many video games. You will learn about complexity and depth and the related problems a game designer needs to solve by using them.

This chapter is probably the most important in the entire book. We will need to look further afield at game design theory and be less practical for a while. It is still going to be a quick overview though. Therefore, we highly recommend that you use this as a base, from which you'll be able to follow up on and deepen your knowledge. Don't be scared if you feel overwhelmed by all this information. Every book, author, and article we're going to quote can be found at the end of this book in the bibliography.

Ready?

Let's go.

Developing an idea into an experience

The main reason for creating a new game mechanic can be described as the need to give the player a novel experience. We learned how the game vision gives us designers a clear direction to follow in order to develop our games. By visualizing the experience we want our players to have, we are taking the first step into the conceptualization of a new game mechanic.

Let's see a practical example.

Modern **First Person Shooter** (**FPS**) games are very different from what we used to play in the 80s and the 90s. When we immersed ourselves in a frenetic shooting game all we needed were some interesting enemies, a few different weapons, and just a bunch of basic controls, such as *move* and *shoot*.

In a quest for better immersion, game designers started to ask questions like: "How can we make an FPS more realistic?", "How can we make shooting more tactical?", and "How can we give players the impression that they are in the middle of a real shooting scenario?"

A real gunfight scenario is miles away from a video game such as *Wolfenstein* and *Quake*, where the player can basically storm the enemies, shooting loads of ammunition at them and withstanding heavy fire with no hesitation. Imagine your task as a designer is to add more strategy to those classic FPS games, in order to evoke a more realistic shooting scenario. Which mechanics would you add to a game with only *move* and *shoot* mechanics?

There are many correct answers to this question, so before we keep reading, try imagining a couple of those!

Done? Great!

A common answer would be: *Adding cover*.

In a real gunfight, you don't usually see people running toward their enemies guns blazing...that's typical of video games and movies! What people do, in reality, is take cover! They try to find a spot where they are protected from the bullets. Only once safe, might they peek out just a little and try to return fire from behind the cover. Imagine if by pressing a button your character can crouch behind obstacles and take cover. And of course, enemies would be able to do the same. Can you visualize how different this game would be compared to the basic **FPS** we started with?

Now you can go even further. Can your character shoot from behind the cover? (In a way, that is different from just leaving the cover and shooting...maybe he is less precise from there? Or can only do suppressive fire...) Can your character move from cover to cover, head down, instead of just walking or running between them?

Naughty Dog's Uncharted and *Ubisoft's The Division* are great examples of third-person tactical combat systems. Finding the right spots to take cover and moving between them is crucial to winning the fight. It also gives the player the freedom to choose how to tackle different encounters and how to exploit the terrain.

Of course, how the enemies react to the players' behavior is as important as the mechanics available. Enemies might use different weapons to drive the player out of covers, such as grenades or heavy fire capable of destroying those covers. Or maybe there could be enemies with melee weapons running toward the player while he's behind cover.

Addressing the need for a tactical and challenging game experience is the key to the creation of interesting mechanics and dynamics. It is important to note that realism doesn't have to always be the experience we want to give to the player. In fact, some game designers might want exactly the opposite. This is the case with games such as the latest version of *Doom* (2016). The idea behind the combat system was to go back to the roots of the FPS genre, offering visceral shootings and frenetic actions. How could you obtain that kind of experience if the game offers mechanics such as cover and stealth actions?

To go back to the most frenetic FPS action, *Doom's* game designers came up with a new game mechanic: *Glory Kills*. In short, by hammering an enemy with bullets, the player can stagger him and then perform a special melee attack that instantly (and quite brutally) kills him.

While performing a glory kill the player is invulnerable and the enemy always drops extra items such as ammunition and health. So, performing a glory kill is a rewarding tactical option that forces the player to approach combat in a very aggressive way and always move forward. All these are great examples of new game mechanics created from the experience we want the player to have. Let's do another example, with a completely different genre and mechanic.

Adventure, role-playing games, and in general, games based on narratives are often based on conversations and interactions with NPCs. In these games, dialogs are as important as action, and the player is challenged with critical choices to make. A classic mechanic to manage dialogues with multiple options is called branched dialogues.

Different lines open different branches of the dialogue, which usually lead to different outcomes and consequences. But how can one add tension and a sense of pressure if the player can take all the time in the word to make his choice? In the internet era, players are even able to pause the game and look for the best answer online in a matter of minutes.

In the early 90s, *Sega's Sakura Wars* answered this question using a real-time conversation system, in which the player has only a few seconds to decide which option to take. This incredibly simple mechanic changes everything. Many modern adventure games have taken inspiration from that mechanic. *Telltale Games* is famous for its narrative games based on real-time conversations, which in the past few years have revamped the interest in the genre.

New mechanics to solve a problem

Sometimes new mechanics are required to solve well-known gameplay problems. This is a typical scenario in live games (for example mobile games or Massively Multiplayer Online Games), where the game is constantly updated and adjusted to meet its audience's evolving needs. But it might as well be the case for sequels, franchises, and final releases after an alpha or a beta test.

One great example is the Chest mechanic in *Clash Royale,* one of the most interesting game mechanics in the history of mobile games (and one that has contributed to the incredible success of *Supercell's* real-time PvP title.)

This is how it works:

In *Clash Royale,* by winning a battle, players win chests. Chests contain Cards and Gold, both essential for player's progression. These chests must be unlocked before the player can get the rewards they contain. Unlocking a chest takes a certain amount of time. Alternatively, this wait can be skipped using Gems (the equivalent of real money). Each player has four chest slots, so they can only have up to four chests waiting at a time. It is still possible to battle when the chest slots are full, but no chests will be won, as all the slots are already taken.

Which issues do you think this mechanic has tackled and solved?
Think about it for a few minutes before reading on. It is clear how Supercell addressed some of the major problems in F2P mobile games, that is, how to organically integrate:

- Sessioning (how long and how often a play session should be)
- Retention (why should a player come back to the game)

- Monetization (if a player can't wait to open a chest...he can always spend some hard currency to do so)
- Progression (opening chests is the main way to obtain new cards and therefore upgrade your deck and progress through the game)

In most mobile games, each of those critical issues is specifically addressed with a set of features that sometimes feel disconnected and sort of artificially constructed. The elegance by which *Supercell* integrated everything in one single mechanic is a testament to their astonishing talent and massive success.

It is quite difficult to find completely new game mechanics in the Console and AAA space. Innovation usually means risk, and big projects are not the best for risk. This is why indie games and mobile games usually present a lot of much more innovative features (and sometimes, they are disruptive in their genre). Always keep an eye on the indie and mobile scene and see what designers are doing to solve common design problems in more efficient and elegant ways.

New mechanics to innovate

Another way to come up with a new mechanic is by asking yourself how things can be done differently. Thinking out of the box is a crucial skill for every game designer. *What if* is a great question to start with something you know or are familiar with and completely re-invent it.

A question like "What if we introduce zero-gravity in *Super Mario*?" can open an ocean of new possibilities and unexplored mechanics and gameplay. When trying to innovate, the *less is more* principle comes in handy again. Many games have innovated entire genres by taking out something from existing games.

"What if in a platform game the character automatically runs in only one direction and the only action available to the player is jumping?" That is why, *Canabalt* (2009) was born, re-inventing the platform genre...actually, inventing (or more precisely, popularizing—see the following information box) a new one: *the Endless Runner*.

While the Endless Runner concept was long known in Korea, journalists credit Canabalt as *the title that single-handedly invented the smartphone-friendly single-button running genre* and generated not only countless clones, by many great original games that rely on that mechanic, including *Super Mario Run* from Nintendo.

The process of innovating is the most difficult to follow, but it's the one that usually raises the bar to the next level. The games (and game designers) that are able to do that are the ones that are leaving a mark on the history of games and gaming. Of course, not all the new mechanics are innovative, as with innovation here we mean something that evolves or revolutionizes a way of doing something.

It is important to note, though, that innovation can spark from any of the previously mentioned approaches. What is different is that some game designers make games (or part of games) with the precise intention of innovating and that this, as you can imagine, requires a specific approach.

Building a new game mechanic

In order to be able to invent a new game mechanic, we need to go back to some theory. Understanding how to classify different mechanics, why they are fun, and what kind of player they appeal to is extremely important if we want to come up with something new. Some sort of *seed* is required to grow our innovative ideas into new game mechanics.

There are many classifications and definitions of *fun*, type of players, and game mechanics: they are all valid, (well maybe some are objectively better than the others…). There will be many opportunities to read and study all of them in your career and I strongly encourage you to do so. Personally, among all the studies I've read, I prefer three authors over the others and I think their approach to such theoretical topics is the best for a book about *Practical Game Design*.

These authors and the respective topics they have covered are:

- Richard Bartle, with his categorization of player types
- Nicole Lazzaro and her study about the four types of fun
- Jesse Shell and his taxonomy of game mechanics

In the next paragraphs, we're going to explore these topics. By understanding them, you will be able to design better game mechanics and ultimately better player experiences.

Many times in your career you will come across decision and designs that are the result of your instinct and *designer sensibility*. There will be times where you will apply game design theory without even knowing it. What defines a good game designer (and game design), though, is how much you will be able to catch all those intuitions and explain them using the knowledge you have acquired through studying and reading. Every time you are not entirely sure of why something *is that way*, go back to the books and make sure you actually know what you're doing!

Bartle's types of players

Richard Bartle is the creator of the first virtual world (it was called **Multi-User Dungeon (MUD)**, 1978) and one of the most important scholars and authors in our industry. In his studies, he categorized the kind of players who enjoy playing in virtual worlds (a categorization that can also be applied to other kinds of games but which it is worth pointing out that was intended by the author for Massively Multiplayer Online Games only).

He identified four main types of player:

- Achievers
- Socializers
- Explorers
- Killers

Let's have a closer look at each category and try to understand why it is so crucial for a game designer to understand them.

The **Achievers** are the players who enjoy setting and reaching the goals set within the game. These goals might be explicitly set by the game itself (such as win conditions, quests to solve, leaderboard to climb, collections to complete) or they might enjoy setting up goals for themselves (such as completing a game without ever losing or in the shortest amount of time possible). **Achievers** want to *Max Out* the game, in a way that could either be intended by its design or not.

The **Socializers** draw fun from the interactions they have with other people in the game. It goes by itself that multiplayer games are the best games for this type of players, but don't forget that social interactions might be built even outside the game world in many ways.

The incredible popularity of *Facebook* and social games, which started around 2008, is basically all thanks to these players. And it is safe to say that even the popularity of the whole video game medium owes much to the players who care about sharing their experiences as much as playing them.

The **Explorers** are the players that enjoy to immerse themselves in every bit of knowledge the game has to offer. It might be the lore of an RPG game such as *The Elder Scrolls: Skyrim*, or the rules and the cards in a Collectible Trading Card Game such as *Magic: The Gathering*. The **Explorers** are the experts of game worlds. They are the players that, most of the time, end up knowing the games even better than the game creators.

The **Killers**, lastly, are players driven by the desire of dominating the thrill of competition. These are the highly competitive players that see video games as a sport and they constantly try to get better to dominate the others. As opposed to the **Achievers**, the **Killers'** desire to get better is driven by the only goal of defeating other players, not so much by the joy of progress:

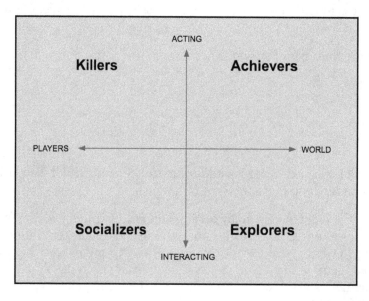

Bartle's four types of player and how they act and interact with both the virtual world and other players

Bartle's study goes much more in depth, analyzing the interactions between these categories and how they influence the design and the entire existence of virtual worlds (by which Bartle means explicitly what we would define as Mass Multiplayer Online Games). Again, his books are a highly recommended read.

In regard to how to use player types to create new game mechanics, it is clear how important it is to understand your audience and then design with that in mind. That said, two things must never be forgotten: great games provide fun mechanics to every kind of player, and some players might well have many facets, enjoying being **Explorers** one time and **Killers** another time.

Lazzaro's types of fun

Nicole Lazzaro proposes a similar model to Bartle's, but instead of focusing on players, she focuses on their emotions and the kind of fun they have while playing games. She defined four *keys to fun* and states that for a game to be fun (generally speaking), at least three out of four of these keys to fun must exist in the game experience.

Each key to fun corresponds to some fundamental human emotions:

- **Hard Fun**: Frustration and Fiero, in the moment of personal triumph over adversity
- **Easy Fun**: Curiosity, Awe
- **Serious Fun**: Excitement and Relief (relaxation)
- **People Fun**: Amusement, Joy

You can already see the connection with Bartle's model. But don't make the mistake of thinking that **People Fun** is the type of fun Socializers might experience or **Easy Fun** is the type of fun Explorers experience. It doesn't work like that and as we said, a good game proposes at least three out of four types of fun to every player:

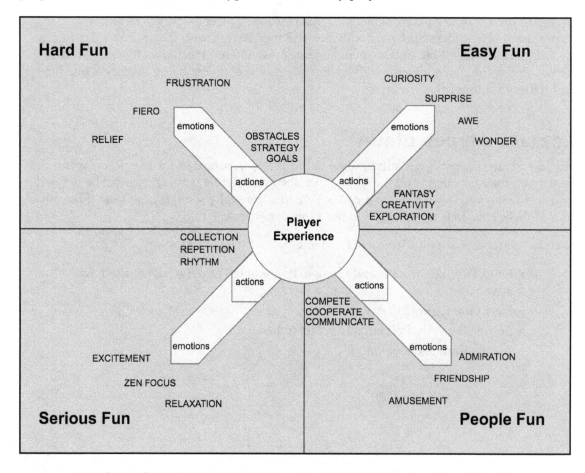

Lazzaro's four keys to fun. A set of actions within the game triggers a specific emotion in the player and therefore enables a specific type of fun

Let's have a look at a practical example of a couple of popular games.

The *Dark Souls* franchise is famous for its difficulty and the great anger and frustration that it causes to players (are you already seeing the point?) That is, of course, its **Hard Fun** component. The frustration of repeatedly dying in the search of an optimal strategy is directly proportional to the triumph experienced for winning. That feeling of obtaining a meaningful victory is something really powerful.

Hard Fun and **Serious Fun** go hand in hand in *Dark Souls*; the difficulty of the fights is what generates the frustration in players who get beaten, but it is also what makes it meaningful to progress, level up, find the right equipment, and strategize.

The adrenaline rush when the boss fight begins is a powerful emotion that only a difficult situation can provide.

What about the **Easy Fun**? You might think that a game such as *Dark Souls* doesn't give many opportunities for **Easy Fun**...but just look at how many memes there are over the internet! The game might not have been designed with those funny moments in mind, but still, by providing a *playground* for players' creativity, the game designers have opened the possibility for a lot of **Easy Fun**.

The gesture feature (the player earns moves such as waving or cheering) and how it has been used to capture funny screenshots of the game is a perfect example of **Easy Fun** (combined with **Social Fun**, as part of it is sharing those screenshots or video on the internet).

Another great example is the **Easy Fun** provided by a compelling control system. If you think that just rolling around in *Dark Souls* or jumping your way to your destination is quicker than just running...you're experiencing **Easy Fun**!

People Fun (or **Social Fun**) is the most straightforward. Whether it is the co-op feature or the PvP, *Dark Souls* provides all you need to experience **People Fun**. But again, when we talk about social fun and interactions with real players, always think out-of-the-box (out of the game in this case). **Social Fun** in video games comes from outside the world of the game. Games that are enjoyable just by being watched or eSports (such as *League of Legends*) that people enjoy watching as much as they enjoy playing offer incredible opportunities, and quite real emotions and fun. Keep that in mind when you design your game mechanics. In modern games, *Watchability* is as important a character as *Playability*.

Shell's taxonomy of game mechanics

Jesse Schell (in *The Art of Game Design*) has done excellent work defining a taxonomy of game mechanics. Each game mechanic you can think about almost certainly falls into one of the following categories:

- Space
- Objects, Attributes, and States
- Actions
- Rules

- Skill
- Chance

By understanding these categories, you will be able to have a clear idea of how to collocate your new game mechanic and therefore deliver a more conscious design.

Mechanic 1 – space

Space is the space in which the game takes place. According to Schell, all game space is:

- Discrete or continuous
- Dimensional

Discrete spaces (such as the grid in *tic-tac-toe*) have a limited number of cells or positions that may be filled or moved into, while continuous spaces (such as a football pitch) allow for unlimited movement within a limited space. By *dimensions*, Schell means whether a game is played on a 2D or 3D space. An improved graphical remake of a 2D platformer, for example, is still only played in two dimensions. Schell draws upon the field of architecture in order to explain how to design effective spaces.

He sets out five types of game spaces:

- **Linear**: A player can only basically move forward and backward (*Monopoly*)
- **Grid**: Movement is restricted by discrete, adjacent shapes (*Chess*)
- **Graph**: Several points connected by discrete paths (*Talisman*)
- **Points in Space**: Several points with no specified connecting path (*Final Fantasy*)
- **Divided Space**: Space carved up into irregular sections (*Risk*)

Mechanic 2 – objects, attributes, and states

A game's space is filled with objects: characters, items, buildings, props, rocks, trees, and other characters. Basically, *anything that can be interacted with in the game*. In computer science terminology, these objects have attributes (position on the screen, visual appearance, statistics...) and a state (dead or alive, current speed, maximum speed, and so on) that help define them and how they interact with other game elements.

Shell associates to objects and states the terms *nouns* and *adjectives*. You can describe each object of your game with a name and you can specify its attributes and states using adjectives. For example, a car (object) might have the following attributes: red (color), fast (speed), and coupè (type). These are all adjectives to describe the car - its attributes. It can also have a state, for example, whether it is moving or not.

Mechanic 3 – actions

If objects and their attributes are nouns and adjectives: actions are the verbs. Steering, accelerating, braking. These verbs describe the actions available to the car object we discussed before.

Schell describes two types of actions:

- Operative actions
- Resultant actions

Operative actions are the basic actions available in the game. Actions such as jumping, moving, shooting, reloading, and accelerating.

Resultant actions are those that emerge from the operative actions. Accelerating and braking at the right time in a car racing game might result in overtaking the car ahead.

Mechanic 4 – rules

We have seen how rules are not always considered proper game mechanics. According to Schell, rules are the most fundamental mechanic because *they define the space, the objects, the actions, the consequences of the actions, the constraints of the actions, and the goals.*

Goals are probably the most important rule in every game. Goals must be always clear to both the designer and the player. Whether you prefer to consider rules part of the game mechanics or something that govern and determines how game mechanics interact together, don't forget that rules are a fundamental part of every game.

Mechanic 5 – skill

To complete the tasks games present to them, players need skills. In order to create an adequately challenging experience, designers must balance player skill with game difficulty so that players stay interested and in a state of flow. Schell describes three types of skills within games:

- **Physical Skills**: Which involve strength, dexterity, coordination, and physical endurance. In video games, this often includes reflexes and fine motor dexterity.
- **Mental Skills**: Involving memory, observation, and puzzle solving.
- **Social Skills**: Which include reading an opponent, predicting their movements, and coordinating actions with teammates.

Mechanic 6 – chance

Chance is the sixth fundamental category of game mechanics. Chance adds unpredictability to a game experience, increasing replay value and diversifying gameplay. Games that include an element of chance leverage one of the basic human emotions: surprise. People like to be surprised, to experience unpredictable events and to challenge themselves predicting outcomes. In fact, Schell notes that the ability to predict outcomes is a skill in and of itself.

Game loops

In his recent book *Advanced Game Design: A Systems Approach,* Michael Sellers – a game designer and professor – identified four principal loops that define a video game experience:

- The game's model loop
- The player's mental loop
- The interactive loop
- The designer's loop

Why do we call these loops? The idea is that a game is not a linear experience, but a looping structure where an action by the player generates an effect (and give a feedback); this effect allow the player to take another action and so on and so forth, in a loop.

Game's model and player's mental loops

The game's model loop represents the dynamic world of the game. It is the combination of all the systems present in the game with which the player can interact. The player's loop, on the other hand, is the mental model of the game world that the player creates.

The player builds his own mental loop based on the actual game model loop. He set his goals and executes actions that generate feedback in the game and continue to do so until his or her goal is achieved.

The important thing about the player's mental loop is that the activities that a player executes in a game might not match with the game's model loop. Players can find their fun by not completing the game goals, but by setting their own and pursuing them. Maybe in an RTS game with the goal to defeat the enemy faction, some players might find it more fun and exciting to build a city of a particular shape, or to collect all the resources in the map. Or, in an open world RPG, they might prefer to go around and befriend all the animals in the world instead of following and completing the main quest.

Interactive loops

The interactive loop determines the actions the player can take to interact with the world and the feedback that the game gives in response to those actions.

The player's actions are basically inputs into the game's model loop, and the game feedback contributes to creating the player's own mental model loop. The interactive loop is made by a core loop and an extended loop, which we are going to describe in detail below.

Core loops

By core loops, we mean the loop of basic actions the player needs to perform in a game.

As we learned, these actions are a set of core mechanics that the player has to interact with. The loop happens when the player interacts with the mechanics over and over again in order to progress into the game.

In fact, some designers have defined core mechanics exactly like that: The core mechanics in a game will usually be the purposeful interaction that occurs the most frequently. In a platforming game, this is usually jumping. In a shooter, it is usually shooting. In a racing game, it will be driving.

There could be other definitions, as with every other game design concept. As we have said many times already, you don't have to stick with one particular definition of a game design concept. On the contrary, knowing more means you'd keep a clear idea of what other people's points of view on each concept or principle are. We call them core loops because the core mechanic is an action that will produce some results, that will trigger a new need to perform the core mechanic...and so on:

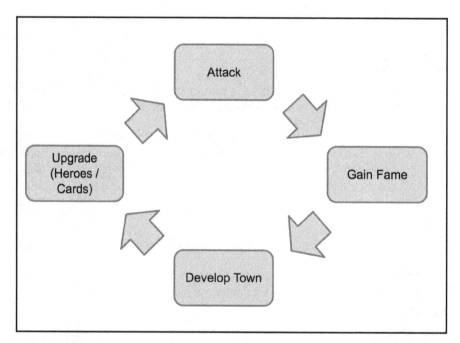

A simple core loop for an action-card game similar to Battlehand. The player fights battles to gain a currency (Fame, in this case). Fame is used to develop and upgrade the player's town. Upgrading the town unlocks the hero and card upgrade. With these upgraded, a more challenging battle can be fought

Extended loops

The extended loop is more complex (and a realistic representation of an entire game). Defining your core loop is part of deciding which new mechanics you might need in your game. Consider games such as *The Witcher III: Wild Hunt* and *Middle Earth: Shadow of War*. Both games' core loop consists of fighting enemies to get rewards and experience points. (You could argue that it's the core loop of most RPG games, and it's true, but not entirely. In fact, how you do that fighting is extremely important and quite different, for example, from a turn-based RPG.)

So what makes *The Witcher* and *Shadow of War* two different games (apart from their settings and lore, of course)?

It's the extended loop, and how all the different game mechanics interact with each other.

In both games, the core loop (fighting enemies to get something) is related to the game's progression, and in both, there is a virtual skill system attached to it. What is really different is what you can do with what you get by defeating enemies and progressing through the game.

Geralt (the protagonist of *The Witcher* saga) can craft a variety of potions and alchemical items and can undertake quests to hunt monsters and interact with various **Non-Playable-Characters** (**NPC**), (with a lot of emphasis on romance). Most of the extended loop is related to expanding the narrative in different and new directions.

Shadow of War approaches the extended loop in a different way: you can collect and organize your personal army of Orcs and then use it to lay siege to enemies' fortress or to defend yours. This feature, which completely changes the gameplay when the player immerses himself in the extended loop, is perfectly integrated with another unique selling point of the Shadow of Mordor franchise: the Nemesis System. The idea behind the Nemesis System is to create emergent stories unique to each player by allowing enemies to develop their own personalities, rivalries, and traits that may grow over time depending on the battles they take part in or the way the players defeat or get defeated by them.

The depth of the system and the meaningfulness of these enemies and their development transformed the way players were playing the game. The core loop of solving the quests to proceed through the storyline and eventually finish the game was almost subverted by the extended loop of hunting those enemies and forging their stories. Of course, this was meticulously planned by *Monolith*'s game designers, with a remarkable result. It is important to understand that different game modes can be seen as part of the extended loop of a game (for example, the different PvP modes in *Blizzard*'s *Overwatch*) but as a designer, it is better to think about the core and extended loop as the actions that happen within a single game session.

From a design perspective, the more the extended loops are integrated into the core loops and mechanics, the more organic and compelling the player experience will be.

Designer's loops

Finally, there's the designer's loop. This is similar to the player's mental model, but this is the designer's mental model of the game. The main difference from the player's mental model is that the designer's loop is a perfect model of what the game and the player experience in the game should be.

The designer's loop is the game design process in itself. Iterating by designing and testing a game form the designer's loop, where the feedback given by someone playing the game and the difference between that player feedback and the designer's intent generates that iterative process has already been discussed.

Games as systems of conflict

According to a formal definition given by Katie Salen and Eric Zimmerman in their famous book *Rules of Play*, a game is "a system in which players engage in an artificial conflict, defined by rules, that results in a quantifiable outcome."

It's an interesting definition, perfect for deeply understanding game mechanics. It is easy to think about conflict in terms of war and triumph through competition, and this is indeed one of the reasons why games that represent fights and battles are so popular. But by *conflict* here, we really mean any kind of problem that is artificially created by the game designer for the player to solve. So why are these conflicts so important for the players and how can we create conflicts that are fun to solve?

Conflicts can arise from three things:

- Opponents
- Obstacles
- Dilemmas

You have to always keep these three things in mind when designing your game because no good game can exist without them.

Opponents

The most obvious cause of a conflict is the fact that an opponent is trying to reach the same goal as the player or to simply prevent the player from getting there. In a single player game like *Dark Souls*, clearly every enemy in the game exists with only one purpose: kill your character and stop you from proceeding further into the game.

Multiplayer PvP games are so interesting because the game world is populated by real humans, all with the common goal of winning the game at the expense of the other players. Some games might have a much more abstract opponent-time, for example. A single player racing game in a time trial race, for example, doesn't feature any opponents (neither human or AI).

Obstacles

Obstacles are very common in all kind of games. They might appear in the form of a physical object that blocks the player somehow from reaching their objective, or they might involve mental skills, such as puzzles in adventure games. Obstacles are different from the opponent because they don't have an objective and they are not driven by any motivation. Nonetheless, they challenge the player's mental and physical skill.

Dilemmas

Dilemmas are probably the most important elements in a game and the type of conflicts they generate are often the most meaningful to the player experience. Dilemmas are the choices players have to constantly make when playing a game.

The legendary game designer Sid Meier (*Civilization* franchise, among others) once said:

"Games are a series of interesting decisions". The more meaningful those decisions, the better the player experience and the game will be. Choices in games are everywhere; how to invest resources in strategy games, which team and formation to select in a football game, which option to choose in a dialogue, which weapon to use in an FPS, which character to leave behind in a narrative game...

Dilemmas have their impact from the macro to the micro. Even the smallest game mechanic needs to include an element of choice.

Modern combat systems in action games express this principle in a great way. If you think about action games with a melee combat system today, you realize how many details are put into designing just the basics of the combat. Sometimes the player needs to make a choice at the start of the game, such as selecting a class, that will influence the entire game. The player also has to choose his gear (that is, which weapon to tackle the next battle with). During the combat, there might be strategic choices about charging the enemy or taking him out stealthily. And also: dodging or blocking with a shield? Using a slow but powerful attack or a series of quick ones?

The choices in those games start from the macro (*which character and gear I am going to use*) to the micro (*how to tackle this horde of enemies*) to the even more micro (*how to approach the fight with the enemy I'm attacking right now*).

No choices mean no agency over what's going on in the game, just button smashing through a repetitive sequence of events. Ultimately, no choice means no fun.

Quality over quantity

It is important to note that with many choices comes great responsibility. A common pitfall in designing game mechanics considering the range of choices they offer is to go for quantity instead of quality.

More choices don't translate into better games unless those choices are meaningful! If a dialogue with an NPC offers a vast range of possible answers, but none of them really affect the game with different consequences, or maybe 50% of them lead to a consequence and the other 50% to just another....that would be a pretty poor implementation.

If striking an enemy with a quick attack produces the same outcome as using a heavy attack...it is as if there is no real choice at all.

More choices, not best choices

Yes, one choice could be the best one for a specific situation or scenario. But if that choice is designed to always be the same one...then, again, the game will be offering very few choices. If one class is stronger than the others in a competitive RPG game, why should a player choose the other? Or if a resource grants access to the best units in a strategy game, how would it be interesting to use or invest in the others?

Sometimes, some choices are the best one a player could make, but there is a price to be paid for choosing them. We're going to see, in Chapter 13, *Balancing*, how the outcome of each choice can be balanced in different ways. For example, how to mitigate a choice that is clearly the best one, with an element of risk (in the aforementioned *Gears of War* reload mechanic, for example).

Wrapping up the theory

At this point of the book, you have probably understood that designing and creating games cannot follow a specific step-by-step recipe that always and universally works. Each game is different and your platform, audience, and scope influence your design dramatically.

This book is trying to convey a practical approach to game design and creating games, but never underestimate the importance of the theory. Behind any best practice or excellent design, there is the knowledge and the application of the principles we described. You have to learn and assimilate those principles by both studying and applying them. This is why the game industry is so avid about *experienced game designers* and why it's so hard to break into it as a junior or trainee game designer. Studying and applying your studies—by creating games—are inseparable parts of what makes a game designer.

I can never recommend enough that you consolidate what you've read in the last few paragraphs. There are many articles online about those studies and, of course, the author's books are an invaluable source of lessons, knowledge, and ideas on game design. Read and study those books!

Combat systems

One of the major epitomes of the conflict metaphor is the combat. There are countless arguments against violence and depiction of fights and wars in video games, and indeed, because there is so much more to video games other than battles, fights, and violence, those arguments are often just empty words. It would be like condemning cinema because there are war movies. The reality about combat in video games (and all kind of games really) is that fighting is part of our nature. And while our society and culture have made it possible for us to avoid fights in our entire real lives, many people will always be fascinated by some of the characteristic elements of combat. Of course, many others won't. Not all games need to include combat, fights or violence at all, and there are millions of players not interested in playing games that involve any kind of violence.

So, why is combat still so popular?

First of all, combat means competition, one of the most powerful drivers in human nature. Combat also means engaging with an activity that challenges the player's skill and intellect. Combat in games perfectly embodies Lazzaro's definition of Hard Fun and goes hand in hand with so many fantasies of our culture: Epic, Heroism, Commanding an army, Cloak and Dagger storylines, and many more.

It is very likely that you will face the challenge of designing a combat system; that's why we decided to include an entire section about it in this chapter. As you are going to read, many of the teachings from this section are applicable to the design of any kind of game, so even if you're not interested in how combat systems work, read on and see what you can learn from them!

How to design a combat system

When we talk about combat systems it is easy to think about games with stunning combat action and incredibly satisfying fights. Games such as *Batman: Arkham Knight* or *Dark Souls* have set a pretty high standard for how combat should be designed in action games. But truth be told, one of the greatest combat systems of all time still belongs to the King (and the Queen) of all games: Chess.

There is only one combat mechanic in Chess: By moving one of your pieces onto an enemy piece, you take it (out of the game). Space represents the only element of Chess' combat mechanic. So how is it possible that just this simple mechanic is at the core of one of the most competitive and long-lived games of all times? The greatness of Chess, like any other games I would say, comes from the interaction of all its mechanics, and the space of possibilities that they open.

The *Move to Take* mechanic, together with the chess board rules and movements available to the different pieces, create a perfect harmony of game mechanics from which an immensely vast range of possibilities emerges. So, to understand how to create a great combat system, you always need to take into account all the elements and the mechanics of the rest of your game.

Holistic game design

Components such as art, animations, and sound effects have a huge impact on how a combat system feels (and on any other game mechanics) and your design should always be influenced and informed by the entire vision of the game you are developing. In modern game development, a new concept of game design has emerged, called holistic game Design; this means that the mechanics, aesthetics, and even every technical aspect of a game cannot exist as a separate entity anymore. And this is especially true in modern games where the level of realism is extreme. There is a great *YouTube* video that shows how awkward *Battlefield 4* would be if it was using 8-bit sound effects from the 80's console era: https://youtu.be/7c1PBufdfcE.

Holistic game design teaches us that it is crucial to look at the big picture. There is a great talk by *Naughty Dog's* Anthony Newman, who goes into the details of the melee combat system in *The Last of Us*. In particular, it gives precious insights on how much the design of the combat mechanics is intertwined with how the characters in the game are animated and scripted. It also gives you an idea of the amount of work required in AAA games to create satisfying combat systems and how specialized the professionals who take on those challenges are. I really recommend that you watch it as soon as you have finished reading this chapter. You can find it at this link on *YouTube*: https://youtu.be/0x2H3kUQByo.

Types of combat system

A comprehensive list of all the combat systems that have been used in video games would be quite long. Surprisingly though, there are basically only two main categories:

- Turn-based
- Real-time

Turn-based games divide in-game actions into a series of distinct parts known as turns (a discrete time-space). Turn-based gaming is often associated with the combat systems in strategy, cards, and RPG games and is at the core of board games (both physical and digital). Typical examples are games such as *Hearthstone*, *XCOM*, or *Civilization*.

In a real-time combat system, all the actions take place in a continuous time-space and therefore characters act as quickly as it takes for an action to be ready. The most prominent examples are actions games and FPS's, such as *The Witcher*, *Call of Duty*, or *Starcraft*.

We could even add a third category: hybrid combat systems, which mix a bit of both real-time and turn-based, but the reality is that most of the time, the system underneath a hybrid combat system is always a turn-based one, implemented in a way that might feel like real time. Classic examples are RPGs such as *Neverwinter Nights*, *Baldur's Gate*, and *Star Wars: Knights of The Old Republic*.

These games, in particular, look like they run in real time, but under the hood, there is a turn system that determines who can attack, move, or act. As you know at this point, there's no such thing as systems that are universally better than others. Every system and mechanic works (or doesn't work) depending on its game context. One important thing to note, though, is that turn-based systems are less dependent on the implementation of characters' animations and actions.

This means that the designer can better control them through prototyping and simulations, which is a precious advantage. Another interesting thing about turn-based systems is that not only the designers are interested in building models to simulate them. Part of the fun for some players who enjoy these kinds of games is, in fact, to build their own game models and analyze them to find the best strategies.

Combat depth

This is going to be valid for games in general, not only for combat systems: what is depth?

It is an interesting concept to analyze because depth comes from the dynamics (the interaction of each mechanics) rather than from the mechanics themselves. Depth in games comes from the number of meaningful choices available to the player. I don't usually look for a formal definition of game design concepts but I love this particular one and I believe it's one of the best.

Let's analyze it.

We have already seen how choices are at the core of every fun game experience. When aiming for depth, it's a common mistake to think that the more choices available, the more depth the gameplay will have. That, of course, is not true, as, for a choice to be meaningful, it is paramount that the amount of options available is limited.

There are moments where giving too many choices becomes the same as not giving any at all. If I am able to attack my enemies with hundreds of different weapons, producing the consistent result of defeating them all, in the same way, all the time...I am not playing a deep game.

A deep game is one where I'd need to choose the right weapon for the right scenario. Let's take a shooter game set in a modern combat environment. A grenade or a rocket launcher might produce the same desired effect in a particular scenario. I might have been successful using a heavy machine gun or a well-placed mine or explosive...but it is very unlikely that I would be successful using a light gun with a suppressor or a sniper rifle.

If all of these weapons were good enough to achieve my goal...what would be the point in having all those differences in the first place?

This is why we talk about meaningful choices. Just choices are not enough to achieve depth.

How to achieve depth

So how to design for depth? The challenge for the game designer here is to design each mechanic with a clear vision of the dynamics they will spark during the gameplay.

Specifically for a combat system, we need to look at these aspects:

- Controls
- Weapons
- Enemies
- Environment

The choices available to the player start with controls. This is particularly true in action games, where the design of the controls (which button does what) is as important as defining the character's actions, weapons, and abilities.

Emergent gameplay

Emergent gameplay refers to complex situations in games that emerge from the interaction of relatively simple game mechanics. It might be part of the initial vision the designer imagined, the result of an attentive design focused on how emergent gameplay could happen. Or it can be something even the designer did not expect. Usually, good games designed with a clear vision of how emergent gameplay could flourish from the core mechanics end up having both those types of emergent gameplay.

Designing mechanics that are disconnected from each other, without any vision as to how they could kickstart emergence, usually results in a chaotic maelstrom of useless mechanics, with no actual ways to interact.

A great example of emergent gameplay is the Rocket Jump in *Quake*. The Rocket Launcher in *Quake* had a knockback effect that players found useful for extending the height of their jumps. By giving up a bit of health (due to the explosion), they were able to jump much higher and reach better strategic positions. None of the designers probably implemented the rocket launcher knockback effect with this in mind. Nonetheless, players have been using this technique to their advantage and the mechanic itself has influenced many other multiplayer shooters over subsequent years.

Of course, this emergent mechanic exists only because *Quake* had a deep enough system for it to emerge. The Rocket Launcher was a unique weapon to use in particular situations and unlike the others had a knockback effect with every shot. Gaining a good shooting position was an important part of the strategy for winning a game. Jumping was an important factor as well, useful for moving faster and in a nonlinear way. All of this prepared the ground for the emergence of a new way to use the weapon.

So, ultimately, depth can be achieved by giving the player different tools to solve problems (or fight her enemies) in different ways. Be warned, though: giving different tools means that even if one might be the best in a specific occasion or scenario...it should never be an optimal strategy for the entire game or for every combat instance.

If the Rocket Launcher is clearly the weapon that does the most damage, with the best accuracy and area of effect.. and it even allows me to rocket jump if I want to...why would I bother using the other available weapons at all?

An optimal strategy is the opposite of depth. There's no depth in a game where something is clearly and always better than everything else. For some players it might be fun to find optimal strategies and stick to the best characters or units or weapons...but you can bet they won't enjoy your game for long. We're talking here of objectively better game elements, not favored ones. There is a huge difference and, in fact, players will most likely stick to their favorite options, but since they won't be optimal strategies, their preference will be constantly challenged by the game. Sometimes difficulty might ramp up just because they deliberately choose to go for their favorite tools, instead of the best ones. Sometimes they could be surprised by how heavily the gameplay might change, just by switching weapon, character, or strategy. This is all great news. Good games empower players to choose their own tools and let them embrace the consequences of their choices.

Depth and complexity

We already talked about quality over quantity, but this is so important that it is going to take its own space.

Are deep systems also complex?

If we think about the simplest system of all, we could say that it is formed by just one basic core mechanic. We also said that depth emerges through the interaction of two or more mechanics. But more mechanics, by definition, make games more complex.

It appears that depth and complexity are, in fact, related, but here is the thing: our job as game designers is to achieve the maximum amount of depth with the minimum amount of complexity.

A very complex game is likely to offer great depth, and that's why we refer to these games as *hardcore* games. But hardcore games are difficult to learn and even if many players would love to understand how to play them and overcome their intrinsic complexity, the effort required is too high and they will never do it.

Much more challenging is to create the same amount of depth of hardcore games while reducing the complexity to a level that is appealing to as many players as possible. If you analyze the history of every AAA game out there, this is exactly what happened and is still happening. We want our games to be played by all the players out there! Not only the ones that can afford to spend hours just learning the basics.

Reducing complexity

If complexity and depth grow together, how can we mitigate the former and favor the latter, then?

The implicit complexity of a game system, its rules and core mechanics, can be simplified only to the extent by which they don't become trivial. This is a fact and there's little we can do, except try to design them in the most elegant way. Luckily, there is something we can do to reduce complexity without affecting depth:

- **User Interface**: We're going to talk about UI more in a later chapter. For now, keep in mind that a simple and elegant user interface is the first and most important way to reduce complexity. No one enjoys a screen cluttered with icons and buttons, even the most hardcore player doesn't want to click through ten screens to find what he's looking for. No *Skyrim* fan ever expected to scroll to an infinite list of text to interact with their inventory. I would argue that the more *hardcore* a game is, the more its UI should be uber-simplified, so the player can focus on understanding the game more than its UI.
- **Pace**: The pace of the game is a major factor in its complexity. The number of decisions the player has to make (which smells like depth) needs to be reasonably balanced against the time he has to make them. Too little time and the player's brain simply won't be able to process everything at once, resulting in complexity sabotaging depth. This is particularly true whenever the player is asked to make uninformed decisions, choices about things she doesn't really know or understand yet. A classic example is the character creation in RPG games. Deciding the character's class and abilities will have a profound impact on the whole gameplay, so be careful about how many choices the player has to make to create her character and how many of those are definitive for the rest of the game.

- **Tutorials**: Tutorials are very important to teach players how mechanics work in the game. They can be included at any point in a game when something new is introduced. Clever level design or pacing can allow the player to experiment with the new tools available in a safe way and funnel the player into their correct use.

In the next section, we are going to discuss how to teach game mechanics and reduce a game's intrinsic complexity with tutorials.

Teaching game mechanics

One of the eternal dilemmas of every game designer is: How do I teach players how to play the game?

In the early days of video games, there was a physical instruction manual that players had to read in order to understand how to play a game. Most of them, of course, never bothered and just jumped into the gameplay figuring out that by themselves. That has been the standard for years.

With the video game audience growing larger and the medium spreading through more affordable and mainstream technology, the average video gamer is today pretty much anyone. It is therefore impossible to take for granted that he'd be able to learn a game just by immersing himself in it. On the other hand, video games themselves have become quite complex systems. Learning a game such as *Doom* back in 1993 was a straightforward task: *arrows keys* to move, *Ctrl* to fire, *Spacebar* to use objects. With those controls in mind, all you have to do in the game is to shoot at the monsters and open some doors by activating switches or collecting keys.

Of course, other mechanics were distinctive of the game: picking up new weapons, avoiding traps like radioactive and toxic pits. Nothing that needed new teaching to the player, though. Got a new weapon? You still shoot by pressing *Ctrl*.

Let's jump 23 years ahead, to the recent *Doom* game released in 2016 by *Bethesda*. The brilliant tutorial phase teaches you how to shoot at enemies, interact with objects, use the alternate fire of your weapon, perform Glory Kills, and access and use your Codex and Mission log. And then: accessing and navigating the automap, destroying Gore Nests, climbing on ledges, jumping, and upgrading your weapons and Predator suit.

That's a lot of stuff! And all of it is taught in the first 10 minutes of the game. It follows naturally, that while the original 1993 *Doom* developers (all hail John and John!) didn't really need to worry about how to teach their game, our friends at id Software must have put in quite an effort to explain all those mechanics in the recent *Doom* game.

How to design a tutorial

There is a famous quote from an ancient Chinese philosopher that says:

"Tell me and I forget, show me and I may remember, involve me and I learn."

This phrase should be a mantra for every game designer working on a tutorial to teach a game mechanic. How many game tutorials have you played that were just a lot of dialogues and instructions, one after the other? And how many times has getting back to a game with such tutorials after a few days required you to go through those dialogues again (or have a look at a guide on the internet)?

A tutorial made of just instructions and text is a bad tutorial, especially if it overwhelms the player with a huge amount of information in a quick succession. Remember that the more text the player has to read to learn something about a game, the less he will actually read.

So what does that quote mean when talking about game tutorials?

Just telling players how something works is never enough. Imagine a tutorial on how to use a shield in *Dark Souls* without having any shields. The tutorial message "Press Left *Ctrl* to parry" would be pretty meaningless, since with no shield equipped, by pressing Left *Ctrl* nothing would really happen. So even if the player knows which key he needs to press to use a shield, chances are that when he eventually comes across one, he wouldn't remember how to use it.

Showing a game mechanic is another classic way to teach how to play.

A great example is in the recent *Far Cry* games. Just before getting into a particular scenario where a new mechanic can be introduced, the game pauses and a series of captioned images are presented to the player explaining how to perform the new mechanic. What is great about the *Far Cry* tutorials is that those tutorial messages are displayed exactly before a perfect scenario to experiment with the new mechanics is presented to the player. And this is where the *Involve me* part begins.

Explaining what a mechanic is in a context where the player can try it out and experiment with it in a safe way means the player will truly learn it before moving on to the next one. The kind of tutorial you will need for your game is deeply connected to the experience you want to give to your players and their behavior and expectations.

Some games are fun because they deliberately don't have any tutorial, so it's up to the player to figure out how things work. If that is part of the fun you want to give to your players, by all means, go ahead! Always remember though that not understanding is the most frustrating experience in video gaming, so be careful! We're going to talk about tutorials again, later, in Chapter 12, *Accessibility,* and have a closer look at how to teach game systems to players.

Tutorials in Free to Play games

Special attention should be given to Free to Play games. This is an excellent example of how your business model, game genre, and target audience can deeply influence every aspect of your game design. Unlike premium games, Free to Play games are downloaded for free, so the initial commitment from your players is very low. They can immediately lose interest or decide to move to the next free game within seconds of their decision to try yours.

Players who buy premium games have already invested money in those games, so their commitment to the game and attention to what's going on on the screen is immensely higher than what they have for F2P games.

This doesn't mean that premium games tutorials can be poorly designed, but for sure they can be designed with more focus on a variety of elements. On the other hand, F2P games tutorials need to be fun, accessible, interesting and promising all at the same time. Accomplishing this is a very difficult task and an incredible challenge for every game designer. Always keep in mind your audience at every step of your design and be consistent with your design choices.

We are going to discuss Free to Play games and what challenges they pose to game designers in Chapter 15, *Games As a Service.*

 The screenshots used in this chapter are for illustrative purposes only. We do not recommend you to misuse these in any way. For more information please consult the terms and conditions of the publishers mentioned in the *Disclaimer* section of this book.

Summary

What a chapter! This has been probably the most difficult so far. We've been through a lot of concepts, principles, and examples. I suggest you reflect on what you have read before proceeding. Let this chapter settle and go back to any part that you think might be worth re-reading, it's a lot to take on!

Our journey started with understanding how it is important to come up with new game mechanics and to transform a vision into a playable experience. We then explained some of the fundamental theories behind game design: how to classify game mechanics, player types, and the fun they enjoy by playing games.

We briefly explored the art of teaching a game using tutorials. We approached games as systems of conflicts and studied how to design a combat system and which elements are important to them - specifically, depth and complexity.

There has been quite a lot of theory, but as Abraham Lincoln once said, "Give me six hours to chop down a tree and I will spend the first four sharpening the ax". We are now ready to deal with one of the most practical chapters of this book, so let's chop the tree and learn how to implement what we have learned so far through prototyping.

7
Prototyping

At this point in the book, you might have realized that, practical as it may be, game design happens in the designer's head first, on a document of some sort second, and only in a third step is it possible to implement it.

To actually *make the game happen*, the designer has to get their hands on a tool that allows them to create working software; to write some code. Not all game designers are programmers, and even if they know how to program, designing and programming are two different jobs both requiring a person's full attention (and the bigger the project, the more this truth cannot be bent).

There is one activity where a game designer is required to turn the design into a playable thing as if he was the only person working on it. This is the quintessence of practical game design.

This is the creation of a game prototype.

What is a prototype?

A prototype is a model built to prove a concept.

This definition is applicable to anything really, not only games. Most of the products we use every day, from the keyboard I am typing on to the complex machines that can fly outside the Earth's atmosphere and reach other planets, all of these things are the result of endless designs, prototypes, iterations, and failures.

Game prototypes are not meant to be representative of what the entire game will look like; in that case, we talk more about tech demo or pre-alpha development builds. If you have a pre-alpha ready, that means you are at a later stage of the development and you have probably already prototyped your core mechanics to get to the pre-alpha stage. Nonetheless, even at later stages, you might need to address problems that were not obvious before. Maybe finally feeling how your game actually plays in the hands of a playtester—or even your own—raises questions about something you could have done differently or better.

Prototyping ultimately means answering those questions. It is crucial to nail down what those questions are as early as possible.

They could be generic questions, such as *Would this work?*, *Would this be more interesting?*, or *Which one is the best?* We will be more specific later, but for now, keep this in mind: if you don't have a clear question, why are you prototyping? And how will you be able to tell whether the prototype is working or not?

Why a prototype?

The main reason why prototypes exist is that we need to narrow down the risk of making something that doesn't work. Imagine that you have infinite time and resources; what would be the point of creating a prototype? Why not just create the entire game, and if it doesn't work, we'd have all we need to try again? Prototypes exist exactly because we need to make the best use of the scarce time and resources we've got.

When we build a prototype for a game, we're generally looking at:

- Whether a mechanic is engaging
- Selecting the best idea from a set of alternatives
- Testing the technical feasibility of an idea (where the idea can be anything from a full game to a graphics technique or AI algorithm)
- If the user can navigate the game UI effectively and intuitively

 Please note that our first point is a huge one! To know what a fun mechanic is and how to judge whether yours is fun or not, you'd need to master everything we said in Chapter 5, *Adaptation of Mechanics*, and Chapter 6, *Invention of Mechanics*; make sure to go back to those chapters whenever you need more clarity!

Prototyping techniques

When it comes to creating a prototype, there are two main options: physical and digital.

You would be surprised to know how many times a physical prototype is used in the video game industry. Many game mechanics can be reproduced through board games, card games, miniature games, or just one sheet of paper with a pen and maybe a few coloring pencils.

Digital prototypes are a bit more complex to put together, but of course, their fidelity to the medium and ability to create real-time environments and handle complex calculations makes them the go-to choice. Most of the time, though, it is always a great idea to start very simply on paper, and then move to digital with clearer ideas.

Paper prototyping

Paper prototypes are my favorites. Making them is as quick as it takes to write on a piece of paper and cut out some cardboard elements. Each time is like creating a little board game! Here's an example:

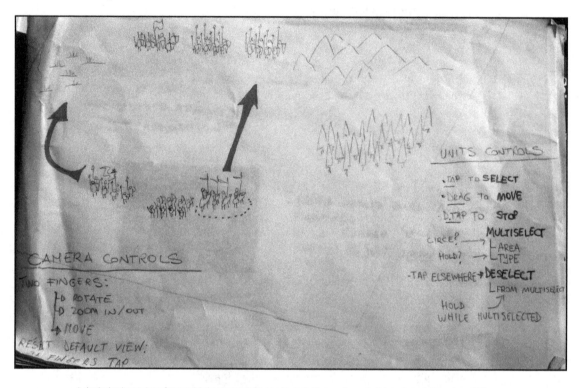

A simple sketch on a piece of paper might be a great start for a prototype; in this case, the emphasis is on the touch inputs for an RTS game

If you're wondering what a paper prototype might look like, have a look at the following screenshot:

A paper prototype for an alternative combat system for *Battlehand: Heroes*. We're going to discuss this particular prototype as a case study later in this chapter

I'm sure you imagined something much more *nice* and *professional-looking*. That's not the case at all!

Never trust a prototype that looks too good; as we said, by definition prototypes are stripped of anything not essential.

It is important to note that there is a huge difference between a UX-UI paper prototype and a game paper prototype. Sometimes a game prototype might include UI and UX elements, but the questions we want to answer by paper prototyping a game are not related to usability or interface—we want to investigate the game mechanics and how fun they are. Always keep this in mind!

Advantages of paper prototyping

So let's have a look at the main advantages of paper prototyping:

- **Cheap**: Paper prototypes are cheap, both in terms of time and resources.
- **No programming involved**: This is straightforward; everyone can create a paper prototype. You can apply your game design knowledge and be in full control of the game creation without involving any programmers or being limited by technology.
- **Easy and quick to create**: You can create a paper prototype by sketching on a sheet of paper with a pencil. No creative process is quicker than this. Most of the prototypes require a bit more work though, such as cutting pieces of cardboard, printing some images or placeholders, and writing cards. Some paper prototypes can even use elements such as miniatures (from other games or easily purchasable online) or dice. No matter how much stuff you might need to create them, it will always be much quicker and easier than creating anything on a computer.
- **Easy to try and iterate**: This is another incredible advantage. You can build a paper prototype in a couple of hours and try it with anyone (friends, family, colleagues) without having to build any working software. Anything that doesn't work can be changed immediately, even during the test itself. Iteration speed is the fastest it could be.
- **Abstraction**: Abstraction is great when it comes to testing prototypes. There are no distractions coming from how the game looks or anything else that is not important. If those pieces of paper come to life and the rules generate fun dynamics, they could only get better by adding a theme and a visual aesthetic on top of them. Abstraction, as we are going to see in the next paragraph, is a double edged sword as it also presents some risks.

Limitations of paper prototypes

Of course, like any tools, paper prototypes present some disadvantages:

- **Abstraction**: To abstract on a system in a way that works on paper before the virtual world, experience is required. You need to be able to distill the essential elements and leave out everything else. You'd need to make compromises and still create something that can answer real questions for the game as it is going to be on screen. Experience is the only way to master abstraction. The good news is that you can start prototype games right now, without studying any programming language, even away from your computer. You don't even have to invent a game, just pick an existing game and imagine how would you paper prototype some of its core mechanics. Don't be afraid of failure. Prototyping is all about making mistakes when they don't have dramatic repercussions. Prototype and fail as much as you can and with everything you can.

- **Struggle to represent complex and real-time scenarios**: This is the main problem of paper prototypes. Just imagine what a paper prototype of a fighting game like Street Fighter would look like. Already giving you a headache, right? Even more difficult, imagine a paper prototype of a VR game, where the main mechanic is based on the navigation of a 3D space. Games that require the use of physical skill, complex calculations, physics, and many others present a huge challenge and sometimes they simply cannot be effectively abstracted into something that works on paper. So be aware that sometimes a paper prototype is simply not the right tool to answer your questions. That is fair enough, as fortunately, you have many more available!

- **Can't fully replace digital prototypes**: Another problem of paper prototypes is that they need to be translated into the digital world at some point. So they are indeed an extra step, as cheap as they are. The value of a paper prototype lies in the chance to catch big problems before any implementation; when your design seems to work on paper and the most evident problems have been discarded, move on to digital as soon as possible. Cheap and fast are the key-words for paper prototypes. As soon as a paper prototype shows signs of being slow and complex, you know this is the time to move on to digital or to realize you have to ask a more specific question and start from scratch again.

Digital prototyping

When your designs and paper prototypes come to life on screen is when things get serious. Be prepared to see what you have imagined in a very different way—be prepared to see things that don't work. The faster you realize something's wrong, the quicker you'll get back to the drawing board, and the better your chance of releasing a fun game. This is the idea behind digital prototypes. Put a working software together as soon as possible and iterate as much as you can on it to define and redefine your vision. Unlike paper prototyping, digital prototyping is a necessary step. If you're not prototyping, you are making a mistake. Period.

It might happen that the prototyping phase is skipped, maybe because there's no time, no resources or the team is extremely confident to just move on to production right away. Remember, prototyping means seeking answers to specific questions. If you already have these answers, there's no need for a prototype. But if the answers are not clear, and the prototyping phase is skipped and the team moves onto development, what is really happening is that a very complex and high-fidelity prototype is being developed with the intention of selling it as a finished product.

You can imagine how disastrous this approach would be if something doesn't work. You'd be surprised how often this happens, even in the most respected studios. And as a professional in the games industry, I guarantee you will hear a lot phrases such as "it's too late to change that", "it doesn't work, but we have to live with it" and so on and so forth. These phrases are the result of designs being implemented without questions, developed for months without early reviews and, in short, with no prototyping at all.

Common prototyping mistakes

The only con of developing a digital prototype is that it will take some time, although it's guaranteed that it will save time in the long run. There are also some other pitfalls, though. Prototypes are tools, and as such, they could be used in the wrong way.

Let's have a look at the most common mistakes and pitfalls of prototyping.

The never-ending prototype

When working on a prototype, it is easy to get attached and try to make it right by iterating on the same thing over and over again. If something doesn't work, the design has to change. The sooner the team realizes it, the more the prototyping phase will serve its purpose. The risk of a quickly built prototype is that it might miss some important elements that might end up being essential for making a final judgment. As part of the iterative nature of prototypes, this is fine. A prototype can start very small (that is, just the core mechanic of a new game), and expand to something larger through successive iterations (that is, core mechanics and a few puzzles or enemies). However, the risk is to keep iterating outside of the scope of the initial question, such as by building a progression system on top of that core mechanic because it felt weak or incomplete. Whenever you feel that a prototype is increasing in scope and starts looking like an entire game, it is probably time to stop and re-assess whether those initial questions have been answered.

Spending time creating systems

Diving into the game's final implementation with the hope of iterating later is always a bad idea. When building software, good engineering is required. The software has to be designed, just like the game. Systems need to be built before actual gameplay. Imagine a car racing game. The programmer needs to engineer a system that can handle different types of cars, with different values of speed, acceleration, braking, stability, and so on. He has to build this data system first, and only then will the designer be able to define the numbers and try them. When working on a prototype, the engineer should just hard-code the values the designer wants to try (maybe with a rudimentary system to expose those variables and make them changeable to the designer, so he can play with different values). The role of the programmer here is to get something playable on screen as soon as possible, by any means possible. System implementation should be always postponed to the implementation stage.

Using the prototype as a code-base for the production project

A good, quick, on-the-point prototype is very likely to be a code mess, full of hacks and horrendous code writing, especially if it was written by the designer himself. You don't want to end up with that code in the final project. When a prototype works and all the questions have been answered, it's time to start from scratch. Now is the time to build those systems and allow an engineer to design the code properly. Again, the mirage of using the prototype code as a base to save time is just that: a mirage. Some time might be saved early on, but rest assured that the first time a problem arises all the time initially saved and more will be lost. This is true even if the prototype worked perfectly fine.

That said, some experienced engineers might be able to create prototypes with perfectly engineered code ready to be taken into production. It is their call in the end and there are surely situations where this would be possible. However, when a designer or another less technical team member is involved in the creation, is always a better idea to let the engineer make this kind of decision.

Spending time adding features, art, and effects

Any time spent adding stuff to a prototype that is not directly related to answering the initial questions is time lost. Not only that, every unnecessary thing added to a prototype is a step toward the prototype code evolving into the final game. Be wary of anything that seems to be working better after some good art, animations, or effects are added. You will be tempted to think that just by *looking good* a game could hide its design flaws.

That is never true.

Seeking confirmations

This is the most dangerous pitfall of prototyping.

If you are convinced you already have an answer and you are building a prototype to demonstrate that it is right at all costs, you're missing a great opportunity. It is crucial to remain open-minded. It is very likely that you'd be building a prototype based on a hypothesis to make something new and better.

Everyone would love to hear how brilliant the solution provided by their prototypes is, and it's great when it happens. If it doesn't, the biggest mistake you can make is to be protective of your work and fail to see how a negative response is as useful as a good one. A prototype that shows how something does not work is a success as much as one that has been proven right.

Remember: the goal is to have answers, not to actually build the game.

A step-by-step guide to prototyping

Here follows a step-by-step process for developing an effective prototype. These steps can be used to prototype an entire game or just a single feature, or maybe just to evaluate a change to an existing system.

Step 1: Ask the right questions

Whether the prototype is for trying out a game idea or a new mechanic or to evaluate and improve something within your game, you need to have a clear problem in mind and how you imagine the prototype is going to solve it. Never start prototyping if you don't know what you need to evaluate or prove.

What would make a good question? And a bad one?
Usually, good questions are specific. Asking whether a mechanic is *fun* or not would be a bad question. What do we mean by fun? A better question would probably be: does this mechanic provide enough decision-making for the player? Are his choices meaningful?

Step 2: Select the framework and tools

Paper or digital prototyping? If paper, is it going to need anything other than just pen and paper? Maybe dice, miniatures, cards? If digital, does it require a game engine? A spreadsheet? A presentation?

Some of these things might not be very clear at the beginning. In that case, start with something and evaluate what else you might need as you go. If you realize something does work—say you find out you're not able to prototype a system on paper—just scrap it and start over with a better tool.

Step 3: Create the rules

This is extremely important for paper prototypes: what are the rules? How do you actually play the prototype? Paper prototype rules look a lot like a board game rule manual. Make sure the rules are simple and clear. Also, digital prototypes need rules. What kind of mechanic do you need to implement? How will you be able to condense a complex game into its abstract and essential version?

Step 4: Implement and create the prototype

It doesn't matter if this is writing the code or cutting out the elements with a pair of scissors. Make something playable happen as soon as possible

Step 5: First Playtest

As soon as you've got something playable, try it. Nothing is going to work as you imagined. The first play of a prototype is crucial because if you approach it with bias, thinking that it is going to work, you are committing one of the common mistakes. The first iteration of any prototype is not going to work. So when you play the first time, take notes and go back to the drawing board to make the changes you need. When we say *play*, we mean to play it with as many people as you can—especially people not involved in the development. At this stage what you really need is an unbiased opinion.

Step 6: Iterate

Re-implement anything that wasn't right the last time, play with your variables, change the rules. Do this until you find an answer to your initial question.

Play and iterate should be quick processes. If you don't find your answers after a few iterations, it might well be that you're asking the wrong question or that you don't want to admit that the answers are just disproving your concept.

If your hypothesis is disproved by your prototype, don't try to pursue that solution anyway.

Prototyping is a process worth doing only if you're willing to accept the consequences and dump what doesn't work.

Step 7: Move on

There are only two possible outcomes from the previous steps: you either prove or disprove your hypothesis. In both cases, the job of your prototype is over. If the answer is not the one you hoped for, don't make the mistake of forcing things to work out your way. If the answer is positive, don't try to add on top of your prototype and make it the feature or the game. Move on and build something new from the answers you have got, not from the prototype you have created.

Prototyping exercise

So, you know the differences between paper and digital prototyping. You can start working and getting experience right now with paper.

In fact, you must start right now.

Before reading on, grab a pen and a piece of paper and try to prototype something. It has to be something doable in under an hour, don't worry about trying something really cool or a real game idea you have. Try to get really practical.

Here are some ideas:

- A racing game for two players A and B, such as *Game of the Goose*
- A simple combat system for a 1v1 card game
- A puzzle level for a platformer game such as *Super Meat Boy*
- A 1v1 strategy game that uses a board and a grid, like *Chess*

Don't worry about the results, just try it and see what you come up with in under one hour.

The hands-on game designer

If you tried to create some paper prototypes, you might have found answers to your questions. If you did right, you might also have even more questions.

One question could be: does it really work like this? Absolutely yes.

Prototyping is about discovering, trying, and making mistakes. If you don't try, you will never learn. The next step would be trying to create something in the digital world. Here things become tougher because you might not have any programming skills and probably not even know where to start. Mark these words: by learning how to use a game engine and program basic game mechanics and small prototypes, you will be ahead of any aspiring game designers who don't have this skill.

This is the real skill that will always give you an edge over the thousands of other designers that will be competing with you for the few design roles available in the game industry. Reading and studying is the bare minimum, so don't think that by reading this and many other game design books you will be any better than your competition. All of them have done the same!

The other factor that makes you a better (more desirable, to be precise) designer is your experience. If you have never worked on a game professionally, it is unlikely that you'll be ever considered better than a designer who did. When you have little or no professional experience there's only one thing that will make you stand out: your personal projects and the ability to design and implement your ideas. I call this game designer *The hands-on game designer*. It is a rare breed, and as such it is in high demand anywhere in the game industry.

Learn how to implement and code your games. You don't need to learn how to go beyond the prototyping stage. You don't have to master computer science or software engineering principles. You just need to know how to make your design happen on screen in a prototype. Do so and you'll have one foot already in your first job as a game designer.

Not only that, as your experience increases in game design, you will find your technical skills to be an incredible tool for communicating ideas, pitching projects, demonstrating your hypotheses, and most of all, for working independently or freeing up the engineers from some implementation work, leaving them more time to focus on more important tasks. You yourself will have more control over how your designs make it into the game. Be a hands-on designer. Be practical and evaluate your work in terms of how many things you can make happen.

A paper prototype case-study

We are going to examine in detail a case study from my personal work experience at *Another Place Productions*. At a certain point during the development of our latest game, *Battlehand Heroes*, we had to address an unexpected problem. The combat system that was good enough for the first title of the *Battlehand* IP was proving problematic in the new game.

Questioning a combat system

Battlehand: Heroes is a turn-based RPG in which the player builds his team of heroes, each with a unique deck of cards to battle. The combat system that worked quite well in the first game, *Battlehand*, was lacking the depth to engage a new generation of players. The first game was released in 2015, and player's tastes and expectations for games always evolve, so games need to also. The players struggled to understand why they should play one card instead of another, how to choose their strategy, and how to correctly react to the enemy's moves.

You might wonder how we actually found out these problems in the game: by playtesting! It is crucial to test your game as soon as possible with real players and note down everything about their experience. We're going to talk more about playtesting and user research later in this book.

We discussed many different solutions for improving the core of the combat systems, but before committing the development team to any of those, we decided to prototype on paper the more promising ideas.

The combat system is based on *2v2* heroes battles, the player can manage each of his heroes and their own deck of 8 cards. Each hero belongs to an element: **Earth**, **Fire**, **Water**, **Air**, or **Spirit**. They are governed by a **rock-paper-scissors** (RPS) strength/weakness relation:

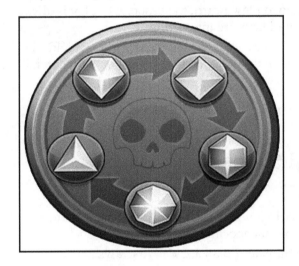

Battlehand elemental RPS mechanic: Fire is strong against Earth, Earth is strong against Air, Air against Spirit, Spirit against Water and Water against Fire

My hypothesis was that the game could have benefited from the introduction of a multi-layered RPS system on top of the elements. Up to this point, each hero could have cards that could be heal, shield, and attack. All of them balanced around their mere power (the more the damage, the shield points, or the HP cured, the better the card, basically). The idea was to try to assign to each card a property that could make it strong or weak against other cards regardless of their numbers. If a shield could block most of the attacks but some attacks can automatically pierce a shield, that would create an interesting scenario where the right card for the right situation may not always be the most powerful one, and it would be up to the player to select it.

Addressing the problem

This is an advanced, real-life scenario; as such, things are never exactly as predicted. In fact, the prototype needed to answer more than one question. But let's get back to the problems again.

The combat lacks depth in the sense that:

- One of the most important strategic choices in the fight is about which hero you select for that specific combat (to be strong against the enemy elements). The strategy should also propagate into the combat itself, not just exist in the pre-fight.
- When it is time to play a card, the best one to play is always the most powerful. The choice could be more interesting.
- All the heroes have access to all the card types (shields, heals, attacks), so each hero can fulfill all the roles in combat (healer, supporter, attacker, defender, and so on).

With these problems clearly in mind, we can ask the right questions.

Asking the right questions – step 1

Does the prototyped system:

- Create a scenario where I don't always choose the most powerful card, but the most useful for that specific situation?
- Allow me to think and plan a few card draws ahead?
- Shift the attention from the RPS mechanic to the cards?

Selecting the tools – step 2

With a clear problem and clear questions to answer, it is time to identify which kind of prototype are we going to need. A great thing about old school turn-based RPG and card games is that using paper prototypes comes just naturally to them! If you consider the few other solutions to evaluate and prototype, paper prototyping sounds like the quickest and cheapest solution.

Creating the rules – step 3

A paper prototype is always an abstraction of what you get in a digital game, so it's more important than ever to get in only the essential stuff.

These are the rules I came up with:

PROTOTYPE RULES

- Each hero has a deck of 8 cards
- For each hero, the player draw 4 cards: his initial hands
- A coin toss determines who goes first, and then the order is: my hero and then your hero
- The turn ends when all the heroes have played a card
- As soon as a card is played, it is immediately reshuffled in the deck and a new card is drawn - the player always have 4 cards in his hand -

Cards

- Single attacks deal 2 damage
- Multi attacks deal 1 damage
- Heal and Multi heals restore 1 HP (Hit Point)
- Shields give 4 shield points
- Multi shields give 2 shield points
- BIG means that the numeric value is doubled, but the hero skips the next turn
  (i.e. a BIG single attack deals 4 damage, a BIG multi shields gives 4 Shield Points)

Effects

- DOT (damage over time) causes 3 damage over 3 turns (the first damage immediately, the rest every turn before the hero who applied the DOT takes his action
- Multi DOT causes 2 damage over 2 turns
- Piercing does direct damage to HP
- Shield Resistant to Pierce resist the pierce effect, but not the base attack damage
- Shield Crush automatically destroys shields
- Return Damage returns 2 damage every time the shielded hero is attacked
- A hero with Taunt must always be the preferred target

Don't worry if these rules are not very clear to you, the point of this exercise is to understand the prototyping process more than the specific example!

For your reference, this is a screenshot of a few *Battlehand Heroes* cards at the time of the prototype creation:

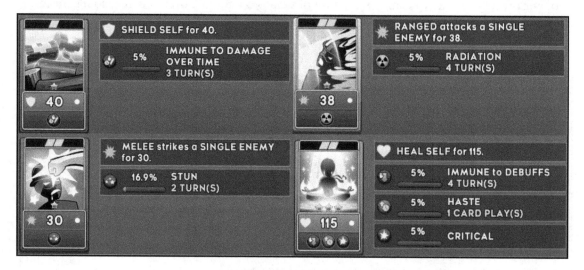

Four cards from an early version of *Battlehand: Heroes*

As you can see, there is a huge difference between the real game mechanics and the prototype's rules, but the core is really the same. The questions we asked can be answered by a much simpler abstraction of the digital game.

Implementation – step 4

This is the part I love the most. To create the prototype, I simply cut 8 cards per hero and wrote the card rules on each of them. Then I created the various tokens needed and used 4 miniatures to represent the heroes.

I also used dice to keep track of the various numbers going on in the game and colored cardboard on which I took various notes related to the heroes during the gameplay.

Each hero's deck was designed to create a compelling experience with just a few cards. We will learn later about balancing and how to set up every number and variable in a game:

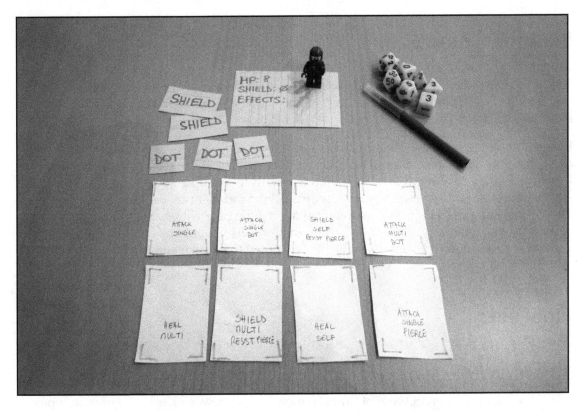

Our Water hero, with his 8 cards and all the necessary pieces to play the prototype

First play – step 5

The first play showed a very promising experience. Playing the prototype was fun and it was clear that the whole thing was on the right track. Of course, the initial questions were really spot-on, as the knowledge of the game we had was deep and based on a previous title for the same IP and a long list of well-known problems and possible improvements.

What really required some more thought were the rules. The damage and HP ranges were too tight: with attacks dealing 1 to 4 damage and heroes having from 6 to 12 HP, some cards were too strong and some heroes were too weak.

Another flaw was the lack of a combination of card plays (COMBO) to get greater advantages (that is, two consecutive DOT attacks dealing extra damage).

Iteration – step 6

With the problems of the first play in mind, the iterative process of improving the prototype started: we tweaked the numbers, added a combo system, and switched some of the cards (for example, we removed all the healing cards from a hero that was supposed to be more focused on attacking).

By continuing to play the prototype, two other flaws emerged. Some battles were dragging on for too long in a sort of stall, so we added a damage crescendo after a certain number of turns passed. We also found that the combo was hard to line up and a bit unsatisfactory, so we decided on an extreme solution: lining up a combo means instant-killing the target hero. This little change spiced up the entire combat a lot, giving a great reward to long-term planning. Of course in the real game nothing that powerful would be implemented, but the game was clearly more fun and engaging. So we noted that down and kept it in mind for our final version of the combo system.

Final step

Were all the questions answered?

I'd say yes, perfectly:

- Having different types of cards be more or less powerful against different types of shields moved the attention away from just the mere numbers, so I found myself going for a less powerful card that had the proper effect to rightly counter the enemy setup. This was happening consistently enough to make me think about new interesting types of cards and abilities and how to build a more effective deck.
- The extreme combo system forced me to always think how to pull out a good combo and added a lot of thrill to the *next card draw*.
- The elemental advantage became almost irrelevant, with the whole focus of the combat shifted onto the battle itself. It even cast some doubts about the elemental wheel, as it made it clear that the RPS mechanic was previously too much on the meta-game side (limiting the strategic choices to the pre-battle phase, when deciding which elements to bring into battle).

With these great answers, we were able to move to digital. As we mentioned, the downside of paper prototypes is that if they work on paper, you have to try them in the digital world too before starting the actual production. There are rare cases where the answer is so clear that you can move to production really quickly, but what you want to do with paper prototypes is to *fail fast* more than really find a working solution. If it doesn't work on paper, it most likely won't anywhere. On the other hand, if it does work on paper, you still have to make sure you can translate that abstraction into something that works in a video game.

From paper to digital

In our specific case, bringing the prototype to the digital game was a fairly easy and quick job.

As the game was already developed to a playable stage, the main job was to modify the current game system to reflect the new changes. Of course, we had to adapt the rules from the paper prototype to the digital game logic, implement them in the quickest and efficient way, play, and iterate:

The cards from the paper prototype were implemented in the digital game

Abstraction versus reality

After we implemented the prototype principles in the actual game, we were ready to start over with the iterations.

In fact, what has been proved on paper was just a quick way to commit to a more serious prototype. It wasn't a definitive answer that the system would have worked. Think about paper prototyping as a *green light* for the actual digital prototyping.

The digital prototype was replicating quite well the experience that we had on paper, but some improvements became obvious and necessary only at this stage:

- The focus on the numbers became too prominent again. Instead of enjoying the immediate action of dragging a card on the enemies and seeing its effect, a lot of calculations were required to understand which card was the best choice.
- The number of cards (8 per hero's deck and 4 in each hand at any given time) was still overwhelming; with so many choices it felt like none were really meaningful (and some were too obviously wrong).
- We needed to introduce the entire library of card effects. Not only Damage Over Time, Piercing shield, and the few others we had in the prototype—the list of *Battlehand: Heroes* card's effects included many others, such as *Speed Up*, various immunities, *Stun*, *Freeze*, and dozens more. The complexity of rumped add a lot, and with those effects at the center of the RPS mechanic, the cognitive overload was a problem.

Moving on

After assessing the reality of the digital prototype, we iterated, again and again, removing everything that wasn't quite working in the more realistic digital scenario. This process took around two weeks and when we felt we had all our answers, we went back to our game in the production environment, leaving the prototype behind. The following is a screenshot of how the battle screen looked prior to our updating:

Battlehand: Heroes before the combat system update. Note the Initiative bar on the right, the number of cards in the hand, and the card layout

We made all the changes necessary to bring across all the good things that truly worked in our prototype, and we were confident in doing so. In the following screenshot, you can see what the game looked like after this process:

Battlehand: Heroes after the combat system update, there are only three cards in each hero's hand and their layout is much more essential

The preceding screenshots can't convey how the gameplay has changed from one version to other, but you can see how everything that we have changed in the layout of the battle screen and the cards reflects our findings from the prototyping:

- The number of cards in each hero's hand has been decreased to three (and those in the decks to six).
- The numbers have been removed from the cards—both the turn counters (top-left corner) and the value of damage/healing/shield from the center of the card.
- The target icon has been made clearer.
- Each card has a clear effect, which can be seen on the round icon in the bottom left corner of the card. The first one, *Smoking Girder*, has the ability to destroy the target's shield in one hit. The second, *Oil Drum*, can weaken the enemy, increasing the damage he takes, and the last one, *Kapow*, always hits regardless of the target evading or any other modifier on the hero's accuracy.

- The initiative bar has been removed and replaced with a turn bar (yellow bar with the five notches) above the HP bar of each character (the green bar underneath each character).

All of these changes reflect the need to change and tweak parts of the game that were simply not possible to evaluate without a prototype. They are the result of an iterative process that, through subsequent changes and evaluation, allowed us to sculpt a final product from a rough initial model.

 The screenshots used in this chapter are for illustrative purposes only. We do not recommend you to misuse these in any way. For more information please consult the terms and conditions of the publishers mentioned in the *Disclaimer* section of this book.

Summary

In this chapter, we have learned how to prototype a game and why it is important to do so. We described in detail paper prototyping and how you can start doing it right now, without any particular technical knowledge. This chapter heavily emphasized paper prototyping over its digital counterpart, because it is really at the core of *what you can do to create a game* and become a better game designer without having to learn anything else. The reader who, at this point of the book, will try to create his own paper prototype and start experimenting with some board game design is the one who already stepped out from being a learner to being a maker.

We moved onto digital prototyping, and how even pretty basic technical skills could make all the difference for a rookie game designer and give them a great competitive edge to break into the game industry and be able to give life to their own vision. We can't recommend enough that you practice with what you have learned so far. Regardless of the platform of your choice, design and create something, right now!

Now that you have understood how to create the atoms of a game and implement them into prototypes, we're ready to learn how to tie them up into a consistent experience that has a beginning and (most of the time) an end. In the next chapter, we're going to talk about the use of Narrative and how to pace the progression of the player throughout the game experience.

8
Games and Stories

We have been discussing how to create a vision and communicate it to the team, and how to design game mechanics and prototype them to answer fundamental questions as soon as possible in the development process. We have learned how to distill what we call *fun* into an interactive experience. It is now time to look at how to take all these elements and make them part of a narrative that can take our players into a virtual world and awaken their imagination, immersing them in the kind of experience that only video games can offer.

Video games (just like books, movies, or plays) can tell stories. Stories are one of the most powerful things human beings can use to communicate. The power of the video game medium, though, lies in one extra thing other mediums rarely have: the enormous potential of interactivity. There's more: this potential is far from being fully known, understood, and accepted at large.

Consider that literature and written stories have been around for millennia (one of the first written stories we know is the Epic of Gilgamesh, dating back from Ancient Mesopotamia, 2100 BC). Theatre was born in Ancient Greece around 600 BC. Even if we think about printed books (a much more recent invention), we are talking about centuries ago (Johannes Gutenberg invented the printing press in 1440). Fast forward in time to the first decades of the last century, where motion pictures arose and films, as we know them today, were born. Television and cinema are things even our great-grandfathers were accustomed to.

Video games, on the other hand, are something that wasn't available to the masses before 1970, and even back then, they weren't used as a form of storytelling. Complex stories, deep characters, profound themes began to appear later, in the late 80's, and flourished in the 90's. That is less than 40 years ago, just think about it! Many people still think that video games are just entertainment for kids and teenagers. Some players don't even consider themselves gamers, especially casual gamers that spend hours playing games such as *Candy Crush Saga* or *Double Down Casino Slots*. The generations born before the seventies didn't grow up with video games. But my generation, which is the generation of today's young adults born between the end of the seventies and the mid-eighties, was fully immersed in them. We witnessed the rise of game consoles and the birth of pretty much every video game franchise. Games are part of our life and culture.

It is safe to say that, a few decades into the future, pretty much everyone will be familiar with video games as a modern form of storytelling.

Narrative

The Oxford dictionary defines Narrative as follows:

"A spoken or written account of connected events; a story"

See what I meant earlier in this chapter's introduction? It's already outdated! Narrative doesn't have to be necessarily spoken or written...it can be told through images, both still (photography, art) or moving (motion pictures and yes, video games!). There is one common mistake though: the belief that interactivity might change the basic rules of storytelling that have been set through millennia of human history. It doesn't.

The story is the goal, regardless of how it is told. So the rules of a good story never change.

In fact, in this chapter, we will just briefly discuss how a good story is written. It is a huge topic that would need a few books in itself. As usual, I can never recommend enough that you pick up this topic and to study it in depth, if that's what interests you the most. Not all designers are story writers. If you'd like to specialize in this particular field...read, play, watch, and study! You can start by reading some books on screenwriting, creative writing, or a specific book about video game writing.

As a game designer, what's really important is to know how to take the pieces of the narrative and recount them in a way that works with your game. Ultimately, a game designer's job is to make a story playable.

Do all games have a narrative?

An everlasting question. And there is no definitive answer. But is worth mentioning that some games are pretty abstract. *Tetris* comes immediately to mind, but any puzzle game or brain game is very unlikely to tell any kind of story. In a game such as *Threes*, the player only needs to slide numbered tiles on a four-by-four grid to combine addends and multiples of three. Of course, comparing those games to narrative rich games (or even to games with an extremely simple narrative, like the aforementioned *Space Invaders)* might give the impression that they don't have any narrative.

But isn't the player playing those games creating a story in itself?
Can the player get such an amazing score in *Tetris* or *Threes* that he will tell the story to all her friends over and over again? "Ah! Have I ever told you about the time I got 999,999 points in Tetris?"

This is exactly a story, a story where the player is the protagonist!

No matter what the final answer to this question is, there is one truth that every designer should keep in mind:
A good game **generates stories** when people play it. It is what Jesse Schell calls the *Story Machine*.

The *Story Machine* concept has been applied in many games. It involves giving the player a toolbox of elements he or she can interact with to create what we defined as *emergent gameplay* in `Chapter 6`, *Invention of Mechanics*. Games such as *The Sims* or *Far Cry* are brilliant examples of this concept. In *Far Cry 4*, the player can decide how to tackle the various challenge in different ways, including exploiting the environments by luring a predatory animal into an enemy camp instead of fighting, or burning down a tree and letting the fire spread in a certain area.

Make sure the game you are designing enables players to create different stories by making different choices.

Why are stories good for games?

"Story in a game is like a story in a porn movie: it's expected to be there, but it's not that important."

This quote from John Carmack, the creator of *Doom* and founder of *ID software*, should give you an idea of the size of the debate around games and stories. On one hand, what Carmack said is understandable, as he wanted to emphasize the fact that games are what they are because they must be played first and foremost. On the other hand, game stories can evoke emotions as deep as those we feel by watching movies or reading books. It is a matter of opinions, but one thing is objective: stories and games work very well together. It's the reason why so many games feature some kind of story and some of the most successful and critically acclaimed games of the last decade involve meaningful and rich stories and great characters.

Why is that? Why are stories so good for games? There are multiple answers.

First of all, stories create an emotional attachment with the *listener* (which is the player, in our case). This is already huge. Also, stories provide a structure (usually with a beginning, a middle, and an end) through which gameplay moments can be organized. It provides a motivation to play that transcends the gameplay. Players will naturally want to know more about the plot, the characters, and the game world.

Lastly, as Raph Koster explains in his book *A theory of fun*, games are naturally played by humans to learn (and not only by humans; animals learn through play too!). Stories serve the same purpose. Games and stories are connected at a very deep level. Structuring one around the other will help you shape your design and, probably, make better games.

Traditional narrative models

We can identify two main models to structure a video game narrative, the three-act story and the Monomyth (or hero's journey). Of course, these are not the only existing two, but they are the most used and the ones from which other structure have developed. The monomyth, as we're going to see, is a more specific and elaborate version of the three-act story that doesn't only cover the story structure but also the characters that live in it.

These two models are a great starting point for understanding the deep relationship between narrative and games. Don't be scared by the fact that most stories share the same core structure. It's been this way for hundreds of years, and nonetheless so many different stories have been told. For sure, there are other ways to tell a story, there's so much more still to discover and invent. But our advice is always to master the fundamental rules before attempting to change or disrupt them!

Three-act story

The concept behind the three-act story is very simple: each story has a beginning, a middle, and an end. This concept is extremely intuitive, as most of the stories we know follow it. Just think about the classic fairy tales that start with *Once upon a time* and end with *and they lived happily ever after*, after a series of events. Movies, books, and many games follow the same pattern.

A better definition of beginning, middle, and end are given by looking at what happens in each of these parts, or *acts*:

- **Introduction (beginning)**: This is where the story is set up. The characters are described and the setting is presented. Everything in this section answers questions such as *who* and *why*. Who are the protagonists of the story and why are they involved in the events that are about to unfold? What are their motivations? Usually, the introduction ends with an event that prompts the protagonist to solve some sort of conflict. A solid introduction allows readers/viewers/players to identify with the protagonist and understand his or her motivations to act.
- **Confrontation (middle)**: This is the biggest part of a story; many events can happen in this act. The basic idea is that the protagonist confronts the conflict and the source of this conflict (traditionally the villain) is presented. The tension increases dramatically throughout this arc and culminates in the moment when the protagonist is about to resolve the conflict.
- **Resolution (end):** The grand finale. The conflict is resolved (either in a happy or bad ending). Once the conflict is resolved the story is quickly wrapped up (as the emotional escalation has peaked and is now fading).

Monomyths

In narratology, the monomyth is a template for stories with a protagonist (the Hero) who goes on an adventure, faces some sort of crisis or conflict, and triumphs over it. By the time he goes back home, he has been transformed by his journey. The study of the monomyth dates back to ancient Greece and monomyths have been at the center of the human experience for millennia.

In 1949 Joseph Campbell popularized the Monomyth in his landmark book: "The Hero with a Thousand Faces."

Campbell described the structure of a narrative as follows:

"A hero ventures forth from the world of common day into a region of supernatural wonder: fabulous forces are there encountered and a decisive victory is won: the hero comes back from this mysterious adventure with the power to bestow boons on his fellow man."

Campbell identified 17 stages of the hero's journey. Not every story contains all 17 stages; some may focus on only a few of the stages, while others may include them in a different order:

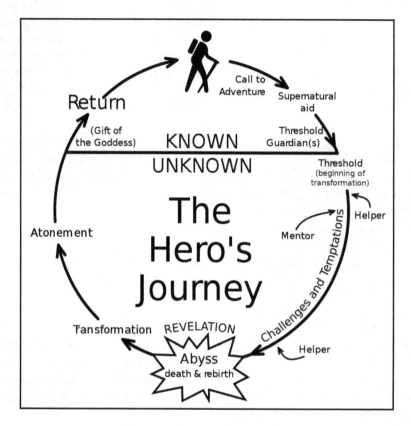

The hero's journey. Source: *Wikipedia* (anonymous)

The hero's journey is now widely used by many creative professionals working not only in games but in movies, TV, novels, and comic books. It is not the only narrative pattern, but it is one of those that works extremely well for video game stories, as they so often involve the presence of a hero and entail them going on some sort of adventure.

17 stages of the hero's journey

The 17 stages are usually organized into three sections:

- Departure
- Initiation
- Return

Let's have a look a closer look at each of them.

Departure

In this act, the hero or protagonist's ordinary world is introduced and the normal routine is shaken when the hero receives a call to go on an adventure. The hero usually refuses the call, but a mentor figure steps in to encourage and advise him:

1. **The call to adventure**: The hero is depicted in his ordinary world, leading an ordinary life. Suddenly, some information is received that calls the hero to a journey into the unknown.
2. **Refusal of the call**: The hero refuses to give up his ordinary life. It might be because of fear, duty, insecurity...any excuse that holds the hero to his current ordinary world.
3. **Supernatural aid**: Once the hero commits to his new mission (consciously or subconsciously), a mentor appears and offers his help. It might come in many forms: advice, training, or aid, often magical, like the gift of an artifact that will help the hero in his quest.
4. **Crossing the first threshold**: The hero finally leaves the ordinary world and enters the unknown adventure world.

Initiation

The initiation act begins with the hero stepping into the unknown, where he faces trials, either alone or with the assistance of helpers. The hero proceeds into his adventure until a crisis of some sort puts him to the test. He must undergo *the ordeal* and eventually overcomes the main obstacle or enemy. This is the *apotheosis* where finally the mission is accomplished and the hero can get his reward.

But the journey's not over. The hero must return to the ordinary world now. He may be pursued by the guardians from the new world, or he may be reluctant to return at all:

1. **The road of trials**: The hero undertakes a series of tests and begins his transformation. Usually the hero experiences failure.
2. **The meeting with the goddess**: The hero gains the help he needs. The goddess here signifies love and its ultimate power against adversity.
3. **Woman as temptress**: In this step, the hero faces those temptations that may lead him or her to abandon or stray for the mission. The woman is a metaphor for the physical or material temptations of life, but of course, it doesn't have to be a woman (keep in mind Campbell wrote all this in 1949!).
4. **Ordeal**: The hero atones from whatever represents the ultimate power holder in his life: might be a person, a culture, a belief, or a fear. The hero's inner monsters represent a life or death crisis. All the previous steps have been moving into this place, all that follow will move out from it.
5. **Apotheosis**: The hero reaches a point of a greater understanding. He is now ready to truly face the more difficult part of his journey.
6. **The ultimate boon**: Armed with all he has learned so far, the hero faces his/her ultimate challenge and wins.

Return

In the *return* section, the hero returns to the ordinary world with the treasure or reward he gained, which he may now use for the benefit of his original world. The hero is transformed by the adventure and gains wisdom or spiritual power over both the new and original worlds. He will never be the same:

1. **Refusal of the return**: The idea of returning to the ordinary world unsettles the hero. Having experienced all the wonders and bliss of the world out there, he faces the challenge of bringing back the enlightenment he has achieved.
2. **The magic flight**: The return journey might still be filled with perils, which the hero can confront with his new self.
3. **Rescue from without**: In the same way the hero needed help during his quest, he might need guides and assistants to go back to where he belongs. Heroes sometimes need someone to bring them back to everyday life, especially if they have been wounded or weakened by the experience.
4. **The crossing of the return threshold**: The hero needs to retain the wisdom he has gained on his quest, to integrate that wisdom into a ordinary life, and then maybe figure out how to share the wisdom with the rest of the world.

5. **Master of two worlds**: The hero lives comfortably both in the inner and outer world, material and spiritual, transcending his ego.

6. **Freedom to live**: Knowledge frees the hero from the fear of death, which in turn is the freedom to live. The hero understands the importance of living in the moment, neither anticipating the future nor regretting the past. He's finally at peace and the journey comes to its end.

Exercise
Take one of your favorite games with a rich narrative and identify the 17 stages of the Hero Journey. Do the same with a movie or book like *Star Wars: A New Hope*, or *The Lord of the Rings* and compare the results. Have you noticed any difference? Are there stages that seem to work better with video games?

Exercise
Can you think of a video game story that doesn't follow at all the Monomyth structure?
List them and try to identify the differences from games with a classic storyline.

Designing narrative for video games

We have briefly seen the structure of a story, but how is narrative designed for a video game? And how is it implemented?

The first thing to note is that a game cannot be simply written and then played out by the system like it was a movie. A game narrative unfolds when someone actually plays the game, so mechanics and dynamics are as important as the story, if not even more so. Interactive storytelling means that players should play and experience the story through their actions. Reading or listening notes and watching cutscenes should give an idea of a deeper immersion in the game world, but should never come before the actual gameplay. The idea is that, even in the most narrative-driven game, the player should be able to bolt through the game skipping any reading, listening, or cutscene...and still be able to make sense of the game story, simply by playing it.

Not an easy task for us designers!

We have already seen in `Chapter 3`, *Scoping a Game Project*, how games are structured. They can be linear, non-linear, open, or endless. Narrative design shares a lot with game structure. The reason is very simple; a game with a narrative is most likely **structured around that narrative**.

Linear narrative

It is safe to say that a linear narrative is the simplest form of interactive narrative. A series of key events develops the story and the player advances from one to the other with gameplay actions. The interactivity is actually pretty limited. Have a look at the following image: the arrows are the story, presented in the form of cutscenes, animated sequences, images, or just plain text. The circles represent the player's actions. This visual representation is usually called the **Strings of Pearls** or **Rivers and Lakes:**

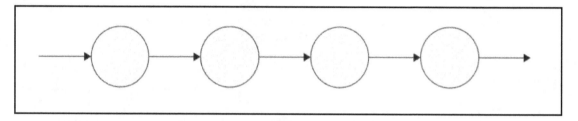

The String of Pearls storytelling method.

It is important to note how the story in a linear narrative is actually non-interactive. Whatever the outcome of the player's actions, the story will remain on track and unfold as the player progresses. The only control the player has over the story is to not actually make any progress.

Don't make the easy mistake of thinking that linear narrative is bad in video games. Not all video games need intricate storylines with multiple endings and branches. A video game can still be amazing and tell great stories using a linear narrative!
Just think about FPS games such as *Doom* or *Call of Duty*, or games with rich storylines such as *The Last of Us* or *Tomb Raider*.

A linear narrative shifts all the weight onto two factors:

- How good is the story?
- How good is the gameplay?

We already talked about this and how delicate the crafting of linear games is. Always keep this in mind!

Linear with extended space of action

Some games might still follow a linear narrative, but the player explore the surroundings. In terms of narrative though, the linearity is still given by the fact that this freedom of exploration doesn't impact the storyline. The story doesn't move forward by exploring; some more story details might be acquired by the player, but there is no overall impact on the story.

A great example of exploration that enhances the storyline without affecting its course are books, documents, or audio files with bits of information scattered around levels. They reward players who explore the game maps, but they don't change anything story-wise. This practice is widely used, especially in FPS games with a linear storyline.

Imagine a game where the finding of a secret document in a suitcase actually opens up a different storyline, where the character finds out that a goal he was pursuing was actually a hoax and he's now able to pursue the right direction. A game with such possibility is leaving the space of linearity and is moving into a modular narrative. The part of the story where the character is tricked into following the wrong path is removed only if the player doesn't find the secret document.

Modular narrative

There are many ways to define a complex narrative; the term I like the most is *modular narrative*.

When a narrative becomes more complex, the design effort should focus on integrating the narrative into the gameplay harmoniously, allowing the player to experience each part of the narrative like it was written to be an actual part of the same story.

To build a modular narrative the story must be crafted in a way that can be cut into different forms, each representing different outcomes according to the player's actions. An important NPC might die (or not) at some point in the game, with a dramatic impact on the rest of the game. Building story modules means designing the story to go on in both cases: either with the NPC alive or dead.

The real challenge that video games can pose to writers is writing articulate storylines for non-linear games, especially open-world games.

Witcher III is a fantastic example of non-linear storytelling with hundreds of different stories going on at the same time. The player is free to jump in and out of those stories, some of them might even progress regardless of the player paying attention to them. Within all this, there is still an overarching storyline that follows the player's journey from beginning to end.

Let's have a look at different types of modular narrative.

Graph

A graph structure implies that choices create a branching narrative. The branches could lead to completely different paths and endings (in which case the graph is actually called a Tree) or can rejoin it at certain points and then branch again:

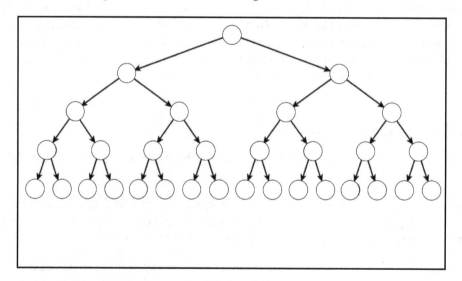

In a graph structure, each node represents a story point where the player can make a choice and proceed to the next node

There could even be multiple graphs, connected only at some specific points. We talk in this case about *Parallel plot structure*, in which two plots or points of view are told at the same time and the point of view switches between the different parallel versions. Once the point of view is switched, the narration could take either a linear or modular form. Eventually, all the storylines will converge in a timeline milestone, where the point of view might change again.

Open structure

In an open structure, story elements are associated with different physical places, so the player can wander around *discovering* and *triggering* different elements of the story. Sometimes, stories with an open structure might not even have a story arc and the player is in total control of the hero's journey. It's up to the player to decide when to confront the various challenges and how. The journey can even never get to a proper end. This is the form typical of simulation-based games, strategy games, and some open world-based games, such as **massively multiplayer online role-playing games** (**MMORPGs**).

It is worth noticing that, while an open structure seems not to follow the classic three-act story or monomyth models, there are always smaller pieces of the game experience that actually do.

If you think about quests in an MMORPG, those are little *stories within the story* that usually follow quite perfectly the three-act model. Even games without quests that rely on emergent gameplay, such as a *Minecraft,* generate stories that follow a classic model. The stories created by the player in the moment of playing the game do precisely this. Just try to listen to any player talking about a gameplay experience he had in any game. Is his story following a model familiar to you?

World state

The idea of a world state comes straight from the notion of the State Machine.

A State Machine is a mathematical model of computation. It is an abstract machine that can be in exactly one of a finite number of states at any given time.

Imagine that the State Machine is your world (or story) and each state is a moving part of the narrative.

In a traditional *branching narrative,* structured in a Tree, for example, a decision opens up a new branch of the three, which now requires moving on in a different direction from the other branches. In a narrative with states, a variable is generated to track the decision, and this variable will only affect the nodes in which it is referenced.

Imagine a story where a character might either die or survive at a certain point. If the state of the story without such character is registered in a variable, the branch of the story might remain the same, but every time the character appears in a node the system can tell whether the character is actually there or not.

You can imagine it like this:

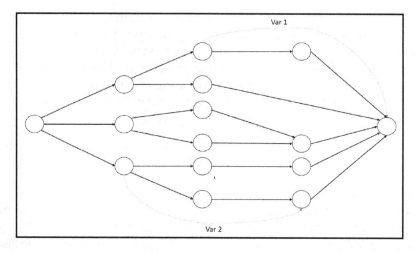

In the preceding example, something might happen in the nodes that affects the variables *Var 1* and *Var 2*. These events will affect later nodes that refer to that variable, therefore the narrative might change according to the state the world is in.

An earlier decision might affect later decisions with no need to branch.

Stories that rely on World State have the enormous advantage of offering meaningful replayability. In fact, even simple state changes might result in very different story developments if there are enough permutations to create more complex interactions between the states.

Environmental storytelling

> *"Environmental storytelling creates the preconditions for an immersive narrative experience in at least one of four ways: spatial stories can evoke pre-existing narrative associations; they can provide a staging ground where narrative events are enacted; they may embed narrative information within their mise-en-scene, or they provide resources for emergent narratives."*

> *–Jenkins, 2004*

The practice of environmental storytelling is well established in visual media. "Show, don't tell" is what many writers aspire to do. This principle applies not only to the actions of physical actors but also to the world, which in itself can be a very important (though sometimes underappreciated) actor.

We are going to discuss this again and in more depth in the next chapter about level design, but for now, it is important to understand the concepts behind "telling stories through the environment."

Of course, environmental storytelling is conveyed to the player through the game's level and environments.

How can we achieve that?

Let's have a look at a few practical examples:

- **Level geometry, artistic theme, and architecture**: These are not just a dressing for your gameplay, they affect the emotional state of your players and can also tell (or imply) a story of their own. It's essential to work closely with the art team (and especially the concept artists) to establish a set of backstories that could be told with each environment. Even if some players were to blast across the content with little attention to detail, an environment with a coherent backstory, art theme, and architecture will help immerse your audience:

This post-nuclear landscape in Metro: Last Light features an airliner that fell from the sky due to the EMP effect of the atomic bomb.

Details in the environment itself:

- **Props (decorations)**: Bottles, crates, cars, and skeletons do not need to be just a filler. You can carefully arrange everyday objects to tell players more about the inhabitants of the space or its history. In *Fallout 3*, a set of two skeletons embracing in bed paints a story of lovers choosing to live their life to the fullest in the face of an impending nuclear apocalypse. Do not be afraid to put things out of their place or proportion bring characterization. Is your NPC a maniac? Why don't you fill his bedroom full of nothing but teapots... Such cognitive dissonance.

- **Writings on the walls, signs, paintings, and pictures**: These can be a very effective tool; just make sure you are ready to localize the art into different languages or display the translation via the user interface:

In Dead Space, very important gameplay information has been presented in an unusual way.

- **Fauna and flora**: The animals and plant life of the game world can make it feel more alive but also help to convey the backstory. In *Dishonored*, the streets are populated by swarms of rats, a telltale sign of a plague engulfing the city.

- **Objects**: Found in the environment. Data disks, diary pages, books, and audio logs are now a staple found in many titles. They can be used for anything from revealing the main narrative to covering supporting characters, side-quests, and world building.
- **Characters**: They inhabit the environment. Overhearing poor citizens talk about the evil ruler can be as powerful as seeing them beg on the streets. Think of the NPCs and their clothing, dialog, and actions as an extension of your game world. Investing time in bespoke animations and audio will definitely increase the budget, so make sure to focus on reusable actions and animations first.
- **Audio:** We are not going to cover audio in this book; as you know, that is a discipline in itself! Never forget though that audio (dialogs, sound effects, and music) is as much as part of a game as the visuals and gameplay. You'll be surprised how much you can get across with the right sound effects or even just music.

Narrative review process

We have discussed how making video games is about creating, evaluating, and iterating to the find the optimal solution. Jonathan Dankoff, expert in User Research, and Corey May, games writer, game a very interesting talk at GDC 2015 (Game Developer Conference `https://www.gdcvault.com/play/1022166`). They pointed out the importance of the implementation of a review process in video games narratives, to assess and address issues with the narrative during pre-production and develop a game with a clearer storyline.

The framework was developed at Ubisoft, therefore it was meant for massive AAA productions, but the takeaways are very useful for games of any size. Underestimating the impact of the story is a common mistake, and the price is usually paid with stories of poor quality or the necessity to stretch the budget (both time and money) to sort out problems that could have been addressed early on with nearly no costs.

A very similar idea was proposed by Mike Laidlaw, former creative director at *Bioware* on franchises such as *Mass Effect* and *Dragon Age,* during the game narrative summit at GDC 2018. He emphasized the importance of peer-reviewing the scripts of a game as early as possible during the production.

The narrative review process consists of three steps on which the team should iterate one or two times:

- **Read**: Groups of different people read a general overview of the story
- **Review**: The readers rate the story, make notes, or fill-questionnaires
- **Analyze**: The reviews are discussed and the process is repeated (not more than once or twice) until all the biggest concern and issues are addressed

Let's have a look at these steps in detail.

Step one – Read

The first step is to create an outline of the game story. One page per act or module would be enough. The idea here is to stay agile. The outline details all the story elements and how the story develops throughout the game.

This outline is then given to two groups of readers:

- **Peer writers**: Knowledgeable about game writing, able to give technical feedback.
- **Team members**: Game director, game designers, level designers, leads. Everyone that would be involved in the decision-making process for the project, expect for writers.

Step two – Review

The reading groups give notes about the script. They might point out what they liked, what sparked their interest in knowing more, and what they didn't particularly understand or enjoy. They can put ask questions to the writer.

A questionnaire can be also added to the script, to more empirically measure the level of enjoyment, interest, and comprehension.

Step three – Analyze

All the notes given by the review groups are analyzed and synthesized into a report, which is then discussed at a roundtable.

The report only contains constructive feedback and relevant issues. The idea is to discuss what to improve, not to collaboratively design the narrative with the review group.

Both the writers and the reviewers participate in the roundtable, briefly discussing the major problems and even brainstorming possible solutions. A final assessment is made and a subsequent iteration is done by the writers on the script.

The benefit of narrative review

This process has multiple benefits:

- **Early enough to act**: The process should happen early in production, meaning the story script is cheap to change and has very little to no impact on the game's production at this stage.
- **Meaningful feedback**: Feedback is practical, actionable, and given by experts.
- **Clear direction**: Organized feedback on the story means that writers can use it for future decisions. There is no guesswork on why some decisions were made.
- **Invest in the narrative**: The team will know the narrative and be invested in it early on. A better understanding of what the narrative is trying to accomplish will benefit game and level design and even art direction.

This framework, as said, was developed and used for AAA productions such as *Assassin's Creed*, but games of any size will definitely benefit from a narrative review process as early as possible in the development.

You don't have to follow each step exactly as described, or you might want to try this and then develop your own framework based on your experience. Whatever you choose to do, don't forget that, if you are developing a game with a deep and rich narrative, the writing process will need the same care as is devoted to gameplay.

 The screenshots used in this chapter are for illustrative purposes only. We do not recommend you to misuse these in any way. For more information please consult the terms and conditions of the publishers mentioned in the *Disclaimer* section of this book.

Summary

We have taken a peek at how a narrative is designed for video games and how stories suit the video game medium very well. Of course, this is really just the tip of the iceberg. Interactive storytelling is a huge discipline, one that a game designer should know but not necessarily need to master unless he wants to specialize in writing or narrative design. For the reader who wants to delve deeper into it, we have established a few starting points.

We looked at two common types of narrative: the three-act story, which has a beginning, a middle, and an end, through which the tension constantly builds up and reaches a final climax, and the monomyth, which is used to represent the archetypal hero's journey through an adventure that takes him out of his comfort zone into a new world of discovery and experiences, and back again.

We went through the structure of different narratives in games, both linear and modular, and underlined the similarity between narrative and the game structure we discussed in previous chapters. Finally, we looked at a technique for reviewing narrative design, a process in which game designers should be always involved, especially when they're not the ones writing the story.

9
Level Design

In this chapter, we'll delve into the process of level design, a huge, nebulous topic that's capable of taking up an entire book in itself. We won't tackle individual tools or focus on a single genre; instead, we aim to provide you with insight into different aspects of the process as well as practical tips on how to best approach creation of content for your game.

Strap yourself in; this is an important one, as even the most elegant rules and most polished mechanics can lead to a poor gameplay experience if your level design is not up to scratch!

What is level design?

Level design is the process of creating playable content that serves as a medium of delivering gameplay and storytelling experiences to players. Some games rely on carefully crafted and strictly planned levels/maps/stages/missions. Others leave room for randomization, but still require human input to create puzzles, challenges, enemy spawn rules, pre-assembled level *chunks*, and even high-level world-building rules.

The craft of level design lives on a flexible cross-section between game design, storytelling, and art. Depending on the needs of the project and team structure, a level designer will either take care of the entire level design from start to finish or ask for artistic input from environmental artists, who'll take care of the visual side of things for them. In smaller teams, it's quite common to have a generalist game designer tackle level design tasks.

Depending on the game you're working on, the tools you'll use to create levels and missions can vary greatly. For 3D games, you're likely to use either proprietary in-house technology or the standard tools available in engines such as Unity or Unreal (learning the basics of at least one of these two editors is highly recommended). For 2D games, it's more difficult to plan ahead as in-house tools dominate the scene, but, that said, the tools are usually far simpler (by the way, if your game uses 2D tiles and grids, try *Tiled*—it's an old but very reliable editor that is available for free).

The level design process

As we already know from the opening paragraphs, level design can span a variety of tasks, from defining enemy spawn patterns to creating puzzles, sculpting, and populating an environment or even defining beat-maps in music games. Nevertheless, there are some processes and steps that can be applied to almost any content creation task, be it in part or as a whole. These steps are as follows:

1. **The premise**: Setting up a high-level vision
2. **The sketch**: Expanding upon the design
3. **Grayboxing**: Implementing and iterating on gameplay
4. **Art implementing:** Dressing up your creation
5. **Final polish**: Bug fixing and final adjustments before release

Let's go through all of them in detail and explore some examples!

The premise

Think of the premise as a succinct but persuasive sales pitch, even if the only person you're selling an idea to is yourself. Usually, all you need is a short paragraph that highlights the purpose (from the designer's point of view) and potentially the value (in the player's eyes) of creating that particular piece of game content. If you have strong references do not be afraid to use them; these can be anything from movie scenes to screenshots of existing games.

It's common for the premise to change and evolve multiple times, especially as it's likely to be written down a long time before you actually get down to creating the described content. Nevertheless, it's always good to write down and present your ideas to other people on the team to help you narrow the design down to what's truly important.

Remember, a premise with too many ideas is usually one that often fails to explore its potential. You're also at risk of confusing your players and creating content that feels bland. If you can't think of a single characteristic that makes your level stand out from the remaining parts of the game, you have just found yourself a good candidate for exclusion. If you have too many good ideas, store them as separate premises; you can always scrap and salvage whatever you can or start anew.

The detail and focus of a premise fully depends on your product. In a story-driven game, your premise can reflect on the single most important plot development and the way you plan to achieve the desired result. On the other hand, a match-3 puzzle game can get away with a trivially short premise such as "Introduction to the mechanics of the new Ice Block, easy difficulty, small size, tall but narrow layout".

Let's take a look at a few levels and reverse-engineer the potential premise:

Left 4 Dead (Multiplayer FPS) – No Mercy Campaign
The first campaign in the game is set in New York City, shortly after the viral outbreak. Our survivors are awaiting rescue on the roof of a downtown apartment complex. A helicopter flies by and tells everyone to make their way to the Mercy Hospital to evacuate. The survivors embark on a 4 or 5-part adventure that takes them through the streets of New York, the metro system, and the sewers, culminating in a grand finale on the rooftop of Mercy Hospital.

Mario Kart (Super Nintendo, Racing) – Rainbow Road
Exciting, multi-colored paths in the depths of outer space! Loads of 90 degree turns and a few long straights. Short length and normal grip. Difficulty is added by removing all barriers and putting in Super Thwomps (falling blocks that knock out racers when touched).

Remember, there are benefits to writing a premise for nearly anything, from levels and missions to weapons, power-ups, gadgets, character classes, enemy types, puzzles, tutorial sections, and boss fights. Having a plan always beats wandering around blindly, even if you do change it halfway through. Just do not treat your premises too seriously; there's a chance your creativity will take you away from the chosen path and throw you onto something far better. Embrace it when it happens, but do not count on it!

The sketch

Let's put your ideas to the test! The purpose of the sketch is to revisit and expand on your plans prior to in-game implementation.

For games with complex and time-consuming content creation pipeline (such as console RPGs), you may find this step in the process absolutely necessary. However, in less risky scenarios that do not require massive investments (for example, physics-based puzzle games), you might want to save time and jump straight into the next stage (grayboxing).

 It is possible that many weeks or even months have passed since you wrote down your initial premise. Catch up with the rest of the team (and especially any other designers) and make sure that the premise still fits with the rest of the game.

Depending on the type of content you're working on, the sketch can contain:

- Written design details
- Dialog or a detailed script for storytelling purposes
- Actual sketches, drawings, or scribbles of potential layouts
- Gameplay flow or timeline (list of major events and any branching paths)
- Artistic references (videos, screenshots, and photos)
- Gameplay references (potentially a video of another game)

 Why shouldn't I simply start by writing very detailed premises early on and then moving on to execution? The later you are in the project, the better and more cohesive the content you create. If you've just finished production on another game feature or level, there's a chance you have amassed new knowledge and expertise, or perhaps a slew of better ideas that you can put to use. Writing detailed designs for every part of the game's content and following with pure execution is tempting (it makes us feel like everything is planned, under control), but often you'll end up executing an inferior design, just because you got attached to the idea. Games are a product of a dynamic craft, not an assembly line. Be agile! If modifying your premise (even drastically) won't carry a huge price tag, don't be afraid to propose changes. There's no point to sticking to a bad plan just for the sake of it, and you're still early enough that design changes will be cheap.

Let's take a look at some examples of potential sketches!

Example – written sketch

As the first example, I created a written sketch for the Water Temple from *The Legend of Zelda: Ocarina of Time*. Not because it's a level design masterpiece, but because it's probably one of the most controversial dungeons in the series.

There should be enough detail in the sketch to help brief the team and brainstorm on ideas. You could also start assembling lists of new assets and functionalities for artists and programmers. At the same time, we've left the majority of gameplay exploration to the grayboxing stage. The dungeons in this game are often sets of individual rooms and challenges that come together to fulfill a larger vision.

On a side note, I wonder if the makers of the original *Ocarina of Time* realized how tedious and confusing this dungeon would get—mainly due to the constant backtracking, the chore of equipping/unequipping the *Iron Boots* and a convoluted, maze-like layout. Some of these problems could certainly be foreseen based on the premise, especially since the hub layout itself is designed to induce backtracking (returning to previously visited locations).

And now, without further ado, let's take a look at a written sketch for the Water Temple:

Legend of Zelda: Ocarina of Time (Action-Adventure) - Water Temple

- **Premise**: A water dungeon with a big, round, water-filled hub with a vertical layout. Players need to visit various wings and use the ocarina to manipulate the water level in the hub (unlocking access to new areas). This will feel like a true maze and test players' navigational and puzzle solving skills.
- **Backstory**: The Water Temple is dedicated to the worship of water spirits and is heavily guarded by Zoras.
- **Placement and Access**: The temple is placed under Lake Hylia. It can only be accessed with the Hookshot and Iron Boots.
- **Art References**: Here, you would typically attach some art you found on the internet. These can be split into the *do* and *don't* categories (sometimes showing what you don't want something to look like is very useful). It's very common to have the artists or the art director participate or take care of this process for you.
- **Size**: Large, multi-level. Desired playtime between 1 and 2 hours.
- **Requires:** Hookshot, Iron Boots (to walk underwater), Zora Tunic (to breathe underwater)
- **Rewards**: Longshot (Hookshot range upgrade, after mini-boss), Water Medallion (boss), and Heart Container (boss).
- **Notable obstacles**:
    - 5 Gold Skulltulas (special spiders needed for the Cursed Family quest)
    - New Enemies: Stingers (manta), Shell Blade (clam), and Spikes (float in water)
    - New Obstacles: Vortex (water trap, upon collision, throws the player back to the spawn point), Rapid Currents (impossible to swim against, will be used in puzzles)
    - Mini-boss: Dark Link (mirrors player's moves)
    - Boss Fight: Giant Amoeba (use Longshot to defeat)

Example – imaginary playthrough

A sketch can take many shapes! In the following example, we are dealing with a game that relies on carefully scripted single-player missions. In such cases, writing a high-level timeline of the events is a very useful exercise. The plan is surely going be modified several times during the implementation stage, but at least you'll have a solid starting point:

The mission has three distinguishable beats. The approach, the assassination, and the extraction

Call of Duty: Modern Warfare (FPS) – Pripyat assassination

Backstory: A retrospective mission set in set in Pripyat, near Chernobyl, telling the story of Captain Price (lieutenant back then) 15 years before the action of the main storyline takes place. The bad guy, Imran Zakhaev, is trying to purchase nuclear material gathered from the Chernobyl power plant. An assassination mission was approved by the US to try and stop Zakhaev and the transaction. Price was sent there with his superior, Captain MacMillan.

The mission itself is split into two parts that naturally fit together. First, we have to get into position (quietly), then we execute the target and try to make it out (all hell breaks loose).

Part One – All Ghillied Up

Premise: A quiet and atmospheric black-ops mission. The player needs to follow their partner, stay patient, sneak around, and time their assassinations to avoid detection. This section can be divided up as follows:

Name	Details	Duration	Intensity
Intro	Follow Captain MacMillan. Lay low and take down your enemies in a stealthy fashion. Infiltrate a nearby church.	3 min	1
Convoy	You'll need to get past an open field undetected. Enemy helicopter, armor, and infantry patrols are on the lookout.	3 min	3

Junkyard	Use stealth to sneak by or eliminate enemies around the junkyard areas filled with decommissioned army vehicles and containers.	3 min	2
Convention	Reach an open area filled with infantry and vehicles. Sprint to cover then sneak under enemy trucks.	4 min	3
Pripyat	Enter the desolate and overgrown town of Pripyat, navigating through the concrete tower blocks.	3 min	2
Hotel	The duo enters the hotel from which they can observe the transaction and carry out the assassination. Part 1 of the mission ends here.	1 min	1

Part 2 – One Shot, One Kill

Premise: Players assassinate the target, after which all hell breaks loose. The mission turns into a full-blown action sequence with enemy helicopters, intense firefights, and a last-stand by the iconic Pripyat Ferris wheel. This section can be divided up as follows:

Name	Details	Duration	Intensity
Transaction	The transaction is about to take place and the target comes into sight. This will be a very long distance shot. You will need to adjust for the wind (based on nearby flags) and the bullet drop.	2 min	3
Escalation	Target down, but your position is compromised. Run! You've got 15-20 minutes to get to the extraction zone (actual timer to add tension).	1 min	4
Apartments	Navigate in close quarters fighting groups of enemy infantry.	3 min	3
Helicopter	An attack helicopter appears, take it down! MacMillan gets wounded by the crashing chopper.	1 min	4
Piggyback	Carry MacMillan to the extraction zone. Face swarms of enemy infantry.	3 min	5
Apartments	Smaller scale, close quarter encounters. Closing in towards the extraction zone.	3 min	3
Ferris Wheel	You and MacMillan prepare to make a final stand by the iconic Ferris wheel. Set up claymores and find a good sniping spot.	2 min	2

| Last Stand | Fight off waves of enemies until the chopper arrives. | 4 min | 6 |
| Outro | Extract into safety. | 1 min | 1 |

Using the data from the imaginary playthrough, the designer can create high-level intensity graphs, which can later help to plan and execute the pace of the mission:

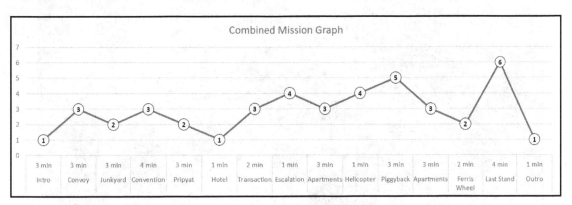

We'll talk at length about pacing, intensity, and the creation of detailed timelines in `Chapter 13`, *Balancing*.

Grayboxing

Gameplay ideas rarely pan out the way you see them inside your head, making grayboxing one of the most important parts of the level design process.

Grayboxing (also known as the *blockout* stage) refers to the process of transferring your vision (or an existing prototype) into a simple but playable in-game version. It allows you to make great strides on playability and validate the base geometry before investing time dressing it up.

The titular *gray box* refers to the boxy, largely untextured look of levels quickly assembled in 3D editors:

A grayboxed (blocked out) level for a game in the *Uncharted series*, as shared by the level designer Michael Barclay (Twitter @MotleyGrue).

When entering the grayboxing stage, it's essential to remain flexible, to open your content to new ideas and improvements based on playtesting, feedback, and experimental iterations. This is often the last time to make sweeping design changes, as they can get exponentially more expensive the closer you get to the end of the level design process.

Why work on gameplay first? Well, the last thing you want to do is invest large amounts of time and resources into making something artistically pleasing, only to realize it's not fun to play at all and needs to be completely remodeled.

 No matter how good the artists on your project are, do not count on their pretty textures, visual effects, sounds, and animations to make up for something that isn't fun in its purest form. You want the art to enhance the game, not mask the shortcomings of its design.

In regard to gameplay, the grayboxing stage is the best time to:

- Validate the base premise and feel of the content
- Verify the geometry/layout/sequence of events
- Set the base difficulty
- Place and configure various gameplay elements such as:
    - Enemies, puzzles, pickups, and obstacles
    - Triggers, scripts, and any other special gameplay scenarios
    - Cutscenes and story elements (possibly in a raw, purely functional form)
    - Tutorials (again, only to a degree that allows you to validate gameplay)

 There are times when the content is not designed around gameplay at all, but instead, around a certain *artistic masterpiece*. For example, a beautiful landscape that showcases the power of your game engine, or an extremely important plot development in a story-driven game. In such situations, you will have to shift your focus towards a different objective, but it's important to acknowledge (and accept) the potentially negative effects on gameplay such a shift can bring. For example, by opting to deliver a huge open vista we may have to remove parts of the geometry and reduce the number of actors in play.

Art implementation

With gameplay proved out and validated in the grayboxing stage, art implementation can begin! This includes creating detailed geometry, placing props and decorating the environment, texturing, lighting, and creating special effects and animations.

Whether the game designer is directly involved in this part of the process depends on their skill set, the project, and the team. Some highly experienced level designers can handle every single aspect of creating a stage, while others focus solely on gameplay and leave the artistic side to the likes of professional environmental artists.

Even if you cannot participate in this step directly, it's important to keep an eye on the process and ensure that essential gameplay elements are getting the correct treatment.

Production timelines can be tight, and artistic efforts often start as soon as you complete the sketch (or even the premise) of the stage. Concept art, animation, and modeling often run in parallel with grayboxing and gameplay iterations. Whenever this is the case, it's important to wait for gameplay iterations to conclude before investing in the creation of set pieces and proprietary art that have to limited re-use value.

Final polish

As the name suggests, final polish is the last step of the process, after which the content is officially *done* and ready for release. This step will often be offset in time and can take place long after all art and gameplay aspects have been implemented, with artists and designers working on something else in the meantime.

Why can't we simply finish everything in one go? You can certainly try, but with the passing of time you'll improve your skills and gain new perspective and insight. You'll also be able to compare your creation with the rest of the game and reflect on it as a part of something bigger. You are also likely to get feedback from multiple rounds of external and internal playtesting of the game.

Extensive iterations and playtesting done during grayboxing will help reduce the number and extent of changes at this stage. If all goes well, final polish will only encapsulate minor tweaks to the geometry, bug fixing, dialogs, rewards, difficulty, and pacing adjustments.

Level design and storytelling

As you may remember from the previous chapters, games are a medium for interaction and storytelling. When creating new playable content, you have a variety of tools and opportunities to tell your stories. As we have seen, these stories can emerge from both the overarching narrative and the gameplay experience.

Sometimes both stories will be tightly connected. In the detective game *L.A Noire*, most gameplay actions (such as gathering evidence, interviewing witnesses and so on) are not only motivated and supported by the narrative but also crucial for its development:

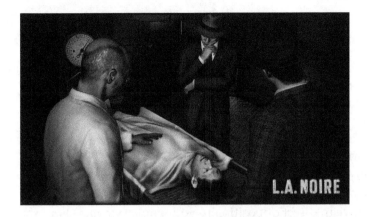

In other cases, gameplay and narrative can be independent entities. In *Puzzle Quest: Challenge of the Warlords*, the orb-matching puzzle gameplay could easily be swapped entirely without affecting the narrative; and on the flip side, the narrative itself does little to influence gameplay:

Puzzle Quest: Challenge of the Warlords offers a strange (and yet fitting) marriage of match-3 puzzle gameplay with an epic role-playing structure and elaborate storyline.

Most games lie somewhere in the middle of this spectrum, with narratives that explain the game world, motivate and justify the player's actions, and at the same time, do not oppose the interactive nature of the gameplay. They allow for player expression within the boundaries of the game world and its rules.

Before integrating any storytelling into your level design, you need to ask yourself a range of questions and establish a set of rules that will guide the content creation:

- What's more important, the narrative or gameplay? If it's the former, will you accept a fragment that isn't fun to play but serves as a good way to deliver your story? If it's the latter, are you ready to sacrifice the narrative for a superior gameplay experience?
- Do you use your narrative to explain and reinforce actions of the player, or is your narrative separate from gameplay?
- Can the game be played without interacting with the story, or is interaction with the story mandatory to progress?
- Is narrative in direct opposition to your game systems? For example, imagine a game in which we play as an FBI agent, and yet we allow (and possibly even reward) hurting innocent civilians.

With these questions answered, you'll need to select from a range of tools to convey the narrative. I've listed the most popular ones below:

- **Cutscenes**: Cinematic sequences where control is taken away from the player.
- **Dialog**: These can be either be passive or interactive. Interactive dialogs can unveil extra information as well as allow for self-expression and branching narratives.
- **Gameplay**:
  - **Directly**: The storyline development depends on players performing certain actions. This gives an opportunity to integrate choice but does not enforce it.
  - **Indirectly**: The player is *a passenger* experiencing the story being unveiled as a result of changes in the game world or actions of other players or NPCs (non-playable characters).
- **Narratio**: *Thomas Was Alone* and *Stanley Parable* are two amazing examples of how narration can be tightly infused with level design to produce highly engaging stories.
- **Environmental storytelling**: A big subject that we have discussed in Chapter 8, *Games and Stories*.

When it comes to architecture and artistic themes, *BioShock,* with its immersive take on a stylish, art deco utopia gone wrong is a go-to example. *Gone Home,* on the other hand, is a short, story-driven experience built almost entirely around exploration and environmental storytelling, featuring great attention to detail and highly effective (yet subtle) presentation.

Level design practices

In the previous sections, we have explained what level design is, and how the process of creating new content can be approached. Now it's time for some practical tips and tricks that should help you with the design process!

Functional level design and realism

Game worlds range from highly realistic to completely made-up, and most fall somewhere in the middle of the spectrum. Worlds do not become more believable because of visual clutter, high-resolution textures, and detailed geometry. They become believable if we can imagine the life that keeps on going when we look away. Even the simplest AI systems can yield surprising results. Humans are naturally prone to connecting strings of random behaviors into larger, more meaningful stories, a phenomenon known as *apophenia.*

A simple way to create more coherent designs is to imagine the inhabitants of the world interacting with their surroundings. Don't settle for a set of walls with haphazardly placed furniture that acts like a filler. An office, a house, or a store all have a set purpose and the objects inside them are in there for a reason. A bath doesn't belong in the living room, and a bed is rarely placed by the front door. If rules from the real world do not suit your creation, then create your own rules and make your fictional world adhere to them.

On top of making your layouts more immersive, realism can help in making game mechanics more understandable by allowing players to use their own non-game experiences and references. Many physical properties of the real world, such as light, gravity, friction, and buoyancy can take little cognitive effort when translated into fictional worlds.

Remember, the world you're creating, its inhabitants, and their stories are there to support your gameplay experience, not govern it. Unless you're working on a simulator, extensive realism can quickly get in the way of the gameplay experience, and become prohibitively expensive to implement. Players do not want a different version of the real world, they want an immersive world that they can understand and care about.

Evolving game features

We can apply the philosophy of *Kishōtenketsu*, a classic storytelling structure often applied to Chinese, Korean, and Japanese narratives. *Kishōtenketsu* divides the story into four segments:

- **Introduction** (ki): Establishing the setting of the story by introducing characters, locations, and any relevant historical aspects.
- **Development** (shō): The story follows the established path with no major changes.
- **Twist** (ten): An unexpected development in the story. There may be more than one twist in a story, but this is the most significant one.
- **Conclusion** (ketsu): The story ends in a satisfying matter.

A similar philosophy can be applied to level design, especially when your content focuses on the introduction and evolution of game mechanics and challenges.

Big thanks to Mark Brown for an insightful video (https://www.youtube.com/watch?v=dBmIkEvEBtA) that inspired me to elaborate on this topic in this book. Search for *Mark Brown* on YouTube to find his channel!

Introduction

Unless you're going for a *Dark Souls*-like *Darwinian difficulty* (that is, you may have to learn from your mistakes, evolution by natural selection); any new game mechanic, be it a tool, an obstacle, an enemy type, or a puzzle has to first be introduced in the most basic (and safest possible) manner.

There are various techniques you can use to introduce new features and mechanics, for example, having another character perform an action first so that players can follow in their footsteps. We'll explore ways in which you can teach your players in Chapter 12, *Accessibility.*

The philosophy of Kishōtenketsu been used in games for quite some time, and some of the best recent examples can be found in modern *Mario* games such as *Super Mario Galaxy 2*, *Super Mario 3D Land*, and *Super Mario 3D World*.

Let's look at an example! In world 2-4 of Super Mario 3D Land, a new platform is introduced that flips between two positions every time you jump. When the platform is first introduced, there are no consequences for failure (falling down as the platform escapes from under our feet), and players have to learn by doing. Here's the approximation of the layout:

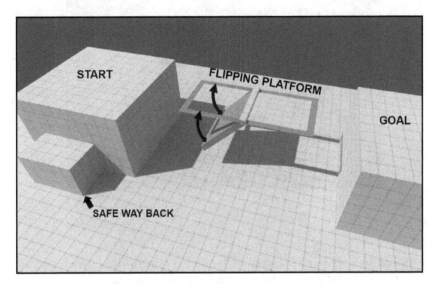

Remember, the novelty factor alone makes the game more exciting and cognitively stimulating (raising our intensity for that segment); save the challenge for later!

Development

Now that the player has been acquainted with the new game element, it's time to introduce a challenge and test their understanding of how the feature works.

Let's continue our example! As the level develops, so does the challenge. Falling will now result in death and there are obstacles and enemies that get in the way and keep players on their feet:

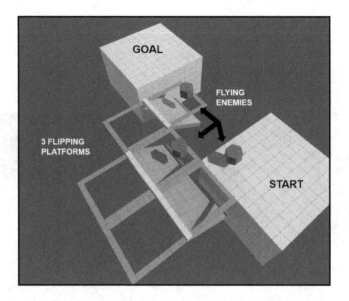

Twist

After players showcase a sense of mastery, it's time to confound their expectations. The twist is all about taking what players begin to take for granted, and twisting it in a fresh new way. This is often done by mixing the new mechanic with something that you've introduced previously or by exposing a property that players did not experience or expect. For example, in many Legend of Zelda games, players get a bow and arrow and use it to activate remote switches. Later on, it's unveiled that you set your arrows alight by shooting them over flaming braziers. This twist is all about discovering a new combination of two seemingly unconnected elements, and can be used to present a variety of spatial puzzles.

When it comes to our case-study, one of the twist segments pairs our flipping platforms with rotating spike obstacles (introduced in previous worlds):

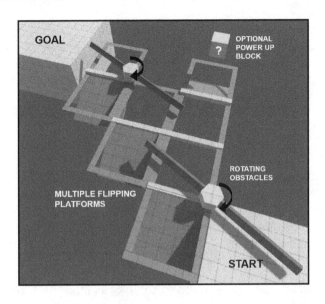

Conclusion

This is the final part of our 4 beat story. Players have already acquainted themselves with a new game element, and they've mastered it and seen it being used in novel, unexpected ways. Treat the conclusion like your closing statement; it does not have to be difficult, it has to be satisfying, and provide a sense of achievement, or at least closure. The new element can now either become a staple or be put to rest, ready to come back whenever you wish to provide variety or mix it with something new.

The flagpole sequence found at the end of most Super Mario platform levels is a perfect place for the ultimate showcasing of the (now mastered) mechanic. In world 2-4 of Super Mario 3D Land, the flagpole segment asks players to climb a set of flipping platforms if they wish to get a score bonus, a positive ending to the story told by the level design.

Pacing from day one

The slow and gradual introduction of game mechanics mentioned above is an example of a pacing exercise. The pace of the game is most often being dictated by the rhythm and intensity of the levels you create. The intensity can stem from both physical and cognitive challenges as well as artistic and emotional stimulation. Novel content and difficult sections raise your intensity while repetitive segments and low difficulty lower it. Prolonged periods of low intensity lead to boredom, while long, overly intense sections can exhaust your players.

Tightly controlled singleplayer content (especially if it's story driven) tends to be much harder to revamp once integrated. Therefore, it's important to think of pacing from the very first day, possibly during the sketching period (as illustrated by our example from *Call of Duty: Modern Warfare*).

We'll cover the complexities of analyzing, planning, and delivering singleplayer and multiplayer pacing at length in Chapter 13, *Balancing*.

Lock and key

Lock and key is a widespread, but somewhat controversial design practice. The basic implementation includes a literal use of a lock and key. You restrict access to a certain area (or reward) until players find the *key*. To do so, they need to venture elsewhere and complete a set of tasks, advancing the storyline or their character.

Turning away your players and asking them to come back later is a form of so-called backtracking. There is value to it but you have to be careful as extensive backtracking and having to manage a list of uncompleted areas can be incredibly frustrating.

One obvious use is to prolong your content's lifespan. You may have spent a long time crafting a beautiful set-piece or a highly functional area, and using a *lock and a key* around it will increase the time spent with your content. Just make sure it's not senseless *running around;* adding a new obstacle, a fresh wave of enemies, or otherwise *twisting* the area will help your content feel fresh.

Locks and keys can also be used to encourage exploration and make for a less linear experience. Creating a large area and hiding key objects around it allows you to set your players free, while simultaneously ensuring they visit the most important segments and complete all of the necessary tasks.

Remember that locks and keys do not have to be literal. The level design of games in the *Pokemon* and *Legend of Zelda* series is filled to the brim with abstracted locks and keys.

In *Pokemon*, the keys are abilities that have to be unlocked and taught to your creatures. Teach your *Pokemon* the *cut* ability and you can now gain access to areas blocked by thick bushes. Needless to say, scouring the map while trying to remember where to apply the newly available *key* can be a tedious and stressful task for some players.

In *Legend of Zelda* games, there are both actual *keys* (used to unlock doors, chests and boss rooms) and *key items*. The latter are usually unlocked in the middle of the dungeon and allow the player to access areas that were previously blocked by a specific puzzle or obstacle. On top of unlocking the rest of the dungeon and granting access to secret areas in the outside world, the key items often come with a secondary use. Some are useful in combat, others can be applied in interesting combinations to solve puzzles.

The hookshot is an example of a key item that has a variety of gameplay uses, from puzzle solving to combat.

To sum it up, lock and key design is a popular and effective technique, but be careful not to overdo it. Extensive use of backtracking and forcing your players to memorize a list of inaccessible areas is a sure way to make your levels tedious and confusing. Content design that relies solely on pattern matching (use A on B, then X on Y, now rinse, repeat) turns your game into a *shopping-list* full of memorized responses, rather than a vehicle for true challenge, choice, and expression.

Geometry and gameplay

Level geometry (that is, the layout) and the spatial properties of the space you're creating can have a profound effect on player's emotions, and therefore on gameplay. We'll explore this subject by first introducing the *prospect-refuge theory* developed by an English geographer and poet Jay Appleton in his 1975 book *The Experience of Landscape*.

In his work, Appleton presented an enlightening insight into the reasons behind certain landscapes being perceived as beautiful and others as bleak, and why some spaces draw us in and make us feel safe, while others make us uneasy and insecure. According to the prospect-refuge theory, humans like to occupy intimate, sheltered spaces (refuge) that are overlooking vast, open areas full of potential (prospect).

Examples of a **refuge** include:

- An explored cave, cavern, or den
- The inside of a parked car
- A bench covered by the protective shade of a tree
- A walled, wooden lookout tower
- A house on a hill

An example of a refuge area in *The Elder Scrolls: Skyrim*.

Examples of a **prospect** include:

- An open square or park in the middle of a city
- A slowly descending valley seen from the top
- Islands surrounded by calm water observed from the safety of the harbor
- Softy ascending mountains and hills in the distance

A vista full of prospect in *The Elder Scrolls: Skyrim*

Knowing the basis of prospect-refuge theory allows you to look at the spaces you create from the perspective of an ancient hunter-gatherer that's lying dormant in each and every one of us.

While making playable spaces, it's up to you to decide what kind of emotions you want to invoke. To satisfy the primal needs of your players, you must protect them from being seen and ambushed, while simultaneously allowing them to peek outside and spot enemies and opportunities alike. On the other hand, if you aim to put your players on edge, make them feel like a *sitting duck*, visible and exposed from multiple sides. For example, force them to carry a torch or a flashlight while walking down a dark path in the middle of a steep valley, with little visibility, difficult terrain, and lots of opportunities for being ambushed.

Manipulating space

The prospect-refuge theory can help us identify the needs, wants, and fears rooted in human psychology. This, in turn, can help us create playable spaces that carry emotional purpose.

Depending on the current status of your player and your game mechanics, the physical shape of the world will present different threats and opportunities. Knowing the theme and functionalities of your game, you should be able to identify the potential emotional responses to any type of space. Predict, analyze, and collect that knowledge, making it ready to be applied when designing your levels:

- **Enclosed Areas**: In the context of a survival horror game such as *Silent Hill,* narrow tunnels and corridors can quickly turn into a claustrophobic nightmare, with enemies able to easily block your movements and pin you down. Moreover, a narrow corridor in a game such as *Dark Souls* can actually prevent you from effectively using certain spells and weapons (as wall collisions stop your swings). But a tight spot does not have to be a bad one! In *Left 4 Dead,* unless you're facing one of a few special enemies (whose attacks deal damage in an area of effect), a corridor or a tiny room can force all enemies into a manageable choke point, effectively turning it into a refuge (a safe and desirable space).

- **Manageable Areas**: These are areas that are big enough to move around in yet small enough to easily explore and master. If the space is easy to traverse (both horizontally and vertically) it can be a very comforting one. Especially if players can use its contents and geometry (including walls and corners) to protect themselves (refuge).

- **Open Areas**: An open area can be an inspiring place for the player (a prospect). For a positive effect, provide the player with freedom of movement and mastery over the environment, making the surfaces, approach angles, inhabitants, and weather conditions unthreatening and easy to traverse. Such space can also promote exploration by sparking curiosity about the features of the terrain (caves, valleys, waterfalls) or man-made structures. Memorable features can also provide helpful landmarks and ease navigation. Good visibility and a low threat of being ambushed are also key to making an open space feel safe. On the other hand, you can make an open space feel incredibly threatening and uneasy by reducing the visibility (through fog, rain, darkness), surrounding the player with a terrain that's ripe with ambush opportunities, or making them feel lost in a desolate, hard to traverse world that has no visible landmarks.

Height

Our response to height in games can vary dramatically depending on several factors, including:

- Our immediate surroundings (enclosed or exposed, safe or dangerous)
- Our ability to traverse in the vertical axis (for example, the power of flight)
- The effects of falling

Imagine standing at the top of a narrow, metal scaffolding, with no railings, suspended high above the ground. You're not only exposed to being seen but also fully aware that any sudden movement can be incredibly risky and therefore, frightening. In the second scenario, place yourself inside an equally tall church tower. This time, you're provided with the cover (refuge) of walls and a set of windows from which you can observe (prospect) any incoming threats and opportunities. The simple act of adding or removing barriers to an elevated walkway can have a big impact on how players approach it.

If the game allows you to fly freely, opening up the vertical space, the frightening effects of height might be removed entirely. On the other hand, if you're punished severely for a seemingly manageable fall, you'll treat height very, very carefully. The same effect can be induced without having to rely on *fall damage* and the threat of death. All you'd need to do is, when the fall occurs, force your players to repeat a difficult or time-consuming jump sequence. I am not saying this is a desirable effect, I am simply highlighting how the consequences of and emotional response to height can vary depending on the geometry, our abilities to traverse it, and the potential consequences of falling.

 Even if your game does not rely on player-controlled traversal, it can make great use of height within its mechanics. For example, in many strategy games, a unit that has a height advantage over its foe can be granted a range of attack bonuses (such as increased damage, range, and accuracy).

Emotional significance of exploration

In the context of physical or virtual space, exploration is the act of traversing an area with the purpose of discovering new information or resources. The levels you create as well as the structure of the game itself can allow for different levels of exploration. Great joy and satisfaction can be found in uncovering the lost lands and hidden treasures of the world.

To understand how to capitalize on exploration in your levels, you'll need to analyze the internal motivations behind each step of the journey.

1. **Planning**: Players project their curiosity onto the game world. They either identify areas of interest ("I want to to go... there!") or specific needs they want to fulfill ("I need to find more mushrooms"). To help in this process, the designer can provide implicit goals (a shrouded area of the map is essentially a big question mark) and explicit goals (*a quest to find the magic tree*). You can also provide visual points of interest in the world, and encourage resource accumulation by making resources scarce and the progression more difficult or less convenient without them.

2. **Execution**: The act of exploration is the act of investment. We put our time and resources on the line, hoping to have our efforts rewarded. It's important to make the players feel like the path they're taking is their own; it's more exciting to be a rogue explorer than a visitor held by a guiding hand. To do that, provide branching paths or open areas that have more than one solution. You may also want to loosen up the structure of the experience (avoid too many scripted cutscenes, turn off automatic path markers, and so on). We want our players to be the authors of their story, even if their every move was predicted and encouraged by the designer.

3. **Pay off**: Venturing into the unknown is much more rewarding if there's a potential to be rewarded for our efforts. To avoid disappointing players, try to limit the disparity between the time, effort, and resources put in by the player, and the perceived value of the reward. That said, be careful of making the pay off feel artificially *fair* and predictable—if each cave is guaranteed to have a loot chest, any sense of exploration wears off the moment you identify a cave. As long as you open up the opportunities for a rare but valuable reward, it's OK to sometimes be a bit disappointing.

Effects of lighting

Light and darkness have always exercised powerful effects on our psychology, and as humans we are all predisposed to fear the darkness and the unknowns it presents. However, when it comes to games, the effects of lighting can shift entirely based on the context. The mood of your game, its artistic theme, and the game mechanics can all influence and distort our natural tendencies. Let's explore the various ways of utilizing lighting in the context of level design:

- **Helping with navigation**: Lights not only illuminate dark environments, they can be used to immediately grab our attention. A natural reaction for any human is to seek the warmth and shelter of light. The stronger the contrast, the stronger the effect. This survival trait has been utilized to great extent in *Left 4 Dead*, where bright lights coming from cars, floodlights, and street lamps are strung together to form a visual path to safety. When players are lost and swarmed by hordes of enemies, they are highly reliant on strong and immediate navigational clues provided by strong lights. This rule works both ways. You should avoid extensively illuminating areas you do not wish your players to pay attention to!

A path of light is guiding the players in Valve's *Left 4 Dead*

- **Light is a commodity**: Fuel for portable lighting sources such as torches, flashlights, and night vision goggles can be turned into a valuable commodity and create a cycle of reassurance (when the light is going strong) and fear (when we run out of fuel). Should an area be completely shrouded in darkness, players will be forced to find a way to illuminate it. This results in a very natural and self-explanatory case of *lock and key* progression gating.

- **Using light for combat:** Many games limit and enforce the use of light sources, but few make them as important as *Alan Wake*, where lights play a paramount role in combat. Shining your flashlight at an enemy will gradually destroy their *shield of darkness*, making them vulnerable to your weapons. You simply cannot fight back unless you use a source of light! Strong floodlights are also spread across the levels, not only guiding the players but also acting as safe zones.

- **Curious shades**: While darkness can be very frightening, shade is much more approachable. Yes, it may obscure some threats, but with a comfortable level of visibility remaining, we can navigate through shaded areas with ease. If players feel adequately equipped and ready for an adventure, a shaded, seemingly hidden and unexplored space is sure to spark curiosity...If an area isn't occupied, then who knows, maybe there's something of value still to be discovered? Shaded areas are also synonymous with refuge spaces, offering protection from being seen by anyone outside while allowing one to see incoming threats.

- **Darkness as a friend**: In many games that put emphasis on stealth, even absolute darkness can be your best friend. In series such as *Metal Gear Solid*, *Thief*, and *Splinter Cell*, standing in the light is synonymous with being utterly vulnerable and exposed. In the context of these game worlds, the veil of darkness provides near-absolute safety in an otherwise hostile environment. But a game does not have to be focused on stealth mechanics to utilize darkness as a safe space; a great example is a first-person shooter from 2002 called *The Darkness* (uh, we are getting quite literal here). In *The Darkness*, the playable character is imbued with special powers that do not work in well-lit areas, turning light into a threat that has to be avoided or dealt with. Level design in such games often puts more emphasis on the use and placement of light and shade as opposed to the actual geometry.

Based on the examples above, we know that imbuing light and shade with gameplay roles defines what a refuge space is for your players. With that knowledge, one can create levels with carefully spaced out refuge spaces that encourage players to plan a path (from refuge, through the prospect space, and back into refuge). If you provide your players with a degree of freedom (multiple refuge spaces to consider) they're sure to start building mental paths between various parts of the space, making them feel more empowered and tactical about the way they approach the environment.

 The effects of using light are often proportional to the level of contrast. If the entire scene has the same level of brightness, nothing can benefit from being particularly pronounced or obscured. A screen filled with bright light does not have as strong an effect as a beaming light at the end of a dark tunnel.

Vision as a mechanic

Light and darkness are not limited to the environmental aesthetic. Vision can be an important part of your game rules, used to create and influence the information horizon: that is, how much players know about the state of the game world and its participants.

With mechanics such as *fog of war* (a staple found in many top-down strategy games), you can reward and encourage exploration, and put an entirely different spin on light and darkness.

In games that utilize this mechanic, any area on the map that hasn't been explored is either:

- **Completely blank**: With black patches on the map
- **Heavily dimmed**: Showcasing the topography, but indicating the player can't see what's going on in that part of the level

Regardless of the initial level of visibility, you have to decide what's going to happen after initial exploration. Two most common examples are:

- Permanently removing fog of war from any area that has been visited
- Only dispersing fog of war from areas that are currently under player's control, or close to a friendly unit or building:

The two states of fog of war in *Age of Empires*.

This may seem like a trivial, low-level choice, but it can have profound effects on gameplay. By removing fog of war after exploration, you permanently empower the player with new information. This promotes players to venture far, and quickly.

On the other hand, reapplying fog of war to uninhabited areas maintains a level of exciting uncertainty. It requires players to anticipate the moves of their foes, rather than to simply react to them. Vision becomes a form of commodity, an extension of any other map control mechanic you may have. It also opens up the possibilities of your level topography. If a unit is positioned above the enemy, it might be able to see and engage the enemy without the risk of effective retaliation.

If you plan on using fog of war or any other vision-oriented mechanic in your game, think of its role and how it may affect player behavior. Are you adding these mechanics because other similar games have it? Or is the added uncertainty and sense of exploration a necessary aspect of your gameplay? Do your vision mechanics reinforce the behaviors you want your players to express, or are they simply slowing down your gameplay?

When working with vision mechanics, be sure to implement (or ask for) a range of parameters that might help you experiment with vision in your game. Examples include multiplying vision radius, persisting vision for a moment after leaving the location, removing fog of war completely, or making it disperse after initial exploration. You might have a standard you think you're set to follow, but your game might feel much more fun with a certain combination that you can't foresee.

Level design in multiplayer action games

Multiplayer level design is a huge subject of its own and each game has its individual dynamic. It's also a prime candidate for extensive playtesting and user research! For the sake of this book, I combined a set of tips that can be applied to most action games and help you design better maps:

- **Follow a premise**: A great way to make your level stand out from the rest of your game is to build it around a unique gameplay premise or a visual set piece (waterfall, windmill, or even a crashed spaceship). Use the geometry, lighting, wall signs, and game objectives to guide the players towards a distinguishable space that defines the level. A strong premise also allows you to stay focused and prioritize parts of the level against one another.
- **Avoid dead-ends**: They stop players in their tracks and disrupt their flow, making them feel lost and foolish for not knowing where to go.
- **Provide flanking opportunities**: Even the most desirable vantage position need some weaknesses.
- **Keep your players moving**: Rewarding risk-taking by hiding powerful items in areas that are densely populated or tough to access is a classic play, but not the only one! You could even keep your players moving by re-balancing or spreading out ammo pickups and lowering the initial ammo capacity.

- **Use heatmaps**: Ask for implementation of death location analytics as early as possible. This will allow you to log the positions of each player death and then transpose them onto the map layout, highlighting areas that are highly popular and ones that see little action. It's okay to have zones that are very *hot*, as long as they're not confined to a single door frame. However, if half of your map is not seeing any action, you may consider changing the geometry or providing additional incentives (such as pick-ups and weapons) for players that venture out there.

- **Think vertically**: We often look at maps from the top, leading us to forget how big a role height plays. Just make sure to provide several ways to traverse between different levels of heights, seeing an enemy above and not knowing how to reach their position can be incredibly frustrating:

The 2Fort map in *Team Fortress* 2 is a great example of a strong premise (two forts separated by a river) and vertical design (the stage has elevated sniping platforms as well as underground sections accessible from the river).

The screenshots used in this chapter are for illustrative purposes only. We do not recommend you to misuse these in any way. For more information please consult the terms and conditions of the publishers mentioned in the *Disclaimer* section of this book.

Summary

Back in this chapter introduction, we described level design as a huge, nebulous topic. Many pages later, and in spite of the overwhelming complexity of the subject, you hopefully feel more confident about approaching the creation of levels for your games.

We started by describing the 5 step approach to level design (from premise to polish), and explored the interactions between level design and storytelling. We then took a journey through a set of practical tips and tricks, from the use of realism and the philosophy of *Kishōtenketsu* (intro, development, twist, conclusion) to the complexities of light and darkness, practical use of space, and tips on multiplayer level design.

But that's not all! The subject of *pacing* (a concept briefly mentioned during our example sketch for *Call of Duty: Modern Warfare)* will be expanded upon in Chapter 13, *Balancing*.

Now that we have our game worlds, we should try and populate them. The next chapter is dedicated to the art and craft of creating game characters.

10
Characters

It is time to see how characters are created and managed in the game world. When talking about characters, it is the game designer's responsibility to translate into gameplay what characters are, what they do, and what their skills, abilities, and behaviors might be. It is no coincidence that we discussed Narrative and how to write characters first in Chapter 8, *Games and Stories*. Even for the simplest character, a few lines are required to answer some basic questions. These answers, no matter how simple or basic, are going to have a deep impact on the player's perception of the game world.

Take *Space Invaders*, for example:

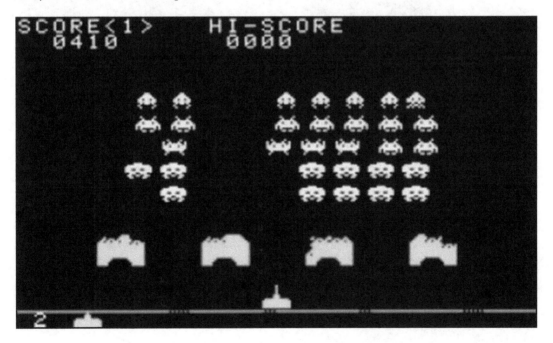

The main characters in *Space Invaders:* the invading aliens and your ship!

It features only four types of enemies: small, medium, and large invaders and the UFO ship. Nonetheless, writing who these characters are, where they are from, and why they are there is crucial to determining their design and implementation. All the invaders have the same speed and the same attack, and they are all destroyed with one hit. But they come in different sizes that make them more or less difficult to hit. The UFO appears only every now and then, quickly crossing the screen from left to right, shooting down at the player. Just four lines for four enemies. Very simple, yet very descriptive and informative for implementation.

Let's jump a few decades ahead.

Ubisoft's *Far Cry* franchise has become famous for its villains. Throughout the five titles released so far, *Far Cry*'s villains have become more and more complex.

In the most recent installment, *Far Cry 5*, the main antagonist is a very complex and controversial character that has sparked many polemics:

Joseph Seed in the famous *Far Cry 5* promotional image

Let's have a look at a brief description from the game's Wiki:

> "*Joseph Seed is a ruthless megalomaniac who is the founder and the leader of the Hope County-based religious cult organization "Project at Eden's Gate" alongside his siblings who he dubs "The Heralds"; Jacob, John, and Faith Seed. Eden's Gate has used both coercion and violence to bring the existing residents of Hope County into its cult, as ordered by Seed, and, as of the events depicted in the game, is in direct conflict with The Resistance and its members.*"

Can you visualize him in an FPS game such as *Far Cry*? How do you think he's going to be in-game? What abilities would he have? What kind of challenge will he pose to the player?

Let's take another example. What about Yoshi?:

Yoshi is an anthropomorphic dinosaur in the *Super Mario* universe

Yoshi can jump, use its tongue to grab distant objects and swallow them, and even lay eggs that can be thrown at enemies.

You might have noticed that I haven't mentioned any playable characters in the previous examples. Most of the times, in fact, the real stars in a game are not the characters you play as but the ones you meet and interact with, both enemies and allies. Enemies and allies (usually called Non-Playable Characters) make the world come to life; they confront or assist the player and are a fundamental part of any game.

Playable characters, NPCs, and enemies

There are three different types of characters in a video game:

- **Playable characters:** These are the characters the player directly controls. In some games there is just one (the main protagonist), while in some other games, there are multiple protagonists. Sometimes the player can temporarily take control of an NPC. In other games, there might not be protagonists at all. In a strategy game such as *Starcraft*, for example, the player controls units. Some of those units might be unique heroes or commanders, some might be vehicles: tanks or even spaceships. The rules for creating a protagonist such as Joel in *The Last of Us* or a Battlecruiser unit in *Starcraft* might be very different, but in the end, the principles you use to conceptualize and design them are not so different.

- **Non-Playable Characters (NPC):** NPCs are characters that inhabit the game world, but are not playable by the player. They are controlled by predetermined behaviors designed by the game designer. They are either scripted to follow a precise order of actions and reactions or driven by some sort of Artificial Intelligence (most of the time, it is a combination of the two).

- **Enemies:** Enemies are entities that interfere with the player goals and pose some sort of challenge. They don't necessarily need to be evil entities trying to kill the player. Some enemies might just block the player from achieving her goals, such as the Crows in *Monument Valley*, and need to be avoided by finding alternative routes. They don't pose any threat to the main character's life...they just won't let her pass!

In the next paragraphs, we are going to have a look at how to categorize, conceptualize, and design all these types of characters.

The function of characters

Each character in a game should have a specific function, whether they are an ally or an enemy. You don't want to populate your world with characters that don't have a purpose and are just there to fill a blank space.

The same is true for enemies. Every time an enemy is introduced in a game, it has to serve a purpose in the overall game experience. Enemies are not just abstract entities on the screen trying to stop or kill the player somehow. Why are they trying to stop the player? Who are they? What are their motivations?

It is not important that all this information is actually conveyed to the player. It might well be that she would never know why those alien ships in Space Invaders were trying to invade our planet. Maybe they just shot the player's spaceship because they felt under threat. Maybe it was a peaceful migration? Okay, probably they really wanted to invade Earth and destroy every human on it, but the important thing is that it was actually really clear in the mind of the designer.

Each NPC or enemy is an opportunity to deepen the player's immersion in the game world, to offer some help, some fresh challenge, some dilemma, or even just some insights. Characters also evoke emotions in the player. We have seen how important and powerful human emotions are for players. Crafting characters, such as crafting game mechanics and narratives, is a great way to build and convey emotions in video games.

Let's have a look at some classic characters you can use, their roles, and the emotions they enable in the player. Keep in mind that these categories are not set in stone; they can be mixed with each other and a single character can well fulfill multiple roles, both at the same time or in different moments of the game. Let's learn about them individually - it will be up to you to find the right combination in your games!

Friend/Assistant

A friend or assistant is a very common NPC in a multitude of games. It might be someone that needs the player's help or is offering it. He can be one of the main parts of the plot or even a playable character. Friendship is a strong thing and it can create a sense of bond and belonging. Trust, empathy, joy, and also envy and competition are all emotions related to a friend. Some of the best examples are *The boy* and *Trico* from *The Last Guardian*, *Joel* and *Ellie* from *The Last of Us*, and *Lydia (and the player)* in *Skyrim*.

Lover

Lovers are similar to friends in terms of function in the game and emotions evoked in the player. Some romances in games are determined by the story itself, but some games, especially RPGs, such as *The Witcher*, or life simulators, such as *The Sims*, allow the player to pursue and live their own romance.

Playing with an emotion like love in a video game has been underrated for a long time. With the media and its audience evolving and maturing, love is becoming a very popular theme and less and less stereotyped. You can find some non-stereotyped, great love stories in games such as *Catherine, Life is Strange, The Last Day of June, Final Fantasy, Baldur's Gate, Dragon Age,* and many many more!

Mentor

Hello, friend. Stay awhile and listen! This memorable line from Deckard Cain in *Diablo* will evoke great gaming memories in any *Diablo* fan. Deckard Cain represents all a mentor should be: a wise, knowledgeable character always keen to help and to guide the hero.

Mentors are pretty popular characters. They always come in handy to teach the player something, either about the game or the game world. They are fantastic for introducing and explaining the lore of the game world, and even game mechanics. You can quite often see mentors teaching the game during tutorials, for example. The usage of a mentor has become extremely popular in F2P games, where the need to introduce the player quickly to both the game's core mechanics and world lore makes the perfect case for the use of this type of character.

Minions (enemies)

We're going to talk about the bad guys in depth later. Enemies, monsters, aliens, dire animals; they all want to stop the player achieving her goal. Their function in a game is to offer a player a challenge to overcome, to stop her, and even kill her character.

But it's not that simple. Creating interesting and unique enemies is an art to be mastered. Their ultimate goal is surely to stop the player, but the real question is how they would do that. We'll have a closer look later in this chapter!

Allies

Allies are different from Friends or Assistants because they bond with the player in a different way. They might be your platoon comrades in an FPS game, such as *Battlefield 1*. They're not quite friends or fully developed characters, but they can create a realistic warfare scenario, where the battle is not centered around the player's characters and a multitude of enemies but can develop on different front lines and end up in different scenarios. The emotions connected to allies depend a lot on the player type but they usually evoke some sort of camaraderie. The player could subconsciously adjust her strategy to protect her allies or to pull out some teamwork even in games where the ally's behavior is heavily scripted and doesn't change according to the player's action at all.

Some games, such as *Gears of War*, have made allies a huge part of the core gameplay. In *GoW* support from your allies is crucial to your success and you can even give orders to the team to select the right strategy.

In games such as *Baldur's Gate*, *Neverwinter Nights* or *Dragon Age* the player controls the main character, but also the entire party of adventurers that go with him or her. In these games, the difference between an ally and the protagonist blurs, but the player's emotional attachment to the main character remains very strong.

Boss

A Boss, such as other enemies, offers a challenge to the player and stops her from progressing further. But there's something more about a Boss. They are milestones for the player's journey. They can usually be found at the end of a level or an area, representing a physical turning point.

They also differ from normal minions in terms of the challenge offered. They are more difficult to beat, usually, as they are designed around new and unique mechanics and require the player to master the game mechanics to be able to defeat them. Some of the emotions related to Bosses are Fear, Anticipation, Anger, Surprise, and Fiero.

Some of the most memorable monsters in video games are Bosses. Some games, such as *Dark Souls*, have made bosses one of the pillars of their core design. Some games, such as *Shadow of the Colossus*, have even brought the Boss concept to a higher level, where every enemy you ever encounter is indeed a Boss.

You will learn more about Bosses in the dedicated section of this chapter!

Antagonist or the Villain

Most of the time an antagonist is a Boss; the Final Boss. The ultimate obstacle the player has to face in its journey. Antagonists, unlike bosses, impend over the player's Journey for the whole game, creating a huge anticipation for the final battle and a real sense of hatred and belligerency in the player.

It is very important that an Antagonist has a solid, believable backstory, and you need to make sure the player can have a glimpse of it. More than ever, creating a compelling Antagonist is what can elevate a game to greatness. There are some things to consider when designing a Villain; we'll discuss them later in 'The Bad Guys' section of this chapter.

Hostage

A Hostage (even better if it's a friend or a lover) is a great narrative device to twist things around. Rescuing a hostage can change the pace of a story and even twist the gameplay. Just think about how different a shooting game becomes when the objective shift from *Eliminate all the enemies* to *Save the hostages*. Players may have to change their strategy and play more carefully, as a stray shot or misplaced grenade can result in a critical failure. Hostage rescue is such an interesting gameplay scenario that some games have been designed exclusively around it, such as *Rainbow Six* and *Hostages*.

Vendor

Games that offer the chance to buy or sell goods...usually need some sort of vendor (unless selling and buying goods happens only using an interface). Vendor characters are very popular in RPGs and action games but they are used across all the genres. The concept of the vendor has evolved further in MMOs, where the player can 'hire' a vendor that enable her to sell her stuff to other players even when the player is not online.
Some other games, such as *Dead Space*, have used the vendor character in the form of a robot, justifying the presence of vendor characters in scenarios where the presence of a human seller is not reasonable or realistic. Usually, vendors are also used to create a feeling of home or a safe place where the player can carry out her business away from dangers. If you are creating a city, camp, or settlement, use vendor characters to give them some life!

Quest Giver

Quest givers are similar to vendors. Instead of goods, they trade missions and rewards. They can also offer some insights on the world lore, or give tips to the player. Characters that give side quests, ask for the player's help, or enable new narrative branches are a great addition to many games. They bring the world to life, giving the feeling that the protagonist is not alone in a static world full only of hostile creatures to defeat. They have needs, motivations, stories.

Obviously, there is extensive use of these characters in RPGs. Try to play a few RPGs or MMOs and focus on the characters that give you a quest. Note down what kind of quests they give and how they contribute to the development of the storytelling.

Competitor

The competitor is quite different from an enemy, a boss, or an antagonist. The competitor's motivations can be far from wanting the player dead or stopped. The competitor, usually, has the same goals of the player, and the challenge he poses is to defeat him in the race to this goal.

Examples might be other pilots in a racing game, an opponent team in a sport game, but also an NPC in RPG or action games. Competitors spark the thrill of competition, the frustration of losing, and the Fiero and excitement of succeeding.

```
Exercise
Play some of the games we have mentioned and focus on the characteristics
of each playable character, NPC, and enemy. Can you identify their
functions? Do they belong to any of the categories we have mentioned? Maybe
to a new one?
```

Character Statistics

How can we represent the attributes that make a character different from the others? How can we represent, in game, character's traits we have defined with a written description?

One classic answer is: "With statistics!" (shortened to just Stats). Stats are a numeric representation of aspects of a fictional character (or unit, or building, or even an entire galaxy). The concept of Stat was introduced in pen and paper RPGs, and indeed is extremely popular in RPG video games, but its versatility and universally understandable concept made stats incredibly useful in many other genres.

Stats can be used to represent the physical or mental attributes of a character, such as Health Points (HP), Strength, Resistance, Speed, and Intelligence:

Diablo is famous for the huge amount of stats and part of the experience is to optimize and max them out

Stats don't have to be numbers though. In *The Sims 4*, for example, you can define character attributes by choosing aspirations, which will impact some mechanics in the game. It's worth noting that, under the hood, all these characteristics are still numbers in the game's code. How these numbers are presented to players matters. Not all the players want to look at the amount of stats we have seen in *Diablo*. And not all of them want to spend time making calculations and optimizing their character's numbers. Different audiences expect and enjoy a different level of complexity, and, even more importantly, not all games need to represent the properties of their world with numbers:

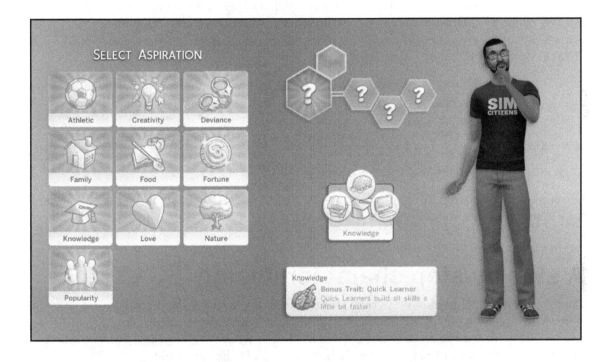

The Sims 4 character creation process includes the choice of a number of aspirations to customize the character and give them some unique in-game bonuses

Using numbers to represent character's attributes is not only simple and immediate; it provides a framework for game balancing. It allows us to compare two characters and determine which one is better than the other.

It allows designers to express mechanics through mathematical formulas. If a character has an HP value and a weapon does a certain amount of damage and they are both expressed in numbers...there will always be a function able to transform the weapon's damage into the HP lost by the player when he got hit. (Usually, the number of damage is **exactly** the number of HP that are detracted).

Even when stats are not represented by numbers, but by adjectives (for example, a character could be *Strong* or *Weak*) there's always a way to translate words or concept in numbers, and as a game designer it's your job to be really comfortable in doing so and using math as much as you can. We will see, later, in `Chapter 13`, *Balancing*, how to use those numbers, but it is not only a matter of balancing. Video games are pieces of software where everything, in the end, is expressed in numbers. When you design a system you should always consider this.

I can never recommend enough rookie game designers to study the basics, such as character creation, by playing *Dungeon & Dragons*. You just need the rulebook, a few dice, a pen, and some sheets of paper.
It's incredible how much you can learn from just creating a D&D character!
If you haven't given it a go yet, just do it!

Ok, enough talking now. We're going do a little design exercise and create a new character for a game you have hopefully played: *Overwatch*.

A step by step character design

Games with multiple heroes are perfect for experimenting and putting to test your design skills. You already have a solid base: an existing game with core mechanics that work. Also, you probably have some ideas about what is lacking or what would make a great addition to any game you like and play a lot...so half of the work is already done!

Read this part very carefully and as soon as you finish, experiment with some character designs for your favorite game. Keep in mind that these sorts of exercises are a very common question asked during job interviews. Always expect to be asked something such as "create a new hero for a game" or "what are you favorite mechanics for this character?" or even "how would you improve this character?"
The more of this you have done while learning game design, the better and more interesting your answers will be!

The steps to design a new character are roughly the following:

- Acquire a deep knowledge of the game
- Write down the design pillars of the game and stick them in a place where you can always see them
- Find out what would be interesting to add in the current balance (or unbalance) of force among the existing characters; what is your character's place in the game world?
- Write a high concept
- Design the character abilities and mechanics
- Define and balance the character's stats
- Prototype
- Iterate
- Final implementation

Keep in mind that all this is done in parallel or by collaborating with the art team. Your job as a game designer is to make a new character that works, regardless of how is going to look like in the end. The high concept and initial concept art always help in defining abilities, weapons, and gear...but your design should be informed by the third step, first and foremost.

Once you find that *sweet spot* for a new character with new compelling abilities and mechanics, no artwork or new concept should take the character off the rails. You don't want to end up with a new sniper when you were designing a character to fill the role of a healer (especially because there's already a character like that!).

Let's analyze each step.

Acquire a deep knowledge of the game

The first step is trivial, but nonetheless extremely important. There is no way you could design some new content for a game if you're not a true expert of it. We already said this and now is a great time to reaffirm it: be an expert of the game you're working on. Understand the problems, the systems, the level design, the strengths and weaknesses of each character, enemies... everything!

Many junior game designers complain that they are asked to have working experience to get game design jobs. There is a way to get that experience without having a job! Deconstruct the games you play, rack up 50+ hours of gameplay and know those games from the inside out. And write it all down.

Can you remember any studying session more fun than this! What a job we have chosen!

However, don't be fooled by the terms *fun* and *play*. Unlike a common video gamer, a professional game designer needs to develop her observation skills and focus on her game analysis much more than simply having fun. My suggestion is obviously to play as many games as possible, but make sure that at least 50% of the time you spend playing is focused on this deconstruction experience and not just playing for the sake of playing.

Write down the design pillars

In order to design new content for a game, you must know what its design pillars are (we won't talk about art pillars, as they are not relevant to this topic). We can't know for sure what they are for *Overwatch*, but we can assume that at the core of the game experience there are things like: teamwork, fluid tridimensional movement, character diversity and uniqueness, and fun to watch.

Everything you design must relate to the pillars. In our case, this means that, obviously, the new character should be unique and diverse, but in a way that makes her (or him) interesting to play in regards to her:

- Movement style
- Specific role and function in the team
- Plus an interesting background that fits with the *Overwatch* universe

Write a high concept

At this point, you should have enough information to write a high concept. It is similar to what you do would do for an entire game, as we have discussed in Chapter 3, *Scoping a Game Project*. Just a few sentences that give an overall idea of what you have in mind.

Examples of some existing characters might work too. Remember, this is an internal document with the goal to explain to artists and developers an idea. So the really important thing is that it does this.

Let's try to write something for our character.

The Princess is a secret agent rumored to have worked in the past with both the Overwatch and the Blackwatch. She's an enigmatic woman, a master spy and infiltrator with a predilection for deceit and sabotage rather than violence and brute force. She has access to an arsenal of ultra-hi-tech gadgets and gears, including a term-optic suit that allows her to blend with the environment and become nearly invisible and infra-sight bugs. She's a mix of James Bond and Major Motoko Kusanagi from Ghost in the Shell.

As you can see, I have used what we have defined for the character to be as a base and then I expanded with a simple narrative that will give me some directions in the next steps. The take away here is that you need to start with something really practical; what kind of character does the game need, mechanically. And then you can start imagining what she's like and what background she has, using this new information to keep going with her abilities, design, and stat balancing.

Of course, there are times where you start with the concept. There are no strict rules about this. Sometimes you might come up with a concept so strong that everything else will come from it.
Or maybe you know you need a number of characters and you start fleshing out their backgrounds and appearance before assigning a specific role or function to each of them.

Define and balance the stats

The great thing about creating a new content for an existing game is that we have a solid starting point.
In *Overwatch*, each character is defined by a set of basic stats (HP..), a weapon, and a set of abilities.
Since we know our character's weapon is going to be a pistol, the first step to define its stats would be to look at every similar weapon available in the game. Once we have our benchmark, we could start balancing this specific weapon against it. We will discuss later in this book how to balance a game (and therefore its smaller pieces, such as weapons or characters).

Weapon

We're going to use all the existing pistol weapons in the game as a benchmark (Wikis online are great tools to quickly find all this kind of information). As we know (because of the concept) that the pistol is going to be some sort of assassin's weapon, we can easily figure out that it should have a suppressor. What would be the suppressor effect in the game? Does it change something from, let's say McCree's revolver?

Let's take a look at what I came up with:

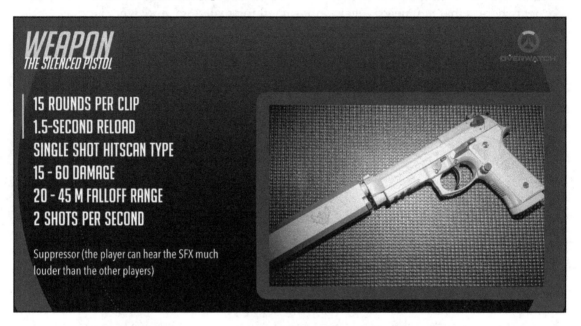

WEAPON
THE SILENCED PISTOL

OVERWATCH

- 15 ROUNDS PER CLIP
- 1.5-SECOND RELOAD
- SINGLE SHOT HITSCAN TYPE
- 15 - 60 DAMAGE
- 20 - 45 M FALLOFF RANGE
- 2 SHOTS PER SECOND

Suppressor (the player can hear the SFX much louder than the other players)

Like the other weapons in the game, our new weapon has the following stats: rounds per clip, reload time, shot type, damage, falloff range, shots per second

Abilities

It is time to design the abilities. We know that every Overwatch character has at least one Primary fire, one to three abilities, and one Ultimate. Sometime they might have a Secondary fire and passive abilities.

We know from the concept that she has to have an invisibility ability.

Are there similar abilities in Overwatch? A few, the most similar is Sombra's Termoptic Camo. So how do we make sure our character relies on that mechanic but feels different? We can obviously play with variables such as duration and cooldown (if it lasts longer, it could have a longer cooldown and vice-versa), but I thought it would feel quite different to balance a longer duration with another mechanic: the more she moves, the less the invisibility is effective, making her more visible as she moves.

The idea here is **to suggest a strategy to use the character with her abilities, strengths, and weaknesses:**

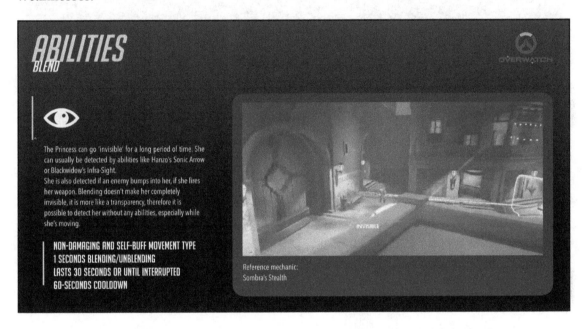

The Princess' 'Blend' ability is designed with an existing ability: Sombra's 'Stealth', which is also used a reference image for the concept document.

I want her to be deadly with her pistol, but not Over Powered (OP), so her passive ability involves a huge skill from the player (to get the bonus damage on the headshots), but she also has an ability to auto-aim for one single headshot:

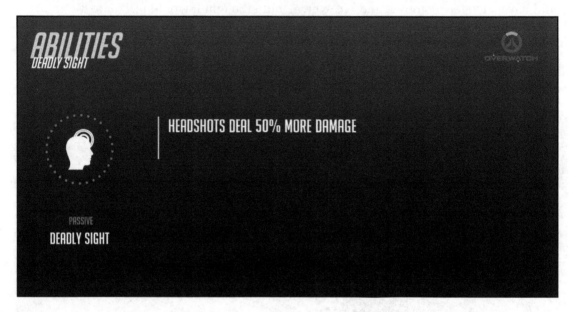

Overwatch's characters might have a Passive ability, one that is automatically used without any input from the player.

The idea here would be to allow a less skilled player to take full advantage of the character's passive ability at least once in a while. At the same time, more skilled players could use the auto-aim at the exact right moment to take out key targets:

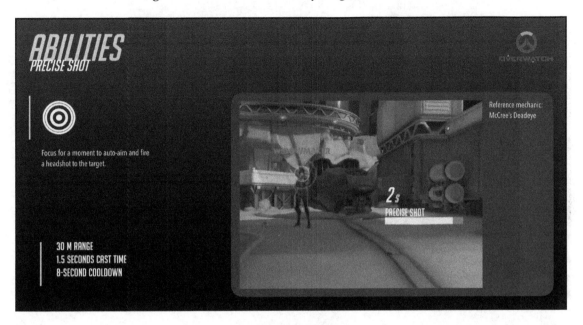

Auto-aiming is a great ability to make a character easier to use. Since it can only be used once every 8 seconds, the player's skill of manually aiming for headshots will still make the difference, but less skilled players can always rely on some help once in a while!

Another interesting ability, 'Mark', would allow for some great team play. This character could cover a very different role if the player plays defensively and alternates her invisibility power with some scouting around the map:

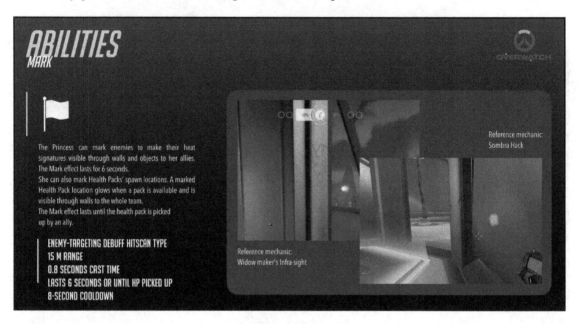

We have discussed how meaningful choices are always fundamental in video games, that's why introducing abilities that allow for more than just one play-style is always a great idea!

And what about her Ultimate ability? Overwatch's ultimates are designed to create epic moments where the tide of a battle can be reverted completely, a 'Wow moment' of great dramatic tension and definitely a lot of fun for the player unleashing them.

As the game is already full of powerful attacks that unleash tons of damage on the unlucky enemy team, I wanted The Princess' ultimate to be a bit different, taking everything she can do with her normal abilities to the next stage. What if she could use her Ultimate to overpower her Blend ability and remain invisible even while attacking and using other abilities...For an insane amount of time?:

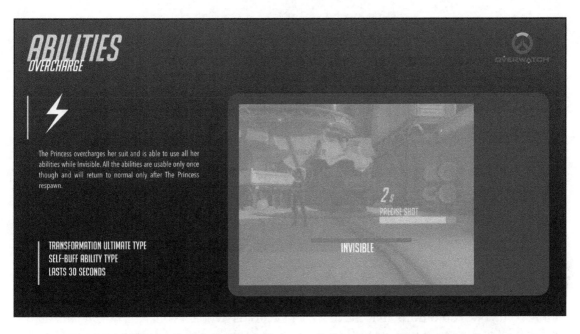

This is the kind of ability that could easily break a game, so let's be clear about this: it's just for the sake of this book...*don't design this at home!*

Yes, this ability definitely sounds too powerful, so how do we counterbalance this? By letting her use her abilities only once after the Ultimate is unleashed. So she would have to take the most out of it and not waste a shot!

Unlike most of the other heroes' Ultimates, this one would allow for a slower type of play, requiring some tactical positioning and a good long-term strategy. Like other Ultimates though, many heroes can easily counter it. Any enemy could easily detect The Princess before she pulls out her diabolic plan, leaving her fully visible...but with all the down-side effects on her normal abilities.

You might have noticed that I put quite an effort in re-creating the Overwatch look & feel in the previous pictures. It doesn't matter if the mechanic is not sketched perfectly, or it is using images from other mechanics (or images of a real pistol which has nothing to do with Overwatch)...as long as it gives an idea of what we're talking about! Remember, a game designer is not a concept artist, so it is not expected to deliver quality sketches or artwork...nonetheless he or she should put any possible effort to deliver its vision. A presentation layer is a powerful tool. The more you master it, the better you will be at your job.

Prototype and iterate

We know this already. Once the design is ready, we need to try it in the game as soon as possible. What works in the designer's head might prove terrible after it's implemented. Mechanics need to be tested and balancing needs to be tested. The earlier issues are found, the easier it will be to go back to the drawing board and fix them.

Iterating, as we have discussed multiple times in this book, is the key to a successful game. Modern game engines and prototyping tools give us no excuse to be too lazy or too confident and just skip to the final implementation.

Unfortunately, we are not able to practically do this and the next steps, as it would require having access to *Overwatch*'s source code...but this is what you'd do in a professional scenario.

Final implementation

At this point, one could think that the designer's work is over. Of course is not. What has been validated in prototyping or testing was sufficient to greenlight a final implementation, but this doesn't mean the new character won't need future re-balancing and some special attention throughout the months following its release.

It might prove to be too weak or too powerful in scenarios the designer had not foreseen, players might find an exploit or simply hate it. When you design something and it makes it to the 'released' stage... you have to play it! There's still a lot you don't know about your creation and how it would interact with the other systems in the game.

The bad guys

We have discussed already that every good story puts the characters in front of some sort of conflict. And nothing is better than the personification of the conflict itself: the bad guys! Villains, monsters, and enemies.

Despite the fact that all these guys intend to kill the player, they serve the higher purpose of letting the player having fun (while he avoids being killed).

But the question is, how are the bad guys designed?

The answer, as often happens in game design, is not a simple one and depends on the type of game we're talking about. Simple enemies, in the same way as the other characters, exist to exert a function. Villains and Bosses do that too, but they also need to be memorable and as interesting as the main characters. Games with deeper narratives rely on well-constructed villains to oppose the protagonist, while more arcade and less narrative heavy games need enemies that offer a challenging focus on the gameplay.

Types of Villains

There are two kinds of villain a player can face:

- Story Villains: A story villain is the kind of antagonist we usually find in books or movies. His function is to drive the story forward, to give the protagonist the motivation to keep going and stop him, to create a dramatic conflict both physical and psychological. Some examples of memorable story villains are The Origami Killer from *Heavy Rain*, Big Boss from *Metal Gear*, and Jon Irenicus in *Baldur's Gate 2*.
- Boss Villains: A boss villain is more focused on the gameplay challenge it poses to the player. It is the boss in *Dark Soul*, Bowser in *Super Mario* or Diablo in...well *Diablo*. They exist to challenge the player to use and master the game mechanics in order to beat them.

Clearly, some Story Villain might also offer the challenge typical of Boss Villains, but what really makes them different is the type of the game they're in and their depth as a character. Like a protagonist, a story villain has his own motivations, backstory, and goals. The less stereotyped they are, the better it is. They're not pure evil entities that act for the sake of evil. From their point of view, they are the real heroes. They think about the protagonist as someone that doesn't understand they are doing the right thing. This is what makes them interesting. Players might even relate to them!

On the other hand, Boss villains can be more stereotyped or driven by more visceral motivations. Even with interesting backstories, they don't evolve as characters in the game and that's totally fine! Just make sure you have the right villain for the game you're creating!

Types of enemies

Of course, villains are the main dish. But what would be a game without the common enemies the player has to heroically defeat one after the other, making his way guns blazing or sword swinging?

Well actually, *Shadow of the Colossus* is a fantastic example of a game where there are no common enemies, but only bosses. But that's an exception and is part of what makes it an extraordinary game.

Generally speaking, a game with enemies needs common enemies. Creating enemies is one of the design activities I enjoy the most. Inspiration can come from anywhere, depending on what kind of game you're doing. Enemies can be soldiers from a hostile faction, monsters, aliens, robots, cannibal plants...the only limit is your imagination!

One of my favorite resources when it comes to enemy design, again, is a *Dungeons & Dragons* manual. It's called the 'Monster Manual' and it contains hundreds of fantasy monsters, each with amazing illustrations, rules, abilities, and lore (based on the *D&D* setting). It is not important if your game is about realistic modern warfare or set in a sci-fi world. The lessons in this book are beyond the nature of the monsters it describes:

Dungeons & Dragons monster's manual: a treasure of information for the enemy and monster design.

What we're going to do is try to categorize some enemy archetypes based on their behavior, functions, and characteristics.

Let's have a look at some classics.

Chaser/Aggressor

This is the most common type of enemy. As soon as the player is in sight, its only objective activates: to kill him. It will chase and attack the player by any means possible until one or the other is dead. You can find this type of enemy in very complex games, such as MMOs (where they decide who to attack depending on how aggressive they are and how much of threat the players nearby are), or it can be more static, like the alien ships in *Space Invaders*.

Patroller

The patroller is an enemy that moves within a pre-determined area. Once the player steps into the area, the patroller can either keep moving regardless of the player presence (such as the Goombas in *Super Mario*) or change its behavior, reacting to the player presence (for example, shooting or chasing the player, as with the guards in *Metal Gear Solid*).

It's important to note that the whole point of the patroller is that it follows a **movement pattern** that the player can memorize in order to plan its actions.

Guard

A guard is similar to a patroller, but its function is to guard a particular object or space. While the patroller might just move back and forth within a space, or transform into a chaser as soon as it spots the player, the Guard's goal is not exclusively to kill the player. So it might prefer to leave the player alone in the case the chase brings him too far away from the place/object it was originally guarding.

Shooter

A shooter is an enemy that keeps his distance from the player and targets her with some sort of ranged weapon. Shooters can shoot regardless of the player's presence (like in some old platform games) or can react to the player's presence. A shooter's behavior can be a subsequent state of a Guard or Patroller. A shooter might be positioned in a particular position, maybe behind a cover - in that case, we talk about a sniper. Snipers are interesting because they force the player to think. Usually shooting them back is very difficult and dangerous, so the player would need to move from his favorite spot and find a way to get around the sniper.

Swarm

Swarming enemies are usually very weak enemies that wouldn't pose any threat to the player if taken alone. Usually, there are many of them and they behave like chasers.

Cannon Fodder

Contrary to the swarming enemies, "Cannon Fodder" is not dangerous even in large groups. They exist to focus the attention of the player, letting him have some easy fun defeating enemies without the risk of losing or being in real danger.

Tank

A tank enemy is able to absorb and sustain the player's attacks for a longer period of time. In case the tank is supporting other types of enemies, it is able to increase the level of threat sensibly, as the player won't be able to get rid of smaller enemy quick enough while the tank is providing cover.

Enemy behaviors and stats

We have defined types of enemies by their behaviors. What about their stats?

We're going to delve much deeper into this later in the book, in `Chapter 13`, *Balancing*, where we'll see how the stats, abilities, and mechanics of enemies are heavily influenced by their function. It is quite intuitive that a Tank type is going to have higher HP or armor values than a Cannon Fodder enemy. A chaser might move much faster than other enemies (and even than the player), but it could lack a ranged attack, or it could be extremely vulnerable to certain attacks.

The whole point here is to identify the enemy's functions and the reasons why it is needed in a particular game level or area. That should always be the first step in designing an effective enemy.

Enemies exist to entertain the player

If a game is based on fighting enemies, make sure the fighting is actually awesome! Animations, visual and sound effects, rewards...all should be tied to fighting and defeating the enemies. There must be a point in fighting them. They must be challenging, but in a way that is fun. If they always outsmart the player, never miss a shot, or always execute the optimal strategy...how could that be fun?

Again, we're going to talk more about this when we'll see how to balance games, but in this chapter, it is important that you understand that enemies in a video game are just a tool for enabling fun. Even in a game such as *Dark Souls*, based on extremely challenging enemies, where the promise is that 'the player will die', enemies are meticulously designed to offer a great experience...once the player has learned how to kill them!
Games such as *Dead Space* have put great effort not only into the enemy design but also into how the player can actually kill them. Different weapons produce different results while aiming at different body parts can disable a leg or a weapon and therefore allow for micromanagement of the combat strategy.

Always design enemies and their systems with a clear vision of their interaction with the players. And give extra attention to their final moment, the one where the player triumphs over the challenge their posing. This has to be great, even for the simplest little creature.

Diversity

I think it is important to spend a few words about diversity in video games. Historically, video games and the games industry, in general, have a problem with the lack of diversity. With few exceptions, most of the protagonist characters are white males. When they are women, they are too often sexualized (Lara Croft is a great character...but we all remember her physique in the first batch of *Tomb Raider* games). When they are homosexual, they are stereotyped, like their sexuality has anything to do with defining what they do and how they act. When they are of different ethnicity, it seems they're there like *tokens*, present just to say 'hey, this game has a non-white Caucasian character!':

The *Overwatch* heroes: each character comes from a different part of the world and represents a different cultural background.

There are no guidelines or design practices for this. This is just a matter of sensibility and willingness to explore different cultures, characters, and scenarios in video games. It's the creator's responsibility to move away from the concept that a white male macho-man or a bombshell action girl would sell more and attract more players.

Equally, just putting a *diverse* character into the game because *we need diversity* would only have the effect of highlighting the ridiculous attempt. The idea here would be not to have to talk about diversity at all, as all these different characters should reflect what is actually just normal in our modern society.

Diversity is not a status quo or a question like *is everyone represented in this game?* All the characters should make sense in the story and the game, with no pre-conceptions about their gender, physical or mental disabilities, sexuality, or ethnicity. All the stereotypes should be left out of your game.

Take your time to play some games like *Hellblade: Senua's Sacrifice*, *Persona 4*, *Life is Strange*, *Overwatch* (yes, look at *Overwatch's* characters a bit closer!), *Remember Me* or Telltale's *The Walking Dead*. Think about this very carefully. You, as a creator, have the chance to make a real contribution to this massive issue of the entertainment industry.

 The screenshots used in this chapter are for illustrative purposes only. We do not recommend that you to misuse these in any way. For more information, please consult the terms and conditions of the publishers mentioned in the *Disclaimer* section of this book.

Summary

We have seen how to create interesting characters and give them a specific function in the game world, whether they are playable characters, NPCs, or enemies. You learned how to define a character through a system of numerical stats, abilities, or a control system. We have walked through a playable character design process and put together a pretty cool new Overwatch hero! We also took a closer look at what makes enemies interesting and villains memorable. Their motivations, backstory, and points of view on the game world.

Finally, we made some important considerations about the concept of diversity and how important it is, in our modern society, to keep that in mind as a part of our creative process. We're close to the end of the second part of this book, the content creation.

Next and final stop: User Interface and User Experience!

11
User Interface and User Experience

In this chapter, we'll introduce you to the basics of **User Interface** (**UI**) and **User Experience** (**UX**) design—a complex craft that often blends art, animation, graphic design, and visual effects with game design itself.

While most professional teams have a dedicated artist taking care of the UI/UX side of the product, it's imperative for any game designer that they learn the principles of designing interfaces and polishing the end-user experience.

Even in a large, well-staffed development team, game designers will have to work side by side with the UI/UX specialists to plan and create interfaces and experiences that are informative, empowering, and delightful to interact with. So, without further ado, let's begin!

User Experience

User Experience refers to a person's overall perception, emotional response, and attitude towards the use of a particular product or system. In the context of game development, UX can encompass anything that affects the overall feel of the game with exception to the rule set and game content. In practice, UX translates into input mechanisms (controls), menu and interaction flows, interface animations and sound effects, camera systems, and game feedback.

Player input

The design and execution of input methods (that is, *controls*) can make or break your game. In this day and age, players expect the developer to adhere to a set of *gold standards* in the input department. For this exact reason, platform holders such as Sony, Nintendo, and Microsoft have created their own set of guidelines to ensure that platform-specific input methods and control functions (that is, how to pause the game) are adhered to.

Nowadays, console action games are almost certain to use the *left analog stick* to move and *right stick* to look around, while PC ones are sure to use *WSAD* keys for movement, mouse to look and *Spacebar* to vault or jump over obstacles. Regardless of game genre, using anything but *Esc* to enter the pause menu on PC can be seen as a cardinal sin.

Although the majority of your controls are not influenced by the platform holder, going against well-established paradigms is a very risky move. Try to give your players a way to modify and personalize their controls, but remember, the default settings are unlikely to be changed by most players. If your default controls are hard to use and unintuitive, you run a real risk of frustrating the audience to a point of leaving the game—no matter how extensive your control options are.

It's more than likely that the games you'll work on come with a strong reference in the controls department (a similar game in your genre), and a set of player expectations (well-established paradigms). Innovation is where things become much more difficult. Novel control methods should be well-justified by innovative mechanics that cannot be effectively expressed with a familiar and well-established control mapping. That is, unless you're planning on focusing your entire game on having the players try to master the controls, as seen in games like the old flash-hit *QWOP* and the hilarious *Surgeon Simulator*.

The principles of ergonomic design (be it of objects, processes, or spaces) revolve around maximizing the productivity of the users and minimizing their fatigue and discomfort. When applied to video game controls, these rules can be summed up with the following statement:

Ergonomic controls are easy to execute in the most common context.

A single key or button press is easy enough on its own. However, pressing *P* while controlling your character with *WSAD* keys and the mouse requires you to stop and lift your hand, and therefore, is not an ergonomic solution.

Actions that require multiple inputs (double taps) or more than one finger to execute are harder to pull off and memorize. This includes specific modifiers such as holding *Alt*, *Shift*, *Ctrl*, or a *trigger* on a gamepad.

Well executed controls match the expected paradigm (for example, pressing *R* to reload in a shooter) and are easy to perform (no need for compound controls). They also shouldn't make us fight our instincts (a practice is known as natural mapping), for example, **holding** a button to **release** something in-game always feels a bit off.

When considering controls and input mechanisms, it helps to list your game mechanics in order of priority and frequency of use. Afterward, go through the list and assign the most ergonomic and fitting actions to the most important and frequently used mechanics first. Following that, any actions that do not need to be performed quickly and efficiently (turning a flashlight, opening the inventory or map screen) can be put on inputs that are less accessible.

Use control prompts if you can afford the space! Control prompts such as press *[E] to Open Door* do not need to end with your tutorial. Unintrusive but persistent on-screen control prompts can be incredibly useful throughout a player's lifecycle. What's obvious to you (or a seasoned player) may not be obvious to someone who picks up the game after a year, especially if you map a whole array of obscure keys to a laundry list of actions.

Control types

When designing your controls, it's important to understand the differences and implications of different input types available on your target platform.

Digital input

This is the most basic input type, capable of returning one of two states, active (1) or inactive (0). A simple example of digital input lies in the keys of a standard computer keyboard. A single key can either be pressed or not pressed at all, there's no other state in between.

Analog input

Analog input can return one or more continuous values. The most popular example would be an *analog stick* found on any modern console controller. When a stick is tilted, the controller tracks separate values for up/down and left/right positions as well as the degree of the tilt. The formatting could look like this: (0, -1) for a stick that's turned left all the way, (-0.5, 0.3) for a stick that's tilted down halfway and 30% to the right. This allows for more subtle and natural control over things like movement or cursor speed.

Just because the controller grants you access to continuous states does not mean you should always use them. You could program the game to detect simple *up* and *down* states based on a single value, a tilt of 75% to 100% in Y-axis would be used for up and -75% to -100% for down. The zone between -75% and 75% is a so-called **dead zone** where the input is deemed insignificant and ignored. In this case, you're essentially turning analog input into digital input.

Complex analog input

Some controllers offer features like motion and position tracking, giving you access to very complex information. A *simple shake* of the controller would result in the creation of a set of *vectors* that track the speed, direction, and acceleration of the movement in all three axes as well as (for more advanced, camera-enabled systems) the starting and ending position in 3D space.

Designing motion controls can be a very complex process that requires close cooperation with a highly-skilled programmer. Compound motion controls (such as doing a figure of 8) are very hard to implement in a way that works reliably for most players and devices. Unless you're working on a motion controlled or virtual reality game and have a team of very experienced programmers, it's advisable to avoid motion controls (and especially complex ones) for core gameplay mechanics. You can, however, try to use the *accelerometer* for cosmetic effects. For example, by making the background of your user interface move as you tilt your mobile device (thus creating an illusion of depth).

Touch screen controls

Some modern touchscreens are capable of tracking as many as 10 individual points of contact. Nevertheless, a simple set of single-finger taps and swipes can usually get you a long way. It's recommended to not rely on more than 4 fingertips as going above that number increases the chances of misinterpreting the input and reduces the number of compatible devices. A touch interface can provide you with:

- A unique ID for each contact point.
- The origin of contact (starting position).
- Current position.
- Change in position and time since last update (used to track movement).

- Status since the last frame (touch started, moved, stationary, released and canceled):
    - Cancellation can happen if more than 5 inputs are detected simultaneously or the device detects being put next to the user's ear (light sensor and position tracking).
- The *intensity* of the touch, which only works on a select few devices that support *3D Touch* or equivalent technology. This feature allows you to distinguish between regular touch input and *force touch*, where the screen has been pressed in a more significant matter.

Similarly to motion controls, you need to tread with great care when integrating complex touch behaviors. Utilizing simple taps, swipes, drags, and pinches or following a pattern on the screen is all very easy and natural, but asking the user to use multiple fingers and *3D Touch* without clear prompts is a recipe for disaster. There's no such thing as a *simple 4-finger pinch*. You may also want to discard any touch input that's too close to the currently active one, as a single finger can sometimes be read as two. It's common practice to manipulate *interactive areas* (hitboxes) of actors or buttons to make them bigger/smaller than their in-game artwork would suggest, making them easier/harder to tap on.

Camera systems

In-game camera is one of the most important interfaces between the player and the game world. A well-designed camera exhibits behaviors and settings that not only help to inform the player but also highlight what's important and improve the player's ability to interact with the game.

There are multiple camera types and perspectives. A game can use a single camera with a fixed setting or switch between different cameras and settings depending on the context.

To create a perfect camera system, you'll often have to work closely with the rest of your team, merging game design goals with technical solutions (intelligent camera focus and pathfinding) and an elusive artistic sensitivity (focused around framing, angles, and transitions).

Let's dive into the complexities of camera design by analyzing different camera types and perspectives.

Camera types

Selection of a camera type often happens on a subconscious level; you simply imagine the game being played one way or another. That said, it's important to acknowledge the reasons behind a particular camera type and remain open to alternatives. By switching from a manual to static or tracking camera one could find a brand new way of presenting the game, reshaping the experience and potentially spawning an entirely new sub-genre of games. Don't be afraid to experiment!

Static

Simple, stationary cameras are used in many games where the game board is entirely contained on the screen such as *Tetris*. There are games that use a series of static cameras and toggle between them as needed. Examples of such systems can also be found in old semi-3D games such as the first *Resident Evil*, which often relied on pre-rendered backdrops. Controlling an avatar in 3D space with fixed cameras that often switch angles is particularly challenging and should be avoided:

In *Resident Evil 1*, ambiguous angles and disconnection between the camera and the character made for difficult controls

Interestingly enough, the effect of static cameras on 2D spaces is entirely opposite, and games like *Super Meat Boy* are a testament to the increased precision one can get from removing camera movement in a 2D environment.

Static cameras are also a very popular choice for puzzle games and mobile titles, where the free-form mouse, touch, and drag inputs are reserved for interactions with the game world and not camera operation. A static camera can also provide a natural parallel to interacting with a fictional workspace or computer interface, as seen in *Her Story,* where the player solves a murder case by operating an old computer.

Taking the static camera to the limit and restricting yourself to one screen can act as a limitation that fosters creativity in level design, and makes the game easier to grasp for the casual audience (not having to move the camera around lowers the cognitive load).

Manual camera

Not attached to any actor, with players being in control of the camera work in varying degrees, including:

1. Two or three-dimensional movement panning the camera as well as zooming in and out
2. Pivot (horizontal rotation)
3. Pitch (angle to the ground or the subject, vertical rotation)

Manual cameras can be found in many strategy games. Some, such as *Black & White,* allow the player to pivot and pitch the camera freely with little limitations. Others, such as *StarCraft 2,* restrict the controls to simple two-dimensional movement (west, east, north, south), zooming in and out.

Restricting the camera pitch and pivot controls can be done to prevent players from getting lost and disoriented by selecting angles that limit playability. Without limitations, players could not only look straight up into the sky but also flip the view of the game world upside down (by adjusting the pitch more than 180 degrees).

A restricted camera can also be designed to automatically adjust certain settings such as pitch. For example, zooming in can lower the pitch to create a more cinematic angle, while zooming out could tilt the camera towards a more tactical, top-down perspective:

In *StarCraft 2*, the camera pitch shifts towards a more side-on angle as you zoom in

Tracking camera

Tracking cameras allow your players to enjoy big playable spaces without the burden of having to manually adjust the framing. Depending on gameplay and portrayed actors, the camera will either follow a single character, a point between multiple characters, or simply focus on the action itself and drag the players along:

1. **Following the actor**: This is the default option for presenting character driven gameplay, from platform games to third person shooters and racing games. Moving the avatar moves the camera—simple, elegant, and effective.

2. **Following the action**: An entirely autonomous first-person camera was often used in old arcade shooters such as *Virtua Cop* and *House of the Dead*. A camera that's *on-rails* sets the pacing and leaves little agency to the players who are simply taken in for a ride. On the other hand, we have third-person action games such as *God of War* and *Bayonetta* that feature semi-autonomous cameras that follow the character's journey across the environment but *aren't directly attached* to it. This design choice caters to the fast and jerky actions and complex encounters with a multitude of enemies coming from all sides. A semi-autonomous camera also allows for some very cinematic moments. There are also games that only use a semi-autonomous camera in some of their multiplayer modes, in order to portray all players on the same screen. From *Super Smash Bros* and *Micro Machines* to *Super Mario 3D World*, the camera will either follow the leader of a race who dictates the tempo or try to zoom out to keep all actors visible at the same time.

The decision on what to track is an important one as it dictates the pace and framing of the action. A degree of autonomous behavior can let players focus on pure execution of gameplay mechanics, but it also opens up the possibility of time-consuming implementation and case-by-case adjustments. If players cannot adjust the camera themselves, you need to make sure they're always offered the optimal view of the action.

Compound Camera

Sometimes, a single solution does not cover the entirety of available gameplay scenarios. A compound camera is one that defaults to one of the above solutions but allows players to tweak or alter its behavior. This gives us two distinct options:

1. **A tracking camera that can be manually adjusted or taken control over:**
   Found in many 3D action adventure games that do not depend on ranged combat or platformers such as Super Mario Galaxy. Such a camera requires no agency until players are required to take aim or identify an area of interest that's outside of their current view.

2. **Manual camera with lock-on or focus options:**
   Fast paced close-quarters combat inside a 3D space can make aiming very tricky. The camera lock-on system allows you to track a chosen enemy target and aims your attacks in their direction. The lock-on camera is an essential element of combat mechanics in games such as *Dark Souls* and *The Legend of Zelda: Ocarina of Time*. On a side note, I've met designers that call lock-on systems an outcome of bad camera design and controls, but most players accept this solution without questioning it (especially if your combat is about timing and positioning, and not analyzing angles between characters on screen).
   As for camera focus, it's a mechanic that can be found in games such as *Gears of War* and *The Last of Us*, where players are sometimes prompted to press a button to move their camera towards a point of interest (something that's relevant to the story or player's current objective). Players are free to *focus* their view for a few seconds, take a quick glimpse, or ignore the point of interest completely. You can never be sure if they followed the hint, but at least you don't take away their controls and interrupt them rudely with a cutscene.

Viewing perspectives

Similarly to camera type, the viewing perspective is often subconsciously set in your brain from the very first moment you think of the game being played.

It's good to be aware of the implications of the perspective of your choosing, and question whether it's the best choice, or if there are alternatives you should prototype. A new perspective can result in a completely different feel and create space for previously unavailable game mechanics.

As pictured by the tower defense genre, changing the camera can lead to a vastly different gameplay experience. From the left: *Fieldrunners, Dungeon Defenders, Sanctum*

First person

We live our lives in first person perspective, and thanks to the depth perception provided by a set of forward-facing eyes, we can judge distance accurately and navigate the three-dimensional world with ease. However, the most natural viewing perspective is not necessarily the easiest to control…

First person games started simple, with slow-paced dungeon crawlers and keyboard only shooters such as *Wolfenstein 3D*. But not long after, the addition of mouse controls and the prevalence of strafing, jumping, and ducking made things much more complicated for the players:

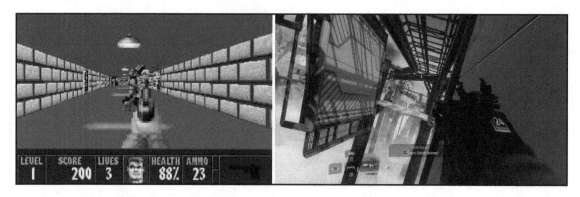

The steady movements of *Wolfenstein 3D* (1992) stand in stark contrast to the highly vertical action of *Titanfall 2* (2017), filled with sliding, wall-running, and grappling hooks

For many casual gamers, learning to move the character and camera separately comes with great difficulty. Contrary to what we *gamers* tend to believe, it's neither simple nor natural. Moreover, fast-paced first person games are known to cause dizziness in a portion of the population. Take these factors into consideration if the audience you're creating for is not very experienced with first person games.

On the plus side, first person perspective puts players right into the middle of the action, creating some of the most immersive experiences (a natural fit for virtual reality). First person cameras are also simple to implement and tweak. And if you're working on a single player title, you could save a lot of time by reducing or eliminating the need for character modeling and animation.

Third person

We'll now explore the wide range of third person cameras where players become an external observer, looking at the game and its world through the portal of the screen.

You could be a god, an army commander or a ZOO manager looking down at their creation. You might be in control of Nathan Drake or Mario, but you do not experience the world through their eyes. You embody a camera floating around in thin air, always close, yet somehow detached from the avatar on screen.

Third person perspective excels in storytelling. A single framing can effectively convey complex interactions between any number of characters and the world they inhabit. No wonder it's arguably the most popular perspective in art and visual media, from graphic novels to theatre, movies, and of course games.

In video games, there are countless iterations of third person cameras to choose from. We tend to narrow down the classification of **Third Person Perspective** (TPP) towards the classic *over the shoulder* games like Tomb Raider, but in fact, we have to consider any perspective that isn't first person. Let's go into the details of the most popular variants!

Behind an Avatar
There are many reasons why cameras positioned behind or over the shoulder of an in-game character are so popular. By exiting the first person perspective, we open the possibilities of extensive characterization through avatar's visual design, customization, and animation. Despite not being in the dead-center of the action, we quickly establish a powerful link between ourselves and the character. The epic on-screen adventures might not happen to me, but they do happen to Lara Croft, and in this world, I am Lara Croft.

Gameplay wise, since we see the actors, we can switch control between multiple characters with ease, something that's harder to pull off in first person games. Moreover, having the camera detached from the character gives us the ability to peek behind corners and cover, and spot dangers and obstacles around/behind our character. This increases our situational awareness and brings it a bit closer to the standard we have in real-life. The nauseating effects of first person perspective are also reduced as the camera moves less erratically and doesn't bob (move up and down) with each step. Interacting with the environment and engaging in full-body movements is also much clearer when the whole character is visible on screen, from vaulting above obstacles to pulling crates and casting spells.

As with everything, there are some downsides to keep in mind. For one, you may need to add complex character animations that could be omitted if you were making a single player game in first person, or if the camera was pulled further away. Moreover, you might need to either be very careful with the level design or invest considerable programming effort into ensuring that the camera behaves correctly in cramped environments. Low ceilings, narrow rooms and layers of obstacles such as tree branches will all make your camera struggle. In combat, having the main character occupy the middle of the screen can get in the way of aiming, forcing you to offset the view to the side (as seen in *Uncharted* and modern *Tomb Raider* games.).

Top Down
Top down perspective is a perfect fit for any game that relies on two-dimensional planning and 360-degree horizontal visibility, making it a popular choice for fast-paced arcade action games, dungeon crawlers, strategy, and management titles. While it may struggle with accurately reflecting height, a top down camera can offer a clear view of countless actors and obstacles with little to no obstruction. Even the most complex buildings and mazes suddenly become easy to navigate floorplans.

Nowadays, a truly top down perspective is rare. Most 3D games opt to tilt the camera while 2D ones cheat with the perspective and show a side-skewed view of the actors and/or the world. This means that characters are rarely reduced to uninspiring sets of heads and shoulders.

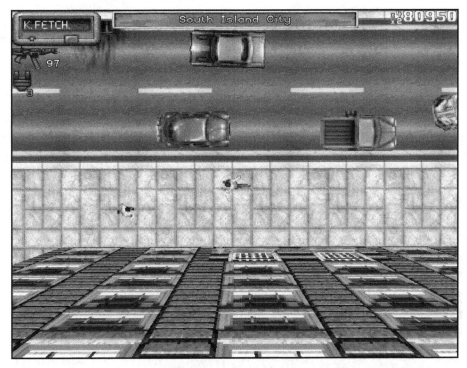

The first *Grand Theft Auto* augmented its top-down camera with an illusion of depth provided by angled building faces

Isometric

In the context of video games, isometric camera refers to a form of two dimensional, axonometric projection (an orthographic projection with an oblique angle but without any perspective). It is a viewpoint that allows to more effectively exhibit depth in a 2D space and create a three-dimensional effect, something that's hard to do in a purely top-down perspective or side view.

Isometric projection can easily be associated with some of the most memorable PC games of the 1990s. This view was applied en-masse to role-playing games like *Fallout* or *Baldur's Gate*, and dominated the huge strategy and simulation genres, from *Age of Empires* to *Simcity 2*.

As we write this book, a set of easily accessible 3D engines is dominating the market, and yet, isometric perspective is alive and well. In fact, isometric games are arguably some of the most popular ones on the planet... After all, casual titles like *Farmville* and *Clash of Clans* were able to easily attract millions of players into their isometric worlds.

Creating high-quality isometric art can be very time-consuming and pose a significant challenge to an inexperienced artist. To help with the process, an artist can either used advanced perspective settings or even 3D tools to model, rotate and export the assets.

Side view

By restricting movements to two dimensions, side view cameras can present an easy to read environment that's not unlike what we see with our own eyes—our world may not be flat, but it's definitely easier to read from the side than from the top. Platformers and fighting games can benefit greatly from more predictable character movements, distances and jump curves. Easy to read contours, angles and environments can also be infused with simple to understand 2D physics, spawning a genre of physics games from *Angry Birds* to *Worms*.

Some games opt to forego some of these benefits in order to infuse their side projections with elements of depth. This can be seen in old 2D adventure games such as *The Secret of Monkey Island* as well as many side-scrolling beats 'em ups:

Trine effectively merges 2D gameplay and physics with 3D assets creating a *2.5D* platformer

Depending on the mechanics and structure of the game you're making, the benefits of using a side view camera can turn into shortcomings. Restricted movement equals somewhat restricted exploration. The *surface level* can get disproportionately insignificant, meaning a big chunk of navigation will result in either climbing or digging. Some games like *Terraria* and *Spelunky* have managed to find ways around the problem with a myriad of navigational tools (ladders, ropes, grappling hooks, jetpacks, and so on), but gravity can often get in the way of your players exploring the environment.

Choosing camera settings

The pitch, field of view, and distance are three key components of any camera. They have to be set and possibly adjusted during gameplay to fit the context and tempo of the game.

The default horizontal field of view should be set depending on the predicted distance from the screen and its size. The closer the players are to the screen and the larger it is, the higher the in-game FOV (field of view) can be. This is due to the screen occupying a proportionally broader angle of your actual vision. If we wanted to create a perfect *window* into the game world we'd need to match the FOV to the angle between the player's eyes and the borders of the screen, and in most cases, we'd end up with a very narrow view space. Fortunately for us, most players are accustomed to slightly higher FOVs, but we still need to make device and platform specific considerations. For example, first person shooters on consoles operate with a horizontal FOV of around 60-65 degrees as players tend to sit far away from the TV. On PC, on the other hand, players sit much closer and thus the FOV should default to 80-90 (and allow for that setting to be raised even higher). As a result, the PC players will see more of the action to the left and right, but the contents of the screen will seem a bit further away (and perhaps even appear distorted). Moreover, if you were to play a console shooter while sitting close to the screen, you could experience a feeling of *tunnel vision* and dizziness, as 90 degrees of your natural field of vision translate to only 60 degrees in the game.

On another note, the larger the FOV, the more processing power you'll use on rendering geometry each frame—always something to keep in mind!

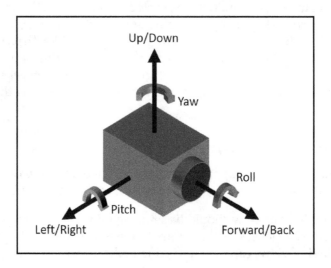

It's helpful to understand the language of camera movement in 3D space

Most modern action games adjust the camera depending on actions performed by the player. A wide, zoomed out camera helps with fast-paced navigation and split decision making, showcasing a larger portion of geometry and the threats and opportunities around the player. For actions that require precision, such as aiming, an alternative camera setting comes into play, with lower field of view, a closer (zoomed-in) state, and possibly a lowered camera control sensitivity.

Horizontal and vertical planes can be easily transferred to the flat planes of our screens, but without VR or stereoscopic 3D technology, depth perception becomes a real challenge. Both of our eyes have to take in the same information, making platforming in third person games a huge challenge. Players can easily misjudge jump distances and have difficulties in aligning themselves with small objects (think of Mario trying to hit a [?] block suspended in mid-air). To help alleviate that, you can raise your camera and pitch it down towards the ground. This will help in assessing the distance between objects. Just be aware that while a more *top-down* perspective can help with horizontal navigation, it lowers the overall vision radius and impedes vertical perception (height).

Depth perception matters more up close (especially in melee combat) than it does at a distance, where its significance is reduced. In first person shooters, aiming at erratically moving enemies who are far away is more of a 2D exercise of aligning the aim with the target, and less of an activity involving spatial awareness. Bring the enemy much closer and you'll realize how much more difficult the combat scenario can get, as players are forced to consider distance and movement speeds in all three dimensions.

 You need to select the camera perspective based on the game mechanics and distance to action. Do not force an up close camera angle if you require players to be aware of what's happening around them. On the other hand, if you want them to more comfortably engage with targets at great distances, a closer camera can help with aiming.

Once you settle on the distance and field of view, it's important to adjust the framing. The default camera settings should focus the camera on what's most relevant to the player's immediate decision making. If players follow a single avatar, you do not need to make it a centerpiece that obscures the most important parts of the screen. There are better places to showcase your character art, be it menu screens, cutscenes, or even a garage (if your avatar is a vehicle). Focus on what changes the most, that is, the environment and the challenges it poses.

Point the camera towards the objective and you'll help guide the players without a single word or a path marker. For this exact reason, in *Super Mario Bros*, the camera always starts offset—with the character standing on the left side of the screen, facing right. From the very first moment, the flow of action is natural.

In the end, you may find that no single camera setting fits every action and situation in your game. Fortunately, there are several solutions, some of which can be combined:

- **Put players in control**: Allow players to pitch the camera, zoom in and out and maneuver it freely.
- **Switch between cameras based on context**: For example, moving into cover or getting the gun out immediately changes the view for one that suits the scenario. For example, by putting our main character to the side so they do not get in the way of aiming.

- **Develop environmentally aware camera**: This can be complex, but ultimately would let the camera decide on the pitch and distance based on player's surroundings. If the player enters a cramped space, the camera is brought in and behind the character (or even transitions into first person view). If the scene features many ledges and jumps in an open space, the camera is pulled out to show more of the terrain.
- **Let the level designer adjust the settings**: This is a technically simpler, but perhaps more labor-intensive way of handling an environmentally driven camera. A set of camera tools can be provided to the level designer. With these tools, the designer can define unique camera presets and place special areas or in-game triggers, which are invisible to the player and activate different camera settings.

Some of the more advanced, environment and context aware camera features are now being supported by modern game engines. For example, the free *Cinemachine* plugin for *Unity 3D*.

No matter what you decide to do, sometimes you'll need to take away the controls and show something that simply cannot be missed. Even wordless cutscenes that simply slide the camera to the object of interest can be invaluable. Adding black *cinematic bars* to the top and bottom parts of the screen may seem cheesy, but nowadays, players are predisposed to sit back and enjoy the cutscene the moment they see them.

Unskippable cutscenes are a cardinal sin, especially if there's no checkpoint/autosave immediately after one. However, accidentally skipping a relevant part of the story is another threat altogether. There are few ways to safeguard against this. First of all, try putting a 2-step confirmation to skip any cutscene, where first input shows a *Press [key] to skip cutscene.* tip and requires a specific action. Secondly, and especially if you have no 2-step process, make sure that skipping is not possible during the first few seconds of a cutscene; this way input from the gameplay phase won't accidentally skip a cutscene someone's keen to see.

Feedback

Games are interactive systems full of interconnected rules and elements. Clearly communicating the results of interactions and the changing state of the game is what feedback is all about. As a rule of thumb, if the player doesn't realize that things are happening, they might as well not have happened at all.

Well incorporated feedback will make your game easier to understand and make for a more satisfying experience. Remember, we're making games, not corporate banking apps; the feedback systems you create can be a source of pure, visceral fun.

There's a wide variety of tools to tap into:

- **UI feedback**: A well-designed interface reacts promptly and clearly to every single input (keystrokes, button presses, tapping, clicking, and so on) as well as to more subtle states such as highlighting objects before input confirmation (for example, cursor hover states, pressing without release). If an action is invalid in the current context, it still deserves a response—either via abstract negative feedback (for example, by using red coloring and *stop sign* iconography) or by communicating the failure with an on-screen text prompt (for example, *You can't use weapons within city gates*). Explaining **why** things don't work can be as useful as providing feedback to successful interactions. Another role of UI feedback is to reflect and highlight any significant changes to the game state. Don't simply update a numerical value from one number to another - many players will completely miss that it happened. Make sure the whole indicator flashes and the numbers pulsate as they go up and down.
- **Character and object animation**: This includes obvious real-world actions such as running, jumping, and opening doors, as well as abstract animations that do not occur in real life. Growing, shrinking, pulsating, moving, rotating, and even re-coloring objects can be done fairly easily in code (without a single frame of animation required). If you can, make good use of these cheap and efficient techniques. For anything else, it'll be down to the use of bespoke, artist-driven animations and...
- **Physics**: Another way to make objects and characters visibly react and move is to introduce them as objects in your physics engine. A collapsing tree does not need to be animated, it just needs to be detached from the ground and allowed to fall.

- **Visual effects**: Smoke, flames, sparks, light—a bonfire is practically made out of *particle effects*, which can either be pre-rendered and exported as flat 2D animations or created dynamically by the game engine. Special effects used in the game-world provide an additional level of feedback and intensity to in-game actions. They are also invaluable in portraying more abstract or immaterial things that cannot be feasibly expressed with physics and animation. You can also use VFX on the UI layer to stylize it and go hand-in-hand with more classic UI feedback. Particle effect editors are not hard to operate and learning their basics can be a helpful skill for almost any game designer!

- **Screen effects**: Color tints, light flashes, screen shaking, and other full-screen effects are a great way of reflecting important information *(Red overlay?! I'm hurt!)* or adding impact *(BOOM! *screen shake*)*.

- **Tactile feedback**: By allowing you to physically connect the players to the game world, tactile feedback can make your game much more immersive. Some developers go as far as to integrate the vibration function right into their cutscenes. Nevertheless, vibration is not for everyone and should only be used as an optional, additional source of feedback. Some players find it distracting, while others, especially on mobile, want to limit the noise produced by constant rumbling. When integrating tactile functions, try to limit the intensity and duration of common actions and reserve the stronger, longer responses to fittingly significant occasions.

- **Audio**: The main roles of sound effects are to reinforce the visual feedback of in-game actions and to convey additional information about the game world that cannot be expressed with visual cues (for example, the footsteps of approaching foes). Music, on the other hand, can have a multitude of roles. It can help to set and reinforce the emotional tone of whatever's going on, build an aural scenery of the game world, and even serve as an additional source of feedback. To provide feedback with music, implement a system that adjusts it dynamically to the overall state of the game *(I hear boss fight music, everyone get ready!)* or a player's individual perspective *(Oh... combat music? I must've been spotted!)*. As useful as sound effects and music are, not everyone can hear them... When it comes to mobile and portable platforms, unless you're working on a music game, you should never depend on audio feedback as the sole way of conveying important information.

- **Textual feedback**: While old-school health bars and combat logs (that is, lists of gameplay actions and calculations) can definitely classify as a part of UI feedback, damage and status indicators are often displayed right inside the game world, usually above the actor. If your game contains systems of progression that rely on manipulating numbers, using text to reflect them becomes near-mandatory. This can apply to anything from damage and healing to combo scores and resource production.

Designing UIs

The main objectives of any UI are to facilitate interaction and communicate the state of the game to the player.

Some products can get away with little UI other than game menus and occasional control prompts, while others try to avoid using any text in their interface and operate purely on iconography. The efforts to try and minimize the amount of UI and communicate the state of the game purely with game feedback and UX are applaudable and can result in very elegant designs.

Nevertheless, the more complex your game systems get, the more complex the states they produce. Deep and extensive user interfaces are often unavoidable, and knowing how to design them (or at least how to support and understand the professionals that do it for you) is a very important skill.

Listing and prioritizing information

As game designers, we often strive to provide our audience with deep, complex decisions. We sometimes think that, if players are confused, perhaps showing more of the stuff that's happening behind the hood will help explain the complexities of our systems. Unfortunately, in spite of our intentions, the tendency to show everything can actually impede decision making. This leads to players getting overwhelmed and struggling to focus on what's relevant and what's not. In short:

Total disclosure can lead to information overload.

Think of it this way. In a racing game, there's often no need to constantly highlight to the player that they're on the *right way*. Instead, we simply opt to display the *wrong way* indicator when they're actually going astray. We can extend this principle further by, for example, hiding the health indicators when the health is full. By not providing health information to the player we signal that health has no significance, which means there's nothing to act on or be concerned about (either health must be full or nothing can hurt me now).

The more complex your game interface, the more you can benefit from a systematic way of prioritizing information based on context. This applies to both working on your own or with a UI specialist. A potentially complex or novel set of screens and features can easily be broken down, analyzed, and put together by following a three-step process:

1. Set the primary, secondary, and stretch goals for the interface you're designing.
2. Define the expected player behavior, possible interactions, and intentions.
3. Make a list of the potential elements and contents of each screen that fit the goals and enable the expected behavior of your audience.

With the goals, intentions, and contents all set, you should be able to map out and categorize each element of the UI based on their role:

*   **Critical**: Objects of high relevance, they directly support primary function of the interface and remain important in most contexts. For example, a **heads-up display** (HUD) marker that points towards the location of the mission objective.
*   **Supportive**: Any part of UI that (in most contexts) is not crucial to player's ability to interact with the system, but should be readily available to support their decision making and guide the interactions. For example, a minimap or weapon and ammo indicator that can be peeked at and assessed with ease.
*   **Contextual**: Information that is only relevant in a particular context is the least important of all and can be hidden behind an additional interaction. For example, a detailed full-screen map is only relevant when we want to plan our next moves or have a hard time navigating with the minimap and the objective markers.

Following such processes can help you design screens that support player behavior and place a manageable amount of information and options in suitable places.

UI mockups

In the context of user interface design, a mockup is a prototype version of the interface, created with the purpose of establishing the design direction, demonstrating or documenting the functionality, and validating the usability.

A UI mockup is likely to contain no actual art aside from basic geometric shapes, placeholder icons and text labels. Thanks to their simplicity and fast turnarounds, mockups allow for quick iterations on different layouts and ways of surfacing information to the players.

Take a look at a simple yet effective wire-frame mockup created by one of SpaceApe's in-house UI and UX experts:

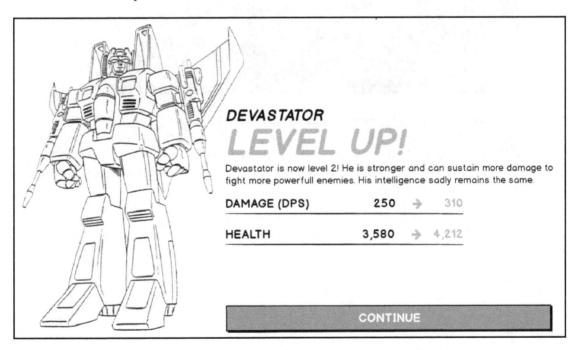

Following that, we have the in-game version of the very same screen, as seen in *Transformers: Earth Wars*:

Try to think of UI mockups as equivalent to the prototypes of game mechanics. Even though most designs are likely to change and evolve once implemented, the process itself greatly reduces the risk of investing many hours of code and artwork, just to realize that a late addition requires a total overhaul.

In case of more complex screens, a wire-frame version can quickly demonstrate usability issues and areas to improve. Let's take a look at another example from the same game:

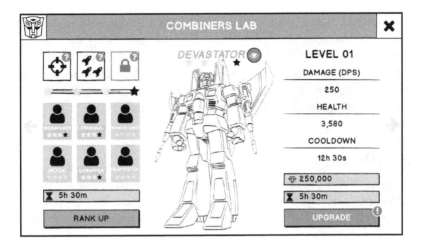

There's a lot going on in there, especially if you consider that we're designing for a 5-inch screen. Fortunately, wire-frames are quick to change and multiple versions can be compared next to one another. Here's the final version:

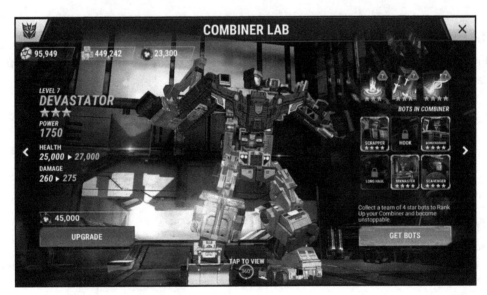

The in-game implementation swaps things around, streamlining and prioritizes the stats and status of the main character. The grid of owned and missing robots takes a backseat. Duplicated or irrelevant information has been removed. The disabled *Rank Up* section was replaced by an active call to action. Relevant resource counters have been added. The little blue *eye* icon has been replaced by a light textual instruction making the whole combiner a big invisible button that can be pressed to enter the *view* mode.

Paper sketches

Paper is a great medium for visualizing simple designs and mapping out rough ideas. It's common for game and UI designers to use whiteboards or post-it notes to explain their ideas to their colleagues, who'll often carry the design towards a more robust prototype.

However, if the design is complicated, highly interactive, dependent on animation, or if you'd like to create a set of many ideas that differ in small details (such as icon size, button placement, and so on), it's best to migrate to a digital medium.

Digital wireframes

Digital mockups often take shape of wireframes—designs that use geometric shapes, flat colors, and simple icons instead of game art.

However, some designers opt to validate the artistic direction of the interface at this stage. To do so, a digital wireframe can be imbued with effects, fonts, and art found on the internet, allowing the designer to swiftly assemble a good approximation of the look and feel.

Animated and interactive prototypes

With the help of modern design tools, one can easily create polished, animated, and interactive prototypes that allow for accurate approximation of the final user experience and interface flow.

This process is especially advised when seeking design validation for features that utilize complicated, nested screen flows, or when trying to establish an animated look-and-feel. An interactive design speaks more than a thousand words. When it comes to the quality and efficiency of communication, even the most basic prototype is better than a five-page-long description of what the interface is supposed to contain and how it should work.

Cloud-based prototyping tools allow you to upload or create your wireframes and link various parts of the screens together and create an interactive flow, which can be sent out and viewed on any device. This is especially useful when designing mobile interfaces and seeking validation on the size of objects and buttons. I've also successfully used these tools to mock-up and present game ideas and even approximate gameplay.

It's hard to pinpoint a single solution, as the market for these tools is evolving fast and each has it's pros and cons. Nevertheless, to get you started, I can recommend you check out *Flinto, Framer, InVision, Balsamiq Mockups, Fluid UI, Axure RP*, and *JustInMind*. That said, a quick search for *UI prototyping tools* is often all you need to get a nice and more up to date lineup.

At the end of the day, you don't even need specific UI design tools to create effective and interactive prototypes. I found great success in using simple presentation tools like *Microsoft Powerpoint*. With the help of the humble shape tool, hyperlinking, and artwork found on the Internet, you can quickly put your UI and UX ideas into an understandable design.

UI Tips and Tricks

With UI and UX design, you learn most by constantly re-evaluating the end-user experience, observing players, gathering feedback, and repeatedly iterating. That said, there's a range of tips, tricks, and good practices that stuck with me over the years.

Choose a fitting state and progress indicator

Information can be displayed in a variety of ways. It's important to evaluate the efficacy of your UI indicators and settle for ones that best fit the context:

- **Progress Bars**: Good for progress, but even better at showing *capacities*, such as ammo or health. We are used to bars changing their state in both directions. A reasonably sized bar allows people to easily recognize ~10 different fill states. This means that our peripheral vision can acknowledge a 10% change in fill-state as a significantly different situation.
- **Circular Indicators**: Great at efficiently representing time! A circular indicator being filled in a radial manner can result in up to 36 unique positions being easily recognizable by the human eye. Radially filled circular indicators are best reserved for parameters that have clear maximum values such as time, speed, fuel, temperature, pressure, and so on.
- **Color Grading**: Color grading relies on shifting between multiple colors and hues to reflect changing states. Think of water temperature going from blue (cold) to red (hot). Color grading is not very effective on its own and should be used as a supplementary solution (with a counter or a progress bar to provide more precise feedback). Subtle color grading also makes things particularly hard to read for colorblind people. An average human can comfortably register ~5-6 different states between two very distinct colors (red-green) or shades (black-white).

Consider using notification badges

Colloquially known as *roosters*, notification badges are displayed next to buttons, category tabs, items, and so on in order to bring them to your attention. Roosters can help you guide players through multiple levels of menu depth, asking them to take specific action or at least acknowledge the presence of new information. If the number of new objects can get very large and hard to track (like in a standard email inbox) consider using a number in the rooster to help players keep track of changes in areas they're aware of but not fully caught up with:

Notification badge with number of actionable items

Match the pop-up with the context

Windows that pop up automatically on top of the screen can be both useful and irritating. There are three distinct types:

1. A *modal dialog* blocks the players and requires action to progress - it is best used for confirmations of any potentially destructive or time-consuming behaviors. For example, loading the save game (but only while playing), selling high-value items, or traveling to a different map. Such dialog should either come front and center or appear right next to the origin of the prompting interaction.

2. A *nonmodal* (or *modeless*) *dialog* can be kept open and acted upon at our convenience. These are usually smaller and tucked away on the side of the screen. They tackle non-essential actions like accepting raid party invites in MMO games and should not interfere with the core gameplay.

3. A *Toast notification*, a non modal, informational dialog that requires no action—Toasts are used to display brief, auto-expiring notifications such as *Game saved* or *Your friend is now online*.

Understand the limitations of tooltips

Tooltips are small boxes containing contextually relevant information on the highlighted UI element. They are used widely in PC interfaces (most likely via mouse-over) and any controls that can support a *highlighted but not activated* state, a flexible cursor some kind of *selector* that can be moved with keys or buttons.

Using tooltips on mobile devices can be tricky! Touch interfaces operate best when pressing directly on the objects (tapping and holding on an object is an awkward and unnatural action). Therefore, on touch interfaces, tooltips should not be put on buttons or other elements that have an on-release action assigned to them. You can, however, put them on elements that do not have such interaction, for example, a *metal ore* resource indicator can be tapped to show a tooltip explaining the purpose of the resource and your current production rate.

Consider labeling your UI

Text labels appear next to, or on top of, other UI elements such as toggles, bars, buttons, and so on. While an icon of a musical note with a checkbox next to it requires no label (it's obviously a sound ON/OFF toggle), players can easily get lost in the crowded interface full of new functionalities. Text labeling is often essential as even the most descriptive iconography can leave your players guessing. It's important to ensure that any labels you use (be it on or under your UI elements) are ready to be localized (translated) and can adjust their font size accordingly to the available space - what takes 5 characters in English may need 15 in another language. Speaking of languages, we'll dive deeper into localization in the following chapter on accessibility.

Do not reinvent the wheel!

The rules of intuitive control design apply to the user interface. Do not break established paradigms unless you have strong reasons to do so. The potential friction caused by changes that go against player expectations can only be offset with ideas that are either simpler or far superior.

Use movement, contrast, and saturation to grab the user's attention

Our eyes are naturally predisposed to prioritize movement; after all, it can signify a potential threat or prey. A pulsating button will draw attention even if placed in our peripheral vision (should it persist, it can also become really annoying). Another tool you can use is color contrast. Some color pairings are stronger than others; red and green have a stronger effect than blue and yellow, even though both colors are considered strongly contrasting and are placed on the opposite sides of the *color wheel*. This could be traced to our ingrown ability to distinguish between ripe and unripe fruit. Differences in color saturation and brightness are more effective if they are used sparsely and consciously. Contrast is a subtle art; if everything is brightly colored, nothing has a chance to stand out. Reserve the contrasting treatment to the critical elements of the UI (going back to the prioritization process described earlier).

Request or create a style guide and enforce it

The person responsible for the visual style of the interface has to develop and maintain a UI style guide. A document that sets the standards for the entire game, starting with the color scheme (including colors behind confirmation, rejection, and neutrality), as well as text and title fonts, the shapes and shading styles of buttons, tabs, text boxes and any other common UI building blocks. A style guide simplifies the day-to-day challenges, ensures the game sends a cohesive message and reduces player confusion. Once the style is set, stick to it. Avoid special cases and exceptions at all costs. If you change something, make sure the change is reflected across the board.

Keep theme and pacing in mind

The style and execution of the UI should reinforce the pace and theme of the game. The subtle UI in *Dead Space*— where indicators and menus are holographically projected onto or from the character—fits the slower pacing of an immersive horror game. It also makes menu management a potentially risky move as the game is not paused when navigating various screens. Since all information is embedded right into the game world, players are driven further into it. Even the health indicator is part of the character's suit, blending with it seamlessly until players get hurt in which case it serves as a constant, brightly flashing reminder of the threat they're in. Embedding the UI into the game world is known as a *diagetic interface*. It may not be the best fit for you, but it serves as a reminder of how to properly consider theme and pacing as part of the design process!

Confirm risky actions

This may sound like a pure formality but you'd be surprised how many games allow you to break valuable objects and lose hours of progress with an accidental click. Confirm anything that has an irreversible (and potentially negative) outcome for the player. You'd be right to be cautious of constant confirmations getting in the way, but you can easily remove them from strictly positive actions. You can also build in a way to opt out of certain confirmations altogether.

Count the time and steps to play

The shorter the play session length, the more important it becomes to get players straight into action. Long title sequences, nested menu options, and confirmations can all get in the way of gameplay. Your players may often have just a few minutes, do all you can to ensure their time is not all spent in menus and loading screens.

Screens differ – often widely

The game interface will often need to support a variety of different devices, aspect ratios, resolutions, and pixel densities. The trend towards responsive design in web development is a good one to adhere to. Objects should not scale endlessly but be capped to a set minimum and maximum size. When it comes to placement, do not use absolute positions, but try to use relative (percentage) distances instead. Anchor all big chunks of the UI to the various parts of the screen (edges, corners, center), then attach all smaller elements (such as buttons inside the pop-up) to their *parent* object. A well thought out interface only has to be implemented once, then verified on the minimum and maximum settings.

Do not analyze mobile interfaces on computer screens. Use paper sketches or put digital mock ups on small-screened devices and see how they fare against people with relatively large fingers.

UI placement is a science

People in western cultures are used to reading content from left to right, top to bottom, in a Z-shaped pattern referred to as the *Gutenberg Principle*:

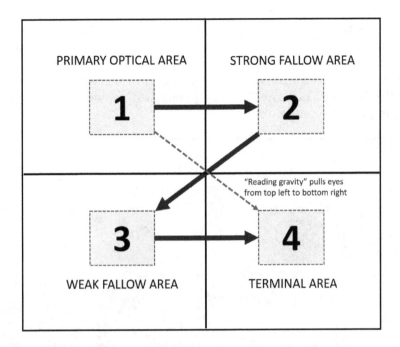

The *Gutenberg Diagram* pictured above divides the reading space into four quadrants and illustrates the Z-shaped reading pattern, as well as the direction of *reading gravity*. Which means that as our eyes sweep in horizontal lines, from top to bottom, they tend to get pulled away from the left edge of the screen and more towards the right.

While the *Gutenberg Principle* finds most use in web-design, its utility can be extended into video game interfaces. It's no coincidence that several years ago, the default interface of *World of Warcraft* adhered to these rules. Player health was attached to the top-left corner, as it's the most relevant information we need to monitor. Minimap occupied the top-right area. The in-game chat was on the bottom-left, and finally, the combat log sat quietly in the bottom-right. That's because the combat log is only relevant if we consciously seek the information contained in it, otherwise, it remains unnoticeable even though it's constantly scrolling.

As screen size gets smaller, a reduced portion of the screen falls into our peripheral vision, reducing the importance of the Z-shaped pattern and placing more emphasis on the center area of the screen. However, the small-screened touch interfaces have a different set of issues. Most importantly, fingers can get into way! This is why status updates and destructive actions (such as deleting something) should be contained to the top, with the bottom part of the screen being dedicated to very popular areas and buttons.

According to the research published by UX Matters (http://www.uxmatters.com/mt/archives/2013/02/how-do-users-really-hold-mobile-devices.php), 49% of users use one hand to operate their phone, 36% cradle the phone with their second hand, and 15% use the device with both hands. Let's take a look at a set of heat-maps that help understand the ergonomics of the dominant use-case, that is, a phone held and operated exclusively with the right hand, in portrait orientation:

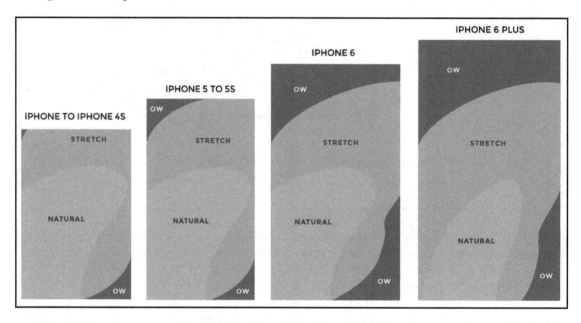

Credit: UX Matters

As we can see, the bigger the display, the harder it is to reach across it! Nevertheless, in most cases, the bottom-left quadrant is the easiest part to access, and the top-left one of the hardest.

For more information and extensive research on mobile UX, visit https://www.uxmatters.com and take a dive into some great articles by Steven Hoober, starting with the three-part article *Design for Fingers, Touch, and People.*

 The screenshots used in this chapter are for illustrative purposes only. We do not recommend that you to misuse these in any way. For more information please consult the terms and conditions of the publishers mentioned in the *Disclaimer* section of this book.

Summary

"A complex craft that often blends art, animation, graphic design, and visual effects with game design itself."

That's how we described UI and UX design in the introduction to this chapter. A few dozen pages later, we've hopefully provided you with a strong introduction to the concepts of input methods, cameras, perspectives, and utilizing feedback , all in the bid of reinforcing your gameplay and crafting a game that's immersive, responsive, understandable, and delightful to interact with.

We strongly encourage that you deconstruct existing games, analyze their feedback mechanics, and even re-create their UI in the form of digital mock ups. As with any blend of art and craft, practice makes perfect!

Next up, we'll naturally extend the concepts of this chapter and apply our user-oriented mindset towards making your games more accessible.

12
Accessibility

In the previous chapter, we learned about the User Experience and the best practices in User Interface design. We'll now learn how to make these, and any other parts of the game, more *accessible;* that is, easier to use, understand, and relate to.

To begin with, we need to find ways to create a steady and frictionless introduction to the game world and the rules governing it. We then have to ensure that the game can provide a highly playable experience to players that are less experienced, skilled, or capable (be it cognitively or physically).

Last but not least, even the best games often start in a bad place, and there's no better way to find things to improve than to test our games on potential players. We'll spend the final half of the chapter on the art of usability testing, and arm you with the expertise required to plan and execute your very own playtesting sessions!

Increasing accessibility

When thinking of making our games more accessible, we often narrow our focus to the overall pacing and difficulty of the in-game challenges. While balancing itself is important enough to warrant a whole chapter (and we've done just that in this book), we first need to identify the ways in which we can make the core of our product fundamentally more approachable.

Reducing cognitive load

Games that require good memory, observational skills, abstract thinking, planning, and fact association are all at risk of being very cognitively demanding.

High-level games of chess immediately come to mind as an example of a difficult mental challenge. And yet, the base rules and mechanics of chess can be understood and memorized by young children, making chess an accessible game.

Complex and mentally demanding games only become inaccessible if the player is stuck or struggles to learn the rules and improve. To make the game more accessible in this department, try the following.

Avoiding mental challenges with binary outcomes

Adventure games in the 1990s were full of abstract puzzles that provided a binary mental challenge—you either got the solution, or you were left to struggle on your own. Players would often end up scouring the game world, scanning every single screen, and trying every possible item combination. Nowadays, a game with that degree of *friction* will likely frustrate the player to a point of quitting. When possible, avoid mandatory puzzles with binary win/lose conditions, or make sure to include a passive or active hint system.

If you are looking for inspiration, try the games in the *Professor Layton* series, where hundreds of clever (and often very difficult) puzzles are paired with a well-implemented hint system. In most cases, a puzzle has three hints that can be purchased for one *Hint Coin* each, and a fourth *Super Hint* (solution) that can be bought for two *Hint Coins*. *Hint Coins* themselves are a limited resource that are awarded for exploring and interacting with the environment (tapping on mailboxes, plant pots, cats, and so on). Players have to work hard to find the hints, which means that using them doesn't feel like cheating.

Limiting initial complexity and interplay between rules

Products that have elaborate rulesets and multi-layered mechanics often require a huge amount of practice on behalf of the players.

As game creators, we often have the desire to design elegant systems where multiple elements affect one another in discrete ways. It's a great ambition to have, but one that can lead us to make an overwhelming experience.

A new mechanic or rule should only enter the stage once the previous one has been fully explored and understood. There's no harm in removing or limiting certain aspects of the game for the purpose of teaching the player. For example, don't ask the players to build a deck of cards before they have a chance to play them, and do not introduce the pressure of maintaining limited time/turns/health/ammo/resources until they are really required.

We'll dedicate more time to the subject of introducing and explaining game mechanics later in this chapter.

Lowering the knowledge cliffs

A great example of a knowledge cliff can be found in many multiplayer arena games like *League of Legends* and *DOTA 2*. Both titles feature dozens of items and hundreds of characters (each with multiple, complex abilities) that players need to understand and memorize. With numbers this high, the knowledge cliff would be significant even if the only variables were simple attribute changes. As it stands, these characters and items are also full of new mechanics—a perfect storm of overwhelming quantity and complexity! No wonder they are some of the least accessible games on the market.

In this situation, limiting the content is the easiest solution. This is why *Valve* has reduced the number of playable heroes in the first 25 games of *DOTA 2* from over 110 to just 20, with new players only able to play against one another. They've also introduced a new *Turbo* mode, which decreases death penalties, changes the pacing, and removes some of the restrictive rules on buying items. Even with all of these changes, there's still a long way to go, as *DOTA 2* remains to be one of the hardest and most punishing games to pick up for newcomers.

Remember, games like *LoL* and *DOTA* are exceptions that managed to survive and reach critical mass without good onboarding, on top of a hugely dedicated player base. The very same strategy can and most likely will sink most other games.

Limiting the complexity of interaction

We've already covered input methods and controls at length in `Chapter 11`, *User Interface and User Experience*. Enabling full control remapping and reducing input complexity goes a long way in increasing accessibility, while rarely leaving a negative impact on the game mechanics.

We can do better though! Can you imagine a way to make your game playable with only one hand? How about one finger? The outlandish one-finger restriction is often an essential requirement for mobile game controls. After all, the second hand may be clinging to a coffee cup or a bus handrail. Certainly, not all games can cater to such requirements, but trying to accommodate to them while maintaining playability for the target audience is a goal we should all aspire towards, for the sake of all players.

 There are often ways in which you can easily bypass the necessity of multiple simultaneous inputs. For example, in first person shooters, aiming down sights, sprinting and crouching can all be toggle actions (press to turn ON/OFF), instead of requiring a key or button to be constantly held down.

Even if your controls are simple, executing them quickly and accurately can be overly challenging. Difficult execution is likely to be a problem in any real-time game, from quick pattern matching in *Guitar Hero* to the expert hand-eye coordination and reflexes needed to play *Counter-Strike*. Make sure to provide a set of slower paced, less punishing challenges for the inexperienced and less capable players. This can be done via difficulty settings, rule adaptations, and multiplayer matchmaking. We'll look into ways of adjusting difficulty in Chapter 13, *Balancing*.

Maintaining visual clarity

If players cannot easily distinguish, read, and understand the state of the game and contents of the screen, they won't be able to interact with the game effectively. Consider the following tips to improve the visual clarity in your games:

- Hide or de-prioritize any unnecessary information in the user interface.
- Separate the enemies and interactive objects from the background. Be it via shapes, outlines, color palettes, or materials and shaders.
- Use clear and uniform visual language in your level design. For example, in *Tomb Raider*, any climbable wall is covered in white paint.
- Do not obscure critical information (player position, threats) with overwhelming and long-lasting visual effects.
- Visualize the state of the game. Use text, icons, and symbols to clearly indicate the state of game-actors. For example, health bars, damage numbers, status symbols, and so on. Adhere to the principles of good game feedback highlighted in the previous chapter.
- Cater to color-blind people, which comprise 10% of your male playerbase. Provide menu options to swap the colors of important elements such as map and target markers, health bars, and so on, and utilize different shapes to distinguish between various parts of the user interface. For example, UI markers could be circular for friendlies and triangular for hostiles.

Making audio optional

Unless your game revolves around audio design, be it spoken lines of dialogue (for example, *Thomas Was Alone, Stanley's Parable*), music *(Guitar Hero, Rock Band, Audiosurf)* or sound cues (for example, footsteps and shots fired in *Counter-Strike* and *Rainbow Six: Siege*), you should avoid relying on audio cues. On top of isolating hearing-impaired players, you're also disadvancing people who play with low or muted sound. The probability of the latter is extremely high in the mobile and portable game market.

As for supporting hearing-impaired players, on top of integrating subtitles, you should also consider putting in options to enable closed-captions (textual descriptions of sound effects). For example, *door creaks* or *loud explosion*.

Restricting negative consequences

Respawning at checkpoints, replaying stages, equipment and character removal, and last but not least, the states of permanent failure (aka permadeath); these are some of the most common examples of negative consequences.

In most cases, taking away a player's progress is a surefire way of making your game less accessible. It's especially true if you pair it with technical issues, failure to teach game systems, and a lack of anticipation and clear feedback. The last thing you want is to leave your audience unaware of the negative consequences and ill-prepared to handle them.

Don't get me wrong, failure can be good and motivating, and we obviously want our players to be challenged. But while it's great to have our audience learn from their mistakes, learning through failure is our last line of defense, and the most frustrating way to teach the player.

I am not advocating against the use of progress-loss as a consequence, in fact, some of my favorite games are incredibly punishing. However, it's important to recognize the negative effects on accessibility, which are brought by progress removal and permanent fail-states. These mechanics are simply not for everyone, and unless they make up the fabric of your game, consider making them optional.

Building on common knowledge

Anchoring your game to another popular product can be handy, but creating a strong reference to the world outside of video games can be even more helpful. This includes popular culture, history, sports, traditions, activities, hobbies, and even the physical properties of the world around us.

Ice is slippery, wood catches fire, diamonds are expensive, and *Rocket League* is kind of like soccer played with cars. The easier it is to draw a parallel between the game world and real world, the less knowledge you'll need to put into player's heads yourself. That said, while removing rules is fine, breaking them in unexpected places can make things very confusing. For example, it's okay if your character doesn't need food to survive, but it's not wise to create a wooden sword that lasts longer than a steel one.

Teaching game systems

Teaching and introducing new rules and mechanics is often as difficult as creating them. The first step is, as always, to acknowledge and respect the differing tastes and preferences of your audience, not only towards certain types of games but also the ways in which they like to learn and tackle challenges. You also have to prepare for different levels of exposure to similar games and relatable life experiences.

We all have our preferred *learning style,* and even though researchers are having a hard time settling on a particular definition and categorization, they all seem to agree that each individual is primed towards a particular set of learning techniques. Some people like to listen, some prefer to read, and others still skip all text and try to figure things out by following visual cues.

A highly successful strategy is to mix several teaching methods into a combination that works well within the confines of the story, game structure, target platform, and audience.

Remember, written information, videos, and scripted gameplay are all valid educational tools, but games are an interactive medium, and the most pleasant and effective way of teaching our players is through play itself. The need for tutorial elements can be greatly reduced by providing players with immediate goal clarity, clear feedback from gameplay and interface interactions, and the gradual introduction of new elements. An elegant and clearly presented mechanic has a chance of explaining itself in action.

In-game teaching techniques

There are times when explaining complex game systems to players with little prior experience may be impossible without the strict guidance of carefully crafted tutorials. These direct teaching techniques include some of the following:

- **Beginner's training**: Scripted and ring-fenced tutorials at the beginning of the game may run the risk of being perceived as unnecessary or frustrating, but they are still a highly effective tool. For one, you have the full control of the game state and the level design and are clear to withhold any progress until all instructions are followed and tasks accomplished. A skilled and experienced player should be able to complete your tutorials quickly; make sure to remove any unnecessary pauses and keep the long demonstrations and speeches for those who really need them. There's nothing more frustrating than being locked away from your controls while a drill sergeant takes 20 seconds to tell you how to reload and pull the trigger.

- **Context-sensitive tutorials**: Well crafted tutorials appear where and when you need them. Try dividing your tutorial content into smaller chunks and implement a set of simple rules and conditions to gauge when and if to launch them. For example, in *Transformers: Earth Wars*, the tutorial for our item fusion mechanic requires that the player has at least eight unequipped items and none of them are level 2. This means that the player did not figure out the feature by themselves, yet they have enough spare items to easily afford it. While it may be easy to preemptively summon a *friendly tutorial fairy* whenever something new appears, it is a much finer art to recognize the stress points in your game and anticipate a good moment to address them. Launching the right tutorial at the right time is the secret to a receptive and grateful player.

- **Optional training segments**: Side-quests, practice missions, and glowing *learn more* buttons next to newly acquired tools. These are some of the ways in which you can inject knowledge without affecting the main storyline. After all, advanced players should not be forced to learn things they already know, and should be given a way to skip past this content safely without losing out. But what happens if they skip by mistake? What if players suffer later because they were simply impatient or misunderstood what they were about to learn? These concerns are valid and can be addressed with a set of fail-safes. Optional training elements should be crystal clear on what they entail (in other words, make sure to expose your curriculum) and accessible later on when players decide they need them.

On the other end of the spectrum, we have indirect teaching techniques, which are either less invasive or naturally intertwined with the fabric of the game:

- **Leaving information in the environment**: Sometimes the state of the environment can provide you with all the clues you need. Back in the previous chapters, we spoke of environmental storytelling; in the case of *Dead Space,* the writings on the wall played a role in teaching the players how to battle the undead. Less obvious clues require more attention to detail and may turn the teaching into a puzzle-solving exercise. Who said that tutorial sections can't be turned into enjoyable obstacles to overcome? As you venture deep into the creepy woods, you encounter metal traps, some of them with their jaws clasped on long forgotten skeletons. There's also a few disabled traps with rocks (which you can pick up) next to them. Soon after, an unsprung trap is blocking your way and a rock lays right in front of you. The connection soon becomes obvious.
- **Teaching by example**: Companion characters (such as Alyx in *Half-Life 2*) do not need to talk to the player to pass on knowledge. As you shoot and bash your way through alien-infested Earth, you observe and copy the skills and behavior of your partner. Should the players have no friendly characters to rely on, they can always follow the footsteps of their enemies. If you see an enemy character (or player) perform a rocket-jump, it won't take you long to try one yourself!
- **Reinforcement**: Since the dawn of time, positive reinforcement is one of the most effective ways to direct human behavior. Players who are rewarded for certain actions with praise, resources, or sheer satisfaction will continue on the path that leads to continued and escalating reward. Investing time and effort into learning new game systems should come with clear rewards and be presented as an opportunity to gain an edge in the future.
- **Accessible information**: Glowing *learn more* buttons, mouse-over tooltips, control hints, and text labels on buttons are just a few examples of supplying players with information that's either out in the open, or easily accessible at their convenience. These tools alone may not be enough to teach players about complex game systems and interactions, but they certainly make the game easier to figure out.
- **Failure**: Teaching solely by trial and error is a certain way of making your players frustrated and the game seem unfair. Nevertheless, it's important to acknowledge the simple yet powerful message that a punishment can hold. If players are losing, the least you can do is explain why and how they've failed and what they can do to improve. Be it by showing a so-called *kill-cam* in a multiplayer shooter, or by explaining the works of the trap, enemy, or game mechanic responsible for the fail-state.

Teaching outside gameplay

A lot of detailed and nuanced information can be exposed outside of the main gameplay experience. However, while these techniques are great at covering specialist knowledge or diving deep into the stats and non-crucial mechanics, they should be used as a secondary source of information—something that cannot be relied upon or expected from players. In this category we can place:

- **Loading tips**: Loading screens are a great place for tips and hints that are not critical to player's progression. Button shortcuts, advanced or obscure mechanics, equipment highlights, and repetition of important information are all valid choices. You can also use this space to place a quick story reminder, a synopsis of the current act/mission or the backstory of various characters and locations. When working on a loading tips system, it's best to ensure it takes player's state into account. This way, a seasoned player who's just about to face the last boss won't be patronized by an unnecessary tip on *how to jump*, nor will a beginner face info about advanced end-game combos.

- **Training cutscenes and videos**: Nowadays, many complex games that are still undergoing heavy development rely on narrated video tutorials on platforms like *YouTube*. This is a good way to transfer knowledge to a dedicated fanbase, but it cannot be depended upon for the final product. If you ever end up creating external video content, make sure to link to it or embed it in your game. In-game cutscenes are a much more dependable way of teaching your players, but they tend to be much more expensive and should not be invested in early.

- **Game manuals and guides**: The paper manuals and guides are largely a thing of the past, and not many users ever seek out the digital versions. Unless you're required to make a manual by the platform holder or are preparing a deluxe printed edition, you should skip this effort and channel it right into the in-game teaching.

- **In-game knowledge banks**: Player journals, PDA's, encyclopedias, and databases are a great way to store easily accessible information. A great example of such a system would be the Codex in the *Mass Effect* series—a place chock full of story content, character bios, backstory, in-game technology, and of course, our beloved tutorials.

- **External wikis**: Official and unofficial knowledge databases (wikis) let highly engaged users dive deep into nuances of your game. Such wikis are chuck-full of detailed unit and equipment stats, patch notes, gameplay hints and walkthroughs. You may not want to invest time into creating an official wiki (especially for a single-player, story-driven game), but no matter what you do, make sure to support the community if they choose to create a knowledge database of their own. As for competitive multiplayer titles, up-to-date wikis can be a pillar of a healthy community.
- **Peer-to-peer knowledge sharing**: The power of engaged fan-base is truly something to behold. Complex and poorly explained games such as *League of Legends* and *DOTA 2* owe a lot of their success to the willingness of their community to on-board and teach one another. Outside of friend lists, guilds, and alliances, you can encourage mentoring behavior by introducing referral programs that depend on the referred player's progress, as well as supporting replay sharing, spectator modes, and a chat system that functions across the whole game.

Best practices

In this section, we've assembled a set of tips and guidelines that can help make your onboarding experiences more focused, organized, and effective.

Don't kill (with) the messenger

Our attempts at teaching the player are at constant risk of making them either bored or overwhelmed. If possible, your tutorial sections should blend in seamlessly with the rest of the game. Longwinded training missions and practice rounds all run a risk of tiring (*when does this end?*) and even patronizing your audience (*I know this already!*). The latter was especially true when it came to *Clippy*, the paperclip from the old *Microsoft Office*. The obnoxious, intrusive, and seemingly clueless nature of *Clippy* became a running joke. Yet, similar training became much more approachable when delivered by an adorable yellow puppy. The tutor, the method, and the ability to skip ahead all play a role in making a less polarizing experience.

Understand the effects of the *training mode*

By playing games, we enter *safe simulations* in which we can learn about the world without any real consequences. Therefore, marking a part of any game as *training* is equal to creating a safe simulation within the safe simulation. So in spite of learning throughout the entire gameplay experience, many players regard in-game training segments as a waste of time, and eagerly anticipate the beginning of the *real game*. If you find yourself relying on such segment, make sure that parts of it are skippable and clearly marked as optional.

You can also turn certain tutorial sections and functionalities ON or OFF based on the difficulty setting selected by the player. If someone is playing a shooter on a *nightmare* difficulty setting they most likely don't have to be told how to move and look around.

Focus your efforts on innovative and obscure

Your teaching strategy should take into account not only the complexity of the game but also the amount of innovation. Focus first on the experimental parts of the game, knowing that the more familiar mechanics have already been successfully taught before (and therefore a solid reference for teaching them can probably be found and adapted).

Following that, look out for parts of your game that may not get in the way of immediate progress, yet run the risk of having a long-term effect. For example, players may not realize the importance of particular resources and throw them away, only to realize 30 hours later that by doing so they're now lacking the necessary materials to upgrade their equipment.

Pick the right moment to work on tutorials

You'd ideally want the core game mechanics to be as close to final as possible before spending significant time and effort on polishing your onboarding experience and tutorials. Early on, the tutorial budget is better spent on in-game text and visual feedback. In the short term, recording a tutorial video or explaining the game in person are also valid approaches. Once you start exposing your game to more people and enter external testing, you'll likely have the basics more or less set in stone, making the time spent on tutorials time well spent.

Make a tutorial plan

Approaching tutorial creation can be a daunting task. To make things easier, you'll need to formulate a plan. If you have a *content lifespan document* or a *player progression flow* at hand (both mentioned in `Chapter 3`, *Scoping a Game Project*), use them as a basis. Otherwise, make a basic timeline of the player's progression and a separate list of important game mechanics.

Now, try to match both lists and note the teaching techniques you could use. Ensure that you do not overwhelm the player with too many unrelated concepts at once. At this stage, you may find out that parts of the game or its level design need to be changed or swapped around to make things fit better. This is a big part of the reason why the beginning areas of the game should be postponed until the base mechanics and the lion's share of the content are finished.

Try a 3 step process

When dealing with guided tutorials that require active participation from the players, it helps to break them down into three steps:

1. **Context**: Tell the players what they are doing and why. For example, *Use your attacks to knock the other contestants out of the arena!*
2. **Interaction**: Guide the players through the execution phase, if possible, more than once and with escalating difficulty. For example, Press X to attack the skeleton... <skeleton defeated> "Great! But... it looks like there's more coming! Get ready!".
3. **Summary**: Solidify the knowledge and highlight the future use of the mechanic, be it with text, images or aspirational goals. For example, *Try to unlock new skills and find new gadgets to see what they do!*. The summary is also a good place to make immediate use of everything that the player's learned so far in a real, unguided scenario.

Test and iterate

No tutorial you create will ever be perfect. As with game mechanics, you have to start somewhere and iron the quirks as you go. If you're struggling to choose between a few different approaches and have access to a big enough pool of test candidates, it's often best to take the extra time to try them all simultaneously on different segments of the player base, then pick the best.

Some things are best left unexplained

We spoke at length about how to explain the complexities of your game to the average player, yet, we need to acknowledge that some games are at their best when players try to figure them out entirely by themselves. Deep, innovative game systems can often be much more interesting if left as a puzzle, and discovering how things work can be a crucial part of the experience. There is also a segment of the population, however small, for whom a certain level of inaccessibility is a big draw. They feel pride in mastering an infamously difficult game, at being in the tiny minority of people who *get it*. This looks like a very niche approach to game design, one that is rarely fitting in the commercial market, yet it deserves to be recognized.

No matter how casual your game is, a degree of mystery and secrecy (a locked door, a seemingly unreachable collectible) can go a long way in driving your players and creating a truly special experience for those who figure things out. Most *Super Mario Brothers* games are very accessible, yet packed full of secrets and optional areas that require extensive thinking and planning to reach.

A good example of a full game following the mystery and mastery paradigm is *The Witness*, a puzzle game set on an abandoned island, with no tutorial and no guidance except for a few pictographs. The only three elements that make the game work (and work brilliantly well) are:

- **Positive reinforcement when puzzles are being solved**: Things on the island activating, lights turning ON, and so on
- **Logic**: The puzzles make sense and can be figured out without the need for speech
- **Level design and environmental art**: The sprawling vistas, different art themes, architecture, and objects (such as closed doors) are crafted in a way that reinforces our natural curiosity

Localization

The term localization was introduced back in `Chapter 11`, *User Interface and User Experience*, when we spoke about putting text labels under your UI elements and ensuring they do not break when translated into different languages.

In the western markets, the long-dominant practice, and often a requirement posed by the publisher, was to support the EFIGS language group (English, French, Italian, German, and Spanish). Recently, in the more globalized era of digital distribution, the western publishers often find themselves expanding the default group, with Japanese, Korean, Chinese, Russian, and Brazilian Portuguese being the most common additions. The inclusion of new alphabets and directions of text flow is something that can pose big UI challenges for those who are unprepared.

Language aside, localization goes above and beyond swapping texts and voiceovers. New markets unlock access to new audiences with different expectations, spending behaviors, pop-culture references, traditions, and cultural sensitivities. Your ultimate goal is to give your players a game that feels like it's made with them in mind.

The best way to approach this is to work with an informed native who can shed light on these differences. Otherwise, a great deal of knowledge can be amassed by observing successful game companies in the sector, looking into local laws that apply to games, and studying the socio-economical situation of your new market.

Examples of localization efforts include:

- Multi-language websites, forums, and customer support channels.
- Tailor-made marketing art and sales messaging.
- A more inclusive character line-up that respectfully represents different races, nationalities, genders, and even sexual preferences.
- Replacement or removal of religious and political symbology.
- Reducing or replacing gore and blood—often a publishing requirement in Germany.
- Different pricing models and/or payment methods. For example, SMS payments are a very popular way of paying for digital goods in India.
- Addition of new characters that appeal to historical or pop-culture references. For example, the Monkey King in China.
- Country-specific leaderboards.
- Localized events and messaging country-specific holidays

To put things into practice, the localized store pages for Transformers Earth Wars not only feature fully translated videos, text, and screenshots but also (in some territories) a completely different set of promotional assets. The first screenshot in the English listing features Optimus Prime. On the other hand, the Japanese version highlights the presence of two regional characters that starred in the Japanese comics and cartoons:

Playtesting

You're likely to have encountered the term *playtesting* before, be it in this very book or elsewhere. In short, playtesting is the process in which you expose your game to the members of your target audience in order to uncover issues and design flaws, and gather actionable feedback that can help improve the game.

However, there's more to playtesting than simply having people play your game and tell you what they think. Varying circumstances ask for different methodologies, and knowing how to apply them is essential in obtaining and analyzing results.

We'll now arm you with practical expertise that should help you decide on:

- Which parts of the game to test and when?
- Who should participate?
- How to run a playtest session?
- How to gather and analyze feedback?

What to playtest?

Anything that cannot be verified within the confines of your development team is a potential playtesting candidate. A well prepared playtest will be confined to a particular set of questions that your team wants to answer, for example:

- Are the controls easy to understand and use?
- Do players like and care about their character?
- Is this area/mechanic/enemy/puzzle too difficult or too easy?
- Are people motivated to keep on playing?

Such questions and hypothesis are often a part of the production milestone and determine whether the game should continue as is, change its course, or even get canceled.

Testing the whole game without focus is rarely a good idea. The broader the spectrum of feedback, the harder it becomes to capture trends and eliminate outlying opinions. Broad spectrum tests are best deployed on groups of people, or even publicly—in the final stages of game's development.

Remember, big innovation requires early validation! The riskier the design the more it will benefit from playtesting. Any fundamental building blocks of your game need to be verified as soon as feasibly possible.

To help you plan and organize your playtesting sessions, a playtesting plan can be formulated between the producer, designers, lead programmers, and anyone else involved in spearheading the development. Such a plan will surely adapt and evolve with the game, but it's important to prepare your team for the upcoming times of pre-test intensity and feedback fueled uncertainty.

We'll now deconstruct a sample high-level playtesting plan of a fictional AAA action-adventure game:

Pre-production

- Controls and base game mechanics (movement and camera, jumping and climbing, aiming and shooting, using cover). Verified internally with individual sessions.

Production Milestone 1

- Controls and base game mechanics (after addressing initial feedback). New and returning players - internal.
- Art direction and brand tests. Done via small-scale social media advertising campaigns targeted at our audience.

Production Milestone 2

- First 30 minutes of gameplay (onboarding experience and usability). The initial appeal of the brand and the game. Individual sessions ran by an external agency on our target audience.

- Multiplayer modes and singleplayer content, 3-5 day long company playthrough resulting in a big show-off match between top players.

Production Milestone 3

- Individual sessions with fans of the brand and/or influential players.
- Iterations on the onboarding experience, difficulty and progression, 2-week long test ran on our friends and family.
- Multiplayer modes and singleplayer content, 3-5 day long company playthrough resulting in a big show-off match between top players.

Alpha

- Closed Alpha test builds are made playable during select weekends for super-fans, influential players, and press.

Beta

- Closed Beta, the game is now accessible 24/7. Extra focus is being put on game balancing and player progression.
- Open Beta established and promoted on available distribution platforms. Main goals revolve around stress-testing our networking, promoting the game, and gathering feedback (some of the suggestions will influence post-release content and schedule).

Release and Post Release

- A **public test realm** (**PTR**) is made available to every player. Having a test server that anyone can opt to play in allows us to pre-deploy game updates and gather feedback on any changes before they're made available to the entire playerbase.

Playtesting formats

In the ideal world, you'd be able to repeatedly tap into a strong and consistent flow of players that represent your target audience and have them engage with the entirety of your game in their natural environment. However, due to costs, time, and manpower required for "lab level" user testing, you'll often have to make sacrifices in either the quality of the players or the extensiveness, robustness, or frequency of the tests.

Fortunately, we're testing entertainment products, not life-saving drugs. Dependable results and useful feedback can be gathered in a variety of ways, some of them available for close to no costs (besides time).

Before you create your playtesting plan, you'll need to acknowledge the advantages and limitations of available solutions, and pick the one that best suits your situation. Playtesting sessions can be divided into three general categories: individual, group, and public.

Individual sessions

As the heading suggests, each player is being exposed to the game separately, with their play session closely monitored and often recorded.

Individual sessions allow you to pinpoint highly specific usability issues, interview the players and confront their opinions with observed behaviors. They are also good at minimizing peer-based bias as players cannot help out or influence the opinions of fellow test subjects.

Frequency is more important than scale. It's better to run the tests every two weeks on just three users than to do it once a month on a group of ten. Big usability issues are easy to find, and if they're repeated by more than one player, you have an obvious problem to address.

Individual sessions tend to be time-consuming as the facilitator of the test needs to dedicate a portion of their time to each player. As the player pool tends to be smaller, poor screening can also hurt your results. The fewer the players, the more unreliable the findings. Try to grade your testers on a scale based on how closely they overlap with your target demographic and adapt this scale to your findings. For example, a 21 year old male *Call of Duty* player is not the best source of feedback for a casual game in the *hidden object* genre, which has a target audience that's primarily female and 34+. Don't just look at the results, but also who is the feedback coming from.

Group playtesting

Sometimes the most efficient way of playtesting your game is to put it into the hands of a whole group of people simultaneously.

Group sessions are often used on the cusp of big production milestones and may also be the only way to validate certain components such as multiplayer gameplay and balance. It's a format that allows you to cover more ground, for the price of introducing peer-to-peer bias, missing minor usability problems, and diluting the feedback.

The playtesting user group is usually composed of a single cohort, be it company employees, fans and influential community members, recruited testers, press, or friends and family. If possible, try your game on various groups to see how the general opinion differs between them.

Supervised playtests have a group of people playing the game at the same time and in the same space. You can run them in your studio or outside, at a conference, exposition show, and so on. Coordinated and supervised tests enable the members of the development team to observe and take notes, but also introduce the risk of peer-to-peer bias. Communication between playtesters can skew the results as they influence each other's opinions and answer their own questions. Moreover, having multiple people in the same space creates a less critical atmosphere, especially if they're playing a multiplayer game against their friends and peers.

On the other hand, unsupervised playtests have the users access the game at their own leisure (within the testing time frame) and return the results via spoken or written feedback, questionnaires, and analytics. These sessions are easy to run but lower the quantity and quality of findings. They may also not be the best choice for testing onboarding as you cannot directly observe the issues. That said, unsupervised playtests can run for weeks on end, a great choice when gathering feedback on storylines, difficulty and balancing, in-game progression, and metagame.

Public testing

Another great way of gathering feedback and testing the game extensively is to release it into the wild, in a limited manner.

Public testing most often takes the form of alpha and beta tests, which correspond to their milestones and can either be open (available to everyone) or closed (with access granted to a portion of registered candidates).

To make the best use of public tests, you'll need to open and gather feedback from multiple feedback channels such as:

- Game forums, fan pages and community sites such as *Reddit*.
- Questionnaires - either e-mailed via newsletters or linked to from in-game.
- Analytics - user retention, equipment usage, win/loss rates, drop off points, and more!
- Built-in rating systems - completed a mission/quest/storyline/challenge? Rate it on a scale or answer yes/no to a sequence of short questions.

- Community outreach by moderators and customer support members.
- Live-streams - you can engage with the audience and take questions/suggestions directly from them.

Once the game is officially live, you can set up a PTR. This is a test version of the game that allows you to gather feedback on new content and changes before they're made live to the entire player base. PTR can be an invaluable tool for competitive multiplayer games but comes with increased server costs and development effort.

In the mobile development scene, you also have the practice of *soft launching*, that is, releasing the game onto a small market (Thailand, New Zealand, Australia, Canada, Netherlands, and so on) with the help of locally-targeted marketing. At this stage, it's also common to run multiple different variants of the game configuration settings in order to find the best performing one. We'll speak more about A/B testing and analytics in Chapter 15, *Games As a Service*.

Remote playtesting solutions

In the last several years, professional user testing companies have begun putting more attention on video game development, and premium playtesting services now extend way beyond candidate recruitment. A quick web search will unveil at least several highly-specialized companies capable of running full blown playtests on your behalf.

These sessions will either be conducted by specialists in a highly controlled environment, or externalized onto candidates themselves. At the end of the testing period, you'll either be granted access to recordings from on-site sessions or self-recorded testimonials from remote playtesters. Some companies are also willing to combine an expert report that not only highlights the most pressing issues but also suggests potential solutions to your problems.

Remote playtesting services are perfect for anyone who lacks the time, people, and expertise to conduct their own tests, but has the money to pay for them. But their utility is not ending there! Remote sessions can be a supplementary source of detailed usability feedback and provide an effective, unbiased control-group for anyone who conducts their own playtesting.

Sourcing candidates

People are the single most important resource when running your playtesting sessions. Each group of potential candidates comes with a set of potential advantages and disadvantages. That said, do not get hung up on trying to find the very best people to play your game, it's often more beneficial to run smaller tests regularly than to find the perfect group of playtesters.

Personal and professional network

If you're working at a games company, using your colleagues as playtesters is one of the most popular practices.

Advantages:

- **Quick and efficient**: Sessions are cheap to run and easy to organize.
- **Inexpensive:** There's no agency fees or fixed *price per player/hour* associated with using your colleagues. That said, be wary of how many man hours are dedicated to your project and get the manager's approval whenever necessary.
- **Repeatable:** It's possible to track changes in test results across multiple versions of the game.
- **Professional feedback is invaluable**: Your colleagues are likely to be full of games knowledge, market insight, and industry expertise. This primes them to share realistic and actionable feedback. They can also help by generating ideas, proposing game mechanics, and giving tips on improving your development process.
- **Enabling extended play sessions**: Using your network opens up the possibility of spending an extensive amount of time with the game and gathering insight into a larger amount of content, the storyline, and the progression systems. It's still good to observe the onboarding section personally, then set the player free and have them report back after several days. You can then set up another interview and compare the new findings and feedback with the initial performance and opinions of the same tester.
- **Confidential**: There is no need for a **non-disclosure agreement** (**NDA**). These are the safest tests you can run.

Disadvantages:

- **Audience mismatch**: It may be impossible to pick users that fit your target audience. Play patterns, age, gender, and interests may differ dramatically.
- **Lack of objectivity**: Many colleagues are less objective and frank with their critique, while others still; are overly pessimistic or have a personal stake in play. The same can be said of your average friend and acquaintance.
- **Diminishing returns on onboarding**: Sessions repeatedly ran on the same person cannot be used to validate your tutorials or first-time user experience. You can only gather objective feedback on your onboarding with help of a fresh pair of eyes.
- **Feedback stagnation**: The more exposure someone has to your project, the harder it becomes to gather fresh and enthusiastic feedback. Repeating the same content for the tenth time is also likely to sprout an unfairly dull and uninspired reaction. They may have nothing new to say but may still feel obliged to *find something* and try to pick holes in the design.
- **Developers aren't exactly players**: Experience with game development processes gives game dev professionals an unfair insight and skews their perception. If you're looking for an inexperienced player, you're unlikely to find them at a games company.

Your personal and professional network is a hugely valuable playtesting resource that can be tapped into one short notice. Colleagues can provide a fresh pair of professional eyes, valuable critique, and a much-needed boost in confidence. Friends, family members, and acquaintances can be screened easily and are sure to at least partially overlap with your target audience.

Spend this resource wisely and avoid over-exposing too many people too early. And remember, your friends and family can be biased towards you and a game industry professional is rarely equivalent to a real player or an average member of your target audience.

Recruited testers

Product testing is a big industry! Requesting help from a local agency is a sure way to offload the time-intensive work of finding suitable candidates yourself. Chances are they already have a strong database of potential playtesters you can tap into on short notice.

Unfortunately, using agencies to handle player recruitment can get prohibitively expensive. In such cases, you can always try to find testers yourself. Online listings are a couple clicks away and offer a large reach for those who put in the time to manage them. Go to forums, *Reddit* subgroups, and fansites where your target audience congregates.

Advantages:

- **Handpicked audience**: A set of entry requirements makes it much easier to pre-screen and recruit candidates representative of your target audience.
- **Controlled, unbiased, recorded**: With proper training and practice, you'll be able to run tightly controlled sessions that provide you with unbiased feedback and even digital recordings of real reactions to various parts of the game.
- **Time Efficient**: Players can be booked for specific days and time slots. It's possible to fit multiple tests in a week and have them witnessed by various members of your team—all without unnecessarily disrupting the development schedule.
- **Ideal for art and FTUE**: This is a perfect way of validating your art direction, brand, and **First Time User Experience** (**FTUE**) against the members of your target audience.
- **Confidential**: People visiting your studio are more willing to sign and abide by the rules of the NDA than the strangers and fans encountered in the wild.

Disadvantages:

- **Requires pre-planning**: Testers, developers, builds, and devices all need to be scheduled for a specific day and time.
- **Costly**: Even if you avoid the agency costs by recruiting players online yourself, you still need to set aside a monetary reward for each player (typically a small shop voucher).
- **Limited duration**: A recruited player can rarely help you validate long-term progression, retention, storyline, or difficulty. It may be possible to arrange for long or recurring sessions, but doing so will increase the costs and yield diminishing returns.

Strangers

Approaching strangers for help is a seemingly common practice amongst indie developers and university students. This can be done on the street, in a public space, or even at an exposition show or a conference.

Advantages:

- **Mobile friendly**: If your project is a mobile title, you can present it to potential players on a moment's notice. Whether you set up a simple stand inside your university building or ask people in the mall to take a look at your prototype, opportunities are abundant.

- **Inexpensive**: The only time you absolutely need to account for is the one spent by the facilitators. Nevertheless, time is money, and you'll increase your chances if you're able to present your candidates with a small shop voucher as an incentive.

- **Suitable for onboarding**: Short tests are perfect for evaluating your tutorials, controls, usability, and the general appeal of the game.

- **Great for art testing**: You don't need a playable version of the game to test the appeal of your brand and the game's art direction. The best way to do that is to present the audience with printouts of several different versions. Have the person pick up their most and least favorite ones and tell you why. Such tests are very reliable and quick to conduct.

Disadvantages:

- **Hard to scale**: Needless to say, there are only so many people you can approach every day and there's a large amount of idle time involved.

- **Require filtering**: It's very hard to screen for suitable candidates and even a short pre or post-test questionnaire may strain the attention span of your candidate, making it harder to determine who exactly the feedback is coming from.

- **More effective with a brand**: If you're testing in a public environment, the attention span will be very short. In general, the bigger the brand or the monetary incentive, the easier it is to recruit. Finding volunteers to try the new *FIFA*, *Call of Duty*, or *Star Wars* game is much easier than recruiting players for an unknown title from an unknown studio, especially with no monetary award for their time.

- **Lack of confidentiality**: Not many volunteers are keen to read and sign a NDA, and even if they do, you're unlikely to be in a position to properly enforce them.

- **Limited use for console and PC products**: Needless to say, getting strangers to visit your studio and sit down in front of a screen is hard!

- **Potential legal roadblocks**: Some countries have strict restrictions put on engaging with minors without their parent's written consent. Malls and other quasi-public spaces also have restrictions on what you can and cannot do on their premises without prior authorization.

Running playtesting sessions

We'll now provide you with a set of guidelines and tips for running your very own playtesting sessions.

At first, the methodology may seem unnecessarily complex and restrictive, but the effort you put into preparing and running your sessions has a direct impact on the quality of the results. Do not fret over your mistakes as a test facilitator. After several sessions, it will all become second nature!

The playtesting scenarios deconstructed below are two of the most commonly encountered permutations. For any other situation, simply pick and choose to find a combination that fits your playtesters, as well as the available equipment, people, and facilities.

Supervised individual sessions

Supervised sessions are best run in a meeting room or another secluded place where you won't be interrupted. The only people present should be the playtester, the test facilitator, and a maximum of two observers. The observers are typically other members of the core development team—everyone should witness at least one test in order to appreciate how their game is performing on an actual player. Instruct the observers to remain quiet and make their presence as unnoticeable as possible.

If you have the capabilities, record each session! This will allow you to distribute the footage to everyone interested, and remove the necessity for observers. In the best case scenario, you'd be able to combine raw game footage with a separate video stream of player's face and body. Seeing the body language of the tester will help you identify their emotional state and better assess their reaction to various parts of the game.

If the candidate is under NDA, make sure to prepare one. As soon as they arrive, greet them, offer them a drink and pass an NDA to read and sign. Once they're all set, the session can commence.

Session introduction

If you do not know the playtester, start by introducing yourself and everyone else in the room. It's good to put distance between yourself and the product. If possible, pretend that you (and everyone else in the room) are not a part of the development team—*We've been asked by some people at the company to run this tests for them*. This setup allows the candidate to open up without fearing they'll hurt your feelings.

After introductions, it's important to explain the purpose of the playtesting session and prime the player to vocalize their emotions and intentions. This is essentially a *script*, which is being run at the start of each session. In fact, you could write and print it ahead, then read it out to each tester. The script is tailor-made for each game and test-group, but it's most likely going to include following statements and questions:

- We will present you a work-in-progress version of a game. We're looking to get your feedback and opinions so that the game can be improved.
- There may be some bugs and unfinished areas, but it's important to get your personal, unfiltered, and honest opinion. If something is terrible, say it's terrible and explain why. Similarly, if you like something, tell us what and why. You cannot hurt our feelings, we are here to learn as much as we can about what works and what doesn't.
- We are here to evaluate the product, not the playtester. You cannot do anything wrong, if something is confusing, it's 100 percent the game's fault.
- When playing the game, try to think aloud and explain what you're doing and why. For example, *I think I need to train more troops. I'll need more gold to do that. Maybe if I go on this mission, I'll get more gold.*
- It's good to ask questions. In fact, you should ask all the questions that pop into your head. One small caveat though, we cannot answer the questions immediately. Instead, we'll give you all the answers you want after we're done!

If you're testing a branded product, consider some of the following:

- How familiar are you with the brand?
    - At this point, it's best to present pictures of characters or other branded material and ask for a run-down of what is what. Often players say they are familiar yet cannot pinpoint more than one or two character names.
- What is your opinion of the brand?
- Who do you think the brand appeals to most?
- Do you have any expectations for a game based on this brand?
- Would you be interested in playing a game in this world?

Unless you know the tester inside out or are running a pre/post-session questionnaire, it's important to understand your player's background:

- Do you play video games? How often? On what devices? PC, console, mobile?
- What are some of your favorite games?
- What gaming genres are you interested in most?

- Are you playing anything now? What is it?
- How much do you spend on games per month?
- Have you ever spent money on downloadable content/in-app purchases? If the answer is YES: What did you spend on? If it's NO: Why not?

Should you have any artistic tests to conduct (most likely mocked-up screenshots and characters in different themes and styles), present them at this point and get feedback on the following questions:

- Which one appeals to the player most? Why?
- Which one appeals to the player least? Why?
- Who do they think the different styles would appeal to most?

Playtesting session

It's time to begin the session! For best results, try to adhere to following guidelines:

- **Provide a comfortable atmosphere**: Keep the disturbances to a minimum and do not respond to player's actions and questions; sit back, observe and encourage the player to keep going. Do not loom over the player, sit next to them and respect their personal space.
- **Encourage the playtester to speak**: Provide positive reinforcement when the player speaks (even if they are wrong) and remind them to vocalize their thoughts and reactions if they are overly quiet.
- **Take notes discreetly**: Do not glue yourself to a notepad as players may feel scrutinized and exposed. An exception to this is when players are voicing their opinions and ideas - writing these down can be encouraging. Recording the session helps reduce the reliance on paper notes, and you can always write things down after the session is over.
- **Do not answer questions**: You're not there to help the playtester have a good time or sell them onto your game. Do not answer questions but encourage them to be asked. Find out why they'd like to know and withhold the answers until the session is over.
- **Prompt players to explain the game to you**: This will help compare player's mental model of the game with the reality. Ask for an explanation of every little detail, as if you were their friend who has never seen the game—Tell me what just happened? What do you think this means? How does this work? Who is this character? Be sure to prompt such explanations whenever the user is struggling (to find out what's wrong in their rationale), as well as at the end of the test (to check if everything aligns and there are no knowledge gaps).

- **Ask if they'd keep playing**: Every 10 minutes or so, ask the tester if they'd keep playing the game on their own volition. This can help you pinpoint potential drop off points. Find out why they'd be willing to stop/continue playing.
- **Avoid leading questions**: A question can be loaded with answers or prompt the player to respond in a particular way. "Would you agree that the controls are easy to understand and intuitive?" is not a good way to ask about controls! "What's your opinion on the controls?" is a much better way to formulate a question.
- **Do not waste time/torture your playtester**: You're not learning anything new from someone who's stuck on a single screen for 20 minutes. Write down the point of friction, apologize for the confusion, and explain what has to be done to move on. Explain only as much as you need to keep the test going, and only when the playtester is stuck for good.

Post-session interview

After the playtesting session is over, it's time to ask about tester's overall experience, gather any outstanding feedback, and answer their questions. Consider the following questions:

- Would you keep playing this game outside the test? Why?
- Would you spend money on this game? Why?
- How would you rate your overall experience? How fun was it on a scale from 1 to 10?
- What's the most memorable moment? Something that stood out to you.
- What's the part you enjoyed most? Something you really loved.
- What's the part you enjoyed least? Something you really hated.
- If you could make changes to this game, what would you change and how?
- Who do you think this game would appeal to most?
- Any other ideas on how we could improve this game and make it appeal more to players like you?

If your game reminded the player of another product:

- How does it compare to that game or other games in that genre?
- What are the biggest differences? What's better and what's worse?

Instead (or in addition to) the interview, you may ask the playtester to fill in a questionnaire. We'll explain the best practices for creating and interpreting playtesting questionnaires in a separate section below.

Unsupervised group playtesting

An unsupervised group session requires far less time and involvement per player, but there's still plenty to organize.

First up, you need to ensure that each playtester has a suitable device and full access to the specific version of the game. The easiest way out is to have every player use their own PC/Console/Mobile phone, sparing you the need to organize equipment.

Make sure to provide detailed instructions on how the game can be obtained and installed. The installing instructions should also explain the intentions behind the test, any areas that require special focus, feedback channels, and any known bugs and issues (in a bid to save everyone's time).

Setting an objective

The success of unsupervised tests depends solely on your players finding the time to try your game and putting in the effort to share their feedback. Unfortunately for us, numbers provide safety. Without direct supervision and time-slots, many playtesters tend to get surprisingly busy with everything but playing the game.

To improve the participation, you'll need to set out a clear, achievable objective for your participants. Try to make the goal rely on time-based progression, not skill. For example: get your character to experience level 10, reach the mountains, finish the first two chapters of the story mode, and so on. This objective will ensure that playtesters engage with the game sufficiently before giving feedback. It also provides a clear way out (excuse) for those who aren't inclined to put in too much of their personal time.

Unsupervised group sessions are often used when a game is approaching a significant milestone. If the project has a large scope, it carries a risk of diluting the results. The sheer amount of new game features and content can make for a very long or very chaotic playtest. Players who are set to roam free across a huge game will likely touch upon everything, but rarely provide a deep analysis of any particular area. To help produce more concrete and thorough feedback, you'll either need to focus the test on a smaller set of areas or features (*This playtest is all about Player vs Player combat mechanics and balancing*) or divide your playtesters into subgroups. Each subgroup would then be served its own instructions, for example Group A focuses on the story mode, Group B on special abilities, and Group C feeds back on the guilds and social features.

You can also increase engagement and the quality of feedback by turning the whole thing into a competition and providing the playtesters with extra incentives. For example, each player has a chance to grab a prize in the following categories: the most useful feedback, the best new idea, the highest score on the leaderboard. If you don't want to hand-pick winners for various categories, you can always run a single prize draw for everyone who submitted their questionnaire in time. As for rewards, if a shop voucher is out of the question, you can always take the winner out for lunch, shower them with their favorite sweets (you can find that out with the questionnaire), or honor them by naming an in-game character, item, or location after them.

Objectives and competitions may seem silly at first, but you'll be surprised at how effective they are at promoting test participation and securing high-quality feedback!

Gathering feedback

For unsupervised group testing, the typical ways to gather feedback would be:

- Face-to-face conversation (make sure to take notes during or immediately after receiving feedback)
- Post-session questionnaire
- Electronic communication (work chat, email, and so on)
- In-game feedback forms (vote a map up/down, rate your experience in last round, and so on)
- Analytics (crash reports, win/loss ratios, drop-off points, average frames per second per device, most/least popular and successful loadouts, and so on)

Playtesting questionnaires

Well executed questionnaires are tailor-made to both your game (in its current state) and the playtesting session itself. Sometimes you'll go for a very short and snappy form, with just a few burning questions to answer, and other times, you'll try to build the profile of the player and seek feedback on every aspect of the game. Consider the following tips:

- **Be mindful of the length**: The length of your questionnaire should correspond to the length of the test and how much area you've covered. A form with 25 questions may be suitable for a week-long *playathon*, but not so much for a few short sessions of gameplay focused on the onboarding experience. Playtesting can be fun, filling forms is not.

- **Build a player profile**: Unless your test is very narrow in scope and the playtesters well known, you should dedicate the first few questions to getting to know your player. This information will help you to add more context and validate the feedback. Player profiling comes down to three components:

  - **Basic info**: Name, age, and gender.

  - **Gaming habits**: Do they play games on your target platform? How often?

  - **Calibrating against genre and competition**: Create a list of similar genres for the playtester to tick, add an open-field at the end for them to add more if they want. Ask what's their favorite game in the genre, ask them to score it. Now that you know who they are and what they play, you can ask them to rate their overall experience in your game on the very same scale. If someone gives their genre showcase a 5/10, and you manage to score a 6, you know that you're faring comparably well in their eyes— perhaps it's not possible for your game to fully satisfy this player, no matter what you do.

- **Use basic questions to track progress**: Repeating basic questions in each test allows you to make quantifiable comparisons across different tests and milestones. Consider making some of the following your mainstay:

  - Rate your overall experience (1-terrible, 10-excellent).

  - Would you play this game after release (1-not at all, 10-absolutely).

  - Rate the default control scheme (1-terrible, 10-excellent).

  - Rate the user interface (1-very hard to use and understand, 10-very easy to use and understand).

- Rate the difficulty of gameplay challenges (1-way too difficult, 3-just right, 5-way too easy). Due to the nature of difficulty questions, they often need to use a different scale; make sure it's visually distinct! (in this case, it's five bullet points instead of numbers from 1 to 10).
- How long did you play?/What level did you reach?/What was your high score?

- **Avoid leading questions**: In here, as in spoken interviews, questions should avoid pointing to an answer. *Do you agree that this game is very easy to use?* is a loaded question. *Rate the difficulty of interaction* is a better phrasing, which will make your players consider their experience, as opposed to having them follow the general trend of agreeing to anything they don't have a strong opinion on.
- **Use 10-point scale**: If a question lends itself to a numbered rating, a 1-10 range provides much more accurate results than a 1-5. With a 10-point scale, you can narrow the score to a tidy number, while providing ample room between the middle and the absolute.
- **Combine questions**: If you're asking the same questions about 5 different components, simply combine them into a single, tidy matrix.
- **Stay consistent**: Do not flip things around! Making a left-to-right scale (where left is bad, right is good) suddenly go in the opposing direction is a surefire way to get false results.
- **Use digital forms**: Do not bother with creating print-out forms that you'll later need to manually gather, input and analyze. Services like *SurveyMonkey* and *Google Forms* are free and easy to use. If your playtesters are nearby, you can secure fresh and immediate feedback by giving them access to a tablet with a survey on it. Another cool thing about digital forms, you can embed links to them directly inside the game!
- **Organize the form**: Order your questions in a logical and repeatable fashion. If one question flows into another without dramatically shifting context, the whole form will take less time and effort to fill. Player info comes first, general questions second, test-specific questions are next, and any open-ended questions last. Try to group your questions either by category (story, combat, social features) or context (there are 5 chapters in the game and each gets a series of questions).
- **Track fill-rate**: The larger the test group, the harder it is to get a 100 percent fill rate. Check the fill-rate throughout the test duration and remind the playtesters about the questionnaire. If needed, send individual messages to players that lag behind. Getting a large group of 50 players to a 75 percent fill rate is a big success.

- **Let the players express themselves**: There are three open questions that I try to fit at the end of my forms:
    - What's an in-game moment you LOVED?
    - What's an in-game moment you HATED?
    - Any closing comments, new ideas, things you'd like to see more or less of?

 The screenshots used in this chapter are for illustrative purposes only. We do not recommend that you to misuse these in any way. For more information please consult the terms and conditions of the publishers mentioned in the *Disclaimer* section of this book.

Summary

Oh, chapter summary... we meet again! Thanks to this (rather lengthy) tutorial, we come armed with knowledge on how to make our games more accessible, how to teach our players, and how to make products that resonate with international audiences. But most importantly, we know how to verify it all with the powers of playtesting, a process that helps ensure the game you're making is at least as good as the one you set out to make!

Speaking of quality, no matter how accessible and well explained your game, it can all fail in the face of underwhelming challenges and overwhelming odds. We'll now take a look at the art of game balance and ways to create perfectly paced experiences. If all goes well, you'll soon know how to keep the difficulty in check and the player on the edge of their seats!

13
Balancing

Gather your notes! We will now combine the knowledge from several previous chapters and explore the ways in which we can plan, structure, and adjust the rules and content of our games in order to create an experience that captures and holds the interest of our audience.

By the end of this chapter, you'll be armed with practical techniques and methods used to adjust the game difficulty, set the pace of the experience, and tune the game's balance to perfection. Let's begin!

Gameplay balancing

The concept of **gameplay balancing** goes far beyond the qualities of individual objects and characters, and into the nature of play itself. Take a look at the classic example of a flawed game design, tic-tac-toe. Why is it flawed? The starting player can never lose. All they need to do is put their mark in the middle. This is a failure of both the design of the rules and the game's balance itself. The game has a single, dominant strategy, and once you figure it out or run into it, you're incentivized to replicate it. The presence of a dominant strategy drastically reduces a player's options. Once introduced into the play pattern, the game loses most of its appeal. Therefore, a wide possibility space is a defining feature of a well-balanced game.

> *"Given the opportunity, players will optimize the fun out of a game."*
>
> *–Soren Johnson, lead designer of Civilization IV, 2011.*

Players are naturally inclined to fall into the safety of senseless repetition, a single move or combo in a fighting game, an optimized building order in an RTS, or the strongest known character class in an RPG. It's our job to make this kind of choice as hard as possible. Speaking of choices, why don't you make one now?

You're stopped by a group of bandits. Pick your weapon: a rusty dagger or the Excalibur sword?

Let's not kid ourselves, this is not a compelling choice; it does nothing to expand your possibilities with an interesting (viable) strategy. And strategies are choices.

Ask yourself, are you designing a puzzle or a game? Puzzles can be great fun, but they rely on a limited set of solutions. Once a puzzle is solved, it offers little replayability. Games that rely on puzzles often require a constant stream of new challenges. Non-puzzle games, on the other hand, are at their best when they are nearly impossible to solve. To get the most out of your game mechanics, you want solutions that are imperfect and shift depending on the situation. When asked "which weapon/gadget/car/character is the best?", the answer you should aim for is *it depends*.

Remember, it's perfectly valid to have an optimal tool for a specific job, but what you should stay clear from is the perfect tool for every job. A compelling choice always comes with a trade-off of some sorts. The trade-off doesn't have to be the cost, time, reliability, or a risk of some sorts, it may just be the inability to do something equally interesting instead.

Game balancing is a war of attrition. It often comes down to thousands of little changes, be it to the level design, the mechanics, or the game's data. In the beginning, everything you do will be an estimation, a ballpark. In these early phases, it's more important to set your data's structure than to achieve the best possible balance. Only after extensive playtesting, and with the help of subjective player feedback and objective analytics, will you be able to move towards true balance. And still, *true balance*, is more of an aspiration than a guaranteed result.

Balancing methods and tips

The following list of tips and tricks should help build an understanding of how to approach the process of game balancing. Right after that, we'll share some of the actual balancing techniques that you can apply to your project!:

- **Start somewhere**
  Is 200 or 2,000 the right number of hit points? Well... that depends. When it comes to game balance, everything is relative. Plant a stake in the ground by setting one element that feels right, and then use it as a reference point for everything else.

- **Narrow your options**
  Avoid iterating in small increments. It's better to overshoot by a large margin to eliminate that option and increase the resolution of changes as you go along. First balancing attempts should be bold; the time for tiny 5% tweaks comes much later.

- **Use big integers**
  If possible, try to base data around values with at least a couple of digits. Numbers in their hundreds and thousands are easier to read and operate on than tens of millions or fractions. They also allow for the right level of in-game granularity; you can deal 25 damage instead of being forced to choose between the large gaps that exists between 2 or 3.

- **Round up/down smartly**
  Using multipliers on your data will often create numbers with lots of digits after the decimal point. On top of that, exponential growth in many game economies can easily turn your starting values in the hundreds into endgame values in the tens of millions. In these scenarios, you'll need to use clever rounding methods based on the factor of the number.

  Spreadsheet formulas are an invaluable tool for any game designer! To achieve good rounding, you can try the following formula: = $Floor(A1,10^{(Floor(log10(A1))-1)})$
  It takes the value (*A1*) and rounds it down (*Floor*) to just two significant digits, creating a set of clean and readable numbers that maintain the right level of detail. This way, 5,421 becomes 5,400, and 1,437,938 turns into 1,400,000. If you'd like to show more significant digits, simply change the **-1** at the end into **-2** and so on. You can also use *Ceiling* instead of *Floor* to round values up.

- **Perception matters**
  Are you familiar with the *weak assault rifle* anecdote? A rumor has it that, in *Halo: Combat Evolved*, playtesters were avoiding the assault rifle like wildfire. They claimed it was too weak, even when the balancing was taken to the extreme, making it completely overpowered. Turns out, all the weapon needed was a louder sound effect with an increased amount of bass. Remember, balance is subjective! If players believe a tool is weak and avoid using it, it is weak, just not from the data point of view. If attempts to popularize a certain strategy with data alone fails, make sure to look for issues in perception. Perhaps all you need to do is work on the feedback including animation, camera, sounds, visual effects, and physical attributes.

- **Self-balancing strategies and countering**

  Rock-paper-scissors is a classic example of a self-balancing system; each choice is valid but comes with a clear strength and weakness. It's also a system built on hard-counters, that is, choices that guarantee success against a particular strategy. Most interesting power relationships are usually a bit more subtle, since they come down to a series of advantages and disadvantages, rather than absolutes. When designing the dynamics of different units and strategies, make sure that the power relationships make sense in the context of the game. The more grounded in reality and less ambiguous your strengths and weaknesses (trade-offs) are, the lower the learning curve.

  For example, in a medieval strategy, the equivalent to the rock-paper-scissors (but with a less binary result) game would be the relationship between archers, pikemen, and cavalry. Archers are strong against pikemen, pikemen counter the cavalry, and cavalry can easily defeat the archers. Another highly popular power relationship is the one of opposing elements, as seen in *Pokémon*, which started simple with *fire* burning *grass*, *grass* absorbing *water*, and *water* putting out *fire*. Relationships of this kind can be a bit confusing though, especially if more ambiguous elements join the mix. Put the likes of *metal, life, death, light, ice, poison, darkness,* and *electricity* into the mix, and you'll have a potential cluster of confusion on your hands. To make a system with such a high level of complexity work, you'll need to introduce it gradually, and ensure a good level of visibility that helps guide the players (in *Pokémon*, a clear efficacy report is given after each attack).

- **Feedback loops**

  Unbalanced systems often spiral out of control due to *feedback loops*. What are those? Let's start by examining a scenario from a fictional city management game. *Due to an unforeseen event, the population in your town shrinks, resulting in a decreased tax income. This, in turn, sabotages your budget and further lowers the satisfaction of your people, making them leave, reducing the tax income even further. Not long after, your town is desolate and out of funds to pick itself up.*

  This is an example of a *positive feedback loop*, where an event creates a ripple effect, which propelled its impact even further. Whenever the penalty for failure or reward for success is not carefully managed, there is a strong chance of having your game balance spiral out of control. Stay vigilant and investigate the systems you create by paying close attention to how player's power grows and shrinks with each outcome, and whether there's anything stopping them from raising or falling completely out of balance. A well-designed game is less of a nuclear reactor and more of a thermostat, keeping the temperature within a desired range.

- **Try Fermi estimation**

  Back in `Chapter 3`, *Scoping a Game Project*, we introduced you to the estimation techniques attributed to Enrico Fermi. The same method can be utilized in game balancing. The initial values are almost always more or less educated guesses, and you can improve your results by considering the minimum and maximum acceptable values, then shooting straight for the average. Is five million the right amount of XP when going from level 49 to 50? I don't know, but I do know that by framing this problem in an approachable way, we can better understand the implications of picking that number. Break it down!:

  - How much experience can a player on level 49 get in an hour?
  - What if he's quite bad, and what if he's an expert?
  - How many hours will people spend on the game a day?
  - What's the minimum, and what's the maximum?
  - Time for some divisions! Do these numbers look right?
    Once you're happy with the time required for different types of players to level up, you've got yourself a great starting point!

- **Unify your units**

  In complex economies with many resources at play, a shared frame of reference empowers you to make more natural comparisons and more informed balancing decisions. Don't compare apples to oranges... just make sure everything is counted in carrots instead!

  To start with, determine your unit! You can pick one of the resources that is already in the game, or you can use a completely imaginary one. I usually create a new one and call it **UU** for short. Next up, you have to set up a cost relationship matrix inside your balancing spreadsheets. This matrix states how much of the other resources goes towards one unified unit. For example, 1 UU equals 200 gold, 350 wood, 100 sulfur, and five minutes of playtime. The breakdown immediately settles that sulfur is twice as valuable as gold. The question is, is it twice as hard to obtain? And is that a conscious decision or an accident? A unified unit is highly effective at helping you assess and tune the *taps* (production) and *sinks* (spend) of multiple resources.

- **Quantities and relative power**
  Who'll win the fight between (A) one tank with 80 health and 50 damage and (B) two tanks with 50 health and 25 damage? The sum of the attributes favors (B), but the relative power does not. In this case, after (A) destroys one of the two tanks, it effectively lowers enemy damage potential by half, securing the margin it needs to win. This is a trivial example, but it goes to show that there's more to balancing than raw attributes. The number of units in play can be either advantageous (the ability to move independently and attack two targets at once, enemy damage can be wasted due to *overkilling,* and so on) as well as disadvantageous (harder to maneuver or engage all enemies at once, requires more space or storage, easily countered by area of effect abilities). Always pay attention to how these factors affect your game!

- **Use analytics**
  Parts of your game will be nearly impossible to balance without the help of analytics. Once the game is in the hands of playtesters, in beta or live, you should be able to gather data on the most and least popular choices and strategies, as well as win/loss ratios associated with them. More information on analytics awaits you in `Chapter 15,` *Games As a Service.*

- **Lost opportunity is a cost**
  Saving money for a single big unit or item? The process of saving resources and withholding actions is part of the cost in itself. This cost varies depending on the game's mechanics and individual circumstances, but it may mean that you're unable to scout ahead, capture ground, or defend against an incoming attack. Make sure that build times, limits, cooldowns, and building or research requirements are all taken into account, and treat them as part of the unit cost, allowing you to scale its power more accurately.

- **Make everything feel powerful**
  A common pitfall for many inexperienced designers is to put absolute trust in their spreadsheet formulas and move everything towards an uninspiring mediocrity. The most rewarding games are those in which most tools, gadgets, abilities, and weapons are not only fun to use, but when applied in the correct scenario, they feel absolutely overpowered. Above all, your game should be exciting, and it's hard to pull that off if differences between strategies are minuscule, and the outcome of the balancing dull.

- **Minimize the iteration time**

  Having to rebuild the entire game just to see a few modified parameters in action is not only a huge waste of time but it also makes the balancing tasks much harder to pull off. After all, it's hard to follow your ideas through if you have to put your thought process on hold for minutes or hours at a time. Before production begins, make sure that the team knows your plans and intentions regarding game balancing. In an ideal world, basic tuning operations are done in the game editor or by using a debugged in-game interface and are immediately reflected in the game. Quick iteration times will help you enter the flow-state and apply your creativity in a more natural manner, with experimental edits that are in direct response to immediate observations.

- **Focus on the end-user**

  As you grow more and more adept at playing your own game (and solving your own puzzles), everything you create begins to feel easy and straightforward. The more experience you have with your game, the higher the risk of creating inaccessible content. Keep track of your target audience and determine who's going to interact with the feature or content that you're tuning. When testing your work, you can try to put an artificial handicap on yourself, for example, by restricting yourself from using more than a few special abilities, or making purposefully sub-optimal decisions and seeing how the gameplay scenario evolves from there.

MBT balancing

The MBT approach takes root in the old real-time strategy games like *Command and Conquer*, where the pillar unit of the army (usually the main battle tank, hence the MBT) is served as the centerpiece for unit balancing. It's a simple but effective technique that can be applied to medium amounts of content (25-100 units).

To start with, pick a well-rounded unit, the focal point of the content. In the case of a real-time strategy game such as *CC: Red Alert*, it would be the main battle tank—the backbone of most armies. Set the stats of your MBT, and tie everything else in the game right back to it. If your game features multiple factions, balancing the MBTs of each faction serves as a cross-faction anchor.

Regardless of final in-game values, you want your initial MBT's stats to be as easy to read as possible: Speed 10, Health 100, Damage Per Second 10, Attack Speed 1, Range 10, Cost 100. The simple, round numbers make every other unit in the game instantly comparable to the common denominator.

Once the base data for most units is plugged inside the spreadsheets, you can use simple formulas to calculate things such as:

- Health per resource spent
- DPS (damage per second) per resource spent
- Time to kill an MBT (derived from using attack speed and DPS)
- Time to be killed by an MBT

Once you're happy with the balance on paper, you can apply multiplications and be rounding to the data to make the numbers work (and look) good in-game.

This technique can get you very far, very quickly, but its value goes down with the amount of complexity in play. Once you introduce elements such as special attacks, the area of effect abilities, different armor types, status resistances, and whole new categories such as flying or melee units, the MBT approach becomes much harder to pull off in an efficient and effective manner.

Layered Modifiers

The titular *Layered Modifiers* are as much of a balancing method as they are a way of structuring and thinking about your data. It is a powerful and highly scalable approach that can help you manage huge amounts of content and variables.

Case in point, I have used this method in a mobile strategy game called *Transformers: Earth Wars* to establish and maintain balance with over 20,000 building and character variants. In terms of combat balancing alone, our data spreadsheets were in control of:

- 9 defensive buildings (with up to 15 upgrade levels)
- 13 utility and production buildings (with up to 15 upgrade levels)
- 6 *Combiners* (super-units composed of 5-6 other robots; each *Combiner* had 2 upgrade versions and 10 to 20 power levels)
- Over 120 *Transformers* characters, equally divided into two playable factions - *Autobots* and *Decepticons*:
    - *Autobot* and *Decepticon* characters were paired against one another. Some pairings were equal, and some were slightly asymmetric. Early on we pushed for variation, but after several months of live operations, we moved towards a near 100 percent equality within each pairing, mostly to maintain the community's sentiment on fairness.

- Each character was given a *star rating* (from 1 to 5 stars). The higher the rating, the more rare and powerful the character. We usually released between 3 and 5 versions of each character.
- All characters had from 20 to 60 levels of experience (20 for 1-star, 40 for 2-star, 50 for 3-star, 60 for 4 and 5-star characters).
- Each character had a special ability with 10 upgrade levels (most abilities were unique within your faction, and were only shared with a bot's counterpart on the opposite side).

- Dozens of unique (and upgradable) pieces of equipment that change the stats and abilities of characters and defenses
- A few dozens of *battle boosts* (single use power-ups)

So, how do you deal with over 20,000 moving parts? By starting from the very top and creating layers of modifiers that help differentiate, scale, and distinguish between your units.

In *Transformers: Earth Wars*, we were able to master our data in *Google Sheets* and used an in-house plugin to import data from the sheets into files for use in-game. Let's break down the organization of character data and how various parts were multiplied and inherited at different levels. Note that a similar (but less complicated) approach was used for buildings, game economy, and other data-heavy aspects of the game.

Tier 1 – Globals sheet

Globals are the very top level of our data structure. By changing values here, you can change the balance of all units in the game. Once established, these values almost never change. The *Globals* sheet contains:

- **Base stats**: HP (health), DPS (damage), and movement speed
- **Level up bonuses**: Set percentage increase to HP and DPS
- **Star-rating multipliers**: Table of multiplications to base HP and DPS depending on the star rating
- **Post-battle cooldown values**: Characters go on cooldown after each battle, and the length grows with character level

Tier 2 – Character Classes sheet

This is another high-level sheet, which is established and iterated early on. There were 18 character classes in the data, which is far too many for an average player to keep in their heads. This is why some of the classes get merged when imported, allowing us to maintain six easily distinguishable in-game character classes. For example, *Melee DPS* exists as a separate class inside the sheets but gets put under the umbrella of the *Warrior* class later down the line. All in all, the *Character Classes* sheet contains:

- **Class-based stat multipliers**: HP (health), DPS (damage), and movement speed
- **Starting abilities**: Basic and special attacks
- **Common passive effects**: For example, *Warriors* get immunity to stun effects
- **Default weapons**: For example, *Gunners* usually use the same grenade launcher, unless it gets overwritten later
- **Base in-game size**: *Warriors* are bigger than *Gunners*, while *Minions* are even smaller
- **And more!**: There's a variety of additional parameters and tags, which are used in battle to tell classes apart, both visually and functionally

Tier 3 – Character Archetype sheet

With foundations set by *Globals* and *Character Classes*, we can now define the characteristics of a single, bespoke unit. The *Character Archetype* sheet is the starting point for any designer who wishes to add a new character to the game. It is the place where the most specific qualities are set, including:

- **Character class and faction**: Pick one of the 18 classes from the class sheet and select the faction for your new robot.
- **Individual stat modifiers**: Characters can be customized within each class by giving them various modifiers. For example, 1.08x HP and 0.96x DPS or additional movement speed.
- **Attack overwrites**: Many attacks are shared between characters, but it's up to the designer to hand-pick the most suitable ones. For example, a *Warrior* with a melee weapon will use sword attacks rather than punches. Additional attacks and abilities are also added on a case-by-case basis.
- **Special ability**: Some special abilities are shared between a few bots in the same class, but most characters receive a bespoke special ability that's been handcrafted by the designer.

- **Additional passive effects**: You can customize the character further by including passive effects such as immunity to stun.
- **Weapon overwrites and other cosmetic data**: We have the full ability to supply the character with a different (or an additional) weapon as well as to change its size and other cosmetic attributes.

Tier 4 – Character Upgrade Path sheet

With the character's class and archetype largely defined, it's time to decide what star-ratings will be available. The *Upgrade Path* sheet contains little bespoke data, but is often imported and referenced across many sheets to build a list of available characters and their star-ratings.

Tier 5 – Troop Level Data sheet

There are tens of thousands of character level files, but none of them have to be managed by hand. The *Troop Level Data* sheet uses the data and multipliers from other sheets to assemble a long list with stats and parameters for each level and a star rating of a character. All you have to do is to import the new parameters from the sheet and into the game files!

Use case summary

Let's sum up our multi-layered setup and extract its key learnings:

- **Globals** are the foundations for everything; they allow us to make sweeping changes to the entire balance from a single place.
- **Classes** allow us to group similar content together and balance different categories of content against one another. For example, ranged characters against melee ones.
- **Archetypes** give us the option to personalize each individual piece of content and retain the control over the minute details.
- **Upgrade Paths** is where we clone a single character into several variants. They let us determine which variants of the characters we'll have in the game and whether there are any special changes between different versions.
- **Troop Level Data** is a data sheet, which uses everything we defined to automatically assemble thousands of character files. All we need to do is to import the data into the game!

This might seem like a lot of spreadsheet work, but the time we'd save on balancing and setting up game data could be counted in hundreds of man-hours. *Layered Modifiers* allow us to hand-craft and personalize each character and building while retaining the flexibility to make sweeping changes to the game's balance on a grand scale. Consider a similar approach whenever faced with a large game economy with thousands of moving parts.

While big spreadsheets are great for handling heaps of game data, new mechanics and abilities are best tuned on a real-time basis. In *Transformers: Earth Wars*, we created and balanced character abilities directly inside *Unity Editor*, which allowed for a quick, and in some cases instant, iteration. As for game mechanics, camera controls, and certain game rules, we built a simple debug menu that gave us control over default parameters and allowed us to switch (flag) components of different features ON and OFF. This level of control enables live experimentation with game features and is invaluable when prototyping new gameplay.

Game difficulty

It's up to the game and level designers to create an experience that's optimal for as many players as possible, and if that seems like a simple task, trust us when we say it's not!

As we have already established in `Chapter 12`, *Accessibility*, our audience varies greatly in their level of gaming experience, real-world knowledge, physical and mental capacity, and even language proficiency. From pattern recognition and memory to spatial navigation, reflexes, and hand-eye coordination, there are many skills at play, and in some departments, the gap between players can be huge. Moreover, some players like to be challenged, and others have little time and patience for a serious struggle, preferring to breeze through levels and experience the story with relative ease.

There are many ways of addressing the difficulty gap. Some rely on pre-set attributes and redesigning the game content, while others are fully automatic and respond to player's performance. No matter which solution you go for, it's important to remember that as the designer of the game, you're sure to know it inside out. By default, you'll make the game too difficult for the average player.

It's paramount to playtest early, and playtest often, even if the sessions end up being quick, informal, and undocumented. Try to expose your work to players on both ends of the spectrum. Looking at how low-skilled and extremely proficient people react to new in-game challenges will help you assess what is and isn't difficult, and where the difficulty is coming from. Is it the number of variables at play, input frequency, accuracy or timing, or is it the game knowledge and mastery over game mechanics? After several sessions of this type, you'll gain insight into the main sources of difficulty in your game. You can use this knowledge in two ways:

- **To develop a set of rules to adhere to**: For example, in an RTS on easy difficulty, we shouldn't have the AI attack the player in the first 6 minutes as they are unlikely to be ready.
- **To help you score your encounters**: Try assigning artificial *difficulty points* and multipliers to various parts of your gameplay challenges. For example, a shielded enemy is 5, a shotgun troop is 3 (but 7 when fought up-close), having at least two enemies at once adds +20 percent to overall encounter difficulty, and so on. These calculations will be very rough at first, but you can make them more accurate by using them on fragments that are known to be easy or hard and adjusting the scoring criteria afterward. After a few days of iteration, you'll be able to measure how easy or hard each part of the game is, even before it's made!

Static difficulty settings

Presenting a set of difficulty settings for players to choose from at the beginning of the game is one of the most common practices for tackling the initial skill gap. If possible, you should allow for this setting to be changed on-the-fly from within the options screen. This ensures that players are not entirely constrained by their initial choice, should they find themselves mismatched to the gameplay challenges at hand.

Difficulty settings may seem like a trivial system at first, but determining what to change and how to change it without sacrificing playability is the hard part (pun intended). The most common and often the easiest approach is to create multipliers for basic game parameters such as time or move limit, player and enemy health, damage and accuracy, cost of equipment, and so on. This practice can often get you quite far, but it can also result in weird and immersion-breaking scenarios where, for example, enemies operate with spot-on accuracy and require a ridiculous amount of hits, while players themselves perish after a single shot in the foot.

A hard difficulty setting should challenge all types of skills. Be careful of reducing your gameplay to a *memory challenge*, where players have to endure constant failure until they develop a bespoke solution to a particular encounter, only to fail repeatedly on the next one. By the same account, playing on an easy or *casual* setting should still involve making gameplay choices and require an understanding of basic game mechanics.

By modifying attributes, costs, and rewards, you manipulate not only the game's difficulty but also player behavior. For example, by making things like health and ammo pick-ups extremely scarce, you are sure to encourage an overly slow and safe play. On the other hand, make these resources overly abundant and players will stop caring about them altogether and resort to the easiest, most powerful solution (no matter how boringly repetitive).

A step up from simple multipliers is to modify the gameplay challenges themselves by:

- **Bespoke challenge variations**: Adding, removing, and swapping out enemies across the whole game can be a tedious task. If possible, strive for a system where you can *flag* different parts of in-game challenges (such as enemies or obstacles) and toggle them ON/OFF based on the flag. For example, out of 7 enemies that can spawn in an encounter, enemy #5 will only spawn on the *hard* setting, and enemy #3 will be swapped out for a weaker one when playing on *easy*. Be careful when making drastic changes, as you can accidentally break the performance (too many actors on the screen), or create an encounter that's so short it feels redundant or so long it gets tedious.
- **Modifying starting states**: This involves changing player's initial units/equipment/abilities/tools and so on, as well as modifying the default state of the world. Now, changing the entire map layout may seem a bit extreme, but making certain traps or pick-ups appear/disappear depending on the difficulty setting is not unfeasible!
- **Changing the winning and losing conditions**: Setting different score requirements, turn and time limits, or adding/removing requirements altogether is usually easy to pull off but requires individual tuning and additional playtesting.

Needless to say, difficulty-specific content variations can add a lot of workload across the whole project, which is why it often pays off to invest time in modifying your game systems and mechanics instead. Let's take a look at a few examples!:

- **Moving the information horizon**: Information is power! You can affect a player's decision-making capabilities by changing the rules around the *fog of war* or by unveiling/obscuring information about enemy strength, position, strategy, and weaknesses.

- **Toggling player assisting features**: Depending on the difficulty setting, you can vary the amount of gameplay assistance offered to players. This includes anything from enabling or disabling hints and aim to assist, to toggling various elements of the user interface such as the mini-map, objective and enemy markers, target reticle, and so on.

- **Adapting major game systems**: Gameplay stretches far beyond the scope of your level design and mechanics. Any optional rules and restrictions can be toggled based on the difficulty. For example, in a puzzle game, the time limit could be turned off on *easy*, while the move undo feature is unavailable on *hard*. Moreover, you can make your in-game challenges more thrilling (but also potentially frustrating) by limiting the quantity of *game saves* or restricting them to a particular place or point in time (be it outside of combat, or in a special shrine). That said, changes to the base rules and systems can be controversial and leave an undesirable impact on some of your mechanics and the structure of the average game session. Apply them with great care.

- **Modifying the Artificial Intelligence**: Look for parts of enemy behavior that can be tweaked across difficulty settings without making the enemies seem either totally incompetent or godlike. For example, modify the likelihood of flanking or aggressive pursuit behaviors, or the chances of using special moves and throwing grenades. Another good trick is to provide the enemies with low initial accuracy, that is, the first few shots are unlikely to hit (and perhaps they even deal lowered damage), giving players more time to react while still feeling threatened.

- **Changing the consequences of failure**: Lowering or increasing the consequences of failure will dramatically change the feel of the game. To increase the tension and make your gameplay more impactful, you can experiment with the loss of progress (experience, items, resources, and so on) or even more extreme features such as permanent death—a defining feature of modern *rogue-like* games like *Faster Than Light* or *Rogue Legacy*. Negative consequences are not for everyone though, so be very careful as to how and when you apply them. You're at a real risk of infuriating your players and throwing them into a feedback loop fueled by failure, where each death makes them weaker and even more likely to fail again. Consider serving these features on an opt-in basis. In *XCOM2*, players can toggle the *Ironman mode* when starting a new game. On *Ironman*, players are restricted to a single save file, which gets overwritten on each turn, making every action and decision irreversible (and by extension, much more thrilling).

Remember, making any changes to game difficulty will cause the ripple on effects in the game's balance (by promoting or diminishing the effectiveness of certain strategies) and the pacing of the experience (by encouraging more reckless or careful play). Do not venture into extremes; try mixing several solutions and observe their effects.

Embracing mono-difficulty

Multiple difficulty settings are a long-accepted practice among players and the industry, but not every game requires them. Even if you normalize your game towards the average player, you can still cater to the far ends of the skill spectrum.

A great way to maintain a single difficulty mode, yet prevent players from getting stuck, is to offer help once they meet a certain condition. For example, being stuck on a puzzle for 15 minutes triggers a hint, or failing to complete the stage five times in a row gives you a power-up.

Successful (and very explicit) examples of such systems can be found in many *Nintendo* products. *Super Mario 3D World* gives you access to a powerful power-up after several deaths, while *New Super Mario Bros. U* – features a *Super Guide Block*—an auto-play mode that can complete the troubling area (or even the entire stage) for the player. These systems are opt-in (players can ignore the help offering) and often have some kind of consequence such as a reduced score.

On the other hand, to cater to the highly skilled players, you'll need to create ample ways for them to show off and receive recognition. The most popular features include optional objectives (in *Super Mario 3D World*, that would be collecting all of the special coins) and difficult side missions, optional bosses, high-score tables, maliciously hidden secrets, accolades, and achievements. Reaching the end of a game may be relatively easy, but mastering it - completing all challenges and unlocking an alternative ending - should be a far harder endeavor!

Mono-difficulty is a great option for story-driven experiences and puzzle or adventure games. Puzzle challenges are not only difficult to grade accurately (what's hard for me may be trivially easy for you), but also pose a challenge to the creation of more discrete difficulty settings - how can you scale your puzzles without giving away the solution? A fixed difficulty setting is also a suitable choice for products with innovative mechanics that do not rely on physical prowess or strong gaming experience—we all start in a similar spot. Budget and time constraints are also valid, though far less glamorous reasons.

Automatic difficulty adjustment

Regardless of whether your game has one or six difficulty settings, there are ways in which you can cleverly adapt individual challenges to a player's current progress or performance.

Rubberbanding

Rubberbanding systems are designed to keep contestants close together, to wrap an imaginary rubber band around them. They try to maintain an optimal level of challenge for each player by creating a *negative feedback loop* and adjusting in-game variables in real time. You can view *rubberbanding* as a systematic equivalent of *Robin Hood;* it helps those who struggle while providing an extra challenge to those who dominate. It can be done with players being well aware of the process or in total secret.

Most racing games do their best to cover their tracks and create an illusion of a tight and fair race. In *Burnout, Need for Speed* and countless other games, an invisible rubber band controls the speed of NPC drivers, linking their performance to a player's position. Get ahead and the rivals will soon follow to contest your position, fall behind and the whole pack of AI drivers will slow down to let you catch up and get within a fighting range.

On the other hand, item box mechanics in *Nintendo's Mario Kart* serve as a good example of *rubberbanding* that's almost explicit. The game features boxes that can be picked up during the race, and each box gives out a seemingly random item from a selection of several weapons and power-ups. However, players are quick to realize that participants at the front of the pack receive far inferior items than those at the end. The gap in item quality between positions 1 and 8 is huge, and the game never tries to obscure it—some items are simply unavailable to well-performing drivers.

The item box modifiers in *Mario Kart* serve as proof that the use of *rubberbanding* reaches far beyond the racing genre. Bonuses and penalties based on a player's standing (be it against the NPCs as well as other players) can be introduced to almost any game system.

Once you determine what to adjust, you'll also need to decide whether to be explicit about it or keep it a secret. As a rule of thumb, any game that tries to maintain a level of credibility and fairness in its competitive play should be crystal clear about the benefits and pitfalls of holding a certain place. In case of single player games, the options are wider and you may employ any tricks you wish. However, bear in mind that enforcing *optimal* difficulty across the board can make for a poorly paced and highly predictable game (we'll speak more about pacing later in this chapter).

Multiplayer matchmaking

Multiplayer games are at their best when played between equal opponents. This is easier said than done, but there are several criteria you can consider when pitting players against one another:

1. **Inexperience**: You may want to safeguard newcomers and have them play against one another until they reach a certain stage. Avoid applying it to the entire population.

2. **Progression**: If players get more powerful over time (for example, by gaining experience levels or building up their kingdom), you might want to calculate their power and use it to match between players who are not too far apart.

3. **Past performance**: This is often done by introducing an Elo rating system, which gives each player a skill rating. This rating can be shown directly as is, translated into a title/medal/league of some sort, or kept invisible (to prevent players from trying to *game* the system and lower their ratings in anticipation of big events). Regardless, after each game, rating points are attributed to the winner and are detracted from the loser depending on their standings. In an uneven match, the higher rated player has more to lose and less to gain and vice-versa.

1. **Current performance**: In some scenarios, the easiest approach might be to match players based on their most recent standing or a winning streak. For example, let's say that the players are to play a total of 10 games; all you need is to match people with similar win rates together. This will make it harder and harder to go on undefeated while giving the players who are below average an increasing chance to win over time. This works best when players start at a similar entry point.

2. **Self-determined matchmaking**: You can also try to offload the burden of matchmaking by letting the players pick their own opponent. Put your players into several categories based on their skill or power, and then let them choose what kind of opponent they wish to fight. Make sure to incentivize punching above your weight while providing an insignificant reward for smashing someone far weaker.

Progression-driven difficulty

Certain games aspire to offer both extensive character progression systems and vast worlds with seemingly unrestricted exploration. This offering creates a balancing risk where players are likely to run into a whole array of encounters, from trivial to impossibly difficult.

To counter this risk, game developers often create systems that automatically adjust game difficulty based on a particular indicator, such as the critical vector of progression (which we introduced as a concept in Chapter 3, *Scoping a Game Project*). This could be a player's experience level, the state of the main storyline, or even the elapsed time since the game began.

The aforementioned difficulty changes often focus on scaling the power of encountered enemies or even replacing them with entirely different ones. Some rewards are also adjusted to remain meaningful, which means that with the very same enemy, the quest or *loot chest* will offer more impressive rewards once your character has progressed. Difficulty scaling does not have to be linear; the average encounter may get progressively more difficult as players grow more accustomed to the game and master its mechanics.

Progression-driven difficulty scaling does not address the differences in skill and capabilities between different players. You may still need to resort to the classic difficulty settings in addition to your scaling.

In some cases, progression-based difficulty management is a very appealing and effective tool by allowing you to:

- **Open up the game world**: There's no right or wrong place to be. Explore! Go wherever you want, whenever you want.
- **Avoid backtracking**: No need to run away from a difficult fight, only to return to the very same spot later.
- **Reduce frustration in combat encounters**: There's little risk of getting stuck or killed by a single hit from a powerful foe.
- **Reward player's time accordingly**: No longer do you have to face the boring grind of pushing through a swarm of completely inferior foes and tasks, with nothing but meaningless rewards to offset your time.
- **Provide life to the entirety of the game's content**: Since the challenges and rewards scale, the entirety of your game content remains viable, so there's no risk of devaluing a large chunk of the game by advancing your characters beyond the relevant range.
- **Help with economy balancing**: Costs that inflate and deflate based on player's status and income help keep things in an acceptable and relevant range.

Nevertheless, employing an auto-balancing system on a wide scale comes with significant pitfalls. By constantly scaling the challenges, you effectively remove the frame of reference between the power of players' avatars and the obstacles they face. This lack of contrast and static difficulty space hurts your game in several ways:

- **Diminished motivation to progress**: Getting killed by a powerful enemy can be annoying, but it can also inspire players to better themselves. Setting your sights on becoming worthy of this seemingly impossible challenge is an amazing motivator.
- **Lack of visible growth**: From time to time, it's best we stop and appreciate how far you've come. It feels great to crush an enemy that used to be a real challenge.
- **A lessened thrill of exploration**: Once you realize that no matter where you go you'll get a fair fight and a fair reward (nothing more, nothing less), the motivation to venture into faraway lands fizzles away.

These cons are something that the designers at *Bethesda* (creators of the games in the *Fallout* and *Elder Scrolls* series) have realized and tried to address in some of their more recent games. While most quest-driven challenges appear to scale with player level, there seems to be a limit to how much the things within the game world can bend. This modified system helps maintain the feeling of progression in the outside world while keeping the core of the experience within a player's ability range and comfort zone.

Pacing

Pacing is all about setting the tempo of your game and keeping the players engaged; it's the heartbeat of your game. Our ultimate goal is to utterly captivate our audience, to suspend their disbelief, and keep them in the state of *flow*.

The psychological concept of *flow* or the *zone* has been recognized and named by *Mihaly Csikszentmihalyi* in 1975, and refers to the mental state of being fully immersed in the task at hand, even to the point of losing the sense of time and space:

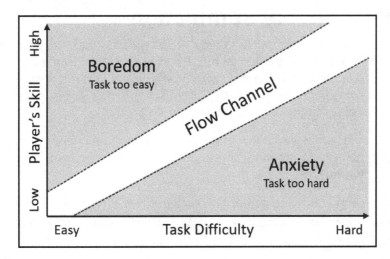

The basic flow graph represents the relationship between difficulty and skill. As players grow more experienced and competent, they require more challenging tasks.

However, there's more to pacing than matching a player's skill and task difficulty! As you may remember, back in the midst of the chapter on level design, we mentioned that the pace of the game is often dictated by the intensity of the levels you create. The aforementioned intensity stems not only from task difficulty but also from mental and sensory stimulation. By this standard, game designers, level designers, writers, and artists are all responsible for invoking and maintaining the flow state in their own regard.

If you were to look at your game as if it was a dish or a musical composition, every bit of content and functionality you have would become an ingredient or an instrument; they all play an important part in something bigger. Exciting plot twists and a whole new planet to explore both stimulate your audience and raise your overall intensity without affecting game difficulty at all.

As a rule of thumb, novel content and difficult sections raise your intensity while repetitive segments and low difficulty lower it. Prolonged periods of low intensity lead to boredom, while long, overly intense sections can exhaust your players. However, this is just scratching the surface. Before we understand how to set and control the pace, let's unpack the meaning of mental and sensory stimulation in the context of games.

Mental and sensory stimulation

Reducing the role of pacing to simply manage difficulty would make us disregard a whole range of more complex aspects of video games. For example, most humans find great joy in exploring uncharted lands, experimenting with new tools, and diving deep into captivating stories. These types of experiences are unarguably useful in making our games more immersive and engaging, and thus should be paced accordingly.

To begin with, any part of the game that encourages thinking and decision-making can be considered as cognitively and mentally stimulating. Actions that stimulate our players include (but are not limited to):

- Learning and mastering gameplay mechanics and controls
- Analyzing new and unfamiliar content, building world knowledge
- Predicting consequences of story developments and reminiscing about past events
- Making meaningful decisions
- Calculating risks and rewards, planning your moves

Sensory stimulation, on the other hand, is all about the visceral experience of inhabiting, observing, and listening to the game world, as well as interacting with it outside the context of game challenges. Sensory stimulation stems from:

- The theme and mood of the game
- Visuals such as 2D and 3D art, animation, visual effects, environments, graphical user interface
- UI interactions
- Background actors and NPCs (animals or people going about their day)
- World interaction and physics (some of us spent hours using the *Gravity Gun* to throw bathroom sinks in *Half-Life 2*)
- Audio music, sound effects, voice-overs, ambient noises
- Passive (non-interactive) storytelling via text, cutscenes, and audio

The preceding mentioned sources of mental and sensory stimulation are often heavily intertwined and impossible to break down without extensive research, but attempting to list them may help us appreciate the roles of various parts of the game in pacing.

To effectively use mental and sensory stimulation in this context, you need to be aware of the inherent diminishing returns. Repeated exposure to any element (be it a type of puzzle, musical piece, animation, or background) reduces its impact and effectiveness. Overly familiar elements get parsed by our brains as a simple background. Just like strangers on the bus, they are rarely memorable or worthy of prolonged attention. There is comfort in familiarity, but too much of it leads to the feelings of stagnation. Every game world needs background noise, but it's up to you to make sure that there is enough going on to maintain a player's interest.

Remember, adding more content and mechanics is not a sure-fire way of making your game more engaging. To start with, piling up more elements will make quality assurance, playtesting, and any gameplay iterations much more expensive. Even then, your attempts at enriching the experience can backfire. The same elements used to inspire the feelings of awe, anticipation, curiosity, and artistic satisfaction can end up overwhelming the player. The story can get diluted by unnecessary plot points and the entire game can get too big to manage, too difficult to balance, and too long to play through. Prepare a *content lifespan* document, set your pacing early on, and only keep what works!

How to approach pacing

Challenging and stimulating experiences are powerful weapons against boredom, but using them to their best effect is a difficult art. Even in a game with a set, unchanging difficulty setting, the intensity of moment to moment gameplay is rarely constant.

Instead, we ought to steadily escalate the physical and mental difficulty but also remember to give players a moment to catch their breath, plan their next moves, invest resources, and start anticipating *the next big thing*. Moments of lower intensity do not need to be empty; they can be populated by scripted events, storytelling, socializing, and sensory stimulation.

Contrast applies to pacing as much as it applies to art. If everything explodes, nothing really does. A game that's all-out intense has no highlights, no ups, and no downs. Flatly paced gameplay and storytelling make up for a series of experiences that easily clump together into an indistinguishable mash.

To put things into a more practical perspective, we'll explore the methods used to pace linear content, follow them with more systemic solutions, and close off with some loose tips!

Pacing linear content

Linear game content is driven by the combined efforts of level design and the narrative, making it expensive and time-consuming to iterate on, but giving you the ability to control gameplay on a very granular, moment-by-moment basis. One of the best ways of exercising this control is to work with a timeline.

This timeline is a long graph spanning the entire length of a single, self-contained fragment of the game that we're about to pace. Gradually, your timeline will be populated with more and more precise details, creating a solid action plan and reducing iteration times dramatically. It's best to start this process early on, during the outline or blockout period, when there's still a potentially high degree of flexibility in terms of gameplay, story, intensity, and structure.

Even though we're working on a single area or level, the pace and progression of the entire game have to be taken into consideration. Make note of what happens before and after your stage, and how your plan fits the overall structure of the game.

Since it's much easier to work on a trusted and effective storytelling structure, try dividing your timeline (and thus, your stage) into three or four distinct acts:

1. Introduction
2. Escalation
3. The Twist (optional)
4. Conclusion

These acts will help you govern the overall flow of intensity in the level and help you provide a sense of progression and closure. They are also a useful scaffolding for framing the narrative. Let's take a look at a fictional example:

ACT 1	ACT 2	ACT 3	ACT 4
We arrive at the island to find the source of mysterious signals.	*We find the alien technology that can be used to harness physical properties of surrounding objects.*	*Our ally turns against us and steals the device. We chase after him and enter an underground bunker*	*The bunker is in fact an alien ship. We fight to reclaim the device and extract before the place blows up.*

Now, use the content lifespan, the script, level sketch, or any other design document to make a list of any elements that you absolutely must have on your level. This includes things like plot twists, puzzle ideas, new content, and mechanics you plan to introduce and so on.

Place these elements on the timeline, and pinpoint the desired intensity and its trend at that point in time:

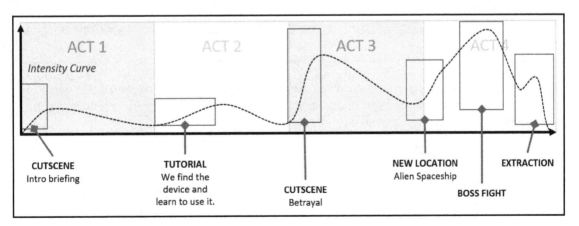

This is a good starting point, but our acts consist of more than a few key points! We can divide them further into areas or *chunks* of various types, such as:

- Gameplay chunks may include various types, for example:
  - Combat
  - Puzzle-solving
  - Platforming
  - Exploration
  - Stealth
- Narrative chunks for important story elements, cutscenes, dialogue sections, and so on
- Tutorials and scripted events

Populate the graph with various chunks and try to maintain a level of variety within gameplay tasks and their intensity. Keep refining the curve as you go along! Even though the intensity may seem ambiguous at first, it will provide a meaningful target to hit during gray boxing and implementation phases and enforce a degree of self-control:

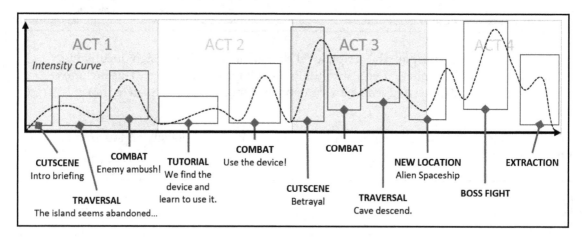

With a complete timeline on hand, you can plan your work more effectively, build up to big events, vary the tasks, and deliver an emotional impact. Do not rush your timelines; a solid plan can help you save lots of time later on!

Pacing via rules and mechanics

By adding and modifying the rules and mechanics, you can evolve your gameplay scenarios, setting the pace and intensity in a highly efficient and repeatable way. Let's look at some examples of using game system pacing:

- **Time**

  Time limits are often used to raise the pace and keep players on the task at hand. Even if things start slow and calculated, the action is sure to pick up as any indecision and inaction slowly accumulate towards an incredibly tense finale. Furthermore, by using mechanics such as overtime (where the game does not end for as long as a losing team is contesting the objective), you can make the game more exciting and give the underdogs a chance to come back from their previous mistakes.

  On a different note, the games in the *Warrioware* series are an extreme example of using time in pacing. Players are presented with a series of quick and silly micro-games, simple tasks that test your reaction time and ask for a few precise inputs. Things start slow, but after a series of several micro-games, the game speeds up and raises the difficulty by reducing the time limits for all tasks.

- **Score**

  Getting close to beating a high score is sure to raise the stakes, but the use of scoring systems extends beyond rankings or the leaderboard, and has great effects on pacing in scenarios involving direct competition. For example, in *Rainbow Six: Siege*, as in many *eSports* games, two teams compete in games that are divided into multiple, individually scored rounds. As the opposing team starts winning points, the intensity naturally grows higher for the losing team. For the leading side, on the other hand, the effect is the opposite. If you need 5 points to win, dropping from 4-0 to 4-1 is still a low-intensity scenario (after all, you have plenty of room for error). As always, the key to sustaining an engaging pacing across both teams is to provide the means for the losing side to come back, and by extension, keep the winning team on their toes.

- **Resource escalation**

  Taking control over resource generation is one of the most effective ways a game designer can raise or lower the intensity of any gameplay scenario. In this context, the resources (minerals, coins, fuel, mana, and so on) are anything that players can use to introduce new elements and options to the game (units, moves, combinations, special abilities, and so on). Resource escalation can be done linearly, exponentially, or in distinct stages. For example, in *Hearthstone* and *Magic the Gathering*, the possibilities for combos and the potential impact of each card grows steadily with the rise *mana*. *Clash Royale*, on the other hand, has 3-minute-long matches, where resource production is kept still for the first 2 minutes. After that, the game goes into overdrive and doubles the resource generation, and thus multiplies the speed and intensity of the gameplay. This practice also increases the chances of resolving the match in 3 minutes without triggering overtime.

- **Pacing in MOBA games**

  Games in the MOBA genre like *League of Legends* or *DOTA 2* are great examples of using rules and systems to manipulate pacing. It pays off to investigate these games, even if you are not a fan. In both cases, the game starts slow, with players largely sticking to their area of the map and methodically accumulating resources and unlocking new abilities. As players grow in power, their options increase and so does the intensity. After several minutes, players are more able to withstand enemy defenses and secure kills. This shifts the dynamic and encourages players to group up, enforcing intense team fights.

  However, the higher your character level, the longer you need to wait to respawn. This may provide a nice break from an increasingly stressful game, but it also increases the consequences of failure. Near the end of a match, the intensity spikes from each encounter can become enormous, especially since both teams are constantly damaging each other's defenses and coming ever closer to securing a victory.

Pacing tips

Now that we have an understanding of what pacing is and how to approach it, let's look at some more concrete examples and tips, starting with the role of actor removal.

Investigating actor removal

Strategy games have a natural pace based on the slow accumulation of power and the results of exercising it. In many cases, the intensity grows as you amass the army, peaks when you go into battle, and either raise through a lost encounter (as you scramble to recover and are left feeling exposed) or lowers with a win (as the threat is reduced).

Moreover, the higher the number of cards, units, or resources under a player's disposal, the more actions and choices they have to make or at least consider. Having little to do is far more relaxing than having to analyze hundreds of combinations and spread the attention across multiple actors and possible locations.

In team-based games, player elimination is sure to put more pressure on the remaining players, especially if there's still a remote chance of winning. In fact, increasing the chance to recover from a losing scenario is a great way of making the game more fun for both sides.

These are just a few simple examples, but hopefully, you'll look at actor removal and player elimination in your games. Analyze the effects they have on pacing, and look for improvements that can be made to address or increase these effects.

High-intensity and storytelling

As things start to blow up and the tempo picks up, the plot might need to take a backseat. Most Hollywood action movies deliberately pause major plot developments for the duration of intense action sequences (car chases, fights, shootouts, and so on). These scenes can be great for light characterization, but suffer when trying to express complex motives, deep emotions, and intertwined storylines. The viewer will be too distracted by everything that's going on to pay attention to more intricate and subtle aspects of the narrative.

Consider applying the same principle to your game and avoid putting heavily involved story elements in very intense sections of your game.

Multiplayer pacing and level design

The layout of your maps is a great tool to modify pacing. You may remember from the level design chapter that providing effective cover will encourage more careful and static play, while rich flanking opportunities and pick-ups will promote movement. However, to further control your pacing, you must look at how gameplay evolves over time.

As an example, in the *Battlefield* series, the *Rush* game mode has one team defending two objectives (radio transmitters or similar) from the attackers who try to successfully detonate them before running out of time or respawns. Upon the successful destruction of both objectives, a new set becomes available and the entire action shifts to a new part of the map. There may be up to 5 different sets of fresh targets, and each set may offer new gameplay opportunities, vehicles, and strategies. In *Rush*, the evolving map layout is constantly shifting the pace.

The map layouts in an RTS like *Starcraft 2* are equally as important. For instance, you can increase or lower the pace of the match entirely by modifying the number of resources available in the starting location, thus changing resource production rates and encouraging or discouraging early expansion efforts. Increasing map size and surrounding players with destructible obstacles or water would further modify the tempo, but at the cost of possibly invalidating certain strategies—ones we worked so hard to enable with careful game balancing.

Utilizing threat and anxiety

In games that revolve around challenge and skill, threat and anxiety play a dominant role in setting the intensity, a role that's often mismanaged or misunderstood. The threat itself does not depend entirely on the actual difficulty of the gameplay scenario. Instead, it is based on the perception of adversity and fueled by the negative consequences of failure.

If the stakes are high, a relatively trivial gameplay encounter can be a source of an immense level of threat. For example, when players die in *Dark Souls* (and other games in the *Souls series*), they drop any *Souls* they've amassed but not spent. *Souls* are a crucial resource that relates to a character's overall progression. If players fail to collect the dropped souls within their next life, the souls disappear forever, and with them, potentially hours of character and world progress.

By raising the stakes and tapping into the *loss aversion bias* (it's in our nature to absolutely hate losing or missing out on things) this mechanic can turn even the most trivial and previously mastered part of the stage into an immensely stressful endeavor. However, there is a positive flipside to this inarguably extreme mechanic. The high game difficulty and consequences of repeated failure are not only raising the intensity and reinvigorating completed content; the successful collection of dropped *Souls* is accompanied by a great sense of satisfaction, pride, and relief. Moreover, even if you were to fail twice in a row, the souls may be gone forever but so is the pressure and tension built around trying to reclaim them. For an average *Dark Souls* player, repeated death is as frustrating as it is motivating:

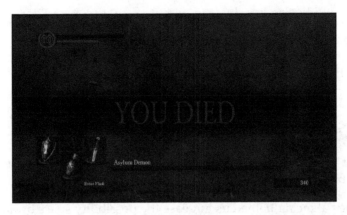

Against all odds, the *Dark Souls* series has popularised the emotional rollercoaster of high-stakes gameplay in the west

Dark Souls aside, an intense game does not need to be a severely punishing one. In *BioShock*, difficult battles often end up with *close calls* and *hard-fought victories*. This is no accident. According to the developers, the game is designed to tip the scale in the player's favor in times of great need. When the player is about to die, the game instead leaves them with a small percentage of health and turns them invulnerable for a short period of time. This gives the player a chance to shoot back and finish the fight with just a tiny portion of their health left. It sure feels great to repeatedly escape death by a razor-thin margin!

There are many more examples of such trickery in the world of game development. Just because we expect our players to play fair, doesn't mean we can't cheat a little to ensure they are having a good time. If done right, these tricks will remain invisible to the players and keep them inside the *flow channel*, but if done badly, they will backfire and break the immersion we worked so hard to build.

A game with no failure states and no punishment is one that poses no direct threat to the player, and some can argue that it is not even a *real game*, but an *interactive experience*. In such scenarios, it's very difficult to maintain a player's interest by directly challenging their abilities. Instead, the game has to rely on other emotions and control pacing by rewarding progress, aspirational goals (difficult puzzles and challenges), as well as mental and sensory stimulation (new mechanics, inspiring art, a captivating story, and so on). Note that having to replay even the smallest part of the game is a form of punishment—repeating tasks without making progress in the game is rarely fun.

The screenshots used in this chapter are for illustrative purposes only. We do not recommend that you to misuse these in any way. For more information, please consult the terms and conditions of the publishers mentioned in the *Disclaimer* section of this book.

Summary

In this chapter, we learned about three interconnected subjects which come together to help you make a game full of varied and exciting gameplay scenarios.

To start with, game balancing helped us increase the possibility space by addressing dominant strategies, tuning mechanics, and changing the parameters of game content. Following that, we explored the methods of setting and adjusting the overall difficulty of the game, helping us match it with the capabilities of our audience. Finally, we looked at pacing, which allows us to maintain a player's interest and keep them in the *flow* by manipulating the structure and relative intensity of each gameplay session.

Next up, we'll dive into the *Final 10 Percent*, which covers practical tips and guidelines on how to raise the quality of your games and turn every interaction into a delightful experience.

14
The Final 10%

Have you ever heard of the 80/20 rule?

It states that 80% of most effects are caused by just 20% of the possible causes.

It is known as the Pareto Principle, named after Vilfredo Pareto, an Italian scientist who postulated a mathematical distribution to describe many social and natural phenomena.

Some examples:

- 20% of the clients of a company account for 80% of its revenues
- 80% of a company's sales come from 20% of its products
- 80% of global world wealth is owned by 20% of the population
- 80% of crimes are committed by 20% of criminals
- 20% of the posts on social networks generate 80% of traffic

It is obviously a rule of thumb, but you'd be surprised how accurate it can be!

In fact, we can safely state that:

"80% of a game is made in the final 20% of the time"

I know, the chapter is called *The Final 10%*. Based on what we've just said, it should have been called *The Final 80%*. But that wouldn't really help with the point we're trying to make here.

The problem with the so-called **final 10%** is that it often takes much longer than the final 10% of budgeted development time. When the game finally comes together, not only will bugs and technical problems with the software inevitably emerge, but some of the systems might prove to be not working as expected. Some design flaws might lie hidden in the game and become evident only at this stage.

This is the reason why so many games' release dates are delayed and so many budgets are burned before the project is done. This is why the dreaded crunch time practice exists in our industry.

It is also the reason why so many games projects fail:

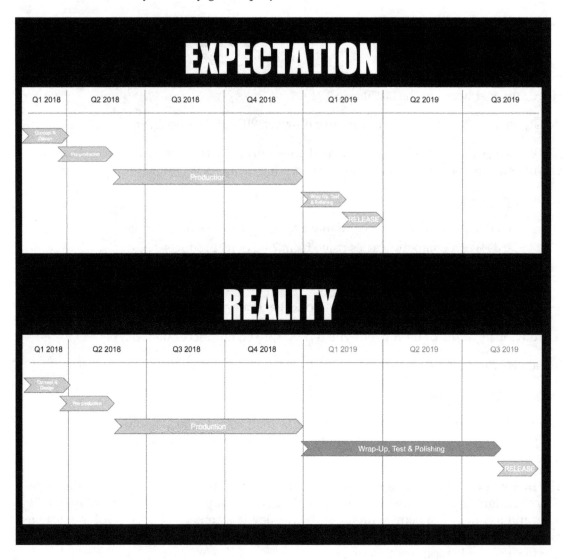

The *Wrap-Up*, *Test* and *Polishing phase* usually takes much longer than what was originally planned, causing great delays in the final release. The purpose of this diagram is to give you an idea of what could go wrong in the game development process

In this chapter, we are going to discuss the activities and issues that make that final 10% so challenging, focusing on those that put the game designer at the center of the action.

This is not a book for project managers or producers (although they would certainly benefit from some game design knowledge), therefore this chapter won't be focused around how to avoid crunch time or meet deadlines.

This chapter is about the activities that must be done in that last 10%. As a designer is your duty to know them and enter the final stage of production confident and ready for the final push before release!

It is important to keep in mind that, in the real world, no project schedule contemplates assigning 80% of the time available to just the final part. The ability and the challenge for the producers and project managers are to make sure that the final stage can be wrapped up in a reasonable amount of time, which is always going to be shorter than the production time. This is one of the biggest challenges of producing a game, but as a game designer, you should stay focused on doing your part and making sure everything you have to do is done in time. We don't live in an ideal world, so be prepared to confront the final 10% with no more than just 10% of the time...or less!

Usually, the final stage of the production begins with the Alpha release. Here follows a list of the activities commonly associated with this final stage:

1. Putting the pieces together
2. Polishing
3. Quality Assurance

Putting the pieces together

It's very unlikely that a game would take its final shape by linearly expanding from its *narrative beginning* to its ultimate ending. During the development, some pieces of the game are developed as modules and all these modules are put together when a playable of some sort is required. But maybe after the Alpha is out, some extra iteration is required to sort out problems and those pieces need to be re-shuffled for the Beta or the next version. Again, it is possible that this task would come at the last moment.

Depending on the size of the project, the designer might have a big responsibility in putting everything together. Usually, the designers are in charge of setting up the whole game content. Maybe the beta version included only a single level or mission, and that one was put together as best as possible for the Beta phase. Now it is time to create and introduce the rest of those missions, quest, dialogs, characters, and levels.

Feature creep

Once the game is finished, or almost finished, it's really easy to see what might be missing. The team, with a clearer picture of a semi-finished product, might come up with fresh new ideas, different solutions, or new content. The feeling is that, with these kinds of additions, it would be a much better game. And you and the team are almost there if only there was a bit more time. Or maybe, while putting the pieces together, it starts to feel like it is not enough. It is not as fun as you thought it would be.

This is the moment where a project might face a dangerous problem: feature creep, the constant addition of features and functionality to a product. Instead of putting together what's already been developed in the best way possible and focusing on increasing its quality, the team makes the collective mistake to think that more new features would make a better game.

An interesting example of deliberate feature creep is the practice of promising stretch goals that we have seen in recent years on *Kickstarter*. *Kickstarter* is a crowd-funding platform where creators can pitch their projects directly to the final user, and ask them for money to make those projects come to life. The idea behind stretch-goals is to promise users more stuff upon reaching extra funding goals after the initial goal is achieved.

So, an original idea is pitched, people love it and back it with their money. The funding goal is achieved and now the developers start adding (promise to add) features to an original design that was already great. There is a great opportunity to make a bigger and better game (and also to raise more money)...but there's also a huge risk of drifting away from the original idea by adding the unnecessary. Of course, the good news for these Kickstarter projects is that feature creep in the design and concept phase of a project is not as bad as coming up with new things when a game is almost completed.

A classic real-life example is adding a multiplayer mode to a single player game. Many game development teams have been almost destroyed by a sudden change in the original plans. To make the game more appealing, a multiplayer mode is announced. Maybe during a big conference or convention. The game is almost finished, and the multiplayer feature is used to increase the hype or attract further investments. Or maybe the team itself think that, now that the game is completed, a multiplayer mode can really be the icing on the cake. When something like this happens and it wasn't planned since the beginning, only bad things can happen.

What a game designer can do to avoid this danger is to find what can be cut, instead of adding more: *Less is more*.

We already discussed this when we spoke about the initial design of a game, now we're going to use it again in the final stage.

Less is more

You should always be on the lookout for features that could be cut from your game. There are three main properties you can look for in features that might make them good candidates for removal from a game:

- **Unintuitive mechanics**: Unintuitive mechanics are always a warning. If players struggle to understand why or how a mechanic works, it might be a good idea to remove it altogether or to strip it down to a much simpler version.
- **Mechanics that don't really appeal to the audience**: Mechanics that don't appeal your audience are a common mistake. A complex crafting system in a casual match-3 game might not be a great idea. Make sure that every mechanic will reinforce and support your design pillars.
- **Unnecessary features**: What might have sounded like a great idea on paper may turn out to be unnecessarily complex in the final game. Maybe you designed multiple different upgrade paths for the character and, during playtesting, some of them simply turned out to be not meaningful enough to be engaging and compelling.

•

Polish

What is polish?

This is another concept that many developers have tried to nail with a formal definition. As you know by now, we don't like formal definitions, so be warned that the notion of what polish is might vary from developer to developer, but most importantly from game to game! To polish a game, basically, means to raise the standard of its quality.

Why and how would you polish a pair of shoes or a plank of wood?

You don't change the shoes or the shape of the plank. Polishing a pair of walking boots won't turn them into a pair of patent leather formal shoes to go with your tuxedo. The goal of polishing is to smoothen the game and the experience. To tweak its values and refine its details until it really feels great and immediately pleasing on an aesthetic and gameplay level.

The (in)famous scenario where the game designer finally plays the Alpha of the game and comes up with a brilliant idea to make things even better...usually is not polishing. It is the dreaded *wouldn't be cool to add this?* scenario. Polishing should not be about adding anything. If a feature is finished or supposed to be finished, and the team feels the necessity to add something on top of it to make it really work, that's a sign that the feature might be broken at its core.

How to polish

Polishing a game is not a game design job only. Actually, most of the polishing work would be carried out by artists, animators, and programmers. The game designer has a crucial role in this phase nonetheless. Entering the final stage of a game production means that the game designer will have to put himself in the shoes of the player and play the game like it is his favorite game of all time. This is the stage where the game designer has to become an expert gamer of their own game.

Most gamers would probably be surprised how little playing of the game happens by most people in game development. Most programmers and artists usually ship games that they have never actually played the whole way through, except those particular moments or scenes here and there where their work was focused.

That's perfectly fine for them, but unacceptable for game designers.

Game designers, along with game directors and the QA department, are the ones that have to keep engineers and artists informed of the final product's quality and determine which areas are in critical need of polish or further attention.

Let's have a look at the most common tasks for polishing a game:

- Stability and performance
- Audio and visual
- Design polish

In the following paragraphs, we're going to briefly mention technical tasks and focus more on the tasks specific to the game designer.

Stability and performance

Stability and performance are the first two things to be looked at during polishing. It involves many procedures and techniques that might keep the engineers busy for a while, but the designers can spot moments or parts of the game that runs a bit too slow or have glitches. Polishing stability and performance means avoiding crashes, glitches, improving and stabilizing the **FPS (frames per second)**, and reducing the functional bugs (even the smallest ones) to zero or as close to zero as possible. It also includes monitoring and optimizing the use of CPU and GPU and the memory usage.

It is worth noting that, even if this sounds like a very technical activity for engineers, sometimes it could take only a designer to solve a performance issue. If a designer has requested features that are within the limits of what can be technically achieved, then the design might have to be reworked, numbers scaled back, the number of enemies reduced, attacks per second changed, visual effects tuned down, or the limits on the number of players in a multiplayer game might have to be enforced.

One way designers can definitely help the engineers solve performance issue is by offering solutions like the above. While an engineer might happily/frustratedly bang their head against a wall of code for a week trying to squeeze another 5% of performance out of a tight section of code, perhaps a simpler solution could be just a designer lowering a number to relieve some strain on the engine. It's worth being vigilant as a designer and involved in knowing the performance bottlenecks of the engines you are most likely making content for; you can save the engineering team potentially days of time and help get the game shipped in time.

Perceived performance

Perceived performance is as important as actual performance. We are talking here about a few minor tweaks that can help give the impression of overall better performance to players. Lowering the max FPS is another common trick, a game capped at 30 FPS might look more fluid than a game that struggles to maintain consistently 60 FPS.

Another common way to improve perceived performance is to enhance the player experience during loading screens.

Loading screens are obviously one of the most obvious and direct feedbacks of a game technical's performance. The bigger the game, the better the graphics, the longer the loading times. Same with online multiplayer games: finding matches or connecting to servers might take a while - even worse, it might all depend from the player's internet connection, and there's very little the engineers can do about that.

During waiting times, there is a multitude of ways to give the player the impression that the game experience is not *blocked* by the loading screen: tips, the game's lore, and tutorials are extremely common, giving the player something to read while waiting.

Some games even feature a mini-game during the loading times, such as *The Sims 3*'s hidden object mini-game.

The art of interactive loading screens reached new heights with titles such as *Bayonetta* or *Fifa*, where the player is able to practice with the mechanics of the game:

The tutorial feature during loading screens was so great in *Bayonetta* that many players started requesting online whether there was a way to stay on the loading screen and keep practicing!

Audio and visual

Audio and visual factors are very important in terms of polishing. Stability and performance remain the top priority, as a fantastic game that crashes or freezes is always worse than a mediocre game that always runs smoothly. Nonetheless, audio and visual are the player-facing layer and every polishing effort will have a tremendous impact on the player experience and enjoyment of the game.

The list of improvements and polishing that can be done with audio, animations, colors, environments, and character design is huge, but we can summarize it in one simple word—**details**. The attention to detail, especially in audio, environments, and animations is what usually takes a game to the next level of quality.

To have an idea of how a polished game looks like, just think about any of the latest *Zelda* or *Mario* games. The graphics, sound effects, animations, response to every player input...they are as great as they can be. It's a pleasure not only to play them but just watching them. Or compare the latest *Call of Duty* to a lower budget indie FPS such as *Insurgency* (far be it from any judgment of the latter, we're comparing two games with a very different budget and audiences here, and that's exactly why the polishing gap is so big).

Another great way to get an idea of how polishing looks like is to compare the various stages of a game, such as alpha, beta, and release:

Pay attention to details such as lighting, particle effects, the lava texture, the user interface on the bottom right part of the screen, and the UI elements for the trigger and the indicator in the upper part of the screen

On mobiles, companies such as *Supercell* or *Zynga* are famous for delivering games with an incredible level of polishing, which is undoubtedly one of the reasons for their success. Polished games are more captivating; just by looking better, they give the feeling to players that the game experience and gameplay are going to be just as smooth as the visual. Beware though, technical and visual polish might be enough to get players to try the game out, but if the design and the gameplay don't live up to the expectations, I doubt any player is going to stick around!

Design polish

Design polish includes a huge variety of activities. Every aspect of the game over which the game designer has direct control can be tweaked and polished. Most likely, we're talking about balancing, especially difficult.

Once the designer finally has the chance to play the game in its entirety, it is possible to go fine-tune values that might have been pre-determined only by data and numeric models. We have seen in the chapter about balancing how a game system is also made of numbers. This is the time to put them to test and tweak them to perfection.

The more time designers have to work and fine-tune all these values, the smoother the player's final experience will be. This is definitely something to think about during planning.

Play

Obviously, the first step in polishing the design of a game is to play it. The designers need to sit down with as many people as possible and play the game with them. We've said this already; this is the moment when the designer becomes the most passionate player of their own game.

 This phase might be neglected by the team. Maybe everyone is exhausted at this point and the idea of playing hours of a game you've been working on for months or even years is daunting. Keep up your team morale! Make the playing activity fun for the team and for yourself. Organize tournaments or challenge with the game and learn from what you see!

Talk

Talk to the team or anyone might be playing the game. Compare different points of view, and note down what doesn't really work or what you feel might be swiftly improved. Take on every criticism and do your best to make every adjustment you can.

There are designers who are very good at taking criticism and some that are not comfortable with it. It's vital to remain open-minded. If you close down and get defensive, you risk losing a channel of feedback as your colleagues don't want to hurt your feelings. Be thankful of all feedback you receive- even if it hurts, try not to show it, because then you will be open to more opinions and the chance to make the game better for all.

Make a checklist of all these little things and then take a significant amount of your daily time to work on improving them, one by one. For bigger games, a producer might help you in this task, organizing and prioritizing each activity.

Show the game to people that have never seen it before and listen carefully to their opinions. Some obvious problems might be invisible to you or others from the team. When you work on a game for a long time, it's very easy to miss those.

Exercise

Consider a game that you like and you think has been somehow polished:
- Identify at least three features that have been visually polished to make the game "feel" better, without having any impact on its core gameplay.
- Do the same, but focusing on design polish, compare similar mechanics for different games and focus on how some of them are more polished than the others.
- Can you spot some technical polishing? Any particular technique to improve the perceived performance?

Quality assurance

There are different methods for game testing, and most methodologies are developed by individual video game developers and publishers. Methodologies are continuously refined and may differ for different types of games (for example, the methodology for testing an MMORPG will be different from testing a casual game). Many methods are borrowed directly from general software testing techniques. Outlined below are the most important methodologies for video games:

- **Functionality testing**: Most commonly associated with the phrase *game testing*, as it entails playing the game in some form. Functionality testing does not require extensive technical knowledge. Functionality testers look for general problems within the game itself or its User Interfaces, such as stability issues, game mechanic issues, and game asset integrity.
- **Compliance testing**: First-party licensors for console platforms have strict technical requirements for titles licensed for their platforms. For example, Sony publishes a **Technical Requirements Checklist (TRC)**, Microsoft publishes **Xbox Requirements (XR)**, and Nintendo publishes a set of *guidelines* (Lotcheck)
- **Compatibility testing**: Compatibility testing teams test the major functionality of the game on various configurations of hardware. This is mostly done for PC or mobile games, as console platforms are more standardized.
- **Localization testing**: Ensures the accuracy and quality of game's localization.
- **Soak testing**: Involves leaving the game running for prolonged periods time in various modes of operation, such as idling, paused, or at the title screen.
- **Regression testing**: QA checks to see whether the bug is still there (regression) and then runs similar tests to see whether the fix broke something else.

All these testings are done following a test plan. A test plan documents the strategy that will be used to verify and ensure that a game or feature meets its design specifications. It tells the tester what to test and look for in every piece of the game.

Game designers and QA

The relationship between a game designer and QA is very important. Game documentation might (and will) be used by QA as a reference for writing and running their test plans. Some specific documentation might be needed for testing specific features.

The more *custom* documentation the designers are able to provide to QA, the easier and more effective the QA work will be. For example, whenever I design a new batch of cards for *Battlehand,* I create an ad hoc document for the QA where I include every card's render with a description of what the card effects are and what numbers are expected to appear on it. This document is quite different from the actual design documentation of each card, which consists of a line in a huge spreadsheet that contains the design of every card in the game. By creating this ad hoc document, I make sure the QA department knows only what it needs to look for, in a more accessible format that includes details that are irrelevant in the design phase (like the card artwork and final appearance).

Remember that QA is your last chance, as a designer, to ship content of the highest quality. Making mistakes is only natural; you will make mistakes. A solid testing is the only way to avoid those mistakes going out to the public, who are going to notice them and who might be pretty unforgiving.

A great way to make the most out of QA is to get your designs reviewed by either a QA manager or the tester that will be assigned to the feature. This way, you will get feedback on your features well before the official QA stage even starts. Getting this kind of thing done before entering the final 10% is a nice way to avoid accumulating too much work in that final stage, and will definitely help to reduce the risk of accumulating delays and falling out of track.

QA might provide game designers some insights about gameplay that goes beyond the actual testing. In the end, we're talking of people that are going to play your game, or parts of it, hundreds of times, and they often have a level of expertise or feeling of the overall balancing that no developer or designer would be able to get in the same time window. Use that knowledge to keep improving the game!

Tips for closing a game project

As we have seen, in an ideal world, the closing phase of a game project should take more time than the sum of each of the previous stages. But that's unlikely to happen in the real world - on the contrary, it is highly probable that you'll find yourself with much less time than expected to wrap everything up.

Here is a list of tips and practices to avoid sacrificing polishing, proper user testing and, in the worst cases, procrastinating a game's release:

- **Review the game concept and game design pillars**: Cut anything that doesn't reflect them. The sooner this review is done, the better it is, but don't be afraid to cut a feature that appears to be in contrast with the original concept, even if it has been partially or fully developed.
- **Have a UX review**: Let a professional UX researcher study your game. A UX review will provide you with extremely useful insights and a lot of actionable points to improve the quality of your game.
- **Get the game out there**: Let other professional game developers try your game, and listen to their feedback. If you can, showcase your game at consumer fairs and show and pay attention to their reactions and feedback. There is a lot that can be learned by watching a real player trying your game.
- **Release as soon as possible**: This is not always possible, but if you can take advantage of an early access version or a soft launch, go for it and test the game with a sensible amount of players.
- **Test and iterate early on**.
- **Keep track of your decisions and don't change them**: If you, or someone else, take the decision of cutting a feature, or adjust a design based on some compromise, note down why and when these decisions were taken. It might not make sense some months down the line and you might be tempted to revisit or reconsider some old decision...only to end up in the same problematic situation of months before. If you know and clearly remember what the reasoning behind a decision was, you are more likely to save time by not reconsidering and overthinking.
- **Stick to the plan**: This is a very simple, but effective, advice. Anything that wasn't part of the original plan should be a red flag. What is the reason it was not part of the plan? Are you slipping into feature creeping?
- **Don't aim for absolute perfection**: Polishing is great, but it can really go on forever and nothing (and no one) is perfect. You should do the best work possible in the time you have.
- **Don't procrastinate**: Fixing bugs and starting polishing during production is the best way to save time when it's time to close the project and ship the game. Whenever you see a bug, if you have time to take care of it, just do it! There will be a final QA phase, but that's when the unexpected bug and problems should be addressed. Postponing every bug to the final QA, even those you were aware of and able to fix early on, is a mistake that will take a lot of your time when you will have very little available.

- **Don't be too passionate about your work, let a project manager decide**: Sometimes you can get stuck with design decisions. Two solutions might be both worth doing or trying. Don't let these moments of indecision block the development process. When in doubt, especially in bigger teams, ask and trust a lead, a producer, or a project manager. The reason to go for one solution rather than the other might be beyond your skills and just a matter of production requirements.

- **Be ready to accept and embrace failure**: Making games is not an exact science; it is also an art. You might follow every step by the book and do everything you are supposed to do and still fail. These moments are hard hits for teams and entire game companies, but there is more to learn from failure than from success. Treasure these experiences and analyze everything that went wrong. This experience is what will make you a veteran game designer.

 The screenshots used in this chapter are for illustrative purposes only. We do not recommend that you to misuse these in any way. For more information please consult the terms and conditions of the publishers mentioned in the *Disclaimer* section of this book.

Summary

You now know how to successfully close and ship a game. We have seen that you need to be conscious about the time required for the final stage in every game's development. We have learned the risks of putting a game together and how to avoid the feature creep danger. We have seen what polish is and how the team and the designers can polish their game to improve the quality of the game.

We had a quick look at the Quality Assurance process and went through a list of useful tips and suggestions for you to keep in mind when the time will come to close your project and finally enjoy shipping your game! The journey's not over yet. In the next chapter, you're going to learn about games as a service, a huge topic which is really dear to us.

15
Games As a Service

For Free to Play, episodic, and subscription-based games, a wide-scale release has always marked the transition from creating a product to running a service. But even for premium titles, a degree of post-launch support is mandatory, and the days of shipping a box and immediately moving onto a new venture are over.

Running a game development business has never been easy, and nowadays, our industry is as competitive and hit-driven as ever. With game development and marketing costs growing ever higher, building, maintaining, and repeatedly monetizing a dedicated fanbase has become a top priority. For players, on the other hand, the landscape is more inviting than ever! The abundance of high-quality Free to Play titles means that players can try as many games as they like, and play them for hundreds of hours without spending a penny.

In this chapter, we will attempt to distill the knowledge required to turn your game into a successful service, from monetization tips and live operations strategy, to addressing game balancing, understanding analytics, customer support, and the tools required to run your games sustainably. Evolving business models presents great (and sometimes controversial) design challenges, but tackling them head-on may be your only chance of making a world-class hit.

Terms of engagement

Before you begin thinking about designing, deploying, and running a live game, you ought to familiarize yourself with a large set of keywords and abbreviations used to describe various parts of the business. At first, these terms may seem a bit unwieldy, yet common language is essential when speaking about increasingly complex and fine-tuned products driven by dozens of people and hundreds of moving parts.

The majority of the list is dedicated to **KPIs** (**Key Performance Indicators**). These are the metrics used to evaluate the performance of the game. KPIs often revolve around financial data, marketing performance, as well as the current size, health, and the overall trends governing your player base.

We'll now unpack several key terms and use this as an opportunity to provide additional insight into the challenges of building and running Free to Play games.

Basic stats

We'll start with some of the most critical KPIs that almost every member of the game team should understand and follow:

Retention
One of the most important KPIs and the basis for your entire business. If you are to have any hopes of making back the costs of developing and running the game, as well as acquiring the user via paid marketing, you need to keep the players coming back regularly. After all, the longer someone plays, the larger the number of repeated opportunities they have to spend.

Retention stats are generally reported as the percentage of players who return in the days after the installation day. The most popular retention KPIs are D1 (one day after installation), D7, D14, D30 (a month after installation), and D365 (a year later), the last being the ultimate testament to a game's longevity. Retention varies dramatically depending on the game's genre and the type of audience you attract. That said, in the mobile games industry, a D1 retention of 40-45% for organic users (players not attracted by paid marketing) is often the target to hit, with outstanding games reaching 60%.

There are a few ways of calculating your retention, and some may be a bit misleading. Rolling retention, for example, considers users who launch the game just twice (on Day 0 and Day 17) as having retained for two weeks, putting them squarely in the D14 retention stat.

Daily Active Users and Monthly Active Users (DAU and MAU)
Two critical KPIs used to monitor the size of the active player base. DAU sums the total number of users who logged into the game on a particular day. MAU, on the other hand, portrays the monthly total, regardless of frequency of engagement.

Concurrent Users (CCU)

A measurement of how many players are logged into the game right now. By tracking the CCU over time, you can find the most and least popular times across the week. This helps you determine the best days and hours to roll out new content, run server scripts, or start a new special event.

CCU is a closely monitored KPI, and a sharp decline in the user count can be a telltale sign of infrastructure errors. Your technical staff will also use the CCU to work out the optimal server bandwidth. Nowadays, server instances can be added and removed remotely based on your current and future needs as well as the historical CCU data. This helps to keep the running costs low while ensuring there's enough capacity to avoid connection problems and server errors.

Conversion Rate (CVR)

The percentage of players who convert from a non-payer to a paying customer by spending money inside the game. The conversion rate varies dramatically depending on the genre, platform, territory, and the average player's age (players who are over 25 are much more likely to monetize). Mobile Free to Play games usually operate with a CVR between 1 and 5 percent.

Average Revenue Per User and Average Revenue Per Paying User (ARPU and ARPPU)

These long acronyms describe the monthly revenue generated by an average user (ARPU) or by an average paying customer (ARPPU). The calculations are simple:

ARPU = Monthly Revenue ÷ MAU

ARPPU = Monthly Revenue ÷ (MAU ÷ Conversion Rate)

The time frame in these KPIs may differ, since some companies look at daily or 24-hour rolling data when calculating their ARPU and ARPPU stats.

Moreover, you may also meet with ARPDAU, and as you've probably guessed from the acronym, it comes down to daily revenue divided by daily active users.

Lifetime Value (LTV)

The combined spend by an average user throughout their entire time with the product is an ultimate testament to the effectiveness of your business model.

Since we do not have data going into the future, the LTV will always be a forecast based on historical performance. By basing your LTV calculations on D1 retained users, you can reduce the noise generated by badly targeted marketing campaigns and lower-quality organic users (often associated with a large store feature).

Marketing and analytics

Following our basic stats, we have a list of KPIs and terms mostly connected to the commercial performance of our game:

Installs

New installs or new users are one of the key marketing KPIs, observed on a daily basis. Nowadays, most marketing campaigns can be tracked, allowing the team to directly attribute the user to a particular channel. Any unpaid install is treated as organic.

K-factor and virality

In marketing, the k-factor represents the viral growth rate of existing users, inviting non-users into the service. It all comes down to a simple calculation of the number of invites sent per average user multiplied by the conversion rate of the invite.

$k = (invites \div user) \times conversion$

Organic Uplift

The *Organic Uplift* represents the unattributed growth in organic (unpaid) installs. This can come as the result of store featuring, increased word of mouth, heightened brand awareness (social media posts, community work, and so on), untracked marketing such as newspaper and street adverts, or players simply seeing an advert online, not interacting with it, then searching for the product by themselves.

CTR

Click-Through Rate, the ratio of users who interact with an advert (or any other, trackable event) to the total number of views (impressions). In games advertising, CTR is used to assess and compare the effectiveness of advertising campaigns.

Cost Per Install (CPI)

Also known as the acquisition cost, this is a crucial KPI for any game that relies on paid marketing. CPIs can be highly volatile and easily inflated by huge marketing budgets of a few big companies who are competing over the same user base.

Nonetheless, in the crowded Free to Play market, the best (and often the only) way of growing your game profitably is to drive down the CPI (by adjusting the daily spend, marketing campaigns, and audience targeting options) and buy as many users as you can at a cost below their LTV.

CPIs can make or break your game. A highly attractive and well-targeted game can get a 2 dollar CPI, while another, less appealing one, may have to spend $20 for a single retained player. And if $20 per user sounds utterly crazy and unsustainable, that's because it usually is, unless your LTV sits comfortably above $20...

It's important to get an insight into the approximate CPI for your game before it enters actual production. To validate your marketing potential, set up a small-scale test ($500-$1000) with a few different versions of marketing screenshots that roughly represent your game and theme. Make sure to add competitive titles to the test to get some benchmark data. If you score way below the competition, consider testing a different theme or premise.

Cost Per Thousand Impressions (CPM)
Even if all you care about is new users, impressions (converted or not) are what you actually pay for. CPM provides strong insight into the actual costs of online advertising and becomes especially useful when assessing the profitability of untracked campaigns such as print, television, and billboards.

Minnows, dolphins, whales
A three-step classification (originating from the gambling industry), used to distinguish between different tiers of monetizing players. While the exact numbers behind each tier often vary across the industry, this classification is tremendously popular in Free to Play games.

To start with, minnows are the minor spenders (below 5 dollars/month), dolphins sit in the middle (*5-24.99 dollars/month*), and whales are the high spenders (*25+ dollars/month*). Occasionally, an extra tier is added above whales and reserved for players who spend more than 50 or 100 dollars/month.

Session stats (number and length)
Knowing the average amount of play sessions per day and their length can empower you to make better decisions when it comes to pacing and balancing your game, for example, by adjusting the length of individual rounds, or the number of resources generated by in-game actions.

Economy and balancing

To wrap up, let's delve into a set of terms and practices used in designing, analyzing, and balancing our in-game economies.

Freemium currency
Also known as soft currency, a relatively abundant in-game resource that can be accumulated by playing the game, without the need to spend money. Usually spent on basic content and gameplay needs.

Premium currency
Also known as hard currency, a scarce resource that is predominantly acquired by spending real money, although small amounts of premium currency may be awarded on a scheduled basis or from tightly limited objectives. Hard currency is used to access premium goods and services as well as to skip time and resource requirements.

Taps and sinks
In game economies, taps (or sources) generate resources while sinks are responsible for removing them. To avoid resource inflation and devaluation of your entire economy, you must maintain a tight grip on resource creation and provide players with deep, desirable sinks.

Energy
Action points, energy, fuel, keys, stamina, lives—these are but a few analogs for a resource designed to limit the amount of time you can effectively spend in the game. Usually, Energy resources replenish themselves over time, to a certain cap, which in some cases might be increased.

Even though you can spend money to replenish energy, it is rarely intended as a significant monetization vector. The primary role of energy mechanics is to help control a player's play sessions and their rate of progression. Without Energy, some players would not only exhaust our content at an uncontrollable rate, but also burn themselves out in the process. What's fun for 10 minutes at a time might not be fun for 3 hours straight. Having a clear incentive to return (*Energy full!*) as well as an excuse to leave the game (*Out of Energy!*) can help maintain a healthy play cycle and establish a play habit around the game.

On a side note, it's important to acknowledge a crucial difference between energy and lives. While Energy is usually spent on any significant action (such as entering a battle), Lives are only decreased upon failure. This means that a losing player will be forced out of the game (or incentivized to spend) sooner than a winning one. The long-term consequences of this difference are hard to predict and should be tested and assessed for each individual case.

Gacha box
Also known as a mystery box, loot box, or loot crate. Gacha boxes distribute rewards (such as resources, items, characters, vanity items, and other goods) in a randomized manner. More on designing gacha systems later in this chapter!

Drop rate
The percentage chance for a player to receive a particular reward in a randomized scenario such as enemy loot drops, gacha boxes, and so on.

Pinch-point

Any part of the game's core progression that relies on artificially inflated difficulty (a moment of increased *friction*) in order to encourage spending. Most mobile level-based puzzle games (such as *Candy Crush Saga*) periodically feature extraordinarily difficult levels that facilitate the need for extra moves and boosts.

Pay-gate

Any part of a game's content that is designed to be assessed primarily via payment can be considered as *locked behind a pay-gate.*

Grinding

The process of repeatedly completing an already mastered part of the game in order to complete a particular meta-objective. For example, amassing a large number of resources to buy an expensive item, or raising the experience level before tackling a particularly difficult challenge.

Churn rate and drop off points

Churn rate is the opposite of retention, it represents the number of players who stop playing the game (churn) after a defined period or at a specific point in time (after a new game update or server reset). High player churn prompts the search for drop-off points, areas of the game and features that prompt significant amounts of players to leave and never come back. To find the drop-off points, you'll need to collect game progression stats (last completed level or task, last unlocked item or game mechanic, total time played and so on) and use them to identify (and hopefully address) the most pressing issues.

Retention funnel

The funnel is a chronological representation of your data. When applied to retention analytics, it allows us to easily identify the biggest drop-off points.

For example, if we wanted to improve our D1 retention, the easiest way would be to look for drop-off points in the key points of our **First Time User Experience** (**FTUE**). The funnel would look like this:

- 10,000 Launched the game for the first time
- 9,500 Created a player profile
- 9,300 Entered the tutorial battle
- 8,000 Deployed units in battle
- 7,900 Finished the battle
- 6,000 Got to the end of the tutorial

A funnel like this immediately highlights a 14% high drop among players who entered the tutorial battle (9,300) and players who deployed their units (8,000). This highlights potential issues with this tutorial step and prompts further investigation and experimentation. Funnels like this can be applied on a wider scale, but the further your players get from the FTUE, the more uncertainty is introduced to your data.

Pay to win (p2w)

A term used to describe games or systems where players can vastly increase their chances of winning by spending real money. The ability to convert money into in-game power does not automatically brand your game as such. The advantages of spending must be perceivable and seemingly out of reach to non-spending players.

Multiplayer scenarios with pay to win dynamics are generally frowned upon in the western market. However, the same is not true for single player experiences, and eastern markets such as China, Japan, and Korea, where the cultural differences (and general maturity of the Free to Play market) play a major role in shifting away from this perspective. In fact, for many Chinese players, being able to afford premium game content is a source of pride.

A/B Testing (also known as Split Testing)

A/B tests are a form of controlled experiments where different versions or configurations of the game are run simultaneously on two (hence A and B) or more groups of players. A/B testing typically allows for efficient and bias-free validation of various theories, from default control layouts to progression mechanisms and game difficulty.

Each test is run for a set amount of time, after which the KPIs of different groups are compared and a winning configuration can be picked. Most tests are best run for at least a few weeks. It's highly possible that the same change that causes a bit of a percentage drop in tutorial completion can also result in a significant increase in long-term retention and conversion rates. In most cases, extensive A/B testing is confined to the beta and soft launch periods, but it's possible to utilize A/B tests for non-critical features across a game's entire lifespan.

Remember, players communicate with one another and it's best if none of your players ever feel shortchanged by their test group assignment. Furthermore, it's best to avoid any A/B tests that have clear, real-money implications, such as trying different price points for the same content. This kind of manipulation will almost certainly enrage the community and erode their trust.

Basics of Free to Play monetization

Setting up and balancing the game economy, player progression rate, and the monetization model can be a daunting and time-consuming job. In well-staffed teams, these duties are addressed by a dedicated specialist, often known as an economy designer. In smaller, less specialized teams, the heavy burden of creating a successful game economy will often fall onto the generalist game designer.

In theory, the business model of Free to Play games is simple. Lower the barrier to entry (free download) to attract a large audience, retain your players with fun gameplay, and provide them with ample opportunities to express themselves, save time, and enhance their gameplay by paying.

In practice, it's a huge challenge, especially since you're operating within a saturated market and with an increasingly savvy audience that often expects to get most of their content for free, even after playing your game for months or even years. To have any hopes of succeeding in this difficult market, you'll need to develop a strong monetization strategy that reinforces an already strong gameplay loop.

While the Free to Play business model is likely to leave a big impact on game design, you should not let monetization drive your prototypes and strip you of your creativity. Gameplay has to come first, since without it, you'll have no users to convert.

 Do not blindly copy/paste monetization models from other successful games. You may not have the brand, breadth of content, and audience size to make them work. As an example, *League of Legends'* monetization works on a multi-million strong user base, that retains for years, but with it's tiny ARPU, its likely won't work for you!

Vectors of monetization

Buying a knife skin in *Counter-Strike: Global Offensive* and purchasing a lollipop hammer in *Candy Crush* are two entirely different experiences. The first is driven by desire, the other by frustration. Knife skins give players a way to express themselves and provide visual variety, but they have no effect on gameplay. The value of the lollipop hammer, on the other hand, is almost entirely dependent on its gameplay impact, since it is a usable tool that helps you get past difficult situations. Your offering has to closely match your game and the desires of your players.

There are four distinct vectors used to drive in-game monetization models:

1. Time
2. Difficulty
3. Playable content
4. Non-playable content

We'll explore these vectors one by one and pay close attention to their effect on gameplay, progression, structure, and a player's emotional state.

Time

This monetization vector is reinforced by the following emotions: anticipation (positive) and impatience (negative).

Time and game progress are strongly intertwined, and Free to Play games often purposely (and gradually) slow down a player's progression rate in hopes of monetizing it. This can be done in two ways:

- **Explicitly via timers**: A centralized server-based clock can support a range of progress gating mechanics, from timers on crafting, building, training, upgrading, and unlocking your units, skills, and structures, to energy mechanics (which directly limit the playtime), and more subtle daily and weekly objectives that grant players important rewards (without which progress slows down significantly).
- **Implicitly via resources**: The prices of in-game content and Experience Points required to level up your avatars are often growing at an exponential rate. In these scenarios, players are given an option to continue playing the game for free, or to spend money and either accelerate resource generation or buy the item outright.

The effectiveness of progression-based monetization depends on game balancing and your ability to maintain an array of escalating goals for players to aspire towards.

However, do not rush the pace of a player's journey. Highlighting end-game content to a beginner will either scare them off (*it's just too much work*) or devalue everything else (*this is all a stepping stone to me getting that one thing I really want*).

Difficulty

This monetization vector is reinforced by the following emotions: mastery (positive) and frustration (negative). By carefully increasing the challenges presented by your in-game tasks (but not the actual complexity of your game mechanics), you're able to create *friction*, that is, pre-planned reduction in a player's rate of progression that is designed to encourage players to spend money.

Friction can be introduced in the form for difficulty spikes (sections that are much harder than their surroundings) or by steeply increasing the overall difficulty curve at a rate faster than a player's growth in power. Difficulty spikes and rises in difficulty curves are not mutually exclusive, and you can combine both solutions.

Once you settle on a method for introducing friction, you can monetize the solutions to the newfound problem by providing:

- **Band-aids** to the temporary problem of a difficulty spike, most likely in the form of consumable goods: premium ammo, powerful boosts, extra moves, lives, and so on
- **Long-term solutions** that help facilitate a player's growth and progression to match the increasing difficulty: permanent upgrades, powerful items and characters, and so on

Monetizing difficulty is risky! In some cases, friction can motivate players and keep them going (and potentially spending), but in others, it will cause players to rebel and leave in frustration. Frequent and obvious difficulty spikes will end up feeling jarring and unfair, and the relentlessly growing difficulty curve can tire your audience and make them feel like everything they do is in vain, removing any satisfaction from in-game progression.

The consequences of monetizing friction can vary between genres and audiences. Soft launching your game and monitoring the progression, spend, and retention of real players is the best way of analyzing and optimizing your friction.

Playable content

This monetization vector is reinforced by the following emotions: curiosity (positive), joy (positive), and boredom (negative). New stories, missions, characters, equipment, environments, and even game modes are all examples of playable content that can be locked behind a *pay-gate*.

To increase the effectiveness of this vector, you'll need to increase the necessity, desirability, and perceived value of your goods, and do it all without pushing the non-paying users out of the game. You can classify your playable content by its lifespan:

- **Permanent**: Game trials, premium expansion packs, and new story episodes have been around for years. Nowadays, we are more likely to get a skeleton of the entire game for free and spend to build up our virtual collections of goods, be it cars, weapons, or heroes. The utility of permanent goods has to be closely planned and monitored. On one hand, satisfying a player's needs permanently removes the chance for repeated sales in that sector of monetization. On the other, making a premium item feel useless and obsolete after 30 minutes will have an equally negative outcome.
- **Consumable**: Satisfying the implementation of non-permanent goods (such as item rentals, game subscriptions, or time-limited access to premium areas) is a great way of maintaining a healthy, long-lasting economy. That said, make sure to diversify your offering! A significant portion of your audience will expect their money to have a long-lasting impact and showcase an inherently adverse reaction to spending on non-permanent content.

Non-playable content

This monetization vector is reinforced by the following emotions: pride (positive), amusement (positive), jealousy (negative), and shame (negative). This category includes content and services that may be useful, desirable, and amusing, but do not directly influence or expand a player's gameplay options and capabilities. The two most common categories are:

1. **Cosmetic items**: Costumes, skins, decorations, icons, companion pets, visual effects, sound effects, animations, and any other content with no utility use and value based solely on the back of look and feel, scarcity, and subjective taste.
2. **Optional services**: Account name changes, server migrations, private chat channels, additional character or loadout slots, and even automatic handling of some of the chores (such as clearing up inventory space). These are all examples of potentially monetizable perks and services that do not have a visible effect on gameplay.

By its very nature, non-playable content is the dominant monetization vector for any game that tries to maintain a level playing field between spenders and non-spenders.

Establishing a game economy

The main goal of any Free to Play economy should be to maximize the LTV of an average player in the most sustainable and positive way possible. This means we need to:

- Adjust the monetization strategy
- Control the rate of player progression by managing difficulty, content burn, resource generation, and resource removal
- Create and adjust the real-money offerings

Adjusting the monetization strategy

You may have a nifty shortlist of items and services to offer, but before you put a single number against them, you need to ask yourself these questions:

- **Who will be playing the game?**: Can your game aspire to create a strong, dedicated fanbase with high retention and LTV, or is it more of a casual affair in a highly competitive genre? What is the age of the average player? People over 25 have more disposable income than teenagers and may be ready to pay for their hobby. Young audiences are very hard to convert and we should actively try to prevent any purchases from minors (for example, by creating an age gate during their first boot-up).
- **How much can you get out of your game content?**: Is the potential LTV for a D365 player capped at a 100 dollars, or is it 100,000? The former highlights a huge problem if you can't acquire a massive amount of users. The latter is often a sign of being either too optimistic or too stingy.
- **Is the audience willing to spend?**: Are there any preconceptions around your genre or brand that may add value or potentially hurt your offering?:
    - A PC or console brand used in a mobile game will likely aspire to players who are used to spending $60 for a finished product. Be careful not to infuriate them with your monetization strategy!
    - On the flipside, brands such as *MARVEL*, *DC*, *Star Wars*, or *Transformers* lend themselves to a market that accepts the need to spend to collect their favorite characters, be it in a physical or virtual form.

- **Are you primed to deliver the value?**: Back in *Transformers: Earth Wars*, we've put incredible effort into tweaking and polishing our character models, animations, preview screens, and the gacha experience. Our aim was to deliver the best digital toys we could, a set of faithful (and sometimes much improved) characters that our players remember from their childhood toys, cartoons, and comics. Thanks to this effort, our game became a legitimate way to collect digital *Transformers* characters, one that requires no shelf space and offers quite a lot for free.

Knowing the basics, you can now adjust your aspirations. For example, a World War II strategy game may lean towards a mature audience and have the content needed to establish a healthy, long-lasting economy. A mobile endless runner, on the other hand, will skew younger players and have a hard time in converting players and extracting revenue without strong upselling techniques. Moreover, if the nature of the game gives little hope for a high D30 retention stat, you might as well try to burn through your content and maximize the ARPPU.

Remember, it's always good to look at successful games within your genre, but there is no guarantee of translating that success onto a game with a different audience, brand, or scale.

Balancing player progression

Pacing and balancing of Free to Play games is a very delicate process. Slow things down too much, too early, and you risk your players growing bored or giving up in frustration. Maintain a quick and steady pace, and you'll burn through your content and remove any time and effort-based incentives to spend.

The only way out of this conundrum is to employ a degree of exponential growth in your economy, but blindly multiplying the costs and requirements can quickly get out of hand. By using a critical vector of progression (described in detail back in the scoping and balancing chapters), you'll be able to model your economy with paying and non-paying players in mind, and better understand the longevity of your content.

Let's see how this process looks in practice! We'll base our example on *Planetside 2*, a Free to Play MMO shooter for PC and PS4.

Example – Planetside 2

Planetside 2 is a **MMOFPS** (**massive multiplayer first person shooter**), a game where thousands of players, divided into three factions, engage in enormous, open-world battles over territory.

The critical vector of progression in *Planetside 2* is a resource called **Certification Points** (**(CP)** or certs). *Certification Points* are primarily acquired through gameplay and spent on the most desirable game content, that is, unlocking and upgrading weapons, vehicles, and the abilities of your soldiers.

Therefore, if we were to balance the economy of *Planetside 2*, we'd need to do it by:

1. Establishing baseline certificate point generation.
2. Approximating CP income over time for different types of players.
3. Modelling the prices for game content based on the desired progression rate.

To begin with, let's tackle the biggest CP source, that is, Experience Points! In *Planetside 2*, players accumulate XP for most gameplay actions such as killing enemies, supporting allies, and capturing territory. The rate for CP generation is set at **1 CP per 250 XP**. This is one of our most powerful variables.

Knowing this, we can begin predicting the amount of CPs generated per day by different types of players, from non-spenders, to light spenders (who subscribe to the premium program and increase their XP generation), and high spenders (who also spend on various XP boosters). The best way of informing our CP calculation would be to use player performance and engagement analytics from closed Alpha and Beta builds, but for the purpose of this example, let's use hypothetical approximations. After all, you'll often have to model your economies with no real data to begin with, and wait for more final adjustments until soft-launch:

	Non-Spender	**Low Spender**	**High Spender**
XP and CP per hour	10,000 XP = 40 CP	12,000 XP = 48 CP	14,000 XP = 56 CP
XP Bonus	0%	50% = 24 CP (premium program bonus)	100% = 56 CP (premium program + XP boosters)
Daily retention bonus	48 CP/day	96 CP/day	96 CP/day
Daily totals for average level of engagement	88 CP (1 h) 128 (2 h) 168 (3 h)	168 CP (1h) 240 CP (2h) 312 CP (3h)	208 CP (1h) 320 CP (2h) 432 CP (3h)

On top of certs coming from the XP and the daily retention CP bonuses (up to 96 CP per day), players are awarded 100 Certification Points for each *Battle Rank* (XP level), up to rank 15 (which requires 120,000 XP). This means we give out an extra 1,500 CPs during the first 10 or so hours of gameplay, a meaningful bonus that should help increase engagement and D7 retention without sacrificing longevity of our economy. Players can also grab additional CPs from various performance and engagement-based *medals*, but their significance as a source of CPs is minimal.

Now that we know how many certs are generated per day, we can better understand that a 1,000 CP weapon requires over a week of highly engaged play for a non-spender, but only 3 semi-engaged days from a high-spender. If our soft-launch data indicates that a lack of variety is hurting retention, then we might want our players to try around 5-10 weapons within their first week . This means we'll need to make sure to include several 100 CP and 200 CP options in the economy.

In *Planetside 2*, the control over player progression is given to the players themselves. There are very few requirements in play, and players have the freedom in choosing what to spend their certs on. Free to Play users can spend minimal amounts of CP on unlocking a wide variety of basic weapons and utility perks across the entire game, but thanks to the exponential pricing strategy, the economy still provides ample room for those who wish to dedicate months of gameplay or hundreds of dollars on specialized equipment and heavily-upgraded abilities.

To illustrate this with an example, let's look at the CP sink provided by a single weapon on a flying vehicle. The *M18 Needler* is a free weapon that can be kitted out for a couple hundred CPs, but the upgrade costs tend to add up quickly:

Optics	Magazine size	Reload speed	Max Ammo
Free (1.25x zoom)	100 CP	150 CP	1 CP
50 CP (1.5x)	200 CP	200 CP	10 CP
150CP (1.75x)	400 CP	400 CP	30 CP
500 CP (2x)	1,000 CP	500 CP	50 CP
		1,000 CP	100 CP
Alternative Optics			150 CP
50 CP (night vision)			200 CP
200 CP (thermal vision)			400 CP

			500 CP
			1000 CP

As you can see, even the default weapon can sink over 7,300 certs and puts the fully upgraded gear out of the range of non-paying customers. The monetization potential of this particular vehicle is further reinforced by secondary weapons, tools, and a variety of vehicle perks. By all accounts, this looks like an economy with a strong, long-term potential.

With CP generation and pricing under wraps, we can set up the relationship between certs and the premium currency. Let's say that 1,000 CP translates to ~6 hours of playtime, and each hour equals 100 premium currency. By pricing the premium currency at 1 dollar per 100, we can effectively translate the value of a 1,000 CP item into $6. With this information at hand, we can estimate the dollar value of the entire economy. To begin with, upgrading the *M18 Needler* alone would cost over $40!

While this kind of calculation is hardly scientific and rarely translates into exact dollar value, it helps you in establishing your pricing strategy and understanding the value of your content. Ultimately, it's up to the players to decide what to spend their time and money on. Most will try to get the things they like for free, some will spend a few dollars for the weapons they like, and others will drop a hundred to treat themselves to a full set of exclusive skins. In the early stages of economy design, the most you can hope for is to create a long-lasting economy, which appears approachable, but encourages spending.

 It's important to note that there are three playable factions in *Planetside 2*, and veteran players are likely to have multiple characters on their account - each with their own rank and cert balance. This simple treatment multiplies CP sinks and the long-term appeal at the cost of a diminished sense of personal investment in each particular character.

Gacha

In Chapter 3, *Scoping a Game Project*, we described gacha as an extreme method of randomized reward distribution. We also mentioned the Japanese origins of gacha, the *gachapon* toy capsules distributed by various vending machines.

What originated in the East is now a common practice in the western market, especially on mobiles. But before you base your Free to Play economy on loot boxes, you have to fully understand the requirements and implications of such systems.

The reception towards gacha varies between platforms, genres, and territories. Evaluate your audience! Are they familiar with the concept of gacha, or will you have to teach them the ropes and constantly manage their expectations? Putting loot crates into any premium product can be seen as a very controversial move.

As with all facets of monetization, taking inspiration from top-games when designing your gacha is a good practice, but it hardly guarantees success. Every gacha model needs to be tailor-made to your game and audience. You may not have the audience, content, or brand required to make your gacha work.

To help you better understand and increase the effectiveness of this monetization model, we'll delve into the five pillars of gacha design, and follow them with additional information, tips, and tricks.

Pillar 1 – Quantity and quality

Since a loot table with ten rewards won't last for long, the very first step in gacha design is to ensure that you have enough content to make gacha a viable monetization strategy.

How many unique pieces of content can you offer? You may not know the final quantities, but it important to look at both pessimistic and optimistic estimates. It's best to aim for at least a 100 unique rewards, but it's possible to get away with less, especially if you can make duplicate rewards useful (or even desirable). More on duplicates later!

Divide your content into three to five tiers signifying its quality and rarity. Why three to five? Anything below three tends to be too shallow, and anything above five tends to be too fragmented and confusing. Find suitable names for the tiers (common, uncommon, rare, epic, and so on), or mark them with symbols (such as stars), or grades (D, C, B, A, S). When it comes to naming and color-coding your content tiers, do not try to reinvent the wheel; the higher the chance some players are familiar with parts of the system, the better.

Speaking of tiers, they are a great way of multiplying your content and expanding your gacha offering. All you need to do is create several versions of the same character/weapon/vehicle (often with the same exact same art and gameplay), but with different starting stats and progression curves. In this way, 40 unique elements can become 120 entries in your gacha economy. Of course, this process has limits and diminishing returns, but I find that sticking to three or so variants works well without muddying the waters too much.

Another way of stretching your rewards is to divide them into pieces, such as asking players to collect 50 fragments/shards/blueprints to unlock an item instead of granting it right away. Be very careful when doing this, as fragmenting rewards delays the payoff and essentially reverses the frequency of content unlocks, as players need to get the same exact gacha reward multiple times to get anything out of the system. As a result, seasoned players (who have accumulated progress on multiple items, over a long time) have a much higher chance of receiving something new than the newcomers (who have little hope of actually unlocking something valuable early on). If you decide on using fragmented rewards, it's best to provide a healthy stream of new content early on, maintaining gameplay variety and keeping players on the optimal path of progression.

After you establish how much content you have to offer and how it's distributed, you have to analyze the speed and price of burning through it. Start by adding up your content and extracting two numbers: the minimum amount of reward drops needed to unlock all available content, and the total drops needed to unlock and upgrade everything. Now, estimate the number of boxes opened per day by different types of player (non-spenders, spenders, and heavy spenders). Using these numbers, you can estimate how long it will take to extinguish your gacha economy, and how much money it will take if you were to accelerate it.

To get a more realistic estimation, try restricting the content to an amount that will satisfy most players. After all, there may be 300 unique weapons in the game, but you may actively use just a few at a time, and your needs may be entirely satisfied with a set of five, heavily upgraded ones. With this point, we segue into the next pillar of gacha design.

Pillar 2 – Player capacity

The long-term appeal of your content is connected to the size of a player's loadout and the utility of growing one's collection.

Imagine a game where players collect various hero characters, but can only take a single one into battle. This will likely create situations where players become completely satisfied with just a few high-class characters, reducing the appeal of unacquired content dramatically.

To keep gacha relevant, you'll need to constantly encourage players to expand their collections. There are few ways of doing that:

- Introduce special game modes or missions, which require a particular set of characters or equipment

- Implement unit cooldowns (penalty for repeated use) or daily bonuses (a more positive take) to encourage interaction with a wider palette of content
- Create counter-strategies in your metagame balance, and consider more explicit, capacity-expanding mechanics such as elemental strengths and weaknesses
- If you come to rely on selling equipment, break it down into multiple pieces (helmet, chest, gloves, shoes, and so on), and maybe even add a few extra rings and trinkets

Regardless of the solution you go for, your main objective is to protect the longevity of the economy. Ensure that the appetite for new gacha content cannot be quenched by a few lucky pulls!

Pillar 3 – Desirability

Is your gacha content desirable? Can you imagine spending $10 on it? How about $10,000? Strong, recognizable brands will help raise the value of your virtual collections, but ultimately, the success of your gacha often depends on utility. It's best if you can make your gacha content an essential element of player progression. Completing an in-game collection should be hard, and upgrading it to its full potential should be near-impossible.

As for cosmetic content, cheap texture swaps may get you part of the way, but players can often tell if you made the effort or not. Take the time to make the premium cosmetics truly outstanding. Go beyond textures and models, and into particle effects, animations, sound effects, and icons.

Pillar 4 – Sustainability

Releasing your game with a decent amount of gacha content is one thing, but sustaining it for many years to come is another (especially with a smaller, leaner team). If it takes you two months to make a new character, but you need to release at least one character per month to maintain healthy monetization, you're heading into trouble.

This is why you must regularly evaluate your content creation capacity and look for ways to optimize the pipeline, be it with tools, processes, training, or outsourcing. The ultimate goal is to turn content creation into a pleasant and risk-free endeavor.

To further reduce the stress of live operations, hold back some of your initial line up and try to establish a backlog of unreleased content. A safety net of at least a month (and ideally three months) will prove essential for all the unforeseen issues that are almost sure to sprout up.

Pillar 5 – Duplicate handling

Allowing for duplicate rewards is often essential to maintaining longevity and stretching your content. Unfortunately, receiving dupes repeatedly can make spending money a downright infuriating experience. It also creates a negative feedback loop where spending money lowers the chances of receiving a valuable reward; hardly an ideal scenario.

To alleviate the problem of meaningless duplicates, we need to create a set of secondary rewards, which are granted for duplicates. These often take form of crafting materials that can be exchanged for rewards of higher rarity. The ultimate goal is to maintain the value of gacha by ensuring that each individual pull is a step towards building up one's collection and accessing more desirable content. Let's look at a couple of interesting examples of successful duplicate handling.

To start with, we have *Hearthstone's* dust system. This collectible card game sells cards in packs of seven, and even with hundreds of cards at hand, duplicates are a very frequent occurrence. However, only two copies of the same card can be used in any deck (one for legendary cards). This renders the third copy of each card effectively useless. Fortunately, any spare or unwanted cards can be disenchanted in exchange for magical dust; the higher the rarity of the card, the more dust you get. A legendary card will net you 400 dust; gather 1,200 more and you'll be able to afford any legendary card you want! By returning between 5% and 25% of a card's value back to the player, and allowing them to pick the card they want to create, *Hearthstone* has created a very effective and player-friendly system.

Clash Royale, on the other hand, treats its cards differently. Premium chests are chock-full of cards, with over 300 cards in a single *Giant Chest*. At the time of writing, there are only around 70 unique cards in the economy, and getting a new type of card is not a frequent occurrence for the player. Therefore, at a first glance, there seems to be an issue of flooding players with a massive amount of duplicates. However, in *Clash Royale*, unlocking a new card is just the beginning! Upgrading cards is the primary means of player progression, and it can only be done via duplicate copies of each individual card. And it takes quite a lot of copies, too… Upgrading an epic card to its limit takes over 386 duplicates, while a common, on the other hand, requires a total of 9,586 copies of the same card! With duplicate-driven economy in place, the cards in *Clash Royale* maintain their value for many months:

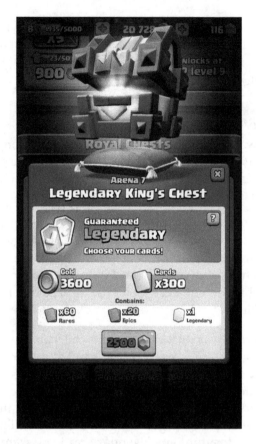

Clash Royale chests are chock-full of card stacks and interesting mechanics. In this case, you can select between different card types as you open the box!

There are many more examples of duplicate handling, but the key lesson is one of maintaining or even reinforcing the long-term effectiveness of your gacha boxes.

It's true that the 100th pull a premium gacha will never be as rewarding as the first couple—full of new, exciting rewards, and endless potential. But it's important we do what we can to maintain the value proposition for as long as possible!

Now that we're finished with the 5 pillars of gacha design, let's take a look at some further tips and insights on the subject!

Weight-based loot tables

As players, we often think of probability in games as flat percentages—this action has a 5% chance of success, that item has a 20% chance to drop, and so on, but assigning actual percentage values to rewards is a very problematic and ultimately futile endeavor. After all, adding a single new reward may require modifications to the entire loot table. Let's look at a simple example!

In a loot table of 5 items, we have 4 common rewards and 1 rare reward, which we want to be 10 times harder to get. Calculating the exact percentage value for our rare item is not an easy task, unless we use weights, in which case it becomes trivial.

In our weighted probability system, each item is assigned a number, which represents its relationship to other items. An item with a weight of 250 is 25 times more likely to drop than an item with a weight of 10. To get a percentage chance, we simply divide the weight of one item by the total weight of the entire loot table:

Item	Weight	Percentage
A	10	10/41 = 0.2439 = 24.4%
B	10	10/41 = 24.4%
C	10	10/41 = 24.4%
D	10	10/41 = 24.4%
E (rare)	1	1/41 = 0.024 = 2.4%
Total	41	100%

By adding more items into the table, we automatically lower the chances of other items. An empty reward entry with a weight of 500 would make all rewards more scarce by reducing the chances of getting any item at all.

We can also nest reward sets together. Our A, B, C, D, and E items could all contain further reward sets with weights of their own, which is exactly how most gacha loot tables operate. You may have a static 10% chance to get a rare item, but the rare reward set itself may contain dozens of entries with varying degrees of probability.

Packaging and opening

Gacha is not just about the reward, it's about the entire experience of receiving it. The design of your packaging and opening sequences can have a big influence on your financial performance.

How do you envision your gacha? Is it a pack of cards that fans out in front of the player? Is it a magical crystal that bursts in a pillar of light? An egg that has to be cracked? A box bursting with treasures? Make sure to set aside ample time to implement and polish both the gacha packaging and the opening experience.

Delivering a good gacha opening experience is a dual faceted challenge. To start with, you want to build anticipation, raise the expectations by improving the sequence for higher reward tiers, and culminate in a celebratory reveal. On the other hand, you need to be efficient and build a sequence that isn't overly long and annoying when seen for a hundredth (or thousandth) time.

If you do your job particularly well, you will have players who try to open 100 boxes in a row. Make sure that doing so is neither problematic nor boring. By implementing an *Open 10 option* for your reward boxes, you can streamline the opening experience without completely devoiding it of its charm.

 When offering multiple rewards from a single gacha pull, it's wise to implement a guarantee of some sort. For example, *Hearthstone's* pack of 7 cards contains at least 1 card that's rare or better. Such a guarantee increases the perceived value and offsets the risk of bad luck on the player's part. But remember, guaranteed rewards may inflate your value proposition and might require you to lower the average quality of remaining rewards.

Maintaining consistency

You want your customers to easily decide between different types of reward boxes based on their theme and contents alone. Constantly shifting the percentage chances for different reward tier chances and introducing ambiguous value propositions will lead to confusion and discourage players from spending.

Set up rules around the distribution of reward tiers inside your premium gacha boxes (for example, a 2%/12%/86% split between legendary/rare/common items) and stick to them! Inconsistent tiers will not only make your life harder (more variables to set up and balance), but they'll also make for less satisfied customers.

With consistent offering, a player who wants a new warrior class character can instantly choose a Warrior Box over a Gunner Box without second-guessing themselves. After all, the chances of getting a legendary character are the same in every premium box. The decision comes down to what I want to spend on, and the value itself never comes into question.

Loot box consistency does not mean you cannot have scarce rewards within a certain rarity tier (for example, a common character that's much less likely to drop than other commons), nor does it prohibit free boxes with different reward tiers, or boxes that guarantee a certain tier. It's all about ensuring that a certain class of premium box offers consistent reward tiers across the entire game, even if the loot tables themselves differ in contents.

Kompu gacha

Kompu or complete gacha refers to a practice of compounding multiple randomized prizes into **powerful sets** (which can be extremely hard to complete). For example, imagine an armor set that comprises of 6 pieces (3 common, 2 rare, and 1 legendary -with an incredibly small drop chance). Thanks to a *set bonus* (for having all 6 pieces), the power of a complete set is much greater than the sum of its individual parts.

By diminishing the value of base components and making the ever-elusive grand prize the ultimate goal of spending money, the model has turned an already popular gacha model into something even more lucrative, but not for long...

In 2012, Japan's Consumer Affairs Agency declared that the disproportionate gap between risk and reward in kompu gacha models puts them dangerously close to gambling, and subsequently banned the use of kompu gacha in Japan. As for the legal status of gacha (be it kompu or otherwise) in the Western market, as of April 2018, we do not have any major restrictions, but it's best to track current legislation, avoid randomized rewards that can be taken out of the game (can be perceived as gambling), and try to protect minors from exposure to paid gacha content.

If you plan on creating sets of loot box rewards and avoid falling into the Kompu gacha category, try to observe the following rules:

- Set components have value on their own, outside the context of the complete set
- Individual pieces are not deceptively rare in comparison to everything else
- The complete set is seen as a bonus, and not the sole purpose of that entire offering

Box gacha

As in normal gacha, the rewards from box gacha come from a randomized loot table, but with one big design change. The box contents are finite and each reward can only be pulled once. If there are 20 items on the loot table, they will all be distributed within exactly 20 pulls, and even if one item has a tiny 0.1% chance of dropping, you can be certain that, in the worst case scenario, you'll only need to pull the other 19 items before receiving your grand reward.

The mechanics of box gacha bring a great level of comfort to the players, and make it the perfect solution for parts of the economy that have a fixed number of duplicates, or wherever a duplicate would be deemed inappropriate. For example, imagine that your players have to spend hundreds of hours and thousands of dollars for a chance of grabbing a box with one of five legendary artifacts. A duplicate, in this case, would not only be inappropriate, but also infuriate the most valuable players.

Bundles and targeting

The more steps you put between players and the content they desire, the higher the chance they'll stop part way in the process. The purchase flow in most online games is a multi-step adventure that's not very user-friendly at all, since our players usually have to:

- Identify something they need
- Check how much currency is required
- Navigate to the premium currency shop
- Decide between different packages, bundles, and offers
- Complete the purchase of the premium currency
- Go back and spend their new resources on the item

In this example, we are assuming that players need to purchase premium currency since very few users stockpile on premiums without a clear spending goal in mind. Now, vast improvements to the flow can be made by simply directing players towards the exact currency pack they need once they attempt to purchase the item (thus effectively removing steps 2, 3, and 4). However, not everyone attempts to purchase something they clearly can't afford in the first place, and so the long shop funnel (along with its many drop-off points) lives on.

Can we make things simpler? The bright minds at *Valve* suggest that developers use real money purchases across the entire game economy, that is, to remove the proxy of premium currency. This might be a solution for you, but many game economies still put an important role onto premium currencies. After all, they are great for tiny, incremental purchases (such as time skips), which can be given out in controlled amounts, and are an elegant way of letting players decide what kind of reward they want.

What if we packed our content into bundles and sold it directly (for real money) to the receptive user base? The short answer: it works. The long answer: themed content bundles at accessible price points are one of the most effective sales techniques in Free to Play video games.

There is no simple answer as to what you should put in your bundles; after all, every game economy is different. But there are a few guidelines to follow:

1. **Timing matters**: Bundles are more effective if they are time-limited and receive the exposure caused by engaging events.
2. **Less is more**: Do not spam your players or flood them with different options. Give them a few different bundles to pick from, and they'll be able to make up their mind in seconds. Give them fifteen bundles with varying themes and price points, and they'll very likely be paralyzed by the sheer quantity of choices and the fear of picking a sub-optimal offering.
3. **Do not put excessive amounts of premium currency in your bundles and sales**: Doing so will lead to players stockpiling on premiums, sitting on it for weeks, and spending it all at once on new game content. Bulk purchases of this kind tend to be a disappointing experience for the user and further shorten the lifespan of your content.
4. **Do not discount heavily and maintain a steady Expected Value (EV)**: You'll find all the information on using and calculating EV in the following section. As for the discounts, the likes of Black Friday may be a good excuse to put on a lot of quality content for sale, but it doesn't require that you devalue it. Try to prevent your offerings from ever going more than 30-40% off. The only exception for insane deals are highly limited (one per user) starter bundles.
5. **Want before need**: I may need more fuel, but what I really want is a new car. Look at usage and purchase data to determine the most desirable content and shortlist it for your most important bundles. Avoid diminishing returns by intertwining less desirable offers at off-peak times (in days with lower DAU), and try not to use your best content back-to-back.

6. **Targeting is everything**: Thanks to machine learning and automatic bundle targeting, it's possible to customize your offerings towards individual players based on their spending pattern and current game state. If you're in no position to deploy such tools, then you can always fall back on manually creating a series of bundles and toggle them based on several profile requirements such as player level, already unlocked content, and past spending (more on that later on).

Utilizing EV in bundle creation

Are your bundles comparably attractive? Are you giving away too much content for too little money? The EV is a simple calculation that helps compare your premium offerings and understand the percentage gain (or loss) of value between them. This is best explained with a simple example.

Let's say your premium currency store offers 100 premium currency for $4, and that a value of a rare character is estimated at 500 premium currency ($20). A special bundle with 200 premium and 2 rare characters is therefore worth an estimated $48. If you were to put this bundle on sale for $29.99, you'd create an offering with an EV of 160% (48 ÷ 29.99 = 1.6), a 60% growth in value when compared to your baseline offering. This is a good deal, but is it too good of a deal? That depends on the average lifespan of your players. If the game is designed to support a year-long player progression, you might want to keep the EVs within 100 and 160 percent. However, if players are easy to acquire but the very nature of your game makes it hard to retain them for more than a few weeks, the EVs could in theory go up to 200%.

Pay close attention to the EVs of all premium goods and don't think of the EV as something you put up or down to sell more stuff. The ultimate objective is to maintain a stable offering across the entire lifespan of your game, with a few exceptions reserved for the likes of highly limited goods such as anniversary sales or starter bundles. Stable EV prevents inflation of your economy and saves your customers the effort (and anxiety) of having to constantly evaluate and calculate your offers in search of good and bad deals.

Adjusting your offering based on individual player spending

If you have a player who is willing to spend $10 but is offered a $5 bundle, you're potentially leaving $5 on the table. Likewise, if your player is looking for a $1 or $2 transaction and you're flashing $50 and $100 offers in their face, the monetization potential dwindles, and you may even evoke a cynical response to your offerings.

We need to make it easy for our players to support the game and consume the content we've crafted for them. To help us cater to player preferences, we need to discover **what each user wants to spend on, and how much**. At first, you'll need to cast your net wide. Present a few extremes and adjust the future offers based on the purchasing pattern. Let's say a user is given a choice between $4.99 and $49.99 versions of the same bundle (that is, the same content but in different quantities). If they go for $4.99, we should try to monetize at $9.99 and $19.99 next. Should they go for $49.99, we are given a signal that a $99.99 offer may be approached with enthusiasm.

This kind of targeting is fertile ground for machine learning algorithms, but huge progress can be made by putting a simple set of requirements based on the last 5 purchases and the top price tier ever achieved. Just make sure to not put a user in the high-spending corner and cut them off from smaller offerings permanently just because they made a once-in-a-blue-moon purchase for their birthday.

Purchase rationalization

Be it culturally or genetically, we are predisposed towards dedicating a large portion of our day to gathering and protecting our resources. For any adult who appreciates the value and purchasing power of money, spending it can be a highly complex behavior. Our decisions originate as emotional and visceral reactions, which are then rationalized before execution.

By acknowledging and embracing the differences in spending habits and patterns, you can consciously expand your offering and cater to a wider portion of your player base. Let's explore a list of common emotional contexts and internal rationalizations used to enable spending:

- **Curiosity**: I really want to find out how this works or what's going to happen next.
- **Necessity**: I need to purchase this to play the way I want to play.
- **Exclusivity**: There is simply no way I can get this now other than paying, so I might as well spend.
- **Opportunity**: I don't want to miss out on this deal. It's 50% off, there's no time to hesitate!
- **Long term value**: I want to maximize my gains and minimize my loses. With a VIP program or premium subscription, the sooner I start, the better. This is even more appealing if the rewards scale and grow with my progress.

- **Permanent value**: I don't want to feel like I have to keep spending repeatedly, but if a single purchase can get me 50% more XP and coins for life, I'm on board!
- **Peer pressure**: My friends have all purchased this boost, and I feel like I should give back and contribute too.
- **Consumer behavior**: A lot of people seem to enjoy this and say it's good, I guess I can give it a try too!
- **Recognition**: This thing will bring me respect and popularity!
- **Altruism**: I can provide benefits to my friends and contribute to the community I care about!

Evaluate your audience!

Spending behaviors are often influenced by cultural differences. To provide an example based on my colleague's many years of experience, American players tend to be more impulsive and lacking in self control, but are also quick to write customer support tickets if they're not fully satisfied. German players, on the other hand, tend to be very analytical, they do their math, internalize their decision, and often blame themselves if they're not happy with their choice. Evaluate the target demographic when planning your monetization strategy; what works in one region won't necessarily translate elsewhere!

Players have limited budgets

Most players have a set amount of money they are willing to spend on gaming in a set period (usually monthly because of paycheck cycles). It's best if players spend consistently over the month, getting small rewards for each individual action. Releasing a high amount of highly desirable content back-to-back will force the players to quickly use up their limit or even go past it. Both of these outcomes are not going to help you sustain the game or your spenders. Should they spend their whole mental cash allocation on the first day of the month, the rest of it may feel very disappointing and bleak in comparison. Similarly, if we put a lot of great content on sale, we'll force some players to spend more than they planned to. Players who overspend are likely to feel angry at the developer, not at their own lack of self control.

To sum things up, spender behavior can vary from highly logical to completely irrational. We need to expand our offering to appeal to a variety of spending patterns and rationalizations, and control the release cadence to prevent overspending.

Live operations

The key objectives of any business are to build, retain, and monetize its customer base. This means that releasing a quality product is just the beginning!

You'll need to maintain a level of support for your game as soon as it becomes permanently available to the public. This could be a public beta, Steam early access, or a so-called soft launch (low-key deployment in a few handpicked territories, for example, Australia, Netherlands, Canada, or the Philippines).

The success of any live title depends on the publisher's ability to double down on their investment and maintain a dedicated team to execute on the key aspects of liveops:

- **Content and feature updates**: Keeping the game feeling fresh, bug-free, and relevant
- **Balancing improvements**: Addressing both dominant and underplayed strategies based on analytics and player sentiment
- **Customer support**: Creating and policing your in-game and online community, and sharing customer sentiments, suggestions, and feedback with the game team
- **Paid marketing and social campaigns**: To profitably grow, maintain, and re-engage your user base
- **Events, bundles, and sales**: Increasing engagement and monetization in a sustainable way

To deliver on this level of support, the development team will need to plan and prepare for live operations in weeks or months before launch. The list of tasks, among other things, includes:

- Planning a few months of events, content, and feature rollouts
- Creating and deploying liveops tools to handle sales, events, and customer support
- Preparing the game code for frequent updates, handling live configs, asset streaming
- Securing the servers and testing the ability to scale them with growing CCU
- Implementing analytics, deep-linking, and marketing tracking tools
- Creating a live marketing strategy and social media content
- Assembling and training the customer support staff

The duration of live support will depend on the success of the game and your team's capabilities. Even if you don't have the resources to create new content and features for more than several months, you should still try and keep your servers going for as long as possible. A minimal level of support a few years into the product's life will help create trust in your products and validate any investment in your virtual worlds.

Staffing

Even after the busiest production period is wrapped up and the game is ready for the full launch, the team size is unlikely to go down. You might be able to release some of the programming, art, and QA staff, but the core development team often has to stay and continue working on new content and updates. Meanwhile, a whole range of support roles enter the picture!

Let's break down a few key roles involved in preparing live games for launch and maintaining them during the live operations period. Depending on your team's composition and capabilities, you may need to distribute some of these responsibilities across any available team members:

Live operations manager
Responsible for planning, designing, and integrating special events, bundles, and in-game sales. Live operations managers are responsible for engaging users, maximizing the financial performance of their games, and simultaneously safeguarding their economies from inflation and excessive content devaluation.

Medium scale mobile games are usually run with 1 to 4 live ops staff, depending on the complexity of the game and the effectiveness of the available tool set. In teams without a dedicated live ops person, it's likely that the game designer will assume these responsibilities, sometimes at the cost of distracting time and attention from creating and balancing new game content.

Data analyst
Throughout a game's production, data analysts and engineers design and integrate analytics solutions that track a wide variety of in-game events from retention, revenue, and session data, to player progression, failure rates, item usage, player inventory size, and even the effectiveness of your marketing (by monitoring the retention of users coming into the game from links embedded into marketing campaigns).

But even the most comprehensive usage data is as valuable as your ability to parse it and turn it into actionable feedback. Data analysts compose dashboards, reports, and detailed investigations into trends and player behavior. Statistically relevant and impartial data is an invaluable tool, which helps inform balancing changes, improve decision making, and shape the future of the product.

Community and customer support lead

Your customer support team is an important bridge between the development team and the player base. Having the CCS lead embedded within the game team ensures that important issues are easily flagged and resolved before anything gets out of hand.

Marketing manager

Live operations require your marketing staff to constantly analyze, coordinate, and scale paid marketing campaigns according to their performance. They also help manage the external relationships with advertising agencies, brand owners, and platform holders such as Apple and Google.

Even though the marketing team itself may consist of many people working on multiple titles at a time, it's often helpful to designate a single owner and point of contact for a particular title.

Social media manager

Growing and retaining a strong social media presence is difficult and time-consuming, but often well worth the effort. Social media managers help to plan, create, and promote engaging content including community votes, game news, photo and video content, and the ever-important live streams.

Efficient live ops

Unless you've made a runaway success, your management may be eager to reduce the team size and allow for most of the production staff to move onto other game projects and opportunities.

This transition will often be done after the game matures (12-24 months after launch) and where there's stable revenue but little prospect for outstanding growth (there are only a few games that can turn into a massive success more than a year after release).

With efficient content and event management tools (more on those later) and T-shaping (training the remaining staff to take up a wide range of tasks and responsibilities), you should be able to run a mature title of average complexity and size with just a few, highly empowered people.

Even without a single coder on board, the live ops team might be able to keep the game alive with events, game balancing, and even basic content updates (based on re-adapted or outsourced art). As for the customer support staff, their numbers will depend on the number of customers who require assistance on a regular basis.

Unfortunately, this is all easier said than done. Creating an efficient live ops machine requires a certain team mentality and preparation, including:

- Writing expandable game engines and designing your games to make them as content-driven as possible.
- Getting creative people into positions of power (to run their own games), and giving them the tools and autonomy they need to thrive. Let people experiment and push their systems to the limits in order to continually delight players with new content, varied mechanics, and twists on old formulas.
- Creating a desire and expectation for automation. You need to recognize the most repetitive tasks and do your best to streamline them. People who use the tools shouldn't expect to have to waste their time.

No matter the size of your live ops team, it's essential to stay organized! Create forms and processes to follow, and always test your content. After several months of recurring events and sales, it will become very tempting to stop updating your planning sheets, skip checklists, and blindly copy/paste data. This will inevitably lead to a gradual decline in the quality of your live operations, and diminished consistency of your offering. It's fine to improve and streamline your processes to match your evolving needs, but these things are there for a reason; do not leave them behind!

Live-game balancing

As you may remember from previous chapters, the game balancing process is sure to continue after release. Live products provide you with invaluable data, but they also introduce heavy limitations, especially for Free to Play games.

Making changes that may affect millions of players is a very delicate act. Players who put significant amounts of time and money into your game are right to expect their content to stay relevant and retain value. Upholding this promise while simultaneously fighting overly-dominant strategies is not easy!:

Use soft-launch and test-environments to validate balance with real players
Beta tests and soft-launches provide you with time and the opportunity for extensive content balancing, especially since it's likely that you won't allow for any spending and may even implement plans to reset the game progress. Moreover, most platform holders (such as Apple, Google, and Steam) can provide you with a clear "beta" or "early-access" badge, which helps to set an expectation that the game is likely to change and evolve.

Once you hit global release, you'll need to slow down. Stagnation may be bad for the long-term health of your game, but it's far better than going back and forth between rash and uncalibrated changes that infuriate your customers.

Vary your data sources
Before you make any changes, you need to know what to address in the first place. Remember that game balance is subjective and does not rely on a single source of information. Mix the data provided by game analytics with internal feedback, player sentiment, and even questionnaires.

Batch your balancing work
Even the most minor tweaks need extensive validation and testing. Changing the spread of a shotgun from 12 to 11 is rarely a good reason to disrupt your live operations schedule. Daily content changes are time-consuming and hard to keep up with, so unless you're trying to address freshly released content, or find a game breaking issue, you should wait until you assemble a set of prospective issues and deal with them once or twice a month.

Batching your changes into bigger releases also gives you an opportunity to manage player sentiment by surrounding negative changes (informally referred to as *nerfs*) with positive ones (known as *buffs*).

Make gradual changes and avoid overshooting
Once a hundred people tell you how badly something *sucks*, you'll be instinctively driven to show the world that you listen by fixing things quickly and decisively. However, once the game is live, you must do your best to curb this reaction, as the risk of going overboard is huge.

It's far better to gradually buff the same strategy three or even four times across two months, than to make it too strong and have to follow up with a nerf.

Nerf by contrast
Although buffing weak content and strategies is often met with great enthusiasm, you must be very careful when making negative changes. Each nerf risks infuriating your players, even to a point of causing a volley of refund requests from dissatisfied customers.

That said, just because you need to reduce the stats of an overpowered character or bring down a dominant strategy does not mean you have to do it explicitly. By introducing new counter-strategies or reinforcing existing ones, you can often restore the balance without resorting to direct downgrades. Remember, context is everything; if you can't bring something down, raise everything around it!

Communicate your intentions as far ahead as you can
An information vacuum breeds rumors and propagates negative sentiments. Try to maintain a two-way communication channel with the community and aim to address any big issues before they escalate. Explain the rationale, share the thinking process, or even part of the analytics data to support your decisions. Utilize a range of tools to address as many players as possible, from in-game news feeds, patch notes, and official wikis, to social media and live-streaming.

Shifting meta can revitalize your economy
Your players are an active component of any multiplayer game and the decisions they make can have a great effect on other players, and by extension, on the overall balance of the game. Tactical adjustments and reactions to strategies exhibited by other players (as well as so-called *mind games*) are the building blocks of your *meta*. The significance and extensiveness of the meta layer varies across games, and often comes down to the knowledge of, and preference for certain card decks, weapon loadouts, building layouts, character rosters, and tactics.

The in-game community at large is constantly evolving the meta by re-evaluating the trends and strategies of other players. Some players expend considerable effort to optimize against the most prolific and successful ones, while others stick to what they like or know best.

Game designers can affect and revitalize (shift) the meta by introducing and incentivizing new strategies and slowly sunsetting (countering) the dominant ones.

On top of making the game more interesting, meta shifting can be a great way of increasing the value of existing content, which wasn't desirable in the *old meta*. By shifting the desire and attention to other elements of the economy, you can also stop a portion of your content from getting overly saturated.

Planning

To have any hopes of delivering on your live operations promise, you'll need to plan well ahead. A few months before the game's global release, you should be able to agree on:

- Content and live ops features (such as events) required for the game's launch. This consists of your liveops MVP (Minimum Viable Product) and should include the content reserved for the first several weeks of live operations.
- The liveops calendar spanning the first few months. More on the calendar in the following section!
- Content production pipeline for the first few months of live operations.
- Live ops features and improvements required in the first few months.

The first few months after global release are as exciting as they are stressful. It's essential to figure out what content matters, and what barely moves the needle. Avoid cutting corners in the hope of turning a quick buck. Do not act on inconclusive data and knee-jerk yourself into trouble. Live games take time to stabilize, and any decisions you make in a rush may end up undermining the game's future.

The first few months of live operations may be rough, but if all goes well, you'll end up creating a well-oiled machine that is set up to succeed for the years to come. The better your processes and plans, the less likely you are to have to *put out fires* on a Sunday afternoon.

Extend the agile development process into live operations! If you're using Jira, or any similar agile tool, try creating a separate *ticket dashboard* for live ops and break down each content update into executable and testable tasks.

Live ops calendar

A live ops calendar tracks everything that's happening in your game and provides an essential insight into the past and future of your live operations. In *Transformers: Earth Wars*, it took the form of a long (but tidy) Google sheet, with each day taking a single row. The rows were populated with the following information:

- Versions of the game client (the actual application installed by the players) and game content (config) across different platforms and environments. It's important to make sure that the game client containing new features or content will be ready for its corresponding event.
- Major real-world events (such as holidays) and in-game affairs (new storylines, game feature releases, and so on).

- Special event information including the name and type of the event, main reward, and start and end dates. More on events later on!
- Sale dates for premium bundles and content. This allows us to easily find out the last time we sold a particular bundle or character.
- Important notes on game economy updates such as new characters entering the gacha pool.
- Newsfeed tracking, that is, which in-game news is live and for how long.

When it comes to releasing new content, it's best to establish a steady, predictable pace. In the case of *Transformers*, a single character per month was much better than a set of three characters in a span of a few weeks followed by a two-month break.

Be very careful to not fire your shells all at once! Setting a release schedule that you cannot sustain will not only increase the pressure on the team, but also inevitably end up creating an impression that the game is *slowing down* and becoming less eventful, thus lowering the trust in its future.

Creating news feeds, preparing events, and implementing new bundles and content takes a lot of time. Use any spare resources, outsourcing, and quiet moments to get ahead with your live ops. Being a few months ahead with game assets and a few weeks with game config gives you the necessary peace of mind, safeguards your operations, and allows members of staff to take a holiday.

Release cadence

The release cycles for your game client (the application you install) and content (config delivered via an internet connection) vary between products and platforms. At *Space Ape Games*, we usually release major content updates on Wednesday or Thursday (ahead of weekend events) and optionally on Monday. Client updates themselves are released at least a few days earlier, with new content and features turned off. The staggered release pattern gives players a few days to update their game without being immediately blocked from playing. It also takes into account the time we need to secure App Store approval.

No matter what release cadence you go for, it's best to reserve a full day to finding and reacting to any live issues. Avoiding Friday releases gives you a good chance to preserve your weekend.

However, it's still necessary to create an on-call roster and designate people to periodically monitor the game's dashboards and inform the team of any issues. After all, if we want to provide a great service to our players, we have to try and keep the game running smoothly and without major disruptions.

Tools and setup

Even the best live ops teams will have a hard time running their game without the help of efficient tooling and a bullet-proof infrastructure. Let's run through the basics:

CMS (Content Management System)
CMS encapsulates any tooling that empowers designers, live ops managers, and any other non-programmers to create, change, and deploy game content.

From game and level editors, to bespoke configuration tools, config files, and online spreadsheets - the fate of your CMS will depend on your game engine and data architecture. Live ops tooling cannot be an afterthought, so make sure to communicate your content management intentions early and request any tools you may need throughout production.

With a well-integrated content management system, editing files is quick, error-free, and well-visualized. Moreover, deploying new balancing tweaks, levels, missions, events, localization files, items, and so on should be done in CMS alone and require no new game code.

New graphical assets may still need an updated game client (until you integrate an asset streaming solution), but balancing tweaks that modify the damage of a *War Axe* from 18 to 15 should never require a new game version. If this isn't the case for your game, your iteration time, bug fixing capability, and live ops flexibility will suffer greatly!

CRM (Customer Relationship Management)
Logging and tracking support tickets means nothing if your customer support team has no way of addressing them. It's essential to have a CRM portal that empowers your team and allows them to monitor, and if necessary, edit player profiles.

The most common use cases include handing out bans and warnings, recovering lost accounts, changing in-game names, sending compensating gifts, and resolving user-specific issues.

At *Space Ape Games*, CRM tools are highly customized for each game, but many companies integrate their entire customer support operations under an umbrella of a single tool such as Desk.

Dashboards

Your analytics are only as powerful as your ability to parse data and quickly react to issues and abnormalities. It's a common practice to compose a live dashboard of the most important KPIs and put them on display in an accessible part of the office. After all, if the team is supposed to feel responsible for the game, they need easy access to information about its current performance. Following links to online dashboards every few hours requires active interest, and catching a glimpse every time you stand from your seat is a much more accessible affair.

As for anyone who's not fully embedded within the game team (or responsible for keeping the service live), automatic daily and weekly reports should be sufficient.

Test environments

The best way of testing client, server, and config updates is to deploy them onto a game environment with actual players. However, the last thing you want is to expose paying customers to untested code and potentially game-breaking issues. To address this conundrum, your server developers and development operations staff will need to establish a range of test environments. From tiny servers for internal use only, to public test realms (PTRs) populated by real players.

At *Space Ape Games*, we often deploy our game updates a few days early onto a single, ring-fenced territory (such as Thailand or the Philippines), where a different version of the game is released. The game in our test market is virtually the same, but contains no in-app purchases (thus removing the risk of hurting paying customers), and its players are separated from the rest of the world. As a result, any issues we weren't able to identify during our internal tests can come to light without damaging the entire game. On a side note, some players really enjoy trying out and giving feedback on new features before they're live for everyone else.

Live ops tools

It's best if your live operations managers can spend most of their time designing engaging events and effective sales strategies, not inputting data by hand. Live ops tools often take the shape of bespoke online portals where one can easily set up and schedule events, bundles, newsfeeds, and notifications. In the best case scenario, you should be able to easily create templates and base new entries on previously used ones.

Asset streaming

When it comes to mobile platforms, the more content you can deliver without updating the game client and going through the submission process, the better. Moreover, Apple and Google both put a limit on the size of the apps and updates that can be delivered over mobile networks (which helps to preserve a user's bandwidth).

By implementing an asset streaming solution, we can keep the initial download size of the game under wraps and deliver the game client without the need for WiFi. And although long asset downloads during the very first loading seem far worse than having to download the entire game on WiFi, based on a few experiments at *Space Ape Games*, it's been proven that the D1 retention is higher if the game client is kept small.

On a side note, small app size also means that potential players can instantly act upon any digital advert for our game. Advertising to people who simply cannot download the game because they are not on WiFi can be a huge waste of money. It's possible to restrict our campaigns to only target WiFi users, but such a strategy would decrease your reach and increase your costs.

Events

Events are special, time-limited activities designed to provide variety, increase player engagement, and potentially encourage spending. Events come in all shapes and sizes, from leaderboard competitions and tournaments, to double XP weekends, Black Friday deals, special maps, and game modes.

The scope of your events will depend on your ambitions, capabilities, and the importance of the period in question. Some events require extensive planning and new content (it's common to theme a large portion of a game's assets after the Olympics, Christmas, or Halloween), while others can be done on a whim and rely on an established event pattern, a few banners, and a selection of available content.

Before you design and implement any event system, you'll have to think of a few potential use cases. For each example you can think of, answer the following questions:

- What's the primary objective of the event? Engagement, the reactivation of lapsed users, revenue generation, and so on?
- Who will interact with the system? Is it targeted at individuals or groups? Casual or competitive players? What's your desired engagement rate?
- How will the event be delivered, presented, and promoted?

- Can players opt into event gameplay when they like, or are they racing against the clock and one another?
- What are the rewards for participation?

Well-designed event systems are made up of a variety of components (such as time limits, leaderboards, and score targets) that can be reused and combined in different permutations.

Event classification

The size and reach of your events has a strong effect on player behavior. A 24-hour long individual tournament feels completely different from a month long faction undertaking. Let's look at a few examples and what they entail:

- **Individual events**: It's just me against the world! Special missions, individual tournaments, and leaderboards can be very appealing and encourage players to return and engage at set times and in set ways. Just make sure to protect weaker and less experienced players against the ultra-competitive elite.
- **Group vs Group**: Few things are as effective in building bonds between players as guild wars, alliance leaderboards, boss raids, and group tournaments. As always, stay vigilant and monitor the effect of various events on your community. Interactions between passionate groups and peer pressure within them can easily turn from fun and engaging to discouraging and toxic.
- **Server-wide events**: Massive undertakings to unlock a game feature or reward on a server-wide scale can be very appealing and encourage lapsed players to return. However, since no one feels particularly responsible or compelled to work extra-hard for a server-wide outcome, you'll need to make sure to recognize and reward individual or guild-based contributions.
- **Faction events**: If your player population is divided in factions, a faction-wide event can unify strangers against a common adversary.
- **League events**: Dividing players and groups into leagues with bespoke leaderboards and rewards is a good way to appeal to engaged and competitive players.

Event components

With the base classification set in place, we need to compose a set of event participation rules. We've listed some of the most wide-spread components that you can deploy in your event design.

Totalizers

In *totalizer events*, players amass event points (or another special, event-specific resource) by playing the game in a set way, for example, by racing their cars across a special track, scoring headshots with a designated sniper rifle, or killing monsters in a specific arena.

Each individual point contribution is added onto the point counter (a totalizer), which usually takes the shape of a long progress bar, with various rewards distributed along the way, and the ultimate reward sitting at the end.

Once the top reward is reached, the totalizer is complete and further event participation loses much of its purpose (unless a separate leaderboard or high score component is present):

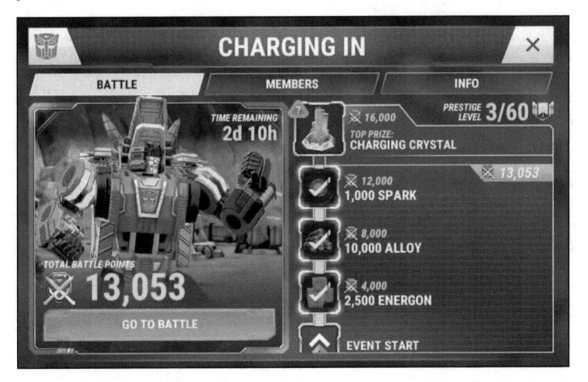

A totalizer event in Transformers: Earth Wars. Players earn points by going into battle, and earn various prizes as they climb towards the top reward.

Prestiging totalizers

Prestiging itself is a concept popularized by *Call of Duty: Modern Warfare*, where players can reset their in-game progress after reaching the maximum experience level, and receive a cosmetic token in exchange. In the context of special events and totalizers, prestiging allows players to complete the same totalizer multiple times, with full rewards gained for each playthrough.

Prestiging shifts the focus from simply finishing the totalizer (which may be hard to do if the score requirement is high), and onto completing a shorter totalizer the maximum number of times. Prestiging can be used to democratize the rewards and make the events more accessible for the weaker players and groups.

In *Transformers: Earth Wars*, we often employed very short totalizers that could be completed up to 60 times, though doing so required a group of experienced and dedicated players. In our case, the top reward on the totalizer was often a gacha crystal, with a small chance of getting a new character. The more times your alliance prestiged the event, the more crystals you amassed and the higher the chances of securing the character. This kind of prestiging rewards hard work, while simultaneously encouraging weak alliances to keep playing, as each completed totalizer gives them a small chance of getting the new character.

There is a caveat for combining prestiging and gacha rewards: the individuals and groups at the very top are often upset about losing the certainty of getting the best rewards. As for everyone else, they enjoy the lower concentration of rewards at the top, and welcome a chance to receive the top reward themselves.

Scored leaderboards

Leaderboards are a video game staple, and to this day, they remain a highly effective component that invigorates competition, and gives recognition to the outstanding performance of the very best players in each game:

Event leaderboard in Transformers: Earth Wars

In the context of live operations, temporary leaderboards can be used to track event performance on a group or individual level. At the very end of the event, various rewards can then be distributed to each participant based on their final standings. The number of different reward tiers can vary greatly and is an effect of a very delicate balancing act.

To start with, you need to make players care about the top tiers on the leaderboard. Following that, place a few tightly packed and meaningful tiers in the middle of the leaderboard. This can help increase the number of players engulfed in the exciting battles at the verges of each reward tier. To put it bluntly, falling dead-center of a reward tier is not nearly as much fun as fighting fiercely to climb (or hold your position) until the very last minute:

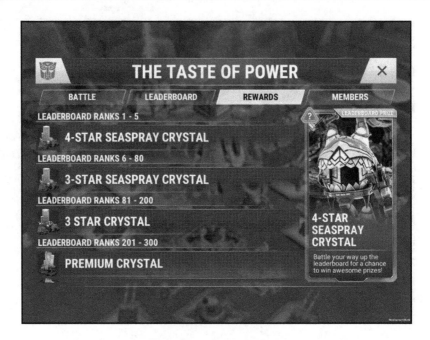

Different reward tiers in Transformers: Earth Wars

In a competition with several hundred participants, the reward tiers can look as follows: 1-5 (top reward), 6-25 (great reward), 26-80 (good reward), 81-150, 151-250 (mediocre reward), 251-400, 400+ (a token of appreciation). For events with a more modest scale, such as localized leagues or mini-competitions with 100 or so players, you can opt for a smaller number of tiers: 1-3, 4-10, 11-25, 26-50, and 51+.

Knockout

In knockout (or elimination) events, players start with a limited number of lives or attempts. They then try to set the high score or complete the event before being eliminated.

To better balance such systems, try using the current winning streak or score when matching players against one another. Natural escalation of difficulty will make things easier at the beginning and far more exiting after several wins:

Challenges in Clash Royale are a good example of an elimination event that works on an opt-in basis

By their very nature, elimination events tend to have a short lifespan, which can be further secured by placing a cap on wins and prizes. The removal of grinding is often welcome by players, but reduces the amount of consumables you can sell. To better monetize these types of events, try using premium *event entry tickets* that can be sold repeatedly to players who dropped out of the event prematurely.

 It's important to note that totalizers, elimination formats, and leaderboards are not mutually exclusive. You can mix multiple event components in the very same event. Experiment with various permutations, rewards, and participation requirements to find the most successful formats for your game.

Event rewards

Medals, trophies, items, perks, characters, costumes, and vanity content—event prizes depend entirely on what you have at your disposal. With rewards, as with events themselves, there is no silver bullet or a one-size-fits-all solution. There are, however, a few tips you can follow!

Set the bar
Always start cheap and increase the quality of the rewards as necessary. Beginning with great rewards in the hope of increasing event participation is a terrible mistake that locks you into a dangerous, ever-inflating pattern.

With rewards, the only way players are happy to accept is up. Bringing the quality of rewards down is a very long and painful process. Doing so incorrectly will cause massive amounts of dissatisfaction and long-term deterioration of player relations. Players never forget...

Pick a theme
Split the categories of rewards to make events feel different or encourage more/less participation. Do not overload the event with 10 different types of content; focus on one vector and make it the top objective. A few good examples of strong themes would be a *4-star crystal event*, where players focus their efforts to get precious crystal rewards at the top of the totalizer, or a *triple XP event* where the main driver of engagement is the additional Experience Points, and the event rewards themselves are purposefully insignificant. Use your rewards to ensure that consecutive events stand out from one another.

Acknowledge the effort
For significant events such as monthly or quarterly leaderboard showdowns, it's advisable to give additional recognition to the winners. If possible, avoid creating an additional reward tier; keeping the best rewards for the top three or five participants is absolutely fine. Instead, give the winners an exclusive cosmetic item, or a permanent place in a virtual hall of fame. The truth is, players at the very top rarely need more resources or better content; they want a reward that no one else can get...

The in-game hall of fame in Transformers: Earth Wars is very efficient (a simple newsfeed) but highly effective

Event participation and engagement

The success of your events can be measured by three factors:

1. **Event Participation**: The percentage of eligible players who participated in the event by completing at least one measurable action. By forecasting and assessing the participation, you can decide whether the effort you spent on preparing the event brings sufficient results. To provide a quantifiable example, for a *mid-core* mobile game with an engaged audience, a participation rate of around 75%-80% in a weekend event would be considered very healthy, and anything below 50% is likely to cast serious doubt on the appeal of the event.

2. **Engagement**: How much time and effort was spent on the event by an average player. For example, if players need to battle their enemies for event points, engagement measures the amount of completed battles. Engagement stats directly influence the intensity of the event, a factor that we'll describe at length shortly.

3. **Sales**: Events are a critical opportunity for monetizing your audience. The financial performance of each event can be broken down into two distinct avenues: direct event sales (players spending to play more, or to improve their event performance) and indirect sales (players being exposed to desirable content that does not influence the event).

Event intensity and player burndown

Grind-fueled totalizers and tight leaderboard showdowns might be your most effective event formats, but they come at a price…

Our communities operate with finite reserves of time, money, and stamina. Running the game at high intensity for too long can exhaust even the most dedicated players, making them feel like they cannot keep up, and are better off leaving the competition (or the game) altogether. We have to do our best to be respectful of the time and effort our players put in our games.

At *Space Ape Games*, we tend to rank event intensity on a scale from 1 to 5, where 1 is assigned to casual and relaxed individual events (in which participation is often seen as optional), and 5 represents group-based efforts with high levels of competition and peer pressure (such as alliance leaderboard events).

Since high intensity correlates to higher engagement, and by extension longer exposure to our premium offerings, we tend to pair intense events with highly desirable content. That said, in many cases, medium intensity events with high participation and engagement rates (but low levels of competitive play) can be an even better place for some of your most desirable sales. After all, players who decide to spend will have plenty of time to try out and enjoy their new weapon/ability/character, or any other piece of playable content, without having to sacrifice their standing in an important competitive event.

The intensity scale may not be very scientific, and at first you'll often misjudge the levels of event participation and engagement. Nevertheless, preparing events with a certain intensity in mind helps to keep things varied, manage player burnout, and set the financial expectations for each particular week.

Populating the live ops calendar far ahead and setting the intensity as early as possible is the easiest way to inform the event design and enforce a healthy event cadence. Take a look at a simple intensity curve spanning ten weekly events: 1, 2, 4, 3, 2, 5, 1, 3, 4, 2.

Now, we may not know the details of each event just yet, but we already know where the strongest (4, 5) and weakest (1, 2) events are placed, and we can plan our content sales around them. We've also ensured that the curve maintains a period of low intensity (1) after the most intense event (5), and have created a space for various event formats all around.

Community and customer support

The video game community at large is not the easiest one to interact with. Players are rarely aware of the realities that you have to deal with and the obstacles you encounter when making and operating games. It takes months and years to gain the trust of players, and a single mistake or a bad (or badly communicated) decision is enough to lose it.

This is where the **community and customer support team** (**CCS**) comes in. They foster, maintain, and police your communities, as well as provide your team with deep insight into the most pressing issues and general player-sentiment.

CCS is an invaluable part of your operations, so try to utilize it to the best of your possibility. Implement daily CCS reports, include CCS in parts of your decision making, and have agents reach out with community suggestions and player feedback on a regular basis.

Supporting players

Helping our players with various game-, community-, and account-related issues is the primary role of each CCS agent. It's hard work that requires a great deal of compassion, assertiveness, and a thick skin. Sometimes, things go terribly wrong and players need to be compensated or refunded; other times, players will try to hack the game, commit fraud, or take advantage of your support team.

Establishing a clear set of rules and guidelines is essential to help the CCS lead to draw the line for compensation, and decide on what can be given out to players, in what circumstances, and in what quantities. The vast majority of players will play fairly, but you'll also encounter a great deal of manipulation. Bending the established rules towards a single player can end up being exposed in the form of screenshots, and used against you later down the line.

Gathering feedback

There are several channels that can be used to gather player feedback:

- Support tickets created from within the game (if your game supports such a channel)
- Emails to your customer support address
- Official chat groups and forums (hosted and moderated by your CCS team)
- Unofficial social media pages, posts, tweets, and forums
- Prominent *Send feedback* buttons that can be placed in test versions of the game (pressing the button begins an email message to your support address)
- Questionnaires and surveys (distributed via in-game newsfeeds or email newsletters)

Newsletters

Monthly and weekly newsletters are a great way of reaching out to the masses to share news, highlight upcoming events, send out gifts, and re-engage lapsed or lapsing players.

Official chats and forums

Setting up and moderating official chat groups and forums is a great way of interacting with the community outside the confines of the game or official support tickets.

Localized customer support

As we've already highlighted in the chapter on accessibility, localization efforts do not stop with translations of in-game text. A game with a large foreign player base should ideally be supported by CCS agents who can speak their language.

At *Space Ape Games*, we've managed to assemble a network of international agents composed of in-house staff and external contractors. These agents can provide us with language-specific customer support in Japanese, Chinese, Russian, German, Spanish, and more! We can also use their skills to help us translate our games with quick turnarounds and affordable costs.

Each agent (be it in-house or remote) can easily highlight and escalate any issues with the CCS game lead embedded directly within the live operations team.

Live streaming

Running official streams on platforms such as *Twitch, YouTube,* and *Facebook* is a great way of bridging the gap between the community and the development team. Live streams are easier to produce than prerecorded videos and trailers (there's no editing involved), and give you a unique opportunity to interact with your fan base in a more casual and spontaneous manner.

To build up a following, you should try to establish a regular cadence (an hour per week works well), promote the streams in-game and on social media, and try to fill them with valuable (but easy to produce) content such as Q&As, team interviews, sneak peaks of new features and upcoming content, and even game-knowledge quizzes.

Tips and tricks

Before we close this chapter, let's delve into a collection of tips and tricks that may help you in designing and running your live games:

Player spending should build up your community, not divide it
Avoid splitting your audience based on their ability to spend. While early access to new content is fine, introducing things such as premium map DLCs is going to split friend groups, reduce matchmaking opportunities, and ultimately hurt both sides of the paying spectrum.

Spending should feel good, but the gratification should not come from gaining unfair advantages and penalizing everyone else. In western markets, most players will quickly rebel against a game that's 100% pay to win (where skill, experience, or strategy mean nothing, and the only way to stay competitive is to outspend their rivals).

Turn premium content into something that makes the game more fun for everyone else:

- Everyone likes to hang around a player with cool-looking gear, impressive visual effects, and amusing animations, and this turns spending on cosmetic content a good experience for everyone.
- While unfair advantages can be very damaging in head-to-head scenarios, the same does not apply to cooperative efforts. Teaming up with someone strong and having them lead the charge rewarding the spenders and non-spenders alike.

Try to embrace reciprocity and drive positive reinforcement within your community:

- Make a spender feel helpful by making their 100% XP boost extend a smaller 10% bonus to their teammates.
- If an area of the game is locked behind paid access, you can ensure that only one player has to spend or grant them a way to sponsor their friends.

- Players spending on big bundles could receive a couple of free gifts to distribute among their peers. This will not only make both sides of the gift exchange feel good, but also increase the chances of the recipient returning the favor (the power of reciprocity). Some people really enjoy giving. In *Team Fortress 2*, a gift box that grants a reward to a random person on the server (excluding the owner) was apparently one of the most popular items.

Disappointments and regrets cost dearly!

As you drive desire and curiosity behind your high-end game content, you must ensure that the payoff is worth the hype. Having weeks and even months of hard work and anticipation end up with a disappointment is a sure way to destroy any trust between you and the player. Regrets over spending are even more damaging and will prompt your players to want a refund.

Think of technical performance holistically

Does the user spend ages on the initial loading screen? Are you respectful of their time and custom? Make sure that players can get to the game as quickly as possible, or you might make them miss their short window of opportunity to spend some quality time with you as an entertainment provider.

Does the game download only what it needs and when it needs it, or are you charging your players dearly in their bandwidth? Be efficient with what assets you need to download and respect the space your players loan you on their devices. If you don't, your game might be the first to be uninstalled when storage gets low.

Does the performance of the game remain stable and smooth even at the most intense and climactic moments? If players spend a lot of time and effort getting to the hardest part of the game and it suddenly crashes or starts to jitter, then they are likely to lose faith in you and your game.

Scarcity influences value

As players grow more experienced and familiar with a game's content, any new findings are sure to excite them. Some goods, no matter how mundane, can increase in value just on the back of being rare and hard (or maybe even impossible) to obtain.

The value and prestige of limited rewards can grow in time. A simple icon or badge may start as a worthless aesthetic reward, and later evolve into a rare and powerful sign of a respectful tenure. However, this is only true if you stand firm and keep scarce rewards truly scarce. Introducing an accessible venue for obtaining the content later (for the sake of a small revenue spike) will forever diminish the value of the entire lineup of content.

Focus on daily retention

Increasing your stickiness and developing a gaming habit translates to weekly and monthly retention. Daily rewards can be a powerful mechanic for increasing your retention and pacing progression. Focus on rewarding gameplay (for example, by giving out daily tasks), rather than simply showing up (daily login bonuses, calendars, and so on).

Optimize your newsletters and notifications

Do not spam your users! When it comes to email newsletters and social media posts, quality beats quantity. Work with your CCS and social and marketing staff to provide players with engaging content such as videos, sneak peaks of upcoming features and events, community highlights, surveys, and Q&As. Localize as much as you can and send the material according to a player's timezone (no one wants an email notification at 2 AM).

On mobile platforms, you'll also have access to push notifications (sent by the server) and local notifications (scheduled from within the app itself). It's often up to the game designer to decide on the frequency and content of this messaging. Aspire to create a smart solution that does not produce 5 notifications within 30 minutes of leaving the app. The most successful communications are context-aware and actionable, inviting players to come back and check on the game just as they become ready for their next session.

The network effect can make and break your game

The network effect can be described as a positive feedback loop where the value of a product or service increases with the rising number of users.

Having your game grow exponentially on the back of its current popularity is great, but the implications of the so-called *demand-side economies of scale* are not always positive. Let's say a player spends a few hours crafting a new hat for their character in an MMO game such as *Second Life*. The next day, said that gets them lots of attention from other players. This kind of positive reinforcement encourages player to spend the next 2 days making a whole smoking outfit. Following that, they will be naturally drawn towards highly populated places in the hopes of gaining the most amount of recognition. Other, like-minded players are inadvertently encouraged to follow the same behavioral pattern.

As a result, the more crowded the location, map, or server, the more popular it becomes. Without sufficient planning, the game may become unplayable due to frame rate issues or server failures, and collapse in disarray, leaving thousands of disappointed customers, and falling victim to its own success.

Put yourself in the consumer's shoes

It's easy for we designers to try and think of individual features that we should and should not monetize based on what other, similar products do. It's far more challenging to take a look at our game through the eyes of multiple players and to identify what they'll actually enjoy spending money on and why.

By embracing a variety of player archetypes, their motivations, and desires, we can hope to better cater to their needs. Ultimately, the most sustainable communities are formed on the backs of players who spend money because they want to, not because they have to.
It's essential for every member of the game team to try and play the game for *real*, including undercover, next to normal players, spending their very own money, and experiencing the same highs and lows as everyone else.

Maintain tight control over your rewards

Anything you give out to players will be remembered and evaluated against everything else you do. Inconsistent policies and sparks of random generosity will ultimately lead to an unhealthy economy and unhappy players. This is as true for live ops (in regard to event rewards, bundles, and gacha offerings) as it is for customer support.

Customer support representatives need to have a coherent policy on compensating players and assuaging angry spenders. Break the rules for one player and you'll set a precedent that sows the seed for mass discontent.

Beware of stockpiling resources

Overabundant resources are one of the biggest threats to any resource-based economy. Put limits on the maximum amount of resources and consumable items players can hold, and be ready to enforce them!

Start strong and hook players onto the long-term premise

Remember, a Free to Play game is as easy to pick up as it is to let go. With zero investment required to install, there is no loss aversion preventing players from uninstalling it at the drop of a hat. After all, there's no need to rationalize your monetary investment and *get your money's worth*. The first-time user experience is everything, an equivalent to a trailer for a Hollywood action film, where you only have a few minutes to win over the audience. Don't worry about naming the player profile, selecting servers, or adjusting difficulty settings. Get players straight into gameplay and tackle the mundane bits later.

Use the little attention you may have (5-15 minutes) to showcase a strong gameplay hook and establish a clearly defined long-term premise—a dream scenario, an aspiration for players to get behind, a reason to return. The premise could be *collect all characters*, *uncover the mystery*, *build up your own city*, or *explore the uncharted lands*. In some cases, you can use onboarding to highlight and perhaps even let the players try out the end-game content. For example, if your sports game has the name and likeness rights to the world-class stars, then give me a chance to play with them for a match or two, to appreciate their value, and only then give me a set of *no-names* and set me on a long path to rebuild that dream team.

Do not worry about polishing the first time user experience until you're well into production. Onboarding segments require tons of iteration and are best made when the game mechanics are nailed down and the team has a lot of experience in making content for the game.

Preview content to spark desire

To build value and desire around your content, the user needs to understand what makes it good. However, in some cases, text, images, and even videos may not be enough to fully showcase the unique qualities of a sleek new weapon, vehicle, or character.
Some things can only be appreciated (and apprised) when you try them for yourself. After all, nothing can explain the taste of a dish as effectively as tasting it!

Do not be afraid to preview and showcase your content. Should the entire value rest on the novelty of trying it for the first time, it means there's little longevity in your content, a symptom of a much bigger problem.

The screenshots used in this chapter are for illustrative purposes only. We do not recommend that you to misuse these in any way. For more information, please consult the terms and conditions of the publishers mentioned in the *Disclaimer* section of this book.

Summary

From decoding your KPIs, to establishing the vectors of monetization, designing loot boxes, and maintaining communities, numerous of mysteries have been exposed in this chapter, and they highlight the countless new challenges that begin to face an ever growing number of game designers. These days, more than ever before, we ought to expand our skill sets and step into the shoes of economists, sales people, community agents, and players themselves.

This is the final chapter of this book, a chance to say goodbye, and an open invitation to revise and reread various parts of the book as you make progress with your next video game project. We wish you the best of luck!

Other Books You May Enjoy

If you enjoyed this book, you may be interested in these other books by Packt:

Mastering C++ Game Development
Mickey Macdonald

ISBN: 978-1-78862-922-5

- Work and communicate effectively in the modern games industry
- Develop simple and advanced gameplay systems
- How to leverage the standard core C++ libraries
- Use modern real-time rendering techniques to achieve immersive 3D visuals
- Achieve a narrative-driven game experience using a variety of data management techniques
- Implement scripting using LUA
- Learn AI algorithms and concepts for handling motion, behavior, and decision making
- Implementation of the OpenGL, Bullet Physics, GLM, SteamVR and other common libraries

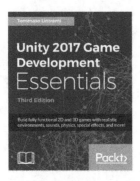

Unity 2017 Game development essentials
Tommaso Lintrami

ISBN: 978-1-78646-939-7

- Script games using C#
- Build your very first 2D and 3D games
- Work through the key concepts in game development such as animations, physics, and scripting
- Test and optimize your games to attain great performance
- Create fully functional menus, HUDs, and UI
- Create player character interactions with AI and NPC

Leave a review - let other readers know what you think

Please share your thoughts on this book with others by leaving a review on the site that you bought it from. If you purchased the book from Amazon, please leave us an honest review of this book's Amazon page. This is vital so that other potential readers can see and use your unbiased opinion to make purchasing decisions, we can understand what our customers think about our products, and our authors can see your feedback on the title that they have worked with Packt to create. It will only take a few minutes of your time but is valuable to other potential customers, our authors, and Packt. Thank you!

Index

CPSIA information can be obtained
at www.ICGtesting.com
Printed in the USA
LVHW011800090921
697458LV00007B/579